Atlas of the Transatlantic Slave Trade

The Lewis Walpole Series in
Eighteenth-Century Culture and History

The Lewis Walpole Series, published by Yale University Press with the aid of the Annie Burr Lewis Fund, is dedicated to the culture and history of the long eighteenth century (from the Glorious Revolution to the accession of Queen Victoria). It welcomes work in a variety of fields, including literature and history, the visual arts, political philosophy, music, legal history, and the history of science. In addition to original scholarly work, the series publishes new editions and translations of writing from the period, as well as reprints of major books that are currently unavailable. Though the majority of books in the series will probably concentrate on Great Britain and the Continent, the range of our geographical interests is as wide as Horace Walpole's.

Atlas of the Transatlantic Slave Trade

David Eltis and David Richardson

Foreword by David Brion Davis

Afterword by David W. Blight

Yale UNIVERSITY PRESS
New Haven & London

Published with assistance from the Kingsley Trust Association Publication Fund established by the Scroll and Key Society of Yale College and with assistance from the Annie Burr Lewis Fund.

Yale University Press books may be purchased in quantity for educational, business, or promotional use. For information, please e-mail sales.press@yale.edu (U.S. office) or sales@yaleup.co.uk (U.K. office).

Maps provided by Mapping Specialists, Ltd., Madison, Wisconsin.
Designed by James J. Johnson.
Set in Adobe Minion type by Julie Allred, BW&A Books, Inc., Durham, North Carolina.
Printed in China.

Library of Congress Cataloging-in-Publication Data
Eltis, David, 1940–
Atlas of the transatlantic slave trade / David Eltis and David Richardson ; foreword by David Brion Davis ; afterword by David W. Blight.
    p. cm. — (The Lewis Walpole series in eighteenth-century culture and history)
ISBN 978-0-300-12460-6 (alk. paper)
1. Slave trade—Africa—History—Maps. I. Richardson, David, 1946–
II. Title. III. Title: Trans-Atlantic slave trade.
G2445.E625.E4 2010
381'.44091821022—dc22
2010018285

A catalogue record for this book is available from the British Library.

This paper meets the requirements of ANSI/NISO Z39.48-1992 (Permanence of Paper).

10 9 8 7 6 5 4 3 2 1

Major support for the *Atlas of the Transatlantic Slave Trade* was provided by:

    THE ANNIE BURR LEWIS FUND AT YALE UNIVERSITY

    THE GILDER LEHRMAN INSTITUTE OF AMERICAN HISTORY

    THE GILDER LEHRMAN CENTER FOR THE STUDY OF SLAVERY, RESISTANCE, AND ABOLITION

    THE KINGSLEY TRUST ASSOCIATION PUBLICATION FUND AT YALE UNIVERSITY

    THE PAPENFUSE FOUNDATION

    THE WILBERFORCE INSTITUTE FOR THE STUDY OF SLAVERY AND EMANCIPATION, UNIVERSITY OF HULL

On this distressing subject, so revolting to every well regulated mind, I will add that such is the merciless treatment of the slaves by the persons engaged in the traffic that no fancy can picture the horror of the voyage—crowded together so as not to give the power to move—linked one to the other by the leg—never unfettered whilst life remains, or till the iron shall have fretted the flesh almost to the bone . . . breathing an atmosphere the most putrid and pestilential possible, with little food and less water. . . . It is to me a matter of extreme wonder that any of these miserable people live the voyage through; many of them indeed perish on the passage, and those who remain to meet the shore, present a picture of wretchedness language cannot express.

"Report on the Coast of Africa made by Captain George Collier, 1818–19," pp. 241–242, Admiralty Library Manuscript Collection, MSS 45, National Museum of the Royal Navy, Portsmouth. Published with permission of the National Museum of the Royal Navy, Portsmouth, England. We are grateful to Mary Wills for drawing this source to our attention.

Contents

Maps

Part III
The African Coastal Origins of Slaves and the Links between Africa and the Atlantic World

Part IV
The Experience of the Middle Passage

Part V

The Destinations of Slaves in the Americas and Their Links with the Atlantic World

Part VI
Abolition and Suppression of the Transatlantic Slave Trade

Foreword

DAVID BRION DAVIS

The transatlantic slave trade, which persisted for 366 years and resulted in the forced deportation of 12.5 million Africans to the New World, ranks as one of history's greatest crimes against humanity. Unlike the Nazis' five-year Holocaust in World War II, it was not driven by hatred and a desire to exterminate an entire people—although one of slavery's long-term effects was a widespread contempt and even racist hatred for people of African descent. The overriding motive that lay behind the uprooting, enslavement, and coerced long-distance transport of millions of sub-Saharan Africans was greed—the desire of European colonizers, including Spaniards, Portuguese, Dutch, British, French, Danes, Swedes, Brazilians, and North Americans, to find the cheapest labor for the production and export of precious metals, sugar, rum, rice, tobacco, cotton, coffee, indigo, and other luxury goods.

The magnitude of the slave trade conveys at least a hint of the magnitude of human suffering. By 1820 African slaves constituted some 80 percent of all the people who had embarked for the Americas since 1500, and mortality on the slave ships averaged at least 15 percent, to which we must add the numerous deaths that occurred as slaves were marched from the African interior to the coast and as they waited to sail, jammed into castle prisons or on board ships. Yet it can hardly be denied—especially in view of the economic dominance of the colonial Caribbean and the essential cotton exports of the American South—that this original black majority of surviving workers became indispensable in creating the prosperous New World that by the mid-nineteenth century began attracting millions of voluntary European immigrants (who, ironically, tended to choose the "freest soil," since free white migrants never wished to compete with slaves in tropical or semitropical regions where plantation agriculture flourished).

Not until the 1400s did the Portuguese and the Spanish construct the kind of ships, and utilize the compass and other navigational instruments, that enabled them to master the major ocean currents and wind systems of the North and South Atlantic—natural forces that had protected the Western Hemisphere from earlier invasions and had isolated it from the deadly diseases of Eurasia and Africa. The sixteenth-century Atlantic slave trade was a product of this larger European breakout that before 1500 had sent Bartolomeu Dias to the Cape of

Good Hope, Columbus to the Caribbean, and Vasco da Gama to India. Columbus himself, a seaman from Genoa who shipped some 500 enslaved Amerindians back to Spain, was part of a larger picture that included colonies of Italian traders, bankers, and sailors in Lisbon, Seville, and other Atlantic ports, men who became deeply involved with black slaves and sugar plantations on the Atlantic islands off the African coast. The connections extended to great German and Italian merchant-banking families who were skilled at raising capital, selling insurance, and handling bills of credit—all of which later became essential for the lengthy transatlantic slave-ship voyages that delayed any return of profit for several years.

Even in its first centuries, what we can term the Atlantic Slave System foreshadowed many features of our modern global economy. We see international investment of capital in distant colonial regions, where low-cost, highly productive gang labor by slaves produced commodities for a transatlantic market. With respect to consumerism, we now know that slave-produced sugar, tobacco, coffee, chocolate, and other luxuries not only altered the European diet but, by the late 1700s, had helped to shape a consumer mentality among the masses, especially in Britain, so that workers became more willing to accept factory discipline in order to afford luxury stimulants and, later, factory-produced cotton clothing, made possible by the cotton gin and slave labor. The long-range effects of slave-based globalization extend even to many aspects of modern culture, as can be seen in the profound impact of the African diaspora on modern popular music.

It is difficult to comprehend the slave trade and the Atlantic Slave System it created without a highly detailed collection of maps. For a considerable period of time, for example, the winds and currents of the North and South Atlantic resulted in two mostly separate slave trades: a southern counterclockwise current or circle connected southwest Africa with Portuguese Brazil, and a northern clockwise circle connected Europe, the Caribbean, and African sources of labor north of the equator. Only maps can accurately convey the changing African origins of slaves, their New World destinations, and, no less important, the degrees to which different European and American nations participated in the slave trade. Only maps can fully illustrate the startling discovery that the region that became the United States, home in 1860 to the largest number of black slaves ever assembled in the New World, imported less than 4 percent of the total migration.

During the past decade specialists led especially by David Eltis and David Richardson, editors of this volume, have made unprecedented empirical discoveries regarding virtually every aspect of the Atlantic slave trade. Beginning with a continually expanding demographic census, they have extended their examination of the slave trade from such topics as the frequency and consequences of slave-ship revolts to an appraisal of the historical consequences of the abolition of the slave trade in 1807–1808 by Britain and the United States. With respect to slave-ship revolts, which occurred on about 10 percent of all voyages, usually when still near the African coast, it is worth noting that such resistance prevented still more African slaves from being shipped to the New World. The fear of revolts significantly increased the cost of the African trade—in terms of added crew, guns, and insurance—and also induced ship captains to move toward African coastal regions, usually farther south, where captives were thought to be less rebellious. Meanwhile, other scholars have greatly enriched our understanding of the political, social, and cultural history of racial slavery in the New World. This landmark atlas is an attempt to combine much of this new information, supplementing 189 maps with literary and artistic material.

Since Brazil and the Caribbean formed the very heart of the Atlantic Slave System, attracting some 90 percent of all the slaves imported from Africa, and since the production of sugar dominated the economies of both regions, even a brief summary of slave-trade history should mention the ancient westward migration of sugarcane cultivation from Asia to the medieval Middle East and then the Mediterranean. Italian merchants were at the forefront in developing sugar production in regions of Cyprus, Crete, and Sicily and finally in helping the Iberians extend the system for slave-grown sugarcane to Atlantic islands off the west coast of Africa in the 1400s: the Madeira Islands, the Canaries, the Cape Verdes, and São Tomé. By coincidence, after the capture of Constantinople in 1204 in the Fourth Crusade, Italians had established slave-trading ports along the northern coast of the Black Sea, much as later European merchants would do along the western coast of Africa. Over the course of nearly two and a half centuries the Genoese and the Venetians purchased thousands of captive Armenians, Circassians, Mingrelians, Tatars, and Bulgarians—peoples whose vague ethnic status as "Slavs" became the origin of the words for *slave* in western European languages. "Slav" slaves were highly prized from Muslim Egypt and Syria to Sicily and eastern Spain, and some were used for the production of sugar, a labor-intensive industry favored by few free workers.

In 1453 the Ottoman Turks captured Constantinople and soon diverted the flow of Black Sea and Balkan captives to Islamic markets. Although this conquest sharply reduced Europe's supply of both sugar and slaves, the Portuguese had already begun importing significant numbers of black African slaves (who by 1550 constituted 10 percent of Lisbon's population), and even in Sicily, Naples, southern France, and Mediterranean Spain the slave population began to "blacken," in part owing to the Arab caravan trade across the Sahara, which led to black slave exports from Libya and Tunisia. In Sicily a notary's record in Latin referred to *sclavi negri,* literally "black Slavs," who outnumbered white slaves there by the 1490s. In short, as the production of Europe's sugar moved westward into the Atlantic and increased in volume—although consumption was still limited to a medicinal and upper-class market—it became almost wholly dependent on black slave labor.

Despite the strong lines of continuity from Mediterranean plantation colonies to the sugar plantations of the New World, the European settlers had no blueprints or master plans for slavery or sources of labor. The first African slaves who arrived in the Americas, in the early 1500s, departed from Europe, not Africa. Not until the mid-1520s did the first slave ship sail directly from Africa; until the early 1600s the sugar plantations in northeastern Brazil relied mainly on Amerindian slave labor. As late as the early 1700s, Indians made up one-third of the slave labor force in South Carolina. The British were unusual in being able to draw on large supplies of white British indentured laborers for the cultivation of tobacco—in the

Caribbean until the 1640s, when Barbados led the way with a revolutionary transfer to sugarcane; and in Virginia until the 1670s, when white immigration began to decline and large planters turned to Africans for their field work. In the late 1670s white servants in Virginia still outnumbered black slaves four to one, but by the early 1690s black slaves outnumbered servants four to one.

In 1492 no one could have predicted the disastrous effect on American Indians of what are called virgin soil epidemics. Millennia of isolation had made them fatally vulnerable to Old World smallpox, influenza, measles, and other contagious diseases. If millions of Caribbean Indians had not died off as the result of pandemics, Spanish cruelty, and the loss of their food base, they might conceivably have provided a significant labor force for later sugar plantations. The near extermination of many native populations hastened the Spaniards' seizure of fertile land from Hispaniola to Peru and the Portuguese seizure of land in Brazil. But in many regions the invasion left only a skeletal native population that could be coerced to perform heavy labor. The more humanitarian leaders, such as Bartolomé de Las Casas and Manuel da Nobrega, called for the importation of many more black slaves as a way of counteracting the Spanish and Portuguese oppression of Indians. Such arguments were reinforced by the familiarity that many West Africans had with large-scale agriculture, labor discipline, and even the manufacture of iron and steel tools. Throughout the New World, colonists agreed that the labor of one black was worth that of several Indians.

The strength and capacity of most West Africans brings us to a subject that is both surprising and upsetting to many uninformed readers: the indispensable complicity of Africans in creating and maintaining the slave trade. Even in the earliest history of the trade, the Portuguese discovered the extreme hazards and counterproductivity of trying to capture and enslave West Africans on their own. West Africans could and did attack and sink some European ships in retaliation; the rulers of Kongo, Benin, and some other regions succeeded at times in temporarily stopping the trade in slaves. Yet the crucial point was the eagerness of African rulers and merchants to sell slaves. Similarity in skin color and other bodily traits, as Europeans viewed them, brought African rulers and merchants no sense of a common African identity with the captives sold. And the sellers of slaves profited immensely from the acquisition of textiles, hardware, bars of iron, liquor, guns and gunpowder, tools, and utensils of various kinds. Between 1680 and 1830, when the trade had its most devastating impact on African societies, the price paid for slaves in Senegambia rose tenfold.

If Africans were themselves divided into many ethnic groups—or, above all, into family or clan lineages based on highly respected ancestors—they quickly learned how to play off one group of Europeans against another and how to maximize the inflow of European and Asian goods. European ship captains soon discovered the need to present ceremonial gifts to African rulers; to pay fees and taxes even to anchor and engage in trade; and to employ black interpreters, often trained in Portugal or São Tomé, who went ashore with the captain to haggle and bargain with local rulers over the price of slaves. Europeans very seldom gained access to the Africans' networks and procedures for producing gold and slaves. The

Portuguese did, however, purchase gold on the Gold Coast in exchange for black slaves whom they had purchased farther east and south, where slaves were cheaper. Moreover, some men of mixed black and white descent commanded Portuguese slave ships, and a few African slave traders journeyed all the way to Brazil and Barbados, where they viewed the western side of the system.

I began by affirming the collective criminality of the Atlantic slave trade, surely one of history's most extreme examples of humanity's inhumanity. In recent years there has been some understandable reaction against the reckless overuse of the word *evil* and its implied dualistic struggle between the supposed Children of Light and Children of Darkness. Yet the sheer evil of the slave trade is difficult to deny, at least today. Nor can we fail to recognize great virtue in the successful antislavery movements that have enabled us to make such historical judgments.

Despite this moral liberation, our Western culture tends to worship the magic of the free market, the invisible hand that allegedly promotes the common good. Yet it was *uncontrolled* market forces that determined how many African slaves could be crammed into the hold of a ship—with the chained and padlocked males lying together for five weeks or more, hunched on their sides and wedged like spoons locked together, unable to stand or stretch out, surrounded by feces and urine-drenched floors— to satisfy consumer demand for sugar, rum, tobacco, and coffee. As it happened, these stimulants did little to improve the world or enhance human health and well-being. Although Britain's first highly contested step toward "regulating" the slave trade, Sir William Dolben's bill of 1788, slightly restricted the number of slaves who could be carried on a ship, the British public launched a boycott of slave-produced sugar when the humanitarian lawmakers initially failed to overcome the defenders of market forces.

The slave trade, though devastating to Africa, was immensely profitable and was in some ways even "progressive." Defenders of the commerce stressed that each slave ship carried a doctor or surgeon; that for marketing reasons captains became increasingly intent on minimizing mortality; and that in good weather slaves were brought up on deck for exercise—indeed, they were flogged if they refused to dance, jump, and sing. The trade reached its all-time peak toward the end of the Enlightenment, in the late 1700s, and was certainly not declining in 1807 and 1808, when Britain and the United States outlawed it. Much mythology about the "backwardness" of slavery notwithstanding, abolitionists were forced to confront the growth and vitality of the New World slave economies. Some 3 million Africans, or about one-fourth of the grand total exported, were shipped off to the Americas after 1807, despite the militant efforts of the British navy. As David Eltis has observed, we can easily imagine the increasingly powerful and steam-driven British and American merchant ships *expanding* the flow of African slaves not only to Cuba and Brazil but to the kind of markets many Southerners dreamed of by the 1850s. What prevented such an expansion was not the operation of supply and demand but a major transformation in Anglo-American public moral perception, spearheaded by a small group of abolitionist reformers.

I do not mean to question many of the benefits of the free market, but if history can teach us some unexpected lessons, here is one: we should recognize that Britain's 1807 law, which ended the country's 130-year dominance of the slave trade and led to the economic decline of the British Caribbean, was a revolutionary move toward *regulating* the global market. That step was followed by a series of treaties and expensive naval interventions aimed at ending the free market in slave labor. This antislavery campaign was complex and acquired more mixed meanings when incorporated in nationalistic and imperialist causes. But there is still much to be said for the historian W. E. H. Lecky's famous conclusion, following the American Civil War, that England's crusade against slavery "may probably be regarded as among the three or four perfectly virtuous acts recorded in the history of nations."

I wish to thank Seymour Drescher for reading an early draft of this foreword and offering some invaluable suggestions.

About This Atlas

The maps in the *Atlas of the Transatlantic Slave Trade* are grouped in seven parts. The introduction contains maps that provide a broad context for the slave trade, as well as an interpretation and an overview. The maps in part I track the participation of the nations of Europe and the Americas in obtaining, carrying off, and distributing African slaves around the Atlantic world. The maps in the following parts are based on the geography of a voyage. Those in parts II and III identify where slave voyages were organized and where the slave ships obtained captives in Africa. Next came the Middle Passage, the voyage itself, portrayed in part IV as far as maps allow us to portray that experience. The maps in part V show where the ships took the slaves in the Americas. Finally, the maps in part VI show the geographic dimension of the suppression of the transatlantic slave trade. None of the maps offers information on the movement of captives before they embarked on their voyage from Africa or on their movements after disembarkation in the Americas, although the captions often include comments on this subject.

Although parts II, III, and V focus, respectively, on the outfitting of slave voyages, places of trade in Africa, and places of sale at the end of the Middle Passage, most of the maps also present a larger picture. In part II, the outfitting ports, labeled in red, are the subjects of the maps, but the slave-trading voyages themselves are at the heart of the maps, linking outfitting ports with places of trade in Africa and the Americas. In part III, the focus switches to Africa. Each major port of embarkation, again labeled in red, has its own map. Many of the maps contain bar graphs that present information about the ports where the slave vessels were outfitted. Part V looks at the slaves that survived the Middle Passage: their African coastal origins and their points of disembarkation. Their ports of arrival in the Americas are shown in red. The bar graph on a map again shows the outfitting ports of the vessels carrying captives, this time for vessels arriving in the Americas rather than for those departing from Africa.

Throughout the *Atlas,* the paths of the slave trade, shown with arrows, connect points of departure and points of arrival, but they are not intended to portray the actual routes of the slave vessels. The width of the paths varies according to the number of slaves that we estimate to have left from a particular region or to have arrived in a particular region. The scale used to draw the paths does not remain constant through the *Atlas*. If a path in one map is wider than a path in another, the wider path does not necessarily represent a greater number of captives. As the legends for the maps make clear, such comparisons are valid only within a given map. To underline this point we have added to many of the paths our estimate of the actual number of slaves carried from one point to another. If the number is located on a path near Africa, it designates departures from the African region or port. If it is located on a path near a region or port in the Americas, it designates arrivals. Because of deaths on the voyages, the sum of departures from all African regions is typically greater than the sum of all arrivals in the Americas.

In one part, however, part IV, the data on the paths reflect not the number of captives but their age and sex ratios, the length of the voyages on which they traveled, and onboard mortality. Again, if a number on a path is located near Africa, it refers to voyages leaving a particular African coastal region. If it is located close to the Americas, it refers to voyages arriving in a particular American region.

Most maps contain tables with summaries of the statistics that label the paths. The table with each map gives some indication of the reliability of the map by showing what share of the data is based on documented information about voyages and what share is based on our estimates. The sum of row 1 in each table (documented statistics) and row 2 (estimated statistics) will correspond to the sum of the statistics shown on the paths (allowing for rounding and the exclusion from the map of some places that only small numbers of slaves left or reached).

Because the range of years covered by the *Atlas* is very large, we have set the political boundaries in the maps according to three benchmark years: 1650, 1750, and 1850. The year used for a given map is indicated in its legend. Because the boundaries for countries in Europe and the Americas are generally well known, we have not always added country names. But for Africa we have provided, in part III, maps displaying both political units and ethnolinguistic terms. For the limits of the African coastal regions used throughout the *Atlas* and their relation to modern nation-states, see map 8. We have used modern names for embarkation points in Africa where these are available. Variations in the dates in the map titles are often the product of the documents available. Readers should note that the trade in African slaves from Europe to the Americas probably began around 1501, but the trade directly from Africa to the Americas began only in 1525. They should also note that the database may have information on departures for a certain span of years, for example, but information on arrivals for a somewhat different span.

Further aid is supplied in a timeline and a glossary of terms, both at the end of this book.

Methodology

Ninety percent of the maps in the *Atlas* are constructed from a set of estimates derived from the Trans-Atlantic Slave Trade Database as it existed in January 2008—almost a year before the launch of the *Voyages* Web site (www.slavevoyages

.org), which includes the database, formerly available only on CD-ROM. Because the database is constantly updated and corrected as new information becomes available, readers cannot replicate the statistics in this atlas exactly by using statistics found via the search interfaces on the *Voyages* Web site. The differences between the statistics on the Web site and those in the *Atlas* are never likely to be major, however, and we do not anticipate that the maps will need to be redrawn anytime soon.

In January 2008 the database underlying the *Atlas* contained details of 34,934 documented slave voyages. We think that these voyages constitute just over 80 percent of all the slave ventures that ever set out for Africa to obtain slaves from all locations around the Atlantic. With the exception of some maps in the introduction and all those in parts IV and VI, the maps in the *Atlas* are based on estimates of the slave trade rather than on the raw data of slave voyages. The procedures by which the estimates were drawn from the raw data are identical to those described at the Web site (see http://www.slavevoyages.org/downloads/EstimatesMethod.pdf, and http://www.slavevoyages.org/downloads/Estimates-2010.xlsx, both cowritten by David Eltis and Paul F. Lachance). Essentially, estimates of the total slave trade allow for voyages that occurred without leaving any known trace in the historical record. The voyages that we know about are all identified in the database with a number. For those interested in investigating further, we have included a unique "voyage id" number in citing some tables and logbook entries. This number allows the reader to identify the voyage in the Search the Voyages Database interface on the Web site.

Slave voyages could last for two years or more from the time a vessel left the port in which it was outfitted. Groupings of years in the maps are always based on the year of arrival in the Americas. The statistics supplied in most maps are rounded. For numbers below 10,000, rounding is to the nearest hundred; for numbers above 9,999, rounding is to the nearest thousand. This convention results in apparent discrepancies, particularly in comparisons across maps and tables. For example, in map 100, "Luanda: Destinations of Slaves and Home Ports of Vessels Carrying Them, 1582–1850," the table shows disembarkations of 2,433,000 slaves, but the figures on the arrows on the Americas side of the map total only 2,429,900.

Most of the maps in this atlas show elements of the slave trade at a broad scale in order to illustrate the intercontinental connections between regions of slave embarkation, outfitting ports of slaving ships, and final destinations of captives. Inset maps present detailed information that would otherwise be lost on a map showing the entire Atlantic basin. Most of the maps use the Mollweide projection centered on the Atlantic Ocean. The Mollweide is an equal-area projection, meaning that it represents land masses at their true relative sizes. Many readers may not be familiar with this projection and may consider the shape of some land masses to be somewhat distorted in comparison to their representation on other maps. We chose to use the Mollweide in order to display the size of Africa as accurately as possible in relation to the other continents and in order to highlight the large regions of the slave trade and their connections to traders and slave markets in Europe, North America, and South America.

The maps displaying the political and the ethnolinguistic terms associated with political boundaries in Africa are identical to those at the *Voyages* Web site and were developed with the aid of specialists in each region of Africa.

Overall, the *Atlas* presents a fuller picture of the geography and the underlying patterns of the largest forced oceanic migration of people in history than has been possible to date. But it represents only a portion of the journey that these migrants were forced to undergo. The term *Middle Passage* describes the middle leg of the typical slave-trading voyage that went from Europe to Africa to the Americas, but it is appropriate in another, broader sense. The ocean voyage was also the middle leg of the journey traveled by the typical slave: from the point of capture to the point of embarkation on the African coast was the first leg, the transatlantic voyage was the second leg, and, if the captive survived the voyage, there was a third leg, from the point of disembarkation to the point of ultimate sale. Perhaps one-fifth of all slaves arriving in the New World faced further arduous travel after their arrival. In all the major Brazilian ports captives could be resold into the gold-producing regions of Minas Gerais and Goías or, later, into coffee estates in the southeast. Slaves taken to the Atlantic ports in the Spanish colonies of the mainland Americas usually ended their odyssey in Peru or the interior of Mexico. Possibly as many as one-third of the slaves taken to the eastern Caribbean were sold on to other markets in the Spanish and British Americas.

Sources

The basic source upon which the *Atlas* draws is the database at www.slavevoyages .org, which contains records of nearly 35,000 transatlantic slave voyages. In the tables on the maps in this atlas, the rows marked "Documented" present the results of analyzing the data on the Search the Database page of the Web site. The Understanding the Database page of the Web site (http://www.slavevoyages.org/tast/ database/sources.faces?type=documentary) provides a full list of sources used in assembling the records. In the tables on the maps in this atlas, the rows marked "Estimated" refer to the Estimates page at the same site (http://www.slavevoyages .org/tast/assessment/estimates.faces). The larger tables included with the introductions to parts I–VI of this atlas are also calculated from the Search the Database and Estimates pages of the database.

For the construction of the estimates see the "Estimates spreadsheet" section of the database (http://www.slavevoyages.org/tast/database/download.faces), where the relevant spreadsheets may be downloaded. The spreadsheets should be read in conjunction with both the methodology essay by David Eltis and Paul F. Lachance, "Estimates of the Size and Direction of the Transatlantic Slave Trade" (2009), which may be downloaded from the same page, and the essays in David Eltis and David Richardson, eds., *Extending the Frontiers: Essays on the New Transatlantic Slave Trade Database* (New Haven: Yale University Press, 2008), especially chapter 1 (pp. 1–60).

Atlas of the Transatlantic Slave Trade

Introduction

Slavery is as old as recorded history; it was present in all ancient civilizations, and in the Mediterranean and the Middle East it was a major feature of empires and societies from the Roman Empire to the nineteenth century. Wherever slavery has existed, it has almost invariably been accompanied by slave trading: the buying, bartering for, and selling of people. Those enslaved were people of all colors; people of different religions; people of every social class. They worked in households and workshops, served in galleys, marched in armies, and, perhaps most important, cultivated crops, including sugarcane.

Sugarcane cultivation emerged in the Pacific in the pre-Christian era, and over the course of more than two millennia it traveled westward around the globe, reentering the Pacific from the Americas in the nineteenth century. In its passage out of the Mediterranean and across the Atlantic, it became indelibly associated with coerced labor. Once Portuguese and Spanish voyages of discovery had initiated conquests around the Atlantic basin, sugar became the economic foundation of a transatlantic trade in enslaved Africans. Sugar plantations producing for export spread first to the islands of the eastern Atlantic (1460s), then to the Gulf of Guinea, in particular São Tomé (1490s), and eventually to northeastern Brazil (1560s). From there it moved first to Barbados (1640s), the most easterly of the Caribbean islands, and then to the rest of the Caribbean.

In the fifteenth and sixteenth centuries the number of Africans traded across the Atlantic basin was modest, perhaps barely exceeding the number of slaves leaving Africa by other routes. Unlike the traffic in slaves in the Mediterranean world, however, the traffic in slaves in the eastern Atlantic islands and the Americas soon became racially based. Europeans considered only Africans, or at least non-Europeans, to be eligible for shipment to the new European colonies as slaves. All societies had fairly clear ideas of who could and could not be enslaved. In the early sixteenth century African conceptions of eligibility embraced a smaller geographic area than the European conception did. Both buyers (Europeans) and sellers (Africans) saw the people traded into captivity on the African coast as outsiders, although the identities that made trading possible did not remain constant over time.

In the seventeenth and eighteenth centuries, most of the economically buoyant areas of the Atlantic world were engaged in the transatlantic slave trade. The fastest-growing states in western Europe helped with the organization of voyages. In the Americas, the regions that had the highest incomes organized the most voyages. The parts of Africa that had passed furthest beyond the agricultural revolution generated the slaves. The first Europeans in the Americas—the Spanish—conquered what in 1492 was the richest part of the two continents in the Western Hemisphere, but 200 years later, the economic center of gravity of the Americas had shifted away from Central America into those parts of the Caribbean and coastal Brazil where the sugar plantation complex had emerged. It was in such highly productive regions that the vast majority of slave vessels from Africa discharged their human cargoes.

Atlantic environmental realities shaped the geographic distribution of sugar production and the slave trade. Prevailing winds and ocean currents created not one but two slave-trading systems, each with its own largely distinct centers of organization, regions of slave provenance, and American slave markets. The division is immediately apparent in map 4. In the slightly larger northern system, trade followed the track of currents north of the equator, which turned clockwise like a giant wheel, or gyre. This slave-trading system was based mainly in Europe and drew almost all its captives from north of the Congo River. Those caught up in this system ended up in North America, especially the Caribbean, or along the Río de la Plata. In the "triangular trade" of this system, vessels sailed from Europe to West Africa carrying trade goods, took captives from West Africa to the Caribbean (the transatlantic voyage was the so-called Middle Passage), and then returned to Europe with New World products to sell. For a century and a half after 1660, as the Caribbean came to surpass Brazil as a sugar-producing region, the English dominated the northern system of the slave trade. The second and much less well-known system was in the South Atlantic. Here, the wheel of currents turned counterclockwise. The slave trade, which was based in Brazil, linked the vast area of West Central Africa with Brazil south of Amazonia. A much less important branch of the trade joined one region of Brazil, Bahia, with an area centered on the Bight of Benin, known as the Costa da Mina in the Luso (Portuguese) world, after a 1678 treaty between Portugal and the Netherlands, which allowed Dutch monitoring of Portuguese ships sailing along the Gold Coast. The Portuguese were virtually the only Europeans who took advantage of the southern winds and currents, although the ships of most European nations did round the Cape of Good Hope and trade in Southeast Africa, an area that in effect was appended to both the North and the South Atlantic systems.

The northern slave-trading system is still the better documented of the two. We know that the price of slaves in the Caribbean increased steadily over the two centuries when the trade was at its height. As similar information for Brazil after 1800 becomes available, an almost identical pattern is emerging for the slave trade south of the equator. As table 1 shows, the number of slaves carried to the Americas increased as the prices of captives (and sugar prices) increased, suggesting a strong demand-driven expansion of the transatlantic slave market. In all, an estimated 12.5 million captives were carried from Africa, of whom only 10.7 million survived the crossing to the Americas.

Table 1 Real Slave and Sugar Prices in the Western Caribbean in Pounds Sterling, 1674–1808

	Real Slave Price (Number of Slaves)	Real Slave Price Index (1674 = 100)	Real Sugar Price (shillings per cwt)*	Real Sugar Price Index (1674 = 100)
1674	20.3 (732)	100	21.9	100
1675–1679	18.5 (9,108)	91.1	20.8	95.0
1680–1684	19.2 (9,259)	94.6	22.5	102.7
1685–1689	21.7 (9,302)	106.9	21.9	100.0
1690–1694	20.3 (4,947)	100.0	36.1	164.8
1695–1699	21.1 (5,392)	103.9	30.8	140.6
1700–1704	25.8 (13,957)	127.1	42.5	194.1
1705–1709	28.3 (10,239)	139.4	34.3	156.6
1710–1714	23.4 (1,984)	115.3	58.1	265.3
1715–1719	20.1 (850)	99.0	32.6	148.9
1720–1724	27.2 (7,205)	134.0	29.1	132.9
1725–1729	28.8 (2,250)	141.9	27.1	123.7
1730–1734	30.8 (2,333)	151.7	22.8	104.1
1735–1739	32.9 (2,514)	162.1	26.5	121.0
1740–1744	33.7 (7,387)	166.0	33.1	151.1
1745–1749	31.5 (1,837)	155.2	37.5	171.2
1750–1754	38.2 (6,324)	188.2	40.1	183.1
1755–1759	36.5 (12,194)	179.8	41.4	189.0
1760–1764	39.8 (7,806)	196.1	38.1	174.0
1765–1769	43.1 (6,795)	212.3	39.2	179.0
1770–1774	46.0 (16,734)	226.6	36.6	167.1
1775–1779	43.8 (17,331)	215.8	39.1	178.5
1780–1784	44.4 (7,292)	218.7	37.8	172.6
1785–1789	55.1 (10,744)	271.4	42.5	194.1
1790–1794	53.7 (18,491)	264.5	52.4	239.3
1795–1799	50.7 (2,174)	249.8	47.8	218.3
1800–1804	50.2 (1,813)	247.3	28.3	129.2
1805–1808	51.9 (2,775)	255.7	30.8	140.6

Source: Derived from David Eltis, Frank D. Lewis, and David Richardson, "Slave Prices, the African Slave Trade and Productivity Growth in the Caribbean," *Economic History Review* 58 (2005): 673–700, especially table 2.

Note: Prices and indexes are five-year averages.

* A hundredweight (cwt) was equal to 112 pounds avoirdupois.

Map 1: The Trade in Slaves from Africa, 1501–1900

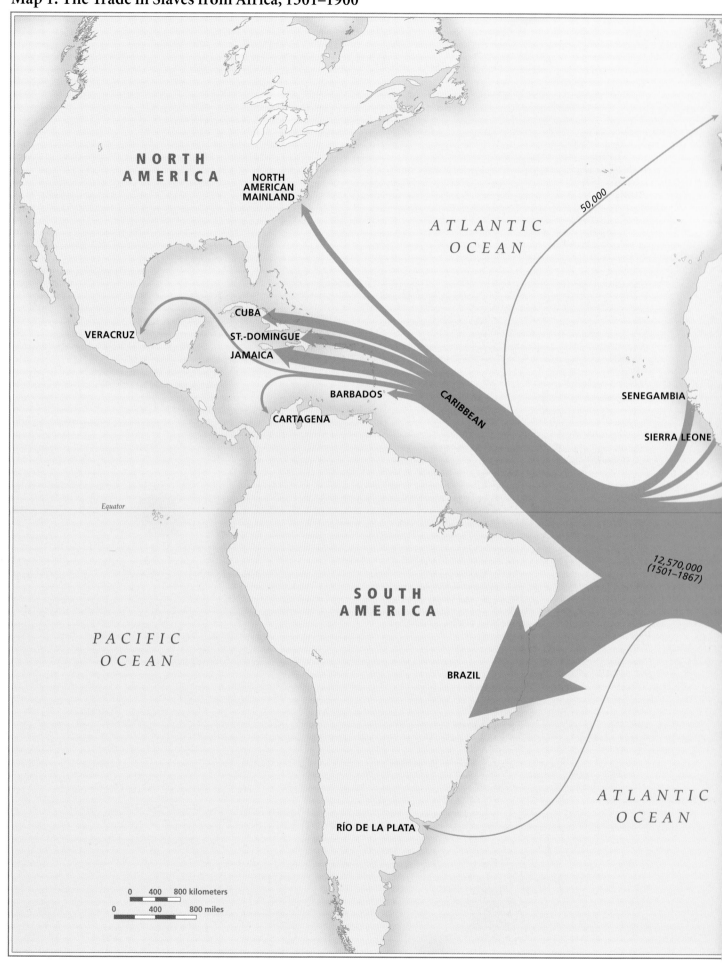

NORTH AMERICA

NORTH AMERICAN MAINLAND

ATLANTIC OCEAN

50,000

VERACRUZ

CUBA

ST.-DOMINGUE

JAMAICA

BARBADOS

CARTAGENA

CARIBBEAN

SENEGAMBIA

SIERRA LEONE

Equator

12,570,000 (1501–1867)

SOUTH AMERICA

PACIFIC OCEAN

BRAZIL

RÍO DE LA PLATA

ATLANTIC OCEAN

0   400   800 kilometers
0   400   800 miles

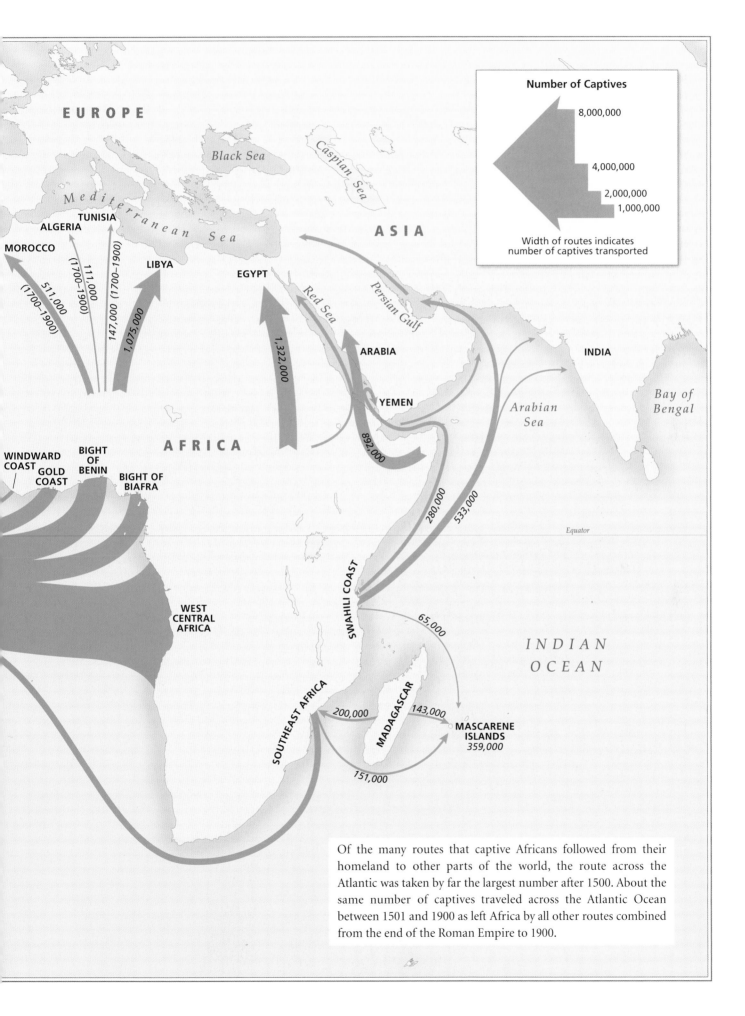

EUROPE

Black Sea

Caspian Sea

Mediterranean Sea

ASIA

TUNISIA
ALGERIA

MOROCCO

LIBYA

EGYPT

111,000 (1700–1900)

511,000 (1700–1900)

147,000 (1700–1900)

1,075,000

1,322,000

Red Sea

Persian Gulf

ARABIA

INDIA

Bay of Bengal

YEMEN

Arabian Sea

892,000

Number of Captives

8,000,000

4,000,000

2,000,000
1,000,000

Width of routes indicates
number of captives transported

AFRICA

WINDWARD
COAST

BIGHT
OF
BENIN

GOLD
COAST

BIGHT OF
BIAFRA

WEST
CENTRAL
AFRICA

SWAHILI COAST

280,000

533,000

Equator

65,000

INDIAN
OCEAN

SOUTHEAST AFRICA

200,000

MADAGASCAR

143,000

MASCARENE
ISLANDS
359,000

151,000

Of the many routes that captive Africans followed from their
homeland to other parts of the world, the route across the
Atlantic was taken by far the largest number after 1500. About the
same number of captives traveled across the Atlantic Ocean
between 1501 and 1900 as left Africa by all other routes combined
from the end of the Roman Empire to 1900.

Map 2: The Diffusion of Sugar Cultivation from Asia to the Eastern Atlantic Islands, 600 BCE to 1650 CE

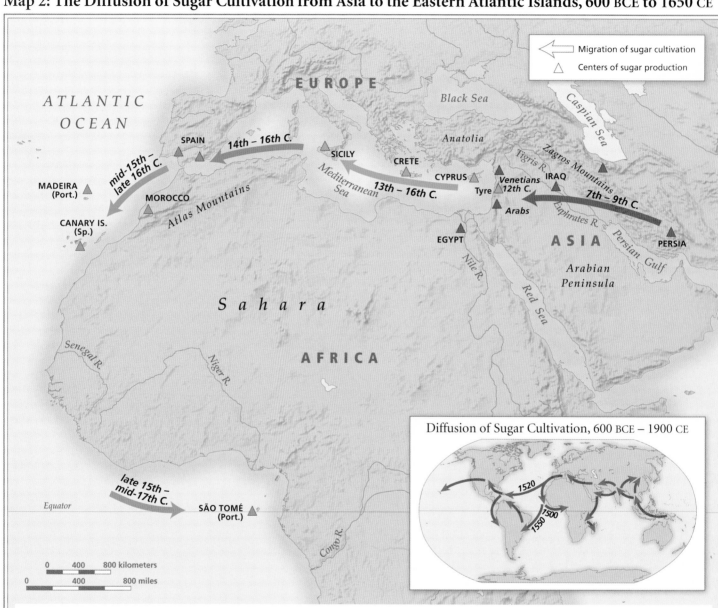

Sugar is the one of keys to understanding the transatlantic slave trade. Cultivation for export (as opposed to cultivation for local consumption) began on Pacific islands before the Common Era and gradually spread across Asia to the eastern Mediterranean, Sicily, the eastern Atlantic islands, the Gulf of Guinea, and Brazil before reaching the Caribbean in the mid-sixteenth century and eventually returning – with greatly changed cultivation practices – to the Pacific islands. Eighty percent of all captives carried from Africa to the Americas during the slave-trade era were taken to sugar-growing areas.

Map 3: The Old World Slave Trade in the Eastern Atlantic, 1441–1758

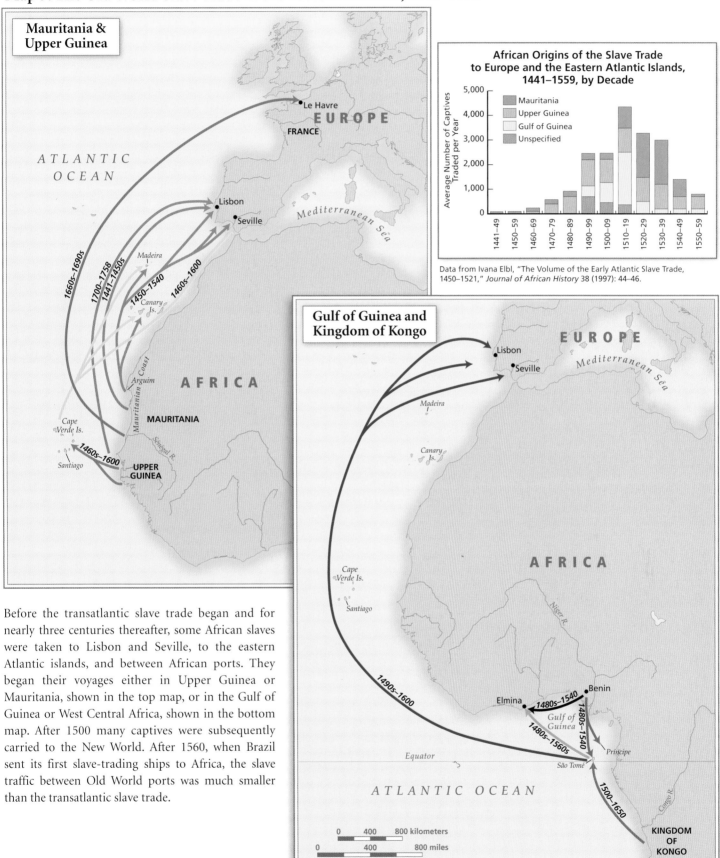

Mauritania & Upper Guinea

Gulf of Guinea and Kingdom of Kongo

African Origins of the Slave Trade to Europe and the Eastern Atlantic Islands, 1441–1559, by Decade

Data from Ivana Elbl, "The Volume of the Early Atlantic Slave Trade, 1450–1521," *Journal of African History* 38 (1997): 44–46.

Before the transatlantic slave trade began and for nearly three centuries thereafter, some African slaves were taken to Lisbon and Seville, to the eastern Atlantic islands, and between African ports. They began their voyages either in Upper Guinea or Mauritania, shown in the top map, or in the Gulf of Guinea or West Central Africa, shown in the bottom map. After 1500 many captives were subsequently carried to the New World. After 1560, when Brazil sent its first slave-trading ships to Africa, the slave traffic between Old World ports was much smaller than the transatlantic slave trade.

Map 4: Winds and Ocean Currents of the Atlantic Basin

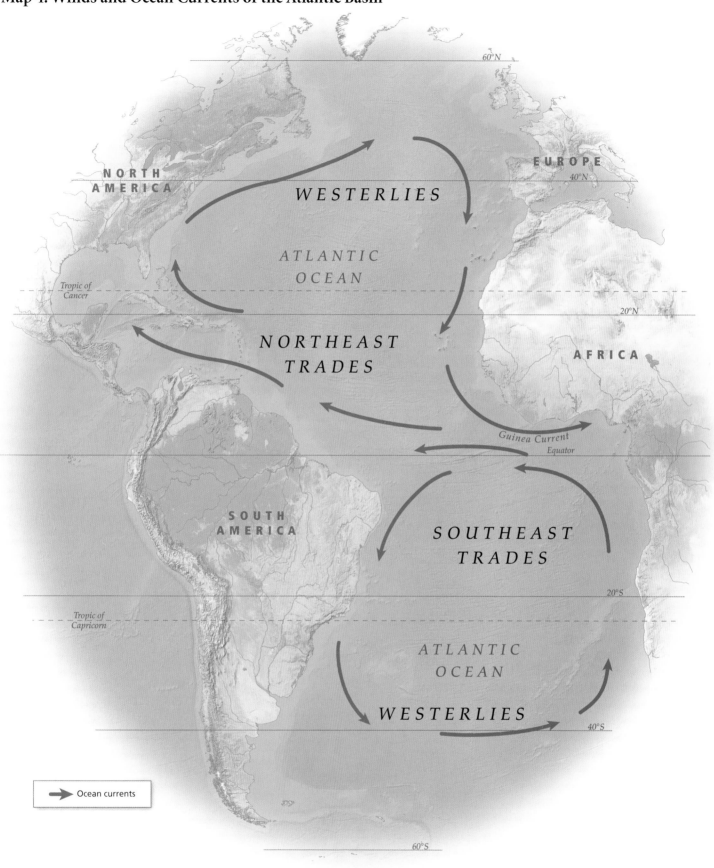

Winds – trade winds and westerlies – and ocean currents determined which Africans arrived in which parts of the Americas, as well as which slave-trading nations would dominate. The winds and currents effectively created two slave-trading systems – one in the north with voyages originating in Europe and North America, and the other in the south with voyages originating in Brazil and the Río de la Plata. For slave traders using the northern circuit, the Guinea Current that carried vessels to West Africa was also important (see Daniel Domingues da Silva, "The Atlantic Slave Trade to Maranhão, 1680–1846: Volume, Routes and Organisation," *Slavery and Abolition* 29 [2008]: 477–501).

Map 5: Voyage of the *Laurence Frigate*, 1730–1731

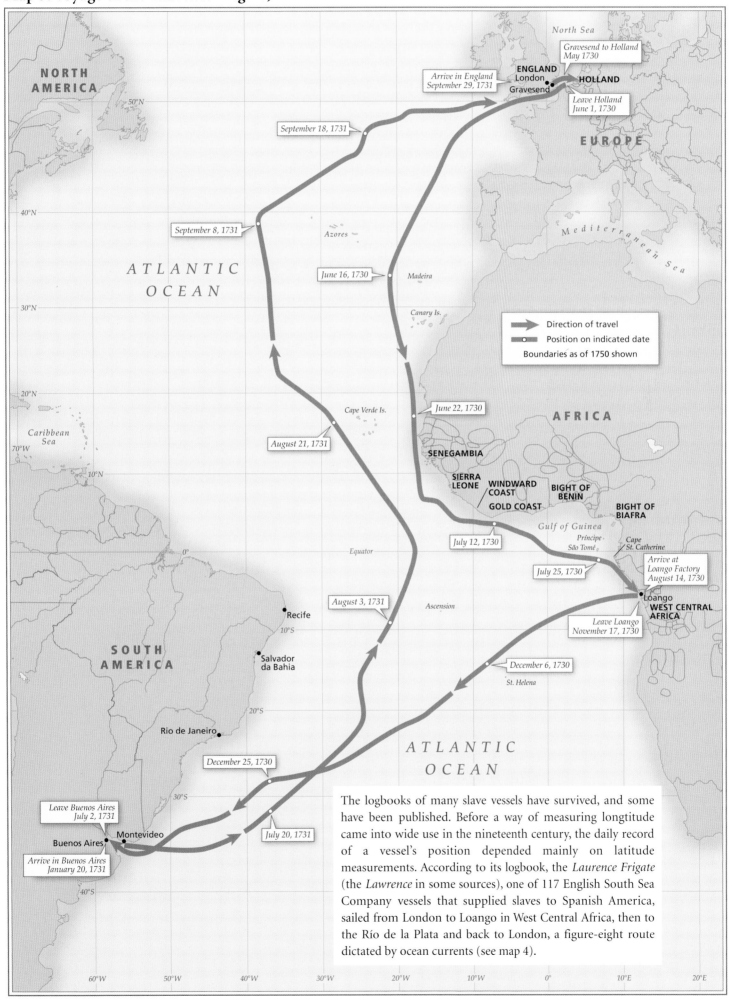

Gravesend to Holland
May 1730

ENGLAND
London
Gravesend

HOLLAND

Arrive in England
September 29, 1731

Leave Holland
June 1, 1730

EUROPE

NORTH
AMERICA

North Sea

September 18, 1731

50°N

40°N

September 8, 1731

ATLANTIC
OCEAN

30°N

Azores

June 16, 1730

Madeira

Canary Is.

Direction of travel

Position on indicated date

Boundaries as of 1750 shown

20°N

Caribbean
Sea

70°W

Cape Verde Is.

June 22, 1730

AFRICA

10°N

SENEGAMBIA

August 21, 1731

SIERRA
LEONE   WINDWARD
          COAST   BIGHT OF
                       BENIN

GOLD COAST   BIGHT OF
                  BIAFRA

Gulf of Guinea

0°

Equator

July 12, 1730

Príncipe
São Tomé

Cape
St. Catherine

Arrive at
Loango Factory
August 14, 1730

July 25, 1730

Loango
WEST CENTRAL
AFRICA

August 3, 1731

Ascension

Leave Loango
November 17, 1730

Recife

10°S

December 6, 1730

St. Helena

SOUTH
AMERICA

Salvador
da Bahia

Rio de Janeiro

20°S

ATLANTIC
OCEAN

December 25, 1730

30°S

Leave Buenos Aires
July 2, 1731

Montevideo

July 20, 1731

Buenos Aires

Arrive in Buenos Aires
January 20, 1731

40°S

60°W   50°W   40°W   30°W   20°W   10°W   0°   10°E   20°E

The logbooks of many slave vessels have survived, and some
have been published. Before a way of measuring longtitude
came into wide use in the nineteenth century, the daily record
of a vessel's position depended mainly on latitude
measurements. According to its logbook, the *Laurence Frigate*
(the *Lawrence* in some sources), one of 117 English South Sea
Company vessels that supplied slaves to Spanish America,
sailed from London to Loango in West Central Africa, then to
the Río de la Plata and back to London, a figure-eight route
dictated by ocean currents (see map 4).

Map 6: Major Regions and Ports in the Transatlantic Slave Trade, 1501–1867

All major and most minor ports in the Atlantic world had strong connections with the slave trade.

The first favourable opportunity you are to sail from hence for Douglass Isleman there to take on Board from Mr Paul Bridson sundry goods as P[er] List inclos'd, From thence proceed for Old Callabar w[h]ere you are to Barter our Cargoe as P[er] Invoice annex'd for Slaves & Elephants Teeth [i.e., ivory], as yr Cargoe is large we would not have you omit any opportunity of purchasing Teeth during your whole stay there & that you dont suffer your people to buy any unless small Scravelas [tusks or teeth] untill you have Compleated, wch has always been ye Custom of trade in that Place, as you are experiencd in ye Customs &c there we need not dictate to you how to act therefore we depend on your prudent Management (wth ye Natives & Ships in the River) in your Trade for our best Interest, should your purchase be very tedious & Slaves scarse we think it advisable that you leave the river when you have got 350 Slaves rather than Risq your own lives by such long detention & what goods remain lay out for Teeth of any Size if possible & then proceed to Barbados and apply to Mr Saml Carter Mercht [merchant] there who will advise you ye State of prices for Slaves at ye Other Islands from wch you will Judge whether to proceed farther or Stop there.

Instructions from Wm Whaley, Robt Hallhead, John Williamson, Peers Legh, Edward Lowndes, John Clayton and Willm. Davenport to Wm Earle, commander of Snow Chesterfield, bound from Liverpool to Old Calabar, 22 May 1751. Earle Family and Business Archive, National Maritime Museum on Merseyside, Liverpool. Published with permission of the National Maritime Museum on Merseyside.

Map 7: Regions Where Slave Voyages Were Outfitted, 1501–1867

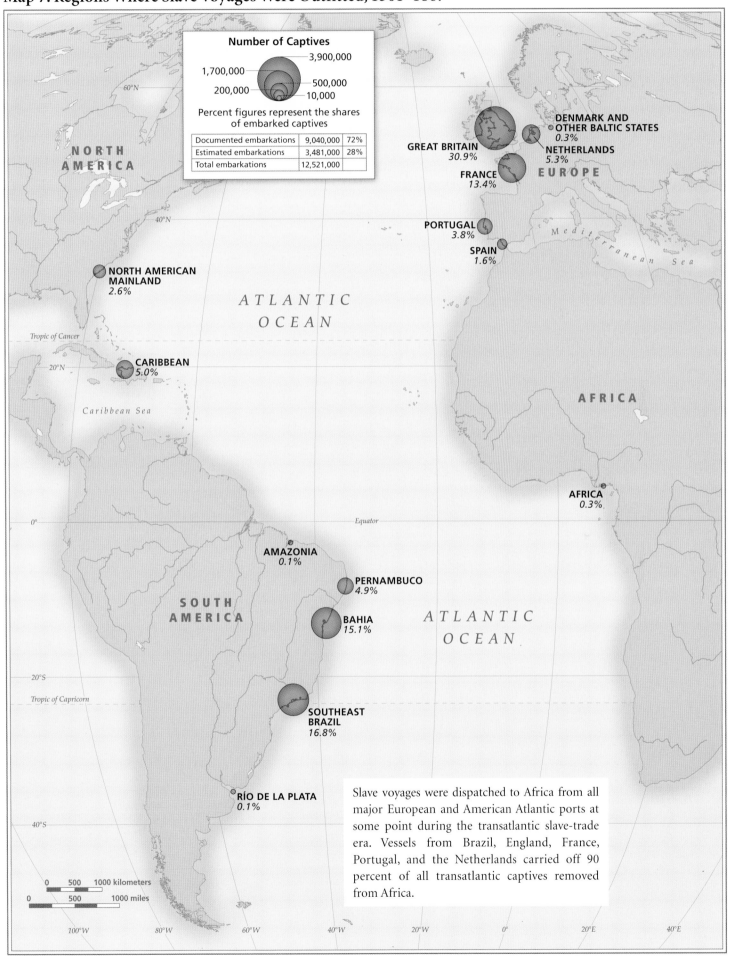

Number of Captives

3,900,000
1,700,000
500,000
200,000
10,000

Percent figures represent the shares
of embarked captives

Documented embarkations	9,040,000	72%
Estimated embarkations	3,481,000	28%
Total embarkations	12,521,000	

NORTH AMERICA

EUROPE

GREAT BRITAIN
30.9%

DENMARK AND
OTHER BALTIC STATES
0.3%

NETHERLANDS
5.3%

FRANCE
13.4%

PORTUGAL
3.8%

SPAIN
1.6%

Mediterranean Sea

NORTH AMERICAN
MAINLAND
2.6%

Tropic of Cancer

ATLANTIC
OCEAN

AFRICA

CARIBBEAN
5.0%

Caribbean Sea

AFRICA
0.3%

Equator

AMAZONIA
0.1%

SOUTH
AMERICA

PERNAMBUCO
4.9%

BAHIA
15.1%

ATLANTIC
OCEAN

Tropic of Capricorn

SOUTHEAST
BRAZIL
16.8%

RÍO DE LA PLATA
0.1%

Slave voyages were dispatched to Africa from all
major European and American Atlantic ports at
some point during the transatlantic slave-trade
era. Vessels from Brazil, England, France,
Portugal, and the Netherlands carried off 90
percent of all transatlantic captives removed
from Africa.

0   500   1000 kilometers
0   500   1000 miles

Map 8: Modern Africa and the Coastal Regions from Which Slaves Were Carried

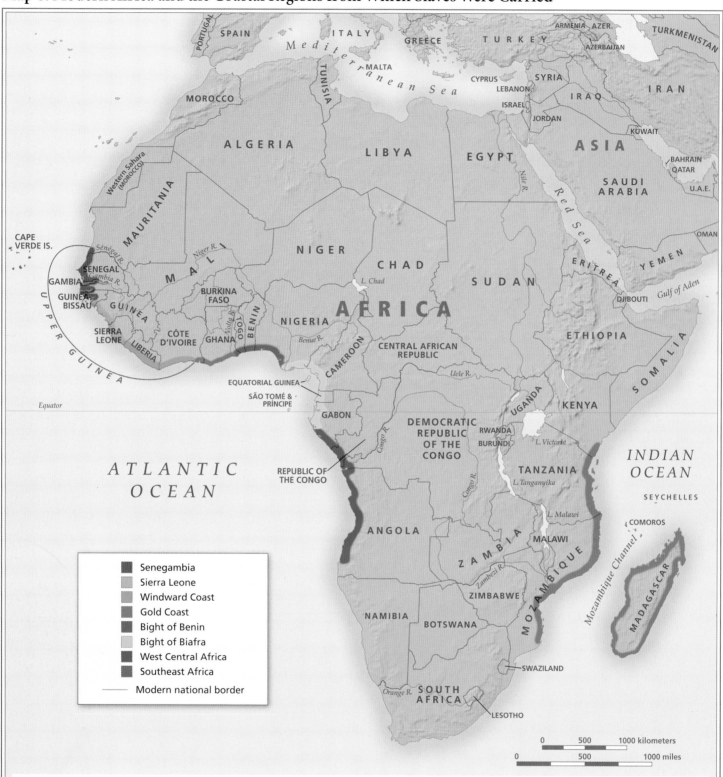

Legend:
- Senegambia
- Sierra Leone
- Windward Coast
- Gold Coast
- Bight of Benin
- Bight of Biafra
- West Central Africa
- Southeast Africa
- Modern national border

In the course of nearly four centuries of Atlantic slave trading, slaves left from six major coastal regions of sub-Saharan Africa – Upper Guinea, the Gold Coast, the Bight of Benin, the Bight of Biafra, West Central Africa, and Southeast Africa. At times in this atlas, Upper Guinea is broken down into three subregions, Senegambia, Sierra Leone, and the Windward Coast. These were in no sense political or ethnolinguistic regions. Rather, they were simply ranges of the coast separated from each other by either major physical features or areas in which little slave trading occurred. They are constantly referred to in the contemporary record as well as in this atlas, especially part III. Map 8 shows the limits of these coastal regions as well as their alignment with modern African nations.

Map 9: Regions from Which Slaves Left Africa, 1501–1867

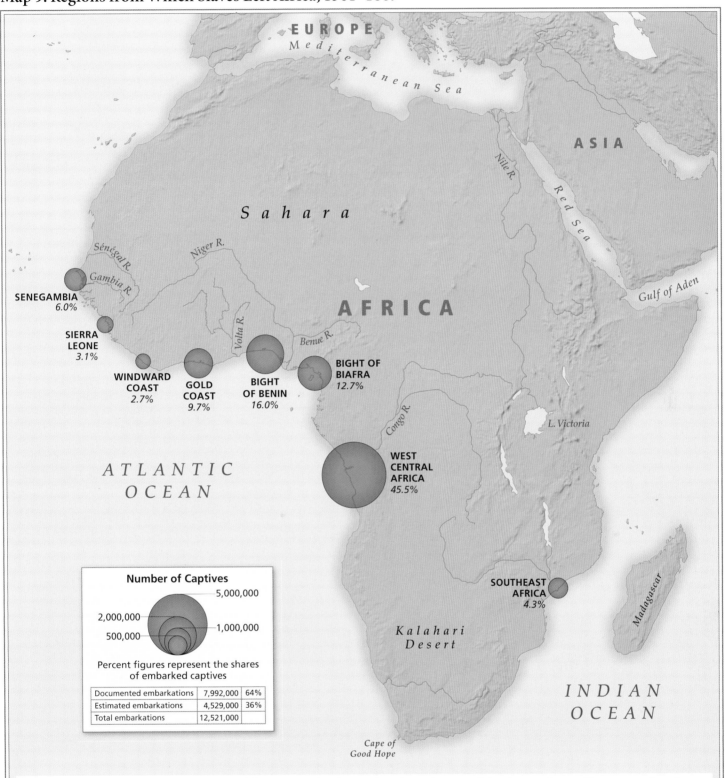

EUROPE

Mediterranean Sea

ASIA

Nile R.

Red Sea

S a h a r a

Gulf of Aden

Sénégal R.

Niger R.

A F R I C A

Gambia R.

SENEGAMBIA
6.0%

**SIERRA
LEONE**
3.1%

Volta R.

Benue R.

**WINDWARD
COAST**
2.7%

**GOLD
COAST**
9.7%

**BIGHT
OF BENIN**
16.0%

**BIGHT OF
BIAFRA**
12.7%

Congo R.

L. Victoria

**WEST
CENTRAL
AFRICA**
45.5%

A T L A N T I C
O C E A N

**SOUTHEAST
AFRICA**
4.3%

Madagascar

*K a l a h a r i
D e s e r t*

Number of Captives

- 5,000,000
- 2,000,000
- 1,000,000
- 500,000

Percent figures represent the shares
of embarked captives

Documented embarkations	7,992,000	64%
Estimated embarkations	4,529,000	36%
Total embarkations	12,521,000	

I N D I A N
O C E A N

*Cape of
Good Hope*

West Central Africa was the largest regional departure point for captives through most of the slave-trade era. Since voyage length was determined as much by winds and ocean currents as by distance, routes were not necessarily quicker from regions closer to the Americas and Europe. Regions west of the Gold Coast generated a relatively small share of the total number of slaves carried across the Atlantic.

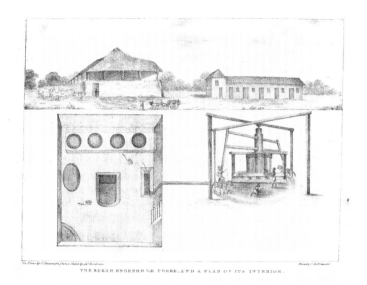

The Sugar *Engenho de Torre* and a Plan of Its Interior, c. 1800

Lithograph by C. Shoosmith from a sketch by James Henderson, from James Henderson, *A History of the Brazil* (London: Longman, Hurst, Rees, Orme and Brown, 1821). Courtesy of the John Carter Brown Library at Brown University.

Exterior of a Distillery on Weatherell's Estate, Antigua, 1823

Aquatint by William Clark from his *Ten Views in the Island of Antigua*, 1823. Beinecke Lesser Antilles Collection, Burke Library, Hamilton College.

Sugar production dominated the lives of many of the enslaved Africans who survived the Atlantic crossing. Work was commonly organized on a gang basis, with strong, healthy adults of both sexes forming the field gangs who planted and harvested the sugarcane. Other gangs of slaves provided essential support services. Cane cultivation was life-consuming, making regular supplies of captives essential to sustain production. Equally arduous was the refining, or "manufacturing," of the raw sugarcane into molasses, rum, and other products for the market. Refining the cane required investment in technology and in skilled African labor. Here we see a sugar *engenho* in Brazil, where juice is being squeezed from the cane, and a distillery in Antigua.

Map 10: Regions in Which Slaves Landed, 1501–1867

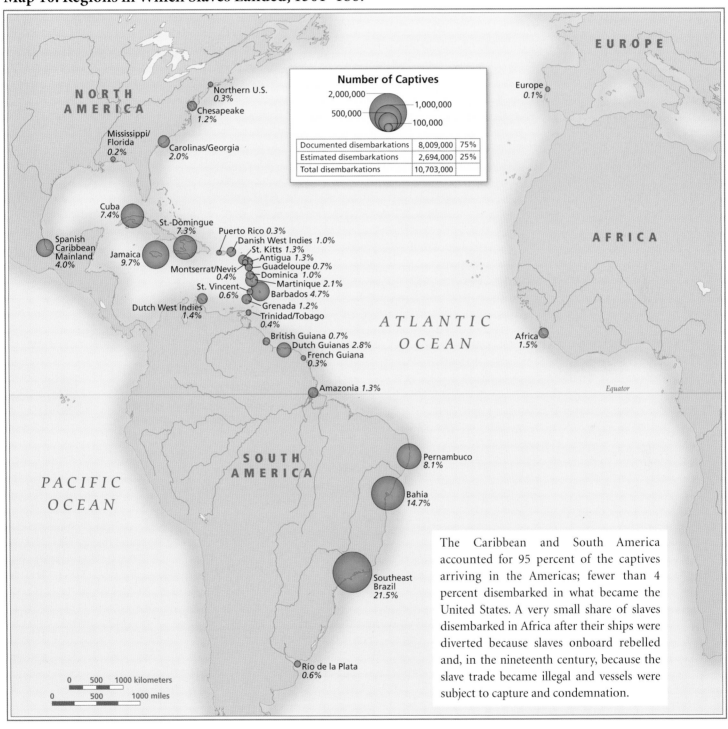

Number of Captives

2,000,000

1,000,000

500,000

100,000

Documented disembarkations	8,009,000	75%
Estimated disembarkations	2,694,000	25%
Total disembarkations	10,703,000	

EUROPE

NORTH AMERICA

AFRICA

SOUTH AMERICA

PACIFIC OCEAN

ATLANTIC OCEAN

Equator

Northern U.S. 0.3%

Chesapeake 1.2%

Mississippi/Florida 0.2%

Carolinas/Georgia 2.0%

Cuba 7.4%

St.-Domingue 7.3%

Spanish Caribbean Mainland 4.0%

Jamaica 9.7%

Puerto Rico 0.3%

Danish West Indies 1.0%

St. Kitts 1.3%

Antigua 1.3%

Guadeloupe 0.7%

Montserrat/Nevis 0.4%

Dominica 1.0%

Martinique 2.1%

St. Vincent 0.6%

Barbados 4.7%

Dutch West Indies 1.4%

Grenada 1.2%

Trinidad/Tobago 0.4%

British Guiana 0.7%

Dutch Guianas 2.8%

French Guiana 0.3%

Amazonia 1.3%

Europe 0.1%

Africa 1.5%

Pernambuco 8.1%

Bahia 14.7%

Southeast Brazil 21.5%

Río de la Plata 0.6%

0 500 1000 kilometers

0 500 1000 miles

The Caribbean and South America accounted for 95 percent of the captives arriving in the Americas; fewer than 4 percent disembarked in what became the United States. A very small share of slaves disembarked in Africa after their ships were diverted because slaves onboard rebelled and, in the nineteenth century, because the slave trade became illegal and vessels were subject to capture and condemnation.

Map 11: Overview of the Transatlantic Slave Trade, 1501–1867

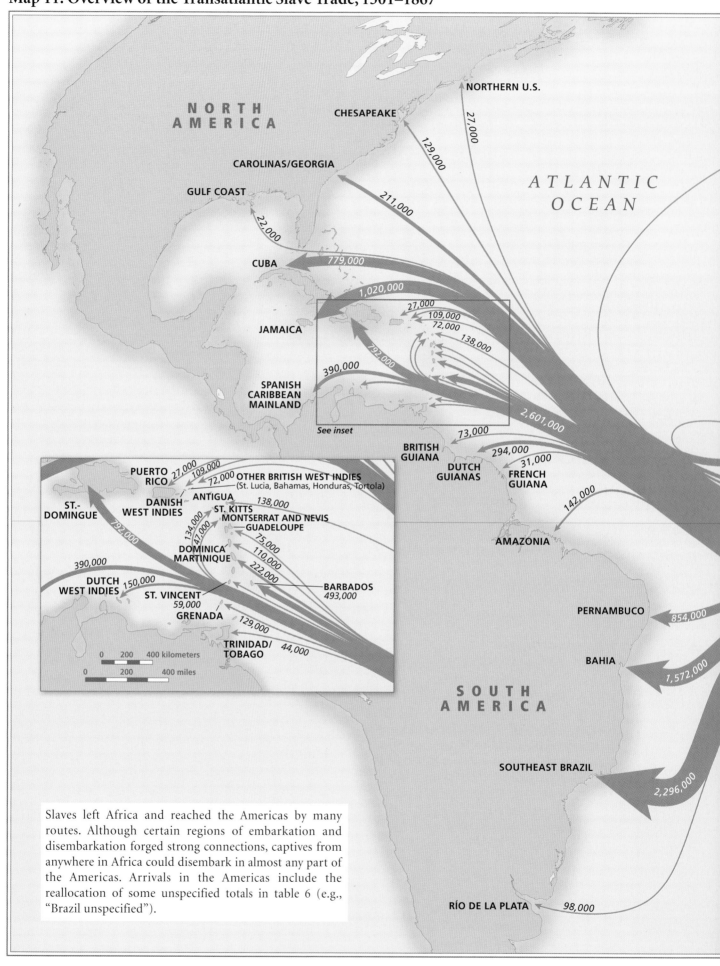

Slaves left Africa and reached the Americas by many routes. Although certain regions of embarkation and disembarkation forged strong connections, captives from anywhere in Africa could disembark in almost any part of the Americas. Arrivals in the Americas include the reallocation of some unspecified totals in table 6 (e.g., "Brazil unspecified").

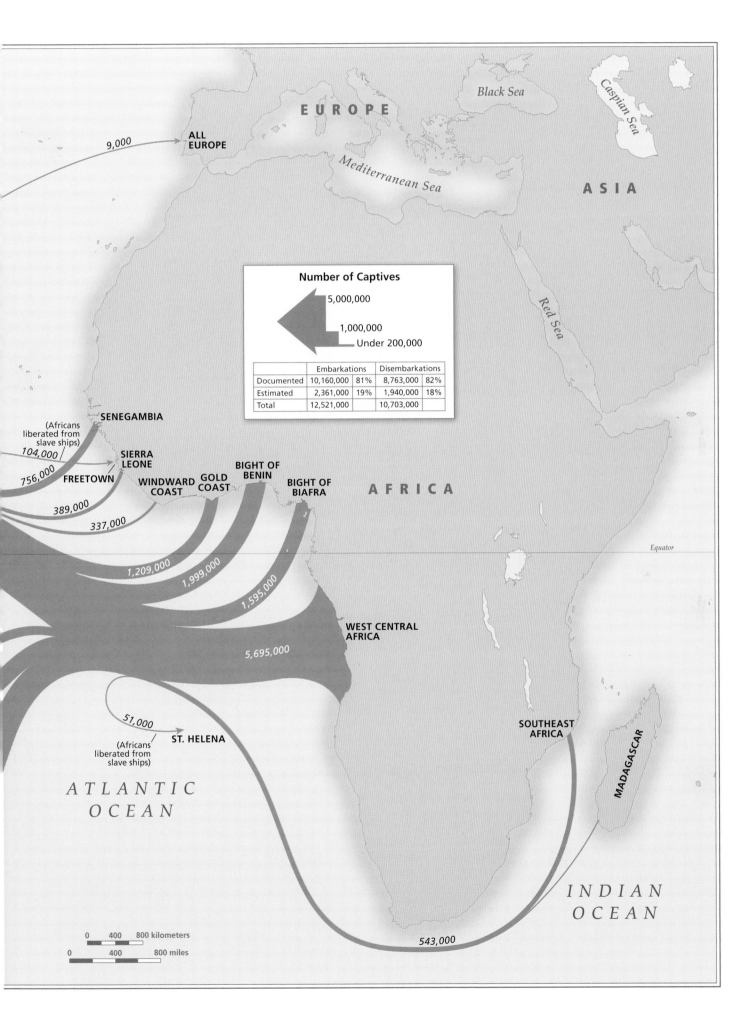

Number of Captives

5,000,000

1,000,000

Under 200,000

	Embarkations		Disembarkations	
Documented	10,160,000	81%	8,763,000	82%
Estimated	2,361,000	19%	1,940,000	18%
Total	12,521,000		10,703,000	

EUROPE

Black Sea

Caspian Sea

ALL EUROPE

9,000

Mediterranean Sea

ASIA

Red Sea

AFRICA

SENEGAMBIA

(Africans liberated from slave ships)

104,000

756,000

SIERRA LEONE

FREETOWN

389,000

337,000

WINDWARD COAST

GOLD COAST

BIGHT OF BENIN

BIGHT OF BIAFRA

Equator

1,209,000

1,999,000

1,595,000

WEST CENTRAL AFRICA

5,695,000

51,000

ST. HELENA

(Africans liberated from slave ships)

SOUTHEAST AFRICA

MADAGASCAR

ATLANTIC OCEAN

INDIAN OCEAN

543,000

0   400   800 kilometers

0   400   800 miles

Part I
Nations Transporting Slaves from Africa, 1501–1867

Every nation that had an Atlantic coastline and merchants involved in Atlantic trade participated in the transportation of slaves from Africa to the Americas during the slave-trade era. The era is generally considered to have begun in 1501, when vessels crossing the Atlantic from Spain began to carry some African captives for sale in the Greater Antilles (the larger islands of the West Indies), and ended in 1867, when the last slave ship from Africa is thought to have disembarked its captives in Cuba (also in the Greater Antilles). For most of this time, buying and selling human beings was no different from buying and selling commodities. Participation in the transatlantic slave trade before the nineteenth century was shaped by opportunity, not morality. A presence in the Americas created the opportunity, and the winds and currents of the Atlantic made the traffic possible. Governments at first tried to channel the slave trade, but thousands of entrepreneurs came to shape the direction and size of the traffic prior to the rise of abolitionism in the nineteenth century.

A breakdown of the slave-trade era into three time periods reflects, at least in part, the principal slave-trading nations' entry into and departure from the trade. In the first period, before 1642, the Iberian powers dominated the trade, with Portugal and Spain being united in 1580–1640 and, in commercial terms, their separation taking place in 1641. By that date a second phase of the trade was under way as the nations of northern Europe began systematically to engage in it. They were subsequently joined by traders from mainland North America. This phase of the trade ended in 1808, when the British and U.S. anti-slave-trade laws of 1807–1808 took effect and other northern European nations began disengaging from the trade. Disengagement ushered in the third period, which lasted through 1867 and during which the slave trade was again dominated by Portuguese and Spanish speakers, operating largely from bases in Brazil and Cuba, against a background of growing abolitionist and suppression activities.

As table 2 shows, the most important maritime powers during the slave-trade era were also the world's leading slave traders. The Spanish and the Portuguese—with large assists from northern Italian capital and maritime expertise—established the first European empires in the Americas and pioneered the early slave trade. By the early seventeenth century, the slave-trading systems of the North and South Atlantic were firmly established (see map 4). The northern wheel of winds and currents, plus the Guinea Current to West Africa, supplied Spanish America. The southern wheel supplied Brazil. The Portuguese flag flew over much of the transatlantic slave trade until the mid-seventeenth century, when northern European nations established their own colonies in the Americas and almost immediately began a steady traffic in slaves. The Dutch, French, and English, as well as the Danes, Swedes, Brandenburgers (later Prussians), and others sent vessels to Africa to obtain captives before 1700.

By 1660 a pattern had emerged that held during the next century and a half. The Portuguese no longer had much of a presence in the slave traffic to Spanish America and the Caribbean but had come to control the South Atlantic slave trade, which was conducted not from Portugal but from Brazil. All other European slaving nations operated largely north of the equator. Regular participation by traders based in North America began after 1730, and the newly independent United States briefly became a major player in the early nineteenth century. England was easily the leading slave-trading power in the North Atlantic; for most of the eighteenth century its ships carried more slaves to the Americas than did those of any other European country, including Portugal. Each nation supplied captives mainly to its own colonies in the Americas.

In the eighteenth century, slave traders competed intensely with each other on the African coast except during periods of European war, which amounted to more than one-third of the century. During wartime, French and, sometimes, Dutch slave vessels remained in port. Nevertheless, certain European countries dominated particular regions for a time. The Portuguese flag was usually the one seen in the major ports of West Central Africa—Luanda and Benguela—and on the southern rivers of the Senegambia region. The English were almost as successful in excluding other nations from the Bight of Biafra in what is now southeast Nigeria: they managed to carry off 87 percent of the slaves taken from the region in the eighteenth century. Also in the eighteenth century the French dominated slaving ports just north of the Congo River prior to the outbreak of the St.-Domingue slave rebellion in 1791. The Dutch had enclave markets on the Gold Coast and at Cap Lahou (now Grand Lahou) on the Ivory Coast. Traders from countries on the Baltic Sea carried off most of the captives taken from the eastern Gold Coast (the area around Christiansborg today).

In the nineteenth century abolition and suppression dramatically altered the pattern of participation in the slave trade. With the gradual withdrawal of the northern European powers, the slave trade came to be dominated once more by the Spanish and the Portuguese, operating largely out of Cuba and Brazil, respectively. Because attempts to suppress the slave trade targeted particular nations, from the mid-1830s slave traders often abandoned their own national flags and flew the flags of other countries, often fraudulently obtained, for at least a portion of a voyage or carried no registration papers at all. Mexican, Argentinian, Sardinian, and Imperial Russian flags, among others, show up in the traffic, and because British antislave-trade patrols were less likely to detain U.S. vessels, the U.S. flag was widely used, even though the number of slave voyages after 1810 sponsored by citizens of the United States remained small.

Table 2   Number of Slaves Taken from Africa by Nationality of the Vessel That Carried Them, 1501–1867

	Spain / Uruguay	Portugal / Brazil	Great Britain	Netherlands	United States	France	Baltic States	Total*
1501–1525	6,400	7,000	0	0	0	0	0	13,400
1526–1550	25,000	25,000	0	0	0	0	0	50,000
1551–1575	28,000	31,000	1,700	0	0	70	0	60,770
1576–1600	60,000	91,000	200	1,400	0	0	0	152,600
1601–1625	83,000	268,000	0	1,800	0	0	0	352,800
1626–1650	44,000	202,000	34,000	32,000	800	1,800	1,100	315,700
1651–1675	13,000	245,000	122,000	101,000	0	7,100	700	488,800
1676–1700	5,900	297,000	272,000	86,000	3,300	29,000	25,000	718,200
1701–1725	0	474,000	411,000	74,000	3,300	121,000	5,800	1,089,100
1726–1750	0	537,000	554,000	83,000	34,000	259,000	4,800	1,471,800
1751–1775	4,200	529,000	832,000	132,000	85,000	326,000	18,000	1,926,200
1776–1800	6,400	673,000	749,000	41,000	67,000	433,000	39,000	2,008,400
1801–1825	168,000	1,161,000	284,000	2,700	110,000	136,000	16,000	1,877,700
1826–1850	401,000	1,300,000	0	400	1,900	68,000	0	1,771,300
1851–1867	216,000	9,300	0	0	500	0	0	225,800
Total*	1,060,900	5,849,300	3,259,900	555,300	305,800	1,380,970	110,400	12,522,570

Source: Voyages Web site, http://www.slavevoyages.org/tast/assessment/estimates.faces?yearFrom=1501&yearTo=1866.

* The column and row totals in this table differ slightly from the data on the *Voyages* Web site because of the rounding rules used throughout this volume and explained in "About This Atlas."

[The Africans are] so crowded, in such disgusting conditions, and so mistreated, as the very ones who transport them assure me, that they come by six and six, with collars around their necks, and these same ones by two and two with fetters on their feet, in such a way that they come imprisoned from head to feet, below the deck, locked in from outside, where they see neither sun nor moon, [and] that there is no Spaniard who dares to stick his head in the hatch without becoming ill, nor to remain inside for an hour without the risk of great sickness. So great is the stench, the crowding and the misery of that place. And the [only] refuge and consolation that they have in it is [that] to each [is given] once a day no more than a half bowl of uncooked corn flour or millet, which is like our rice, and with it a small jug of water and nothing else, except for much beating, much lashing, and bad words. This is that which commonly happens with the men and I well think that some of the shippers treat them with more kindness and mildness, principally in these times . . . [Nevertheless, most] arrive turned into skeletons.

"Description of Africans on a Slave Ship (1627)," in
W. D. Phillips, Jr., *Slavery from Roman Times to the Early Transatlantic Trade* (Minneapolis: University of Minnesota Press, 1985), p. 174. Published with the author's permission.

Map 12: Slaves Carried Off from Africa by Nationality of Slave Vessel, 1501–1641

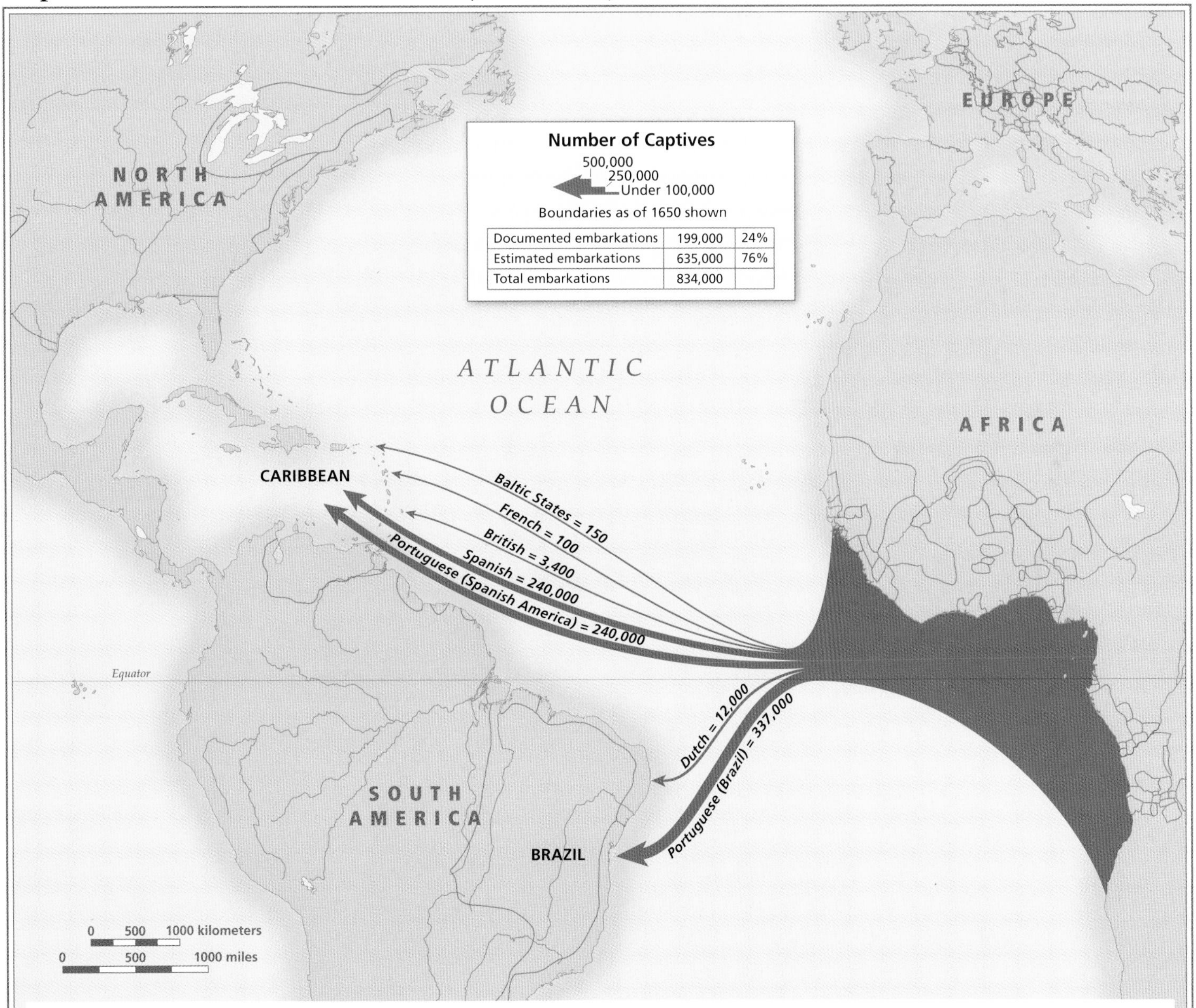

Number of Captives

500,000
250,000
Under 100,000

Boundaries as of 1650 shown

Documented embarkations	199,000	24%
Estimated embarkations	635,000	76%
Total embarkations	834,000	

NORTH AMERICA

EUROPE

ATLANTIC OCEAN

AFRICA

CARIBBEAN

Baltic States = 150
French = 100
British = 3,400
Spanish = 240,000
Portuguese (Spanish America) = 240,000

Equator

Dutch = 12,000
Portuguese (Brazil) = 337,000

SOUTH AMERICA

BRAZIL

0   500   1000 kilometers
0   500   1000 miles

Before 1642 the transatlantic slave trade was dominated by Spain and Portugal. From 1580 to 1640, when the countries were ruled by one monarch, probably well over 75 percent of all slaves sailed in Portuguese ships, the majority of which left from and returned to Brazil. Spanish America and Brazil were the destinations of almost all other African captives who crossed the Atlantic, whatever the national flag of the vessel.

Map 13: Slaves Carried Off from Africa by Nationality of Slave Vessel, 1642–1807

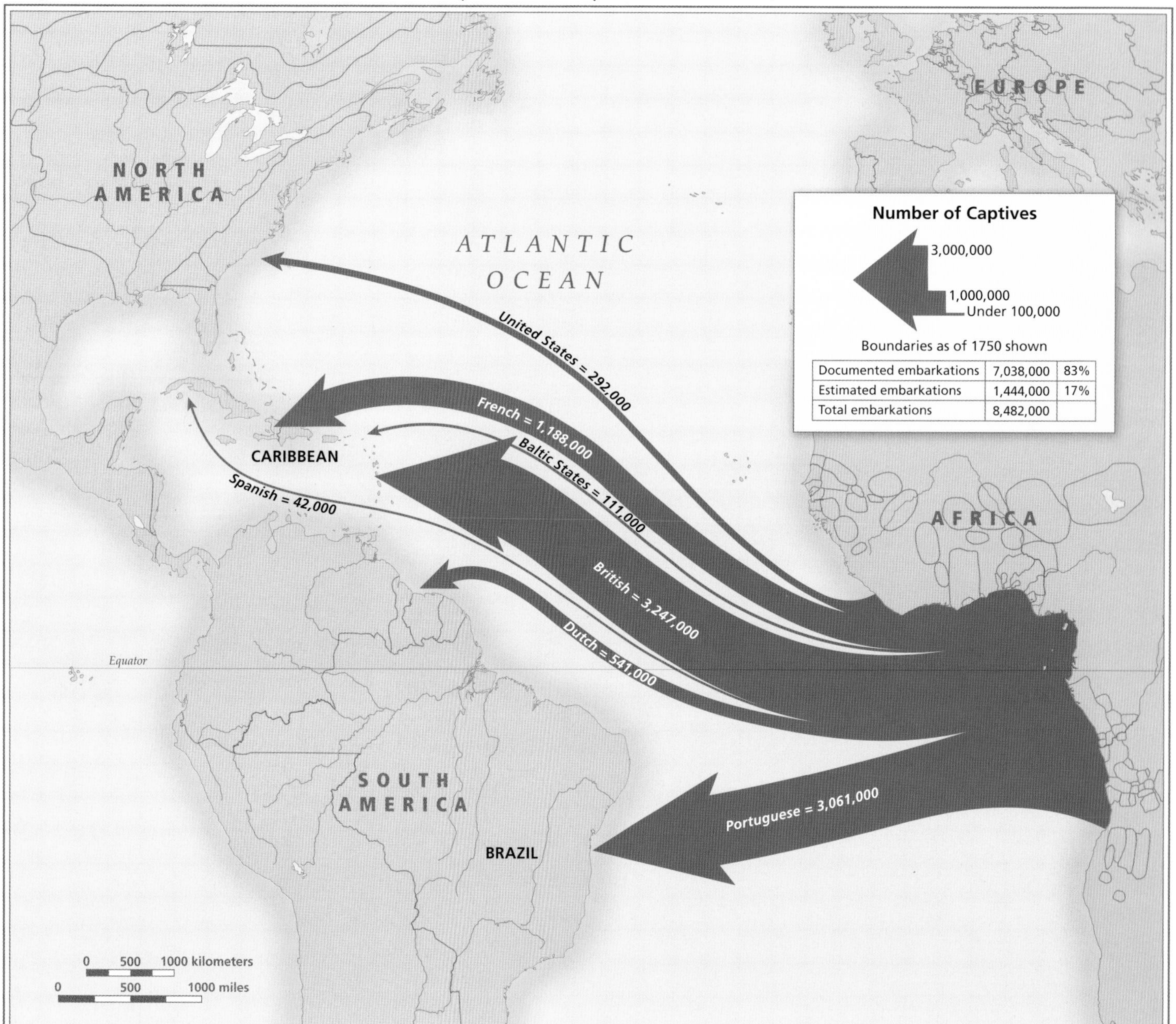

Number of Captives

3,000,000
1,000,000
Under 100,000

Boundaries as of 1750 shown

Documented embarkations	7,038,000	83%
Estimated embarkations	1,444,000	17%
Total embarkations	8,482,000	

United States = 292,000
French = 1,188,000
Baltic States = 111,000
Spanish = 42,000
British = 3,247,000
Dutch = 541,000
Portuguese = 3,061,000

The British and the Portuguese transported nearly three-quarters of all slaves taken from Africa between 1642 and 1807, although merchants in almost every European country, as well as the North American colonies that became the United States, also outfitted voyages. (See maps 15 to 20 for more detailed destinations of each national carrier.)

Map 14: Slaves Carried Off from Africa by Nationality of Slave Vessel, 1808–1867

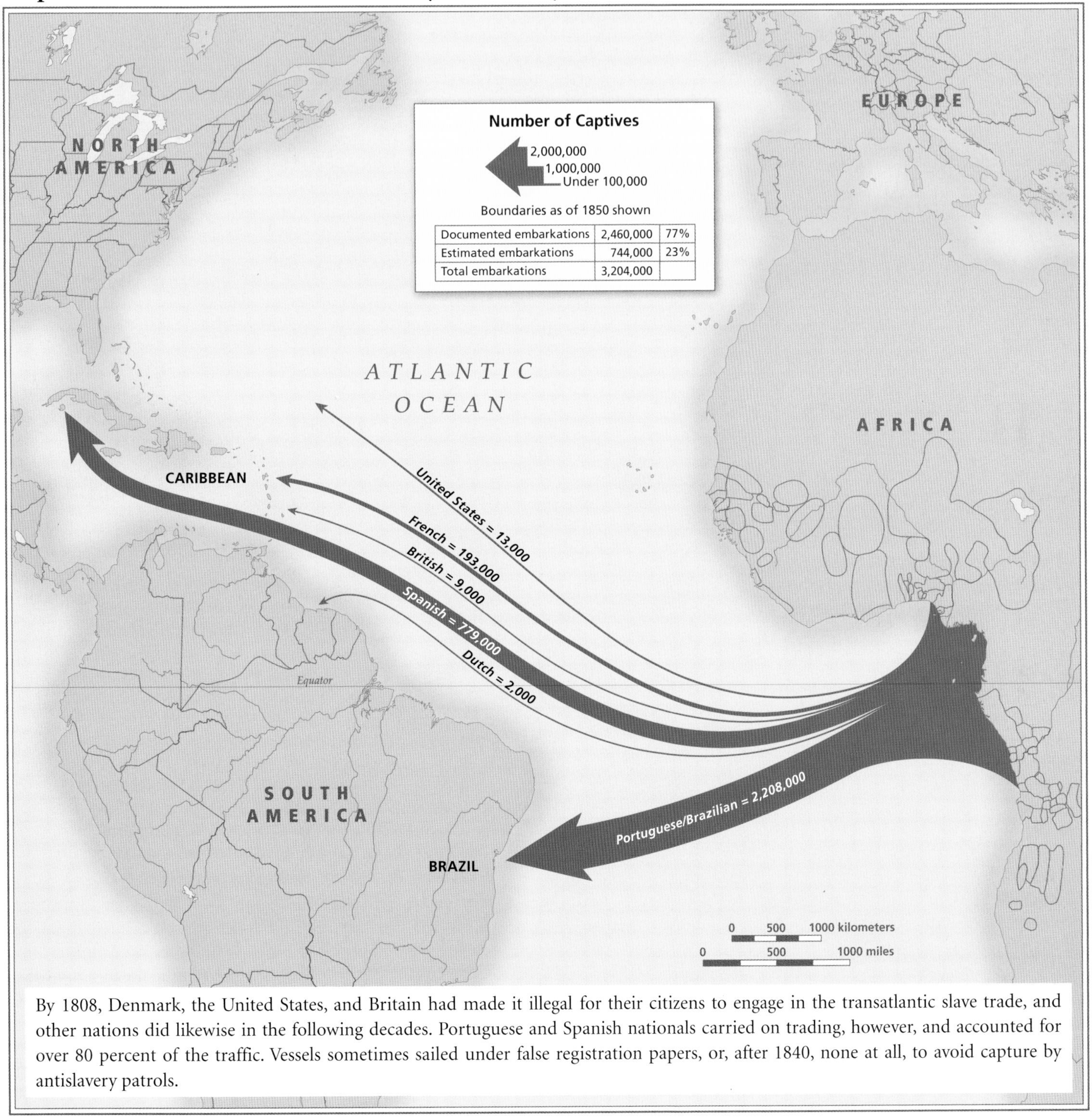

Number of Captives

- 2,000,000
- 1,000,000
- Under 100,000

Boundaries as of 1850 shown

Documented embarkations	2,460,000	77%
Estimated embarkations	744,000	23%
Total embarkations	3,204,000	

NORTH AMERICA

EUROPE

AFRICA

ATLANTIC OCEAN

CARIBBEAN

United States = 13,000
French = 193,000
British = 9,000
Spanish = 779,000
Dutch = 2,000

Equator

SOUTH AMERICA

Portuguese/Brazilian = 2,208,000

BRAZIL

0   500   1000 kilometers
0   500   1000 miles

By 1808, Denmark, the United States, and Britain had made it illegal for their citizens to engage in the transatlantic slave trade, and other nations did likewise in the following decades. Portuguese and Spanish nationals carried on trading, however, and accounted for over 80 percent of the traffic. Vessels sometimes sailed under false registration papers, or, after 1840, none at all, to avoid capture by antislavery patrols.

Map 15: The Spanish Transatlantic Slave Trade, 1526–1867

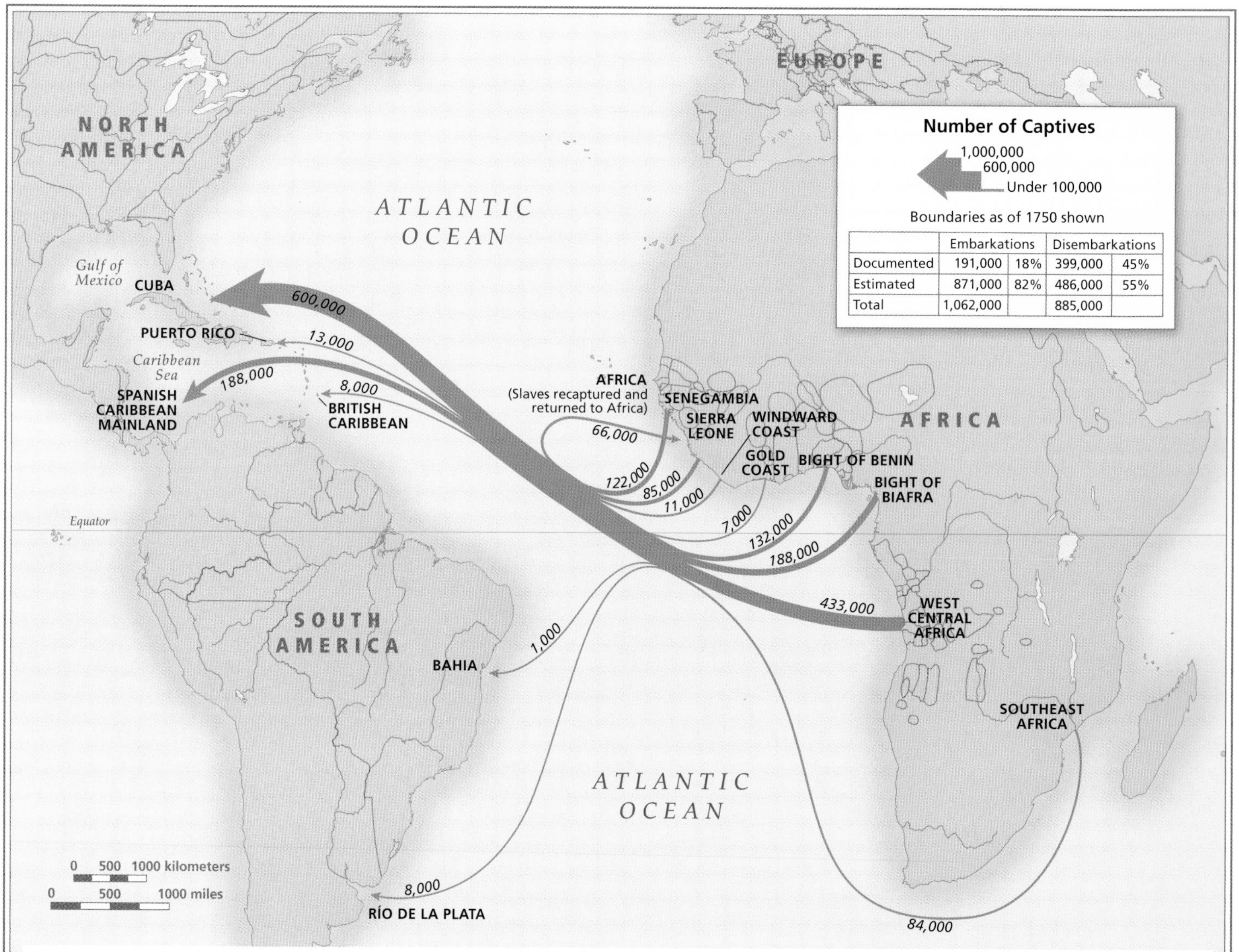

NORTH AMERICA

EUROPE

ATLANTIC OCEAN

Gulf of Mexico **CUBA**

Number of Captives

1,000,000
600,000
Under 100,000

Boundaries as of 1750 shown

	Embarkations		Disembarkations	
Documented	191,000	18%	399,000	45%
Estimated	871,000	82%	486,000	55%
Total	1,062,000		885,000	

600,000

PUERTO RICO — 13,000

Caribbean Sea

188,000

SPANISH CARIBBEAN MAINLAND

8,000

BRITISH CARIBBEAN

AFRICA
(Slaves recaptured and returned to Africa)

SENEGAMBIA
SIERRA LEONE **WINDWARD COAST**

AFRICA

66,000

GOLD COAST **BIGHT OF BENIN**

BIGHT OF BIAFRA

122,000

85,000

11,000

7,000

132,000

188,000

Equator

SOUTH AMERICA

433,000

WEST CENTRAL AFRICA

1,000

BAHIA

SOUTHEAST AFRICA

ATLANTIC OCEAN

0   500   1000 kilometers

0   500   1000 miles

8,000

RÍO DE LA PLATA

84,000

Spanish-owned vessels were important in the slave trade at first, but from 1545 to 1789, the Spanish also contracted vessels from other countries to bring in captives for their colonies under a system known as *asiento* (contract). After 1788 the supplying of slaves to Spanish America was thrown open to all nations. Britain and the United States withdrew from the trade in 1808, and by 1820 the Spanish had become major slave carriers once more, selling most of their slaves in Cuba. After 1836 an Anglo-Spanish treaty made it difficult to use the Spanish flag for slave-trading purposes, but Spanish slave traders continued to operate, sometimes under a variety of other flags.

Map 16: The Portuguese and Brazilian Transatlantic Slave Trade, 1526–1867

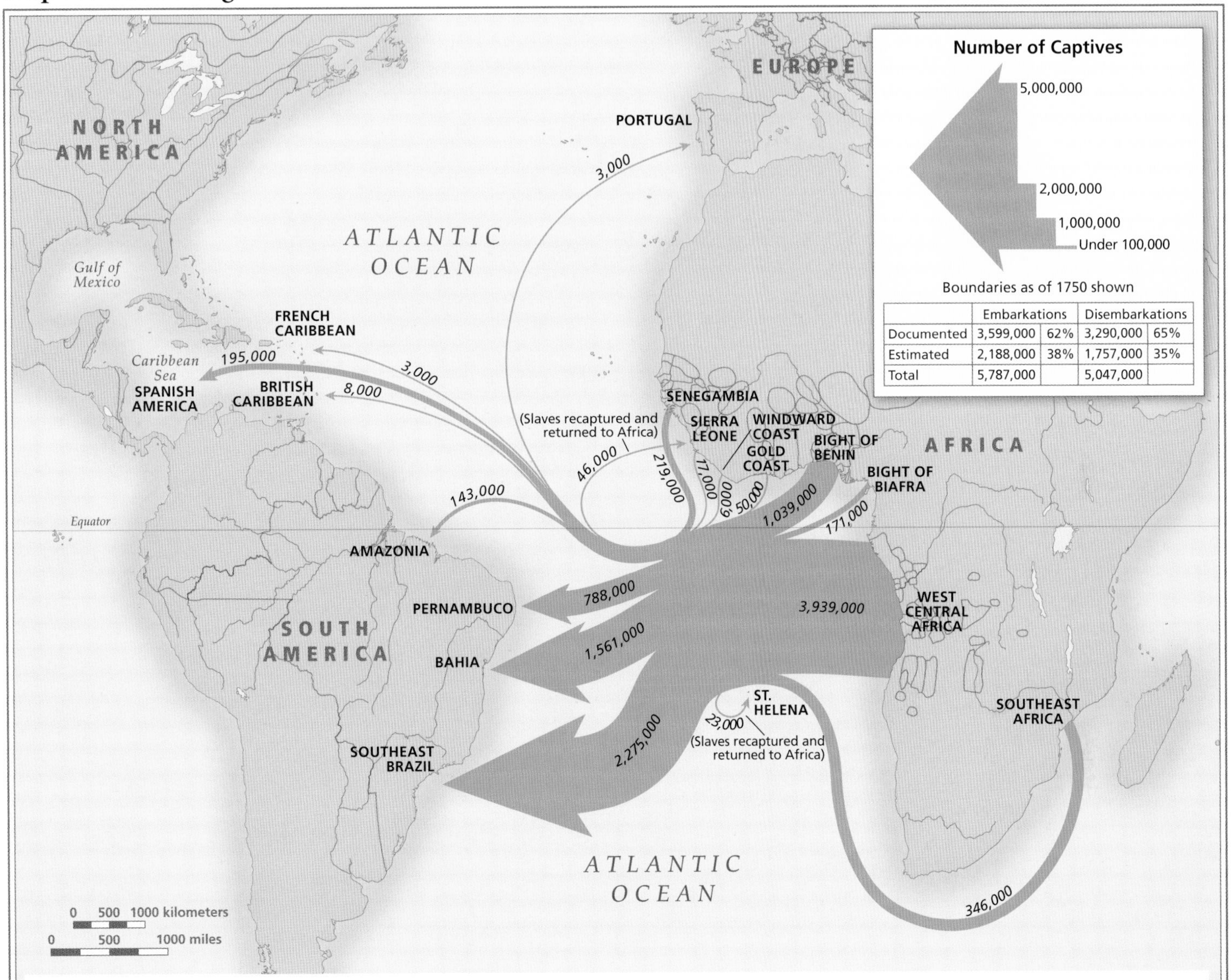

Number of Captives

5,000,000

2,000,000

1,000,000

Under 100,000

Boundaries as of 1750 shown

	Embarkations		Disembarkations	
Documented	3,599,000	62%	3,290,000	65%
Estimated	2,188,000	38%	1,757,000	35%
Total	5,787,000		5,047,000	

EUROPE

NORTH AMERICA

PORTUGAL

3,000

ATLANTIC OCEAN

Gulf of Mexico

FRENCH CARIBBEAN

Caribbean Sea

195,000

3,000

SPANISH AMERICA

BRITISH CARIBBEAN

8,000

SENEGAMBIA

(Slaves recaptured and returned to Africa)

SIERRA LEONE

WINDWARD COAST

GOLD COAST

BIGHT OF BENIN

AFRICA

46,000

219,000

17,000

6,000

50,000

BIGHT OF BIAFRA

1,039,000

171,000

Equator

143,000

AMAZONIA

PERNAMBUCO

788,000

WEST CENTRAL AFRICA

3,939,000

SOUTH AMERICA

BAHIA

1,561,000

ST. HELENA

23,000

SOUTHEAST AFRICA

SOUTHEAST BRAZIL

2,275,000

(Slaves recaptured and returned to Africa)

ATLANTIC OCEAN

346,000

0   500   1000 kilometers

0   500   1000 miles

The Portuguese dominated the southern transatlantic slave trade and, overall, accounted for nearly half of the total traffic. The Portuguese trade quickly came to be based in Brazil rather than in the Iberian Peninsula. Even after Brazilian independence in 1822, most vessels carrying slaves to Brazil and, after 1836, to Cuba flew the Portuguese flag.

Map 17: The Dutch Transatlantic Slave Trade, 1596–1829

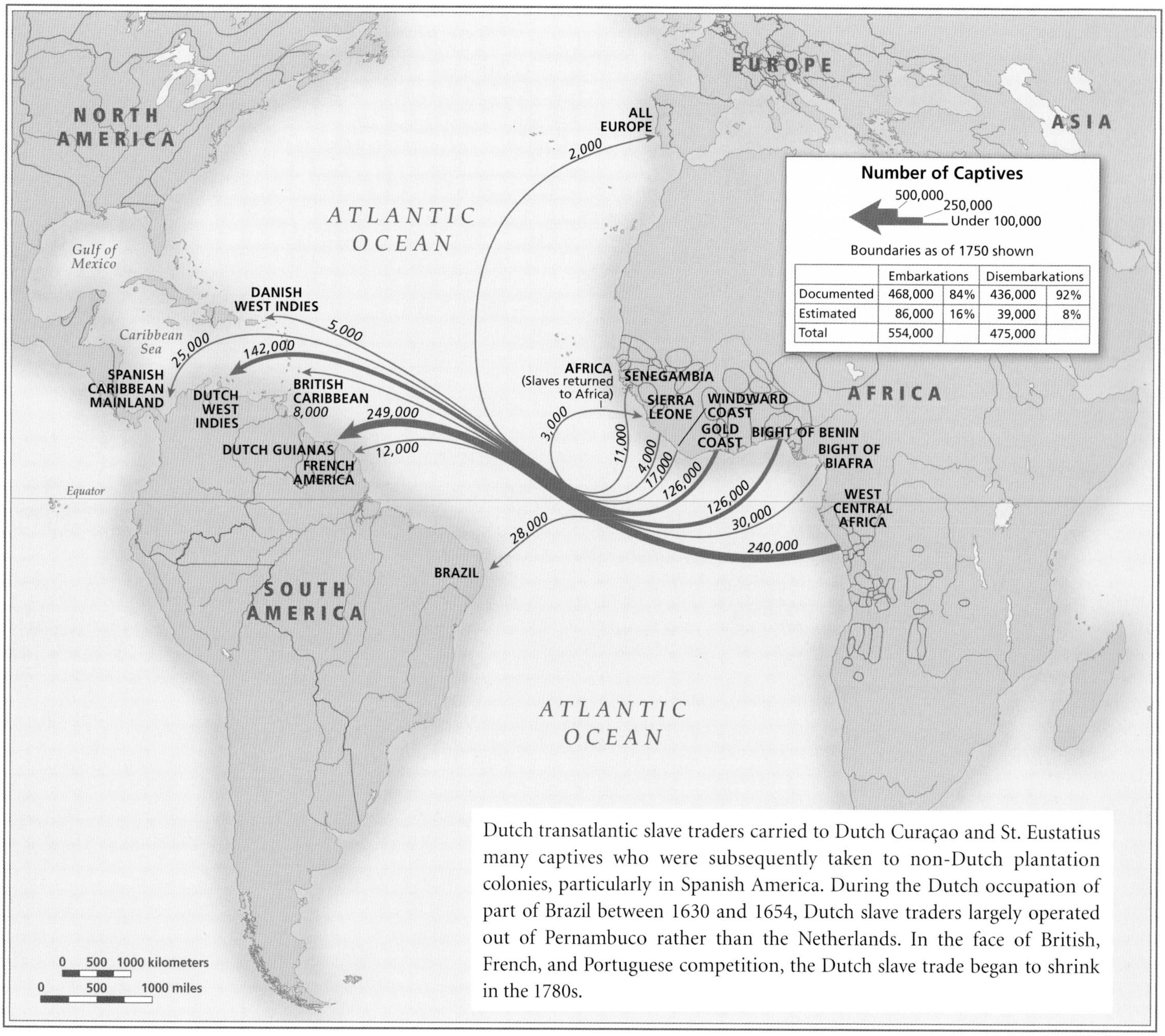

NORTH AMERICA

EUROPE

ASIA

ATLANTIC OCEAN

Gulf of Mexico

ALL EUROPE
2,000

Number of Captives

500,000
250,000
Under 100,000

Boundaries as of 1750 shown

	Embarkations		Disembarkations	
Documented	468,000	84%	436,000	92%
Estimated	86,000	16%	39,000	8%
Total	554,000		475,000	

Caribbean Sea

DANISH WEST INDIES
5,000
25,000
142,000

SPANISH CARIBBEAN MAINLAND

DUTCH WEST INDIES

BRITISH CARIBBEAN
8,000

249,000

DUTCH GUIANAS
FRENCH AMERICA
12,000

Equator

AFRICA
(Slaves returned to Africa)
3,000

SENEGAMBIA

SIERRA LEONE

WINDWARD COAST

GOLD COAST

BIGHT OF BENIN

BIGHT OF BIAFRA

AFRICA

11,000
4,000
17,000
126,000
126,000
30,000

WEST CENTRAL AFRICA

28,000

240,000

BRAZIL

SOUTH AMERICA

ATLANTIC OCEAN

Dutch transatlantic slave traders carried to Dutch Curaçao and St. Eustatius many captives who were subsequently taken to non-Dutch plantation colonies, particularly in Spanish America. During the Dutch occupation of part of Brazil between 1630 and 1654, Dutch slave traders largely operated out of Pernambuco rather than the Netherlands. In the face of British, French, and Portuguese competition, the Dutch slave trade began to shrink in the 1780s.

0   500   1000 kilometers
0   500   1000 miles

I arrived safe in L[iverpool], August 1754. My stay at home was intended to be but short and by the beginning of November I was again ready for the sea: the Lord saw fit to overrule my design. During the time I was engaged in the slave trade, I never had the least scruple as to its lawfulness. I was upon the whole satisfied with it, as the appointment Providence had worked out for me; yet it was, in many respects, far from eligible. It was, indeed, accounted a genteel employment and is usually very profitable, though to me it did not prove so, the Lord, seeing that a large increase of wealth would not be good for me. However, I considered myself a sort of gaoler or turnkey and I was sometimes shocked with an employment that was perpetually conversant with chains, bolts and shackles. In this view I had often petitioned in my prayers that the Lord (in his own time) would be pleased to fix me in a more humane calling, and (if it might be) place me where I might have more frequent converse with his people and ordinances and be freed from those long separations from home which very often were hard to bear. . . . I was within two days of sailing and to all appearances in good health as usual; but in the afternoon, as I was sitting with Mrs N[ewton], by ourselves, drinking tea and talking over past events, I was in a moment seized with a fit, which deprived me of sense and motion and left no other sign of life than that of breathing. I suppose it was of the apoplectic kind. . . . Accordingly by the advice of my friend to whom the ship belonged I resigned the command the day before she sailed; and thus I was unexpectedly called from that service and freed from a share of the future consequences of that voyage which proved extremely calamitous.

John Newton, "An Authentic Narrative," in *The Journal of a Slave Trader (John Newton), 1750–1754,* ed. Bernard Martin and Mark Spurrell (London: Epworth Press, 1962), pp. 95–96.

Map 18: The British Transatlantic Slave Trade, 1563–1810

	Embarkations		Disembarkations	
Documented	2,393,000	73%	2,454,000	90%
Estimated	867,000	27%	279,000	10%
Total	3,260,000		2,733,000	

NORTH AMERICA

EUROPE

ATLANTIC OCEAN

OTHER BRITISH WEST INDIES
(St. Lucia, Bahamas, Honduras, Tortola)

DANISH WEST INDIES — 58,000 — 26,000

ST. KITTS 129,000

MONTSERRAT/NEVIS

ANTIGUA 125,000 — 47,000 — 106,000

DOMINICA

GUADELOUPE AND MARTINIQUE — 91,000

Caribbean Sea

BARBADOS — 458,000

ST. VINCENT — 59,000

GRENADA — 123,000

39,000

TRINIDAD/TOBAGO

ATLANTIC OCEAN

| 0 | 200 | 400 kilometers |
| 0 | 200 | 400 miles |

NORTHERN U.S.

CHESAPEAKE

CAROLINAS/ GEORGIA

GULF COAST

2,000

121,000

138,000

ALL EUROPE

3,000

BAHAMAS 4,000

Gulf of Mexico

SPANISH CARIBBEAN

JAMAICA

Caribbean Sea

60,000

HONDURAS

SPANISH CARIBBEAN MAINLAND

15,000

995,000

See inset

1,261,000

SENEGAMBIA

SIERRA LEONE

WINDWARD COAST

GOLD COAST

BIGHT OF BENIN

AFRICA

BIGHT OF BIAFRA

227,000

163,000

201,000

718,000

354,000

1,031,000

WEST CENTRAL AFRICA

534,000

BRITISH GUIANA 72,000

DUTCH GUIANAS 32,000

Equator

SOUTH AMERICA

MADAGASCAR

ATLANTIC OCEAN

SOUTHEAST BRAZIL

4,000

Number of Captives

2,750,000

1,000,000

500,000

Under 100,000

Boundaries as of 1750 shown

RÍO DE LA PLATA

28,000

| 0 | 500 | 1000 kilometers |
| 0 | 500 | 1000 miles |

32,000

British slave traders dominated the northern segment of the Atlantic slave-trading system almost as much as the Portuguese dominated the southern segment. They distributed slaves across a greater range of New World territories than traders from any other nation did, and after the relative decline of the Dutch in the late seventeenth century they were the primary international carriers, reaching a peak in 1799–1802. Traders from London, Bristol, and Liverpool dominated this large traffic. About 5 percent of the British traffic in slaves, however, was organized in the British Caribbean. The British entered the slave trade relatively late and left it suddenly upon passage of the abolition act in 1807.

Map 19: The French Transatlantic Slave Trade, 1643–1831

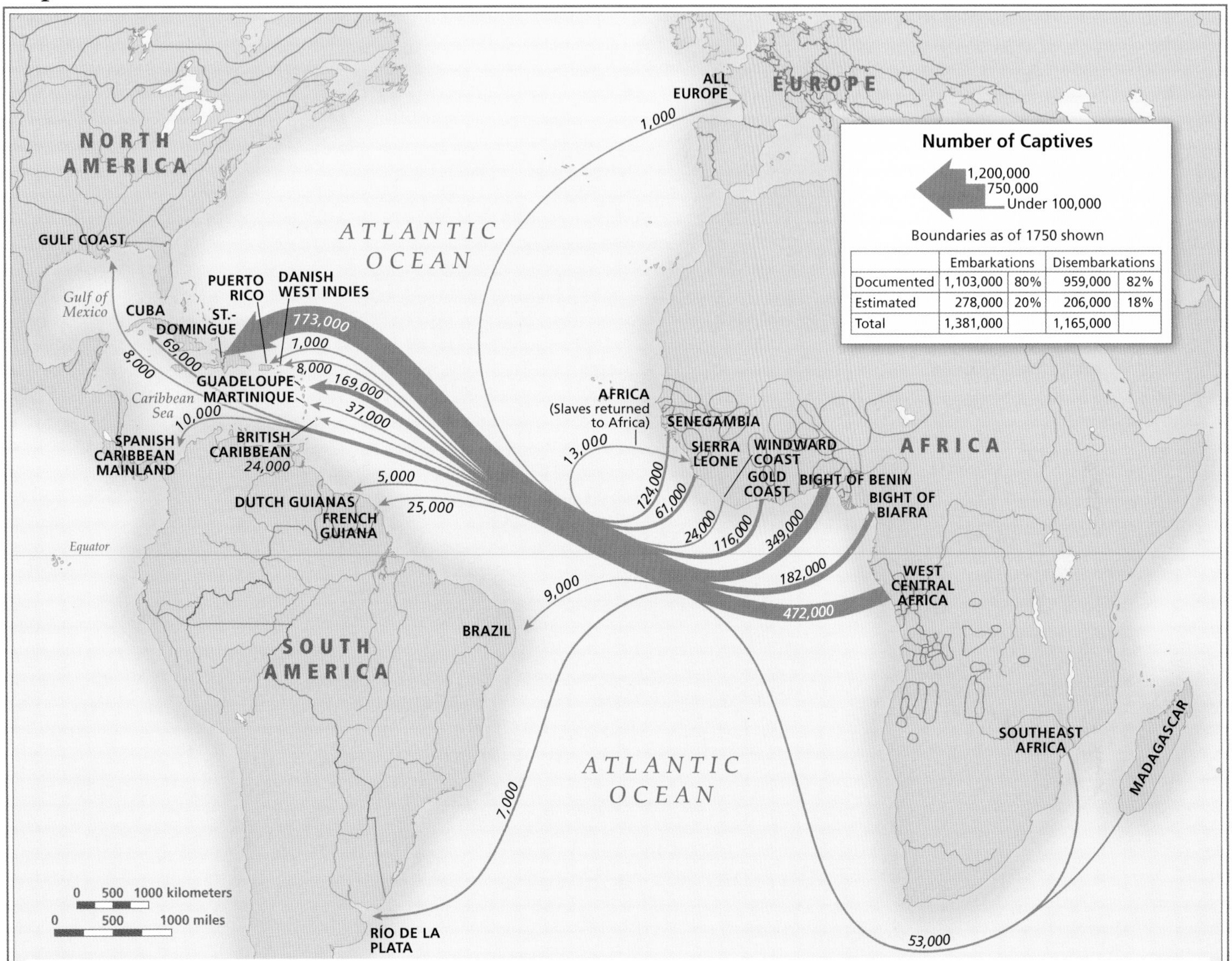

ALL EUROPE
EUROPE
1,000

NORTH AMERICA

ATLANTIC OCEAN

GULF COAST

Gulf of Mexico
CUBA
PUERTO RICO
DANISH WEST INDIES
ST.-DOMINGUE
173,000
8,000
69,000
7,000
8,000 169,000
GUADELOUPE MARTINIQUE
37,000
Caribbean Sea
10,000
SPANISH CARIBBEAN MAINLAND
BRITISH CARIBBEAN
24,000
5,000
DUTCH GUIANAS
FRENCH GUIANA
25,000

Equator

SOUTH AMERICA
BRAZIL
9,000

7,000

RÍO DE LA PLATA

ATLANTIC OCEAN

Number of Captives

1,200,000
750,000
Under 100,000

Boundaries as of 1750 shown

	Embarkations		Disembarkations	
Documented	1,103,000	80%	959,000	82%
Estimated	278,000	20%	206,000	18%
Total	1,381,000		1,165,000	

AFRICA (Slaves returned to Africa)
13,000

SENEGAMBIA
SIERRA LEONE
WINDWARD COAST
GOLD COAST
BIGHT OF BENIN
BIGHT OF BIAFRA
AFRICA
124,000
61,000
24,000
116,000
349,000
182,000
WEST CENTRAL AFRICA
472,000

SOUTHEAST AFRICA
MADAGASCAR
53,000

0 500 1000 kilometers
0 500 1000 miles

France was the third largest of the national slave-trading groups (after Portugal and Great Britain) owing to the importance of St.-Domingue in the eighteenth century, a state subsidy for slave traders until the French Revolution, and the dispatch of French slaving expeditions into the early 1830s. Except for a decade at the beginning of the eighteenth century and the 1820s, the French slave trade overwhelmingly supplied captives to the French colonies; merchants in the French Caribbean colonies organized very few slaving expeditions.

Map 20: The North American Transatlantic Slave Trade, 1645–1860

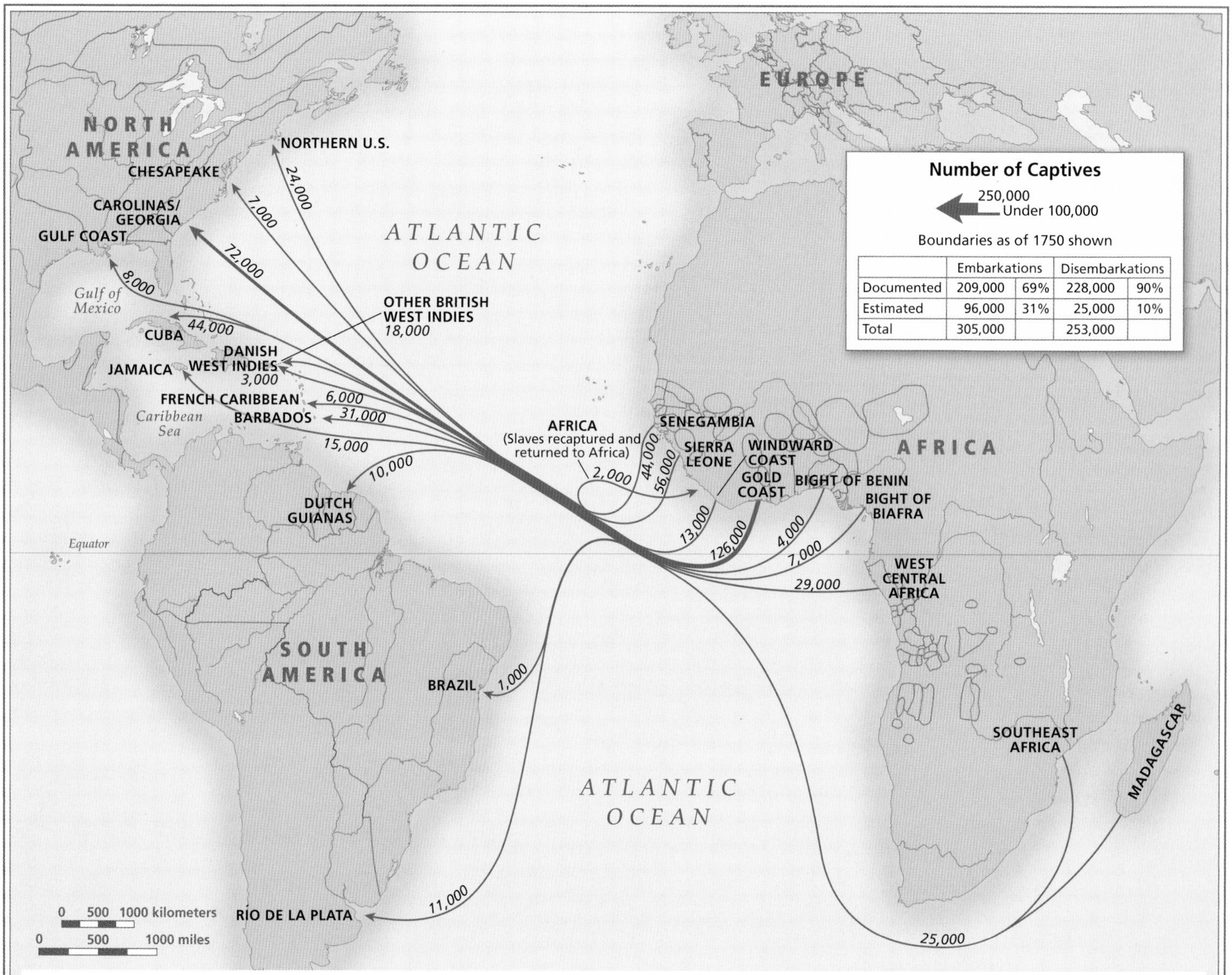

EUROPE

NORTH AMERICA

NORTHERN U.S.

CHESAPEAKE

CAROLINAS/ GEORGIA

GULF COAST

Gulf of Mexico

CUBA

DANISH WEST INDIES
3,000

JAMAICA

FRENCH CARIBBEAN

BARBADOS

Caribbean Sea

OTHER BRITISH WEST INDIES
18,000

24,000

7,000

72,000

8,000

44,000

6,000

31,000

15,000

10,000

ATLANTIC OCEAN

AFRICA
(Slaves recaptured and returned to Africa)

2,000

SENEGAMBIA

SIERRA LEONE

WINDWARD COAST

GOLD COAST

BIGHT OF BENIN

BIGHT OF BIAFRA

AFRICA

44,000

56,000

13,000

126,000

4,000

7,000

29,000

WEST CENTRAL AFRICA

DUTCH GUIANAS

Equator

SOUTH AMERICA

BRAZIL

1,000

ATLANTIC OCEAN

SOUTHEAST AFRICA

MADAGASCAR

RIO DE LA PLATA

11,000

25,000

0   500   1000 kilometers
0   500   1000 miles

Number of Captives

250,000
Under 100,000

Boundaries as of 1750 shown

	Embarkations		Disembarkations	
Documented	209,000	69%	228,000	90%
Estimated	96,000	31%	25,000	10%
Total	305,000		253,000	

The slave trade of the mainland North American colonies, though small, grew rapidly after 1730 and declined after the American Revolution, when one state after another banned the trade. However, American traders experienced a resurgence of business when they found new markets outside the United States late in the eighteenth century and when South Carolina rescinded its prohibition on the arrival of slaves between 1804 and 1807. Briefly in 1806 and 1807 one-quarter of the captives from Africa sailed under the U.S. flag.

Map 21: The Transatlantic Slave Trade of Denmark, Northern German Towns, and Other Baltic States, 1642–1807

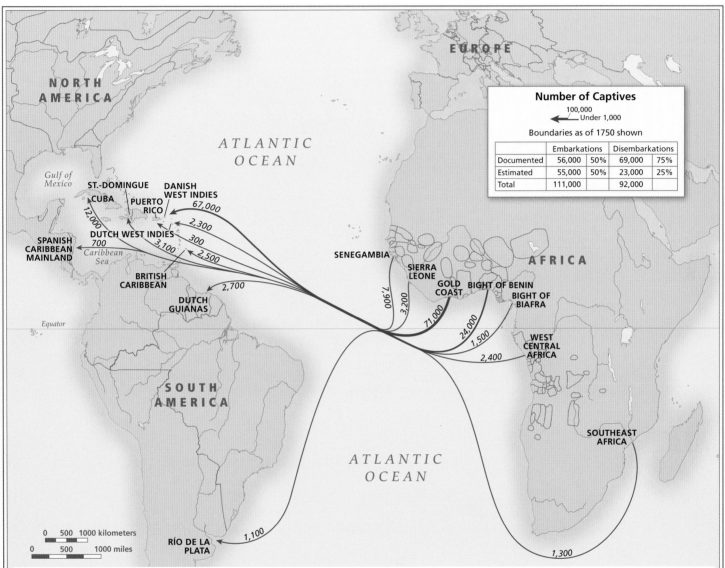

	Number of Captives			
100,000				
Under 1,000				
Boundaries as of 1750 shown				
	Embarkations		Disembarkations	
Documented	56,000	50%	69,000	75%
Estimated	55,000	50%	23,000	25%
Total	111,000		92,000	

Merchants in Scandinavia and the Hanse towns of northern Germany, though considered minor slave traders, carried off more than 100,000 slaves from Africa. Their trade was at its greatest relative importance in the late seventeenth century, but it grew once more in the 1790s, when several European countries, noticeably Spain, opened up free ports, where slave traders of all nations could bring in captives without paying duty. More than half of the voyages organized in the Baltic States set out from Copenhagen, and most of the captives who passed through Danish-built forts on the Gold Coast in Africa spent the rest of their lives in the Danish West Indies. Denmark's ban on its transatlantic slave trade took effect in 1803, but slaves continued to be carried to other parts of the Americas under the Danish flag through 1807.

Part II
Ports Outfitting Voyages in the Transatlantic Slave Trade

The transatlantic slaving business was probably the most international of all commercial activities before the nineteenth century. The trade routes passed through various jurisdictions as they crisscrossed the Atlantic, and much of the merchandise that was exchanged for captives was assembled from many parts of the globe. Textiles from Asia, cowrie shells from the Indian Ocean, and tobacco, rum, and gold from the Americas were packed together with manufactured goods from all over Europe. The mix of the cargo had to be targeted for the particular region in Africa where slaves were to be purchased. Add to this the financial, insurance, and shipping requirements of a typical voyage, and it is clear how complex the organization of a slave voyage was.

As table 3 shows, merchants organized slaving voyages in many of the important Atlantic ports in western Europe and the colonial Americas; the United States and Brazil remained major bases after achieving independence. The largest slave carriers, the Portuguese, accounted for more than two out of every five captives crossing the Atlantic and dominated slaving activities in Africa south of the Congo River. They also established a lasting and substantial presence in the Bight of Benin, taking most of the slaves they acquired there to Brazil. Nine out of ten Portuguese voyages were organized in Brazil, not Portugal. The British, the second most important carriers of captives, accounted for about a quarter of all slaves entering the transatlantic trade. In Africa, the British traded at numerous coastal outlets, from the Sénégal River to Ambriz (Angola), 4,000 miles south, and shipped the great majority of their captives to the Caribbean.

The *Voyages* database has records of slave vessels' departures for Africa from 188 ports around the North and South Atlantic, but no fewer than 93 percent of all slave voyages left the largest twenty ports. The relative importance of different ports varied over time, however. In the Portuguese case, the organization of voyages initially centered on Lisbon but then migrated to Brazil, where, in the later sixteenth century, Recife (Pernambuco), Salvador da Bahia, and Rio de Janeiro emerged as the principal centers in the Portuguese-speaking world for the dispatch of slaving voyages to Africa. In the case of northern Europe, ports like Plymouth, where the first slaving voyages were organized, gave way in the seventeenth century to major ports like Amsterdam, London, Bristol, Nantes, and Liverpool, as well as to a series of less prominent ports, including Bordeaux, Lancaster, La Rochelle, Le Havre, Middelburg, and St.-Malo. In North America, some voyages were organized at ports in the British Caribbean, but they were overshadowed by voyages organized at New England ports between 1750 and 1807 and at Havana thereafter. Overall, Europe was in the ascendancy before 1800 and the Americas after that.

Several factors shaped the changing organizational geography of the slave trade. The political decline of Spain and Portugal and the seizure of territory in the Americas by states in northern Europe in the mid-seventeenth century allowed ports outside Iberia to expand their slaving activities. The ports with established financial and trading resources, such as Amsterdam and London, had a clear advantage in organizing voyages; they were able to draw on networks that spider-webbed across Europe and reached to Asia for trade goods. Their advantages did not prevent other ports from participating in the slave trade, however. Northern European ports facing the Atlantic gained the advantage of shorter voyage times to Africa compared with those whose oceangoing ships had to overcome the prevailing westerly winds of the English Channel. Similar environmental factors help to explain the rise of slaving ports in Brazil, but their growth as bases for slave voyages was also made possible, as with Amsterdam and London, by links with suppliers of Asian trade goods to be exchanged for slaves in Africa. It was further reinforced by their proximity to major centers of plantation agriculture and precious metal production, including gold in Minas Gerais and Goiás (Brazil) in 1695–1750 and silver beyond the Río de la Plata. These areas not only generated large demand for slave labor within the hinterland of major ports such as Rio de Janeiro but also furnished some of the trade goods dispatched to Africa to purchase slaves. In some cases, then, a concentration of goods and services for the organization of slaving voyages, whether in Europe or the Americas, could become self-perpetuating, generating more business. The most important factor in breaking the cycle was the rise of the abolition movement in Europe in the 1780s.

Table 3   African Captives Carried on Vessels Leaving the Largest Twenty Ports Where Slave-Trading Voyages Were Organized, 1501–1867

Port	Number of Captives
Rio de Janeiro	1,507,000
Salvador da Bahia	1,362,000
Liverpool	1,338,000
London	829,000
Bristol	565,000
Nantes	542,000
Recife	437,000
Lisbon	333,000
Havana	250,000
La Rochelle	166,000
Texel	165,000
Le Havre	142,000
Bordeaux	134,000
Vlissingen	123,000
Rhode Island*	111,000
Middelburg	94,000
Seville and Sanlúcar de Barrameda	74,000
St.-Malo	73,000
Bridgetown, Barbados	58,000
Cádiz	53,000
Total	8,356,000
All 188 known slave-trade ship-outfitting ports combined	9,024,000
Top twenty ports as percent of all known slave-trade ship-outfitting ports	93

Source: Voyages Web site, http://www.slavevoyages.org/tast/database/search.faces?yearFrom=1514& yearTo=1866&ptdepimp=10104.10111.10112.10203.10404.10432.10433.10703.10712.10713.10715.10720 .10726.10829.10851.20100.31312.50200.50300.50400: go to the tables tab and create the table of "port where voyage began" and "sum of embarked slaves."

* Newport, Providence, Bristol, and Warren combined.

Sir John Hawkins (1532–1595)

Oil on panel by an unknown artist of the English School, 1581. © National Maritime Museum, Greenwich, London.

Sir John Hawkins sought to break the Iberian monopoly on slave trafficking in 1562–1571 by leading several English slave-trading ventures to Sierra Leone and seeking to sell his African captives on the Spanish Caribbean mainland in exchange for precious metals. The Spanish refused to allow Hawkins to trade in their American possessions, but his voyages signaled a growing northern European interest in American colonization and slaving activities that was to be realized in the seventeenth century. Undertaken with the tacit approval of the English Crown, for whom Hawkins served as treasurer of the Royal Navy, Hawkins's voyages highlight the importance of the alliance between private enterprise and the state in promoting the growth of transatlantic slavery.

Map 22: European Ports Where Slave Voyages Were Outfitted, 1501–1641

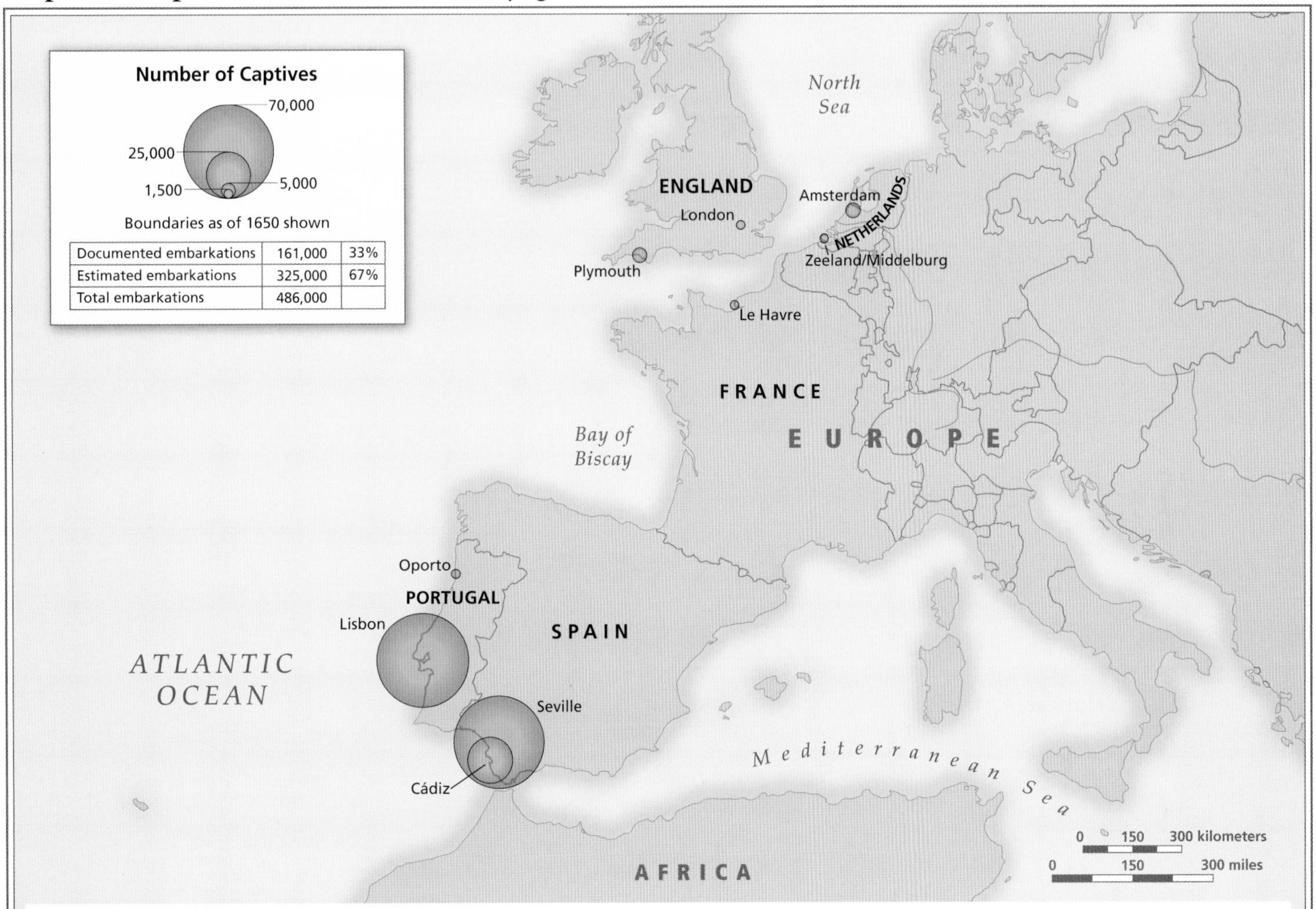

Number of Captives

70,000

25,000

1,500 — 5,000

Boundaries as of 1650 shown

Documented embarkations	161,000	33%
Estimated embarkations	325,000	67%
Total embarkations	486,000	

North Sea

ENGLAND

London

Amsterdam

NETHERLANDS

Plymouth

Zeeland/Middelburg

Le Havre

FRANCE

Bay of Biscay

E U R O P E

Oporto

PORTUGAL

Lisbon

S P A I N

ATLANTIC OCEAN

Seville

Cádiz

Mediterranean Sea

0   150   300 kilometers

0   150   300 miles

AFRICA

Iberian ports accounted for 97 percent of the slave trade organized in Europe up to 1641. From 1501, ships left Spanish ports for the Americas carrying slaves that had previously arrived in Spain directly from Africa. By the 1530s, however, Iberian ports were organizing voyages to Africa to collect captives, then proceeding to Spanish America.

Map 23: Regions of Trade for Slave Voyages Outfitted in Lisbon and Seville, 1501–1641

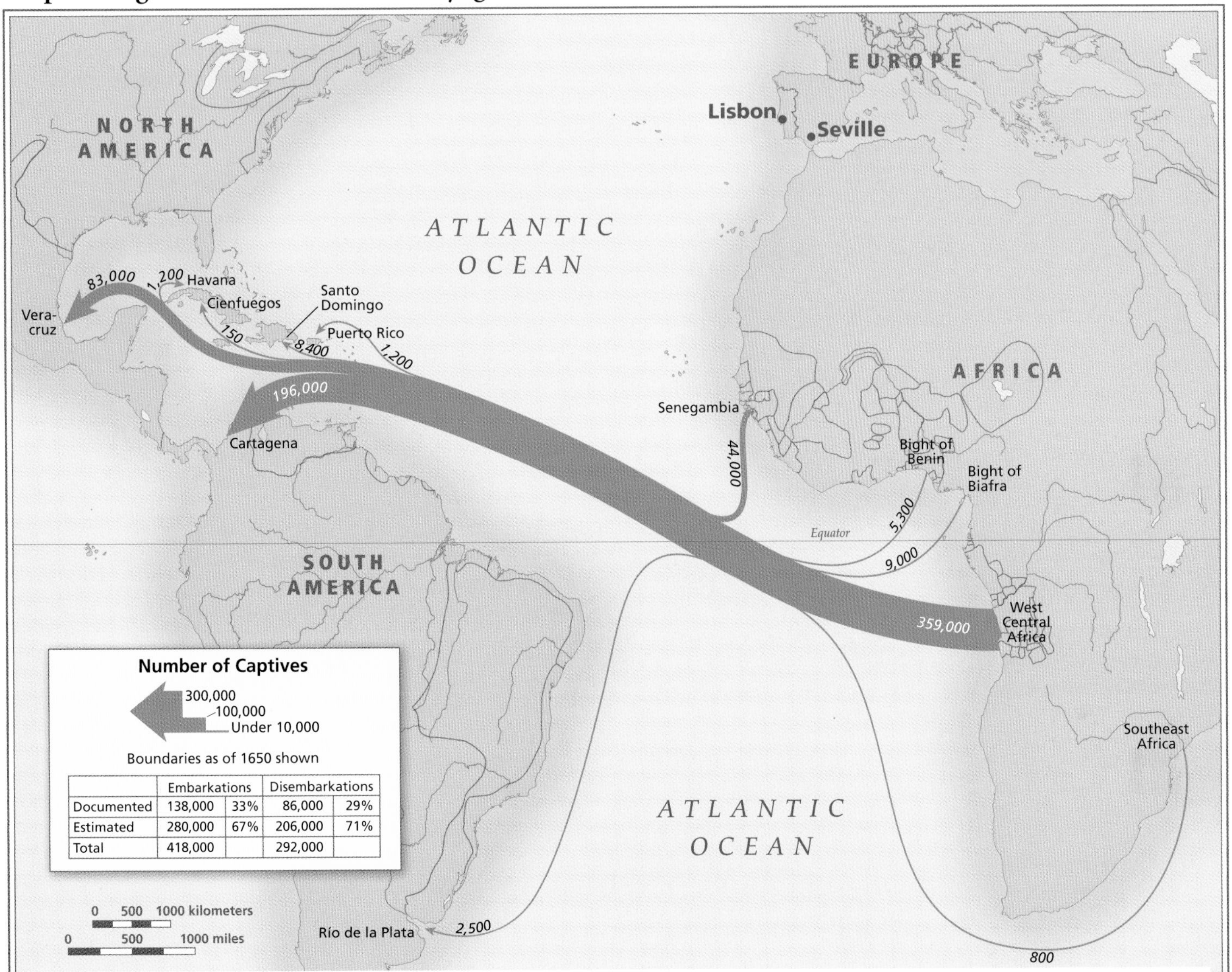

EUROPE

Lisbon

Seville

NORTH AMERICA

ATLANTIC OCEAN

83,000

1,200 Havana

Cienfuegos

Santo Domingo

Vera-cruz

150

Puerto Rico

8,400

1,200

196,000

Cartagena

AFRICA

Senegambia

44,000

Bight of Benin

Bight of Biafra

5,300

Equator

9,000

SOUTH AMERICA

359,000

West Central Africa

Southeast Africa

Number of Captives

300,000
100,000
Under 10,000

Boundaries as of 1650 shown

	Embarkations		Disembarkations	
Documented	138,000	33%	86,000	29%
Estimated	280,000	67%	206,000	71%
Total	418,000		292,000	

ATLANTIC OCEAN

0   500   1000 kilometers

0   500   1000 miles

Río de la Plata

2,500

800

Lisbon and Seville were the organizational centers of the Old World slave trade (see map 3), and their role continued when the transatlantic traffic began. Between 1580 and 1640, Portugal and Spain had the same monarch, and in the records it is often unclear whether a slave ship was sailing under the Spanish or the Portuguese flag. The Spanish Crown used the expertise of Portuguese captains and slave merchants to supply its American colonies with slaves; Portuguese vessels had full access to Spanish America. This branch of the traffic drew on Portuguese "factories" (as slaving establishments were called) in Senegambia, São Tomé (Bight of Biafra), and Angola (West Central Africa).

Master John Hawkins having made divers voyages to the yles of the Canaries, and there by his good and upright dealing being grown in love and favour with the people, informed himself amongst them by diligent inquisition, of the state of the West India, whereof he had received some knowledge by the instructions of his father, but increased the same by the advertisements and reports of that people. And being amongst other particulars assured that Negroes were very good merchandise in Hispaniola, and that store of Negroes might easily be had upon the coast of Guinea, resolved with himselfe to make trail thereof, and communicated that desire with his worshipfull friends of London; namely, with sir Lionel Ducket, sir Thomas Lodge, M. Gunston, his father-in-lawe, Sir William Winter, M. Bronfield, and others. All which persons liked so well of his intention, that they became liberall contributors and adventurers in the action. For which purpose there were 3. good shippes immediately provided. The one called the Salomon of the burthen of 120. tunne, wherein M. Hawkins himselfe went as Generall; the 2. the Swallow, of 100. tunnes, wherein went for Captaine M. Thomas Hampton: And the 3. the Ionas, a barke of 40. tunnes, wherein the master supplied the Captaine's roome; in which small fleete, M. Hawkins tooke with him not above 100. men, for fear of sickenesse, and other inconveniences, whereunto men in long voyages are commonly subject.

Excerpt from *The First Voyage of the right worshipfull and valiant knight, sir John Hawkins, now treasurer of her Majesties navie Royall, made to the West Indies 1562,* in Sir Clements R. Markham, ed., *The Hawkins' Voyages during the Reigns of Henry VIII, Queen Elizabeth, and James I,* Hakluyt Society series, vol. 57 (London, 1878).

[T]here came to us a Negroe, sent from a King, oppressed by other Kings his neighbours, desiring our aide, with promise, that as many Negroes as by these wares might be obtained, as well of his part, as of ours, should be at our pleasure: whereupon we concluded to give aide, and sent 120. of our men, which the fifteenth of Januarie, assaulted a towne of the Negroes of our Allies adversaries, which had in it 8000. Inhabitants, and very strongly impaled and fenced, after their manner, but it was so well defended, that our men prevailed not but lost sixe men, and 40. hurt, so that our men sent forthwith to me fore more helpe: whereupon considering that the good success of this enterprise might highly further the commodotie of our voyage, I went myselfe, and with the helpe of the King of our side, assaulted the towne both by land and sea, and very hardly with fire, (their houses being covered with dry Palme leaves) obtained the towne, and put the Inhabitants to flight, where we tooke 250. persons, men, women, and children, and by our friend the King of our side, there was taken 600. prisoners, whereof we hoped to have had our choice: the Negro (in which nation is seldome or never found truth) meant nothing lesse: for that night he removed his campe, and prisoners, so that we were faine to content us with those fewe which we had gotten our selves. Now had we obtained between 4. and 500. Negroes, wherewith we thought it somewhat reasonable to seek the coast of the West Indies, and there, for our Negroes, and other our merchandize, we hoped to obtaine, whereof to countervaile our charges with some gaines.

Excerpt from *The 3. unfortunate voyage made with the Jesus, the Minion, and four other shippes, to the partes of Guine, and the West Indies, in the yeere 1567. and 1568,* in Sir Clements R. Markham, ed., *The Hawkins' Voyages during the Reigns of Henry VIII, Queen Elizabeth, and James I,* Hakluyt Society series, vol. 57 (London, 1878).

Map 24: Regions of Trade for Slave Voyages Outfitted in Northern Europe before 1642

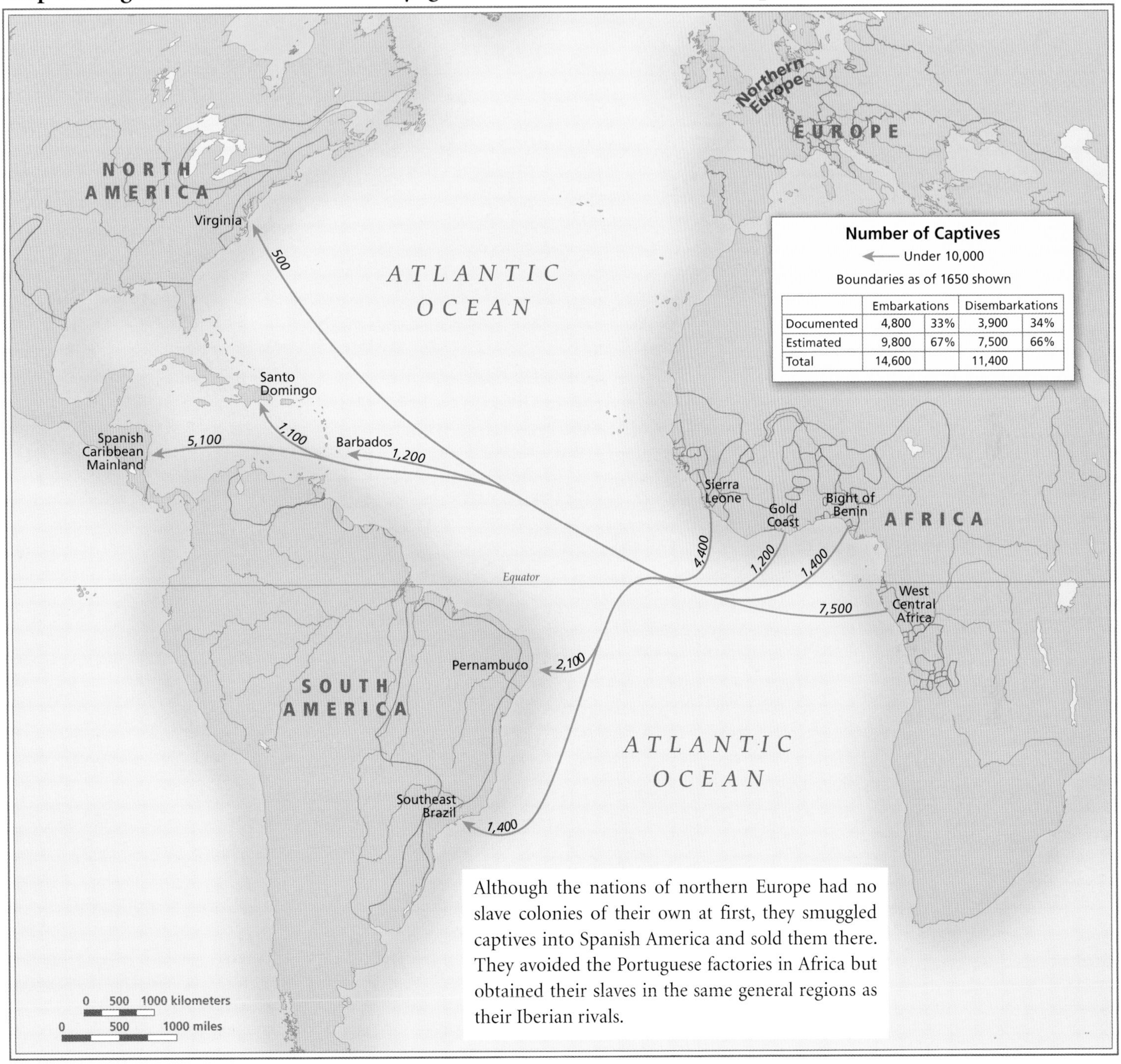

NORTH AMERICA

Virginia

500

ATLANTIC OCEAN

Santo Domingo

1,100

Spanish Caribbean Mainland

5,100

Barbados

1,200

Number of Captives

← Under 10,000

Boundaries as of 1650 shown

	Embarkations		Disembarkations	
Documented	4,800	33%	3,900	34%
Estimated	9,800	67%	7,500	66%
Total	14,600		11,400	

Northern Europe

EUROPE

Sierra Leone

Gold Coast

Bight of Benin

AFRICA

4,400

1,200

1,400

West Central Africa

7,500

Equator

SOUTH AMERICA

Pernambuco

2,100

ATLANTIC OCEAN

Southeast Brazil

1,400

Although the nations of northern Europe had no slave colonies of their own at first, they smuggled captives into Spanish America and sold them there. They avoided the Portuguese factories in Africa but obtained their slaves in the same general regions as their Iberian rivals.

0   500   1000 kilometers

0   500   1000 miles

Map 25: Regions of Trade for Slave Voyages Outfitted in Brazil, 1560–1642

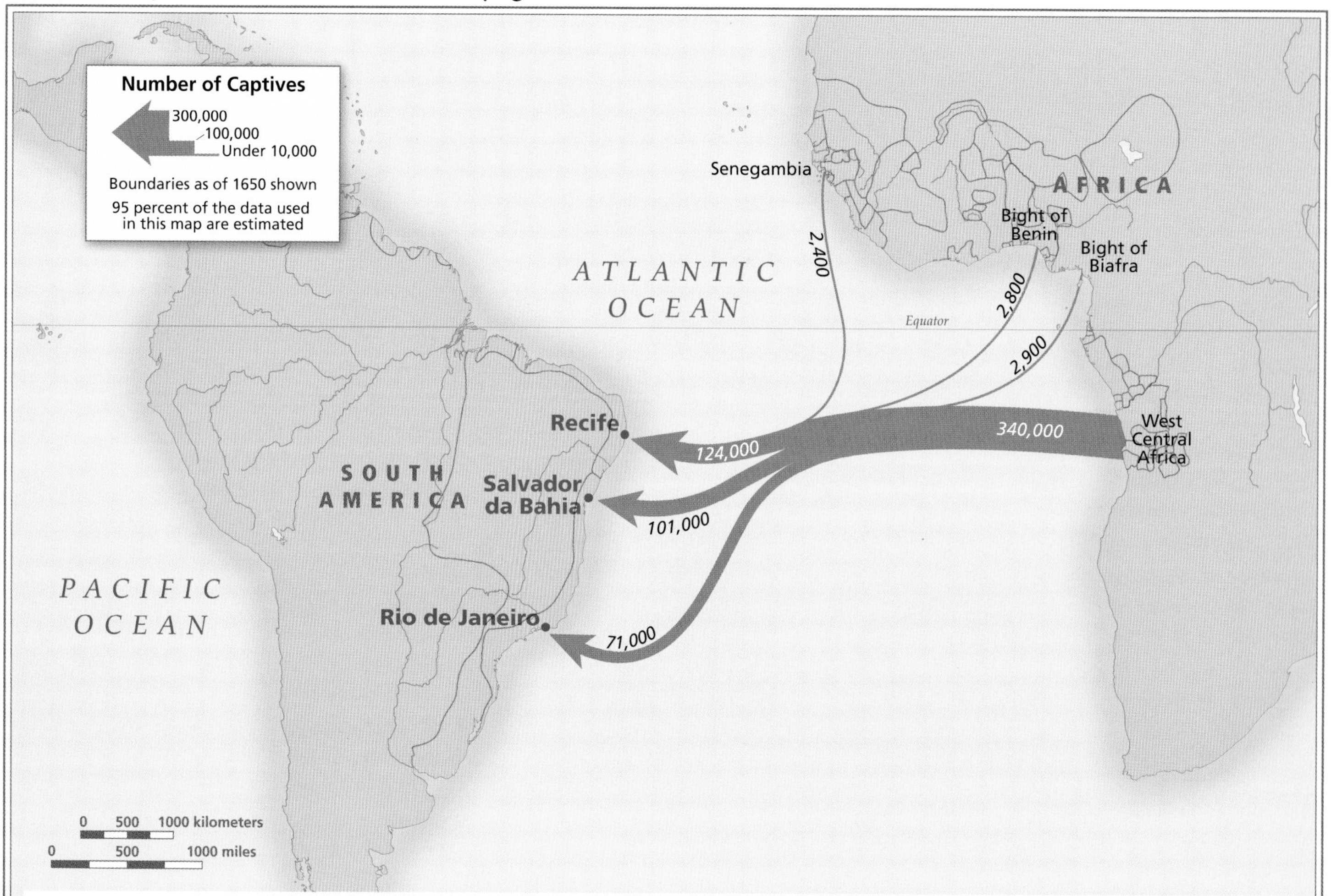

Number of Captives

300,000
100,000
Under 10,000

Boundaries as of 1650 shown

95 percent of the data used in this map are estimated

ATLANTIC OCEAN

PACIFIC OCEAN

SOUTH AMERICA

AFRICA

Senegambia

Bight of Benin

Bight of Biafra

West Central Africa

Equator

Recife

Salvador da Bahia

Rio de Janeiro

2,400

2,800

2,900

340,000

124,000

101,000

71,000

0   500   1000 kilometers
0   500   1000 miles

The first slave-trading voyages to Brazil may have set out from Portugal, but the earliest ports of departure on record were Brazilian, suggesting that the organizational base shifted quickly to Brazil to take advantage of the trade winds and currents of the South Atlantic. Recife, Salvador da Bahia, and Rio de Janeiro each established a two-way rather than a triangular trade with West Central Africa. After the Dutch conquest of the Pernambuco region (the Recife hinterland) in 1630, Dutch voyages carrying captives to Brazil were also mainly outfitted there rather than in the Netherlands.

Map 26: European Ports Where Slave Voyages Were Outfitted, 1642–1807

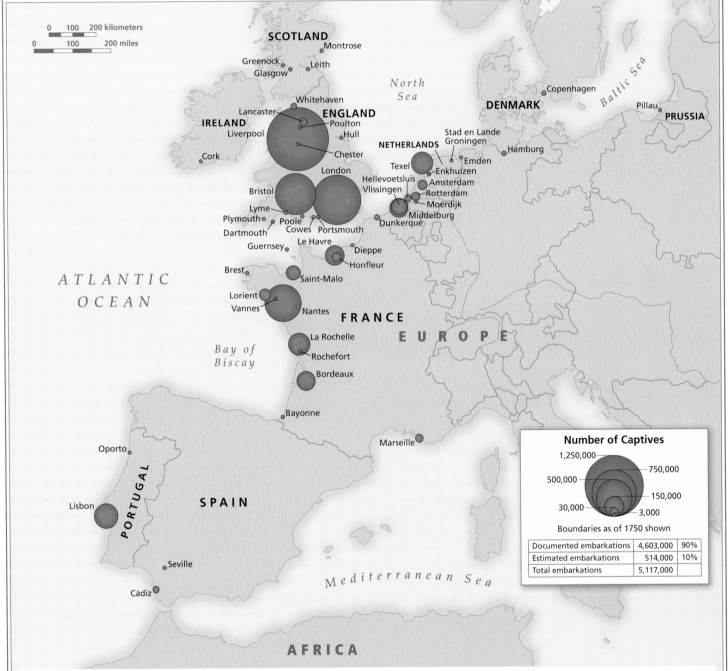

Number of Captives

1,250,000
750,000
500,000
150,000
30,000
3,000

Boundaries as of 1750 shown

Documented embarkations	4,603,000	90%
Estimated embarkations	514,000	10%
Total embarkations	5,117,000	

After 1640 the organizational center of gravity of the African slave trade shifted sharply northward (compare map 22). Liverpool, London, Bristol, and Nantes were as dominant now as the Iberian ports had been in the previous century. In addition, merchants at every northern European port with significant Atlantic commerce sent out slaving expeditions.

We spent in our passage from *St Thomas* to *Barbadoes* two months' eleven days, from the 25th of *August* to the 4th of *November* following: in which time there happened such sickness and mortality among my poor men and negroes, that of the first I buried 14, and of the last 320, which was a great detriment to our voyage, the royal *African* company losing ten pounds by every slave that died, and the owners of the ship ten pounds ten shillings, being the freight agreed on to be paid by the charter party for every negroe deliver'd alive ashore to the *African* company's agents at *Barbadoes*; whereby the loss in all amounted to near 6560 pounds sterling. . . . The negroes are so incident to the small-pox, that few ships that carry them escape without it, and sometimes it makes vast havock and destruction among them: but tho' we had 100 at a time sick of it, and it went thro' the ship, yet we lost not a dozen by it. . . . But what the small-pox spar'd, the flux swept off, to our great regret, after all our pains and care to give them their messes in due order and season, keeping their lodgings as clean and sweet as possible, and enduring so much misery and stench so long among a parcel of creatures nastier than swine; and after all our expectations to be defeated by the mortality. No gold-finders can endure so much noisome slavery as they do who carry negroes; for those have some respite and satisfaction, but we endure twice the misery; and yet by their mortality our voyages are ruin'd, and we pine and fret our selves to death, to think that we should undergo so much misery, and take so much pains to so little purpose.

Excerpt from Thomas Phillips, *A Journal of a Voyage made in the Hannibal of London, Ann. 1693, 1694*, in Awnsham Churchill and John Churchill, eds., *A Collection of Voyages and Travels*, 6 vols. (London, 1732), vol. 6, pp. 236–237.

Map 27: Regions of Trade for Slave Voyages Outfitted in London, 1642–1810

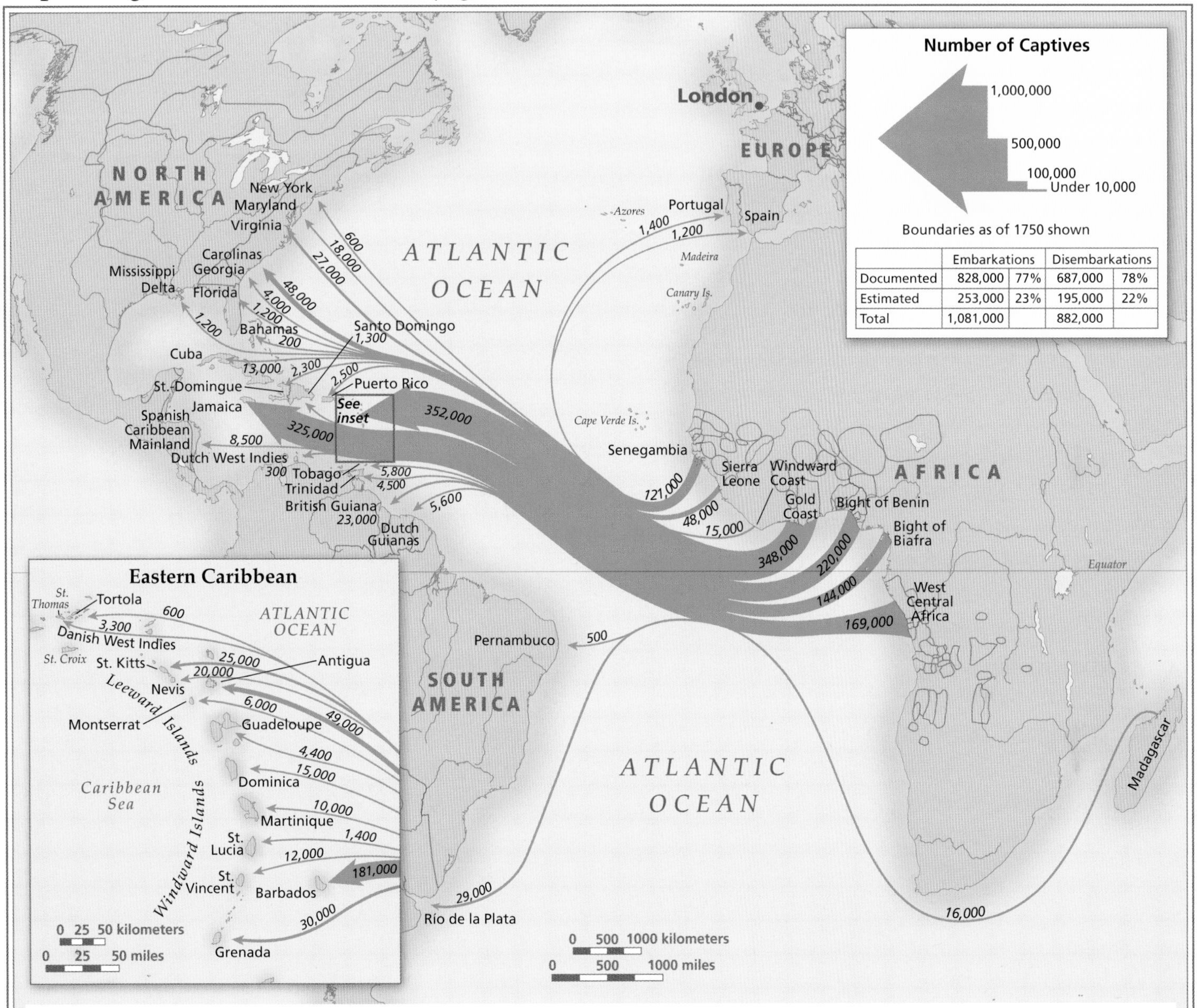

London

EUROPE

NORTH AMERICA
- New York
- Maryland
- Virginia
- Carolinas
- Georgia
- Mississippi Delta
- Florida
- Bahamas
- Cuba
- St. Domingue
- Jamaica
- Spanish Caribbean Mainland
- Dutch West Indies
- Santo Domingo
- Puerto Rico
- Tobago
- Trinidad
- British Guiana
- Dutch Guianas

ATLANTIC OCEAN

Azores • Portugal • Spain
Madeira
Canary Is.
Cape Verde Is.

AFRICA
- Senegambia
- Sierra Leone
- Windward Coast
- Gold Coast
- Bight of Benin
- Bight of Biafra
- West Central Africa
- Madagascar

Equator

SOUTH AMERICA
- Pernambuco
- Rio de la Plata

ATLANTIC OCEAN

Number of Captives

- 1,000,000
- 500,000
- 100,000
- Under 10,000

Boundaries as of 1750 shown

	Embarkations		Disembarkations	
Documented	828,000	77%	687,000	78%
Estimated	253,000	23%	195,000	22%
Total	1,081,000		882,000	

Values on map arrows: 600, 18,000, 27,000, 48,000, 4,000, 1,200, 1,200, 200, 13,000, 2,300, 2,500, 1,300, 325,000, 8,500, 300, 5,800, 4,500, 5,600, 23,000, 352,000, 1,400, 1,200, 121,000, 48,000, 15,000, 348,000, 220,000, 144,000, 169,000, 500, 29,000, 16,000

Eastern Caribbean

- St. Thomas
- Tortola
- Danish West Indies
- St. Croix
- St. Kitts
- Nevis
- Montserrat
- Antigua
- Guadeloupe
- Dominica
- Martinique
- St. Lucia
- St. Vincent
- Barbados
- Grenada

Leeward Islands
Windward Islands

ATLANTIC OCEAN

Caribbean Sea

Values: 600, 3,300, 25,000, 20,000, 6,000, 49,000, 4,400, 15,000, 10,000, 1,400, 12,000, 181,000, 30,000

0 25 50 kilometers
0 25 50 miles

0 500 1000 kilometers
0 500 1000 miles

London's prominence in the trade derived, not from its location (its vessels could take weeks to get through the English Channel), but from its status as a global commercial center. The largest city in Europe, it offered an unmatched range of merchandise, as well as shipping and financial services, to long-distance traders of all kinds, including slave merchants.

For insurance on the Fly Walker Mastr at and from Bristol to the Coast of Africa during the stay and trade there and from thence to her port or ports of discharge in America—on Ship & Goods—Free from the Loss of trading in Boats— The Insurers free from any Loss or damage that may happen from the Insurrection of Negroes— In case the same shall not exceed Ten Pounds p Ct. to be computed on the nett Amount of the Ship Outsett & Cargo—Negroes valued at Thirty Pounds p Head

£200	James Laroche
200	James Rogers
200	Richard Fydell
100	John Purnell Jnr
100	Richard Blake
£800 @	6 Gs. p Ct & Policy 9/- 50.17.-

Rogers, Blake & Co. to Rogers & Fydell & Co., 9 October 1788, in Outset notes of Fly Schooner, 1788, Chancery Masters' Exhibits, C 107/3, The National Archives, Kew, London. Published with permission of The National Archives, Kew, London.

Map 28: Regions of Trade for Slave Voyages Outfitted in Bristol, 1686–1807

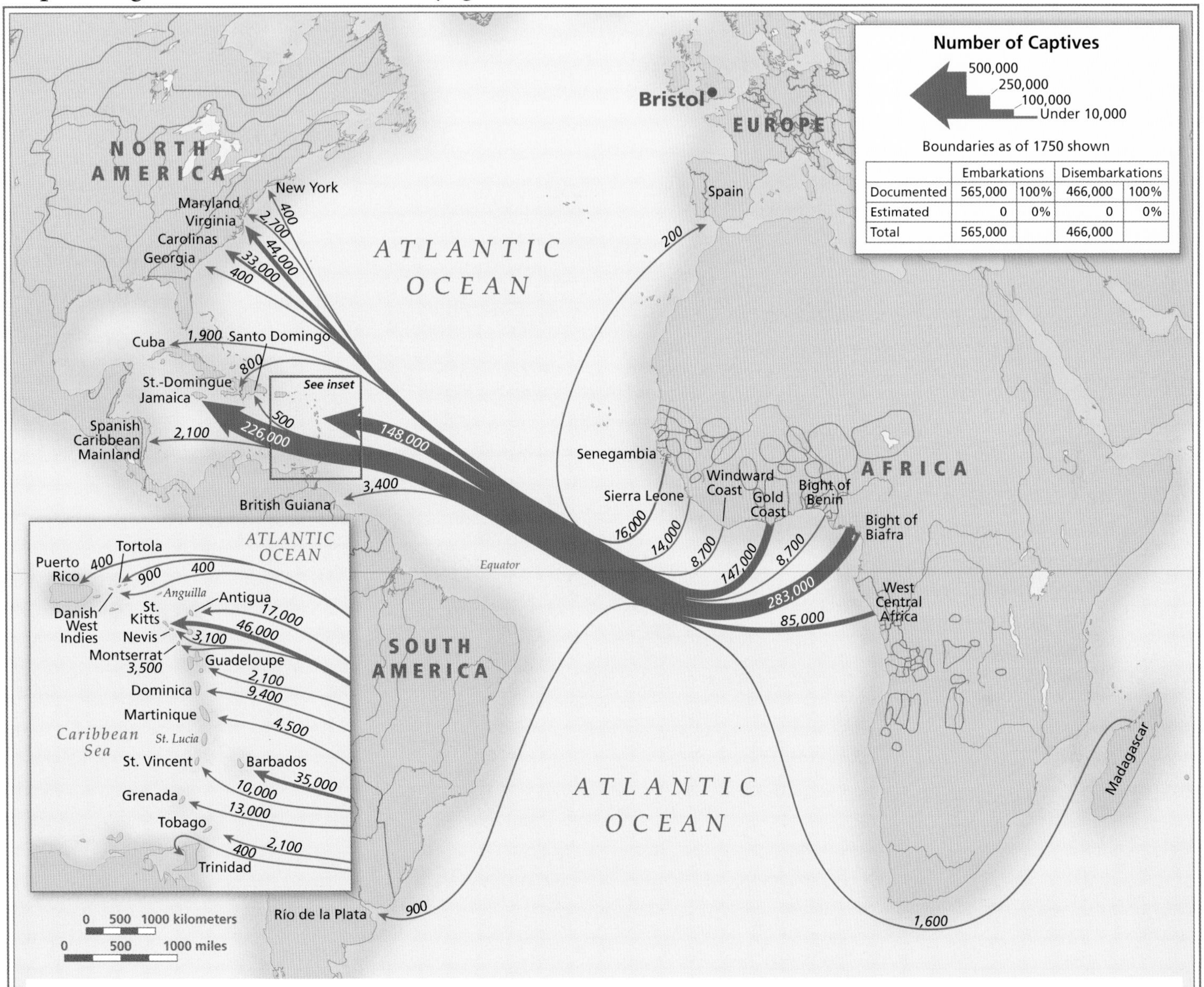

Number of Captives

- 500,000
- 250,000
- 100,000
- Under 10,000

Boundaries as of 1750 shown

	Embarkations		Disembarkations	
Documented	565,000	100%	466,000	100%
Estimated	0	0%	0	0%
Total	565,000		466,000	

Bristol
EUROPE

NORTH AMERICA

New York
Maryland
Virginia
Carolinas
Georgia
400
2,700
44,000
33,000
400

ATLANTIC OCEAN

Spain
200

Cuba
1,900 Santo Domingo
800
St.-Domingue
Jamaica
500
Spanish Caribbean Mainland
2,100
226,000
148,000
3,400
British Guiana

See inset

Senegambia
Sierra Leone
16,000
Windward Coast
14,000
8,700
Gold Coast
147,000
Bight of Benin
8,700
AFRICA
Bight of Biafra
West Central Africa
283,000
85,000

Equator

Inset (Caribbean):

ATLANTIC OCEAN

Tortola
Puerto Rico
400
900
400
Anguilla
Danish West Indies
St. Kitts
Nevis
3,100
Montserrat
3,500
Antigua
17,000
46,000
Guadeloupe
2,100
Dominica
9,400
Martinique
4,500
Caribbean Sea
St. Lucia
St. Vincent
Barbados
35,000
10,000
Grenada
13,000
Tobago
2,100
400
Trinidad

SOUTH AMERICA

ATLANTIC OCEAN

Madagascar

Río de la Plata
900
1,600

0 500 1000 kilometers
0 500 1000 miles

In the second quarter of the eighteenth century, Bristol was the largest slave-trading port in Europe and supplied the major portion of the slaves sent to Jamaica, with its booming sugar economy, most of them drawn from the Bight of Biafra and the Gold Coast. However, owing to its small and increasingly congested harbor, Bristol eventually fell behind Liverpool.

Map 29: Regions of Trade for Slave Voyages Outfitted in Liverpool, 1696–1810

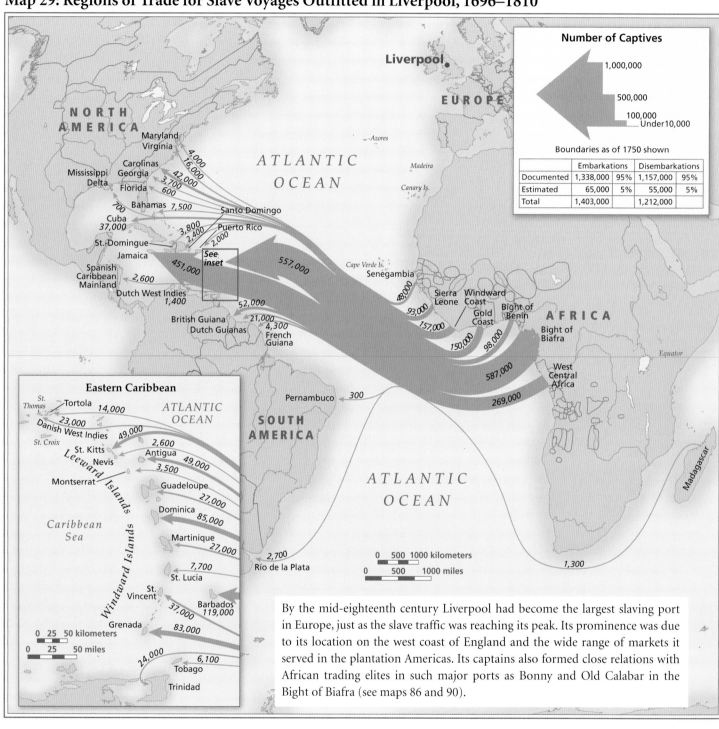

Number of Captives

1,000,000
500,000
100,000
Under 10,000

Boundaries as of 1750 shown

	Embarkations		Disembarkations	
Documented	1,338,000	95%	1,157,000	95%
Estimated	65,000	5%	55,000	5%
Total	1,403,000		1,212,000	

Liverpool

EUROPE

NORTH AMERICA

ATLANTIC OCEAN

Azores

Madeira

Canary Is.

Maryland
Virginia 4,000
16,000
Carolinas 42,000
Mississippi Georgia
Delta 3,700
Florida 600
700
Bahamas 7,500
Santo Domingo
Cuba 37,000
3,800
2,400 Puerto Rico
St. Domingue 2,000
Jamaica
451,000 **See inset**
Spanish Caribbean Mainland 2,600
Dutch West Indies 1,400
52,000
British Guiana 21,000
Dutch Guianas 4,300
French Guiana

557,000

Cape Verde Is.
Senegambia
78,000
Sierra Leone Windward Coast
93,000 Gold Coast Bight of Benin
157,000
150,000 98,000
587,000
269,000

AFRICA

Bight of Biafra

West Central Africa

Equator

SOUTH AMERICA

Pernambuco 300

ATLANTIC OCEAN

Madagascar

2,700
Río de la Plata

0   500   1000 kilometers
0   500   1000 miles

1,300

Eastern Caribbean

St. Thomas
Tortola 14,000
23,000
Danish West Indies 49,000
St. Croix
St. Kitts 2,600
Antigua 49,000
Nevis 3,500
Montserrat
Guadeloupe 27,000
Dominica 85,000
Martinique 27,000
7,700
St. Lucia
St. Vincent
Barbados 119,000
37,000
Grenada 83,000
24,000 6,100
Tobago
Trinidad

ATLANTIC OCEAN

Leeward Islands

Windward Islands

Caribbean Sea

0   25   50 kilometers
0   25   50 miles

By the mid-eighteenth century Liverpool had become the largest slaving port in Europe, just as the slave traffic was reaching its peak. Its prominence was due to its location on the west coast of England and the wide range of markets it served in the plantation Americas. Its captains also formed close relations with African trading elites in such major ports as Bonny and Old Calabar in the Bight of Biafra (see maps 86 and 90).

Map 30: Regions of Trade for Slave Voyages Outfitted in La Rochelle, 1643–1793

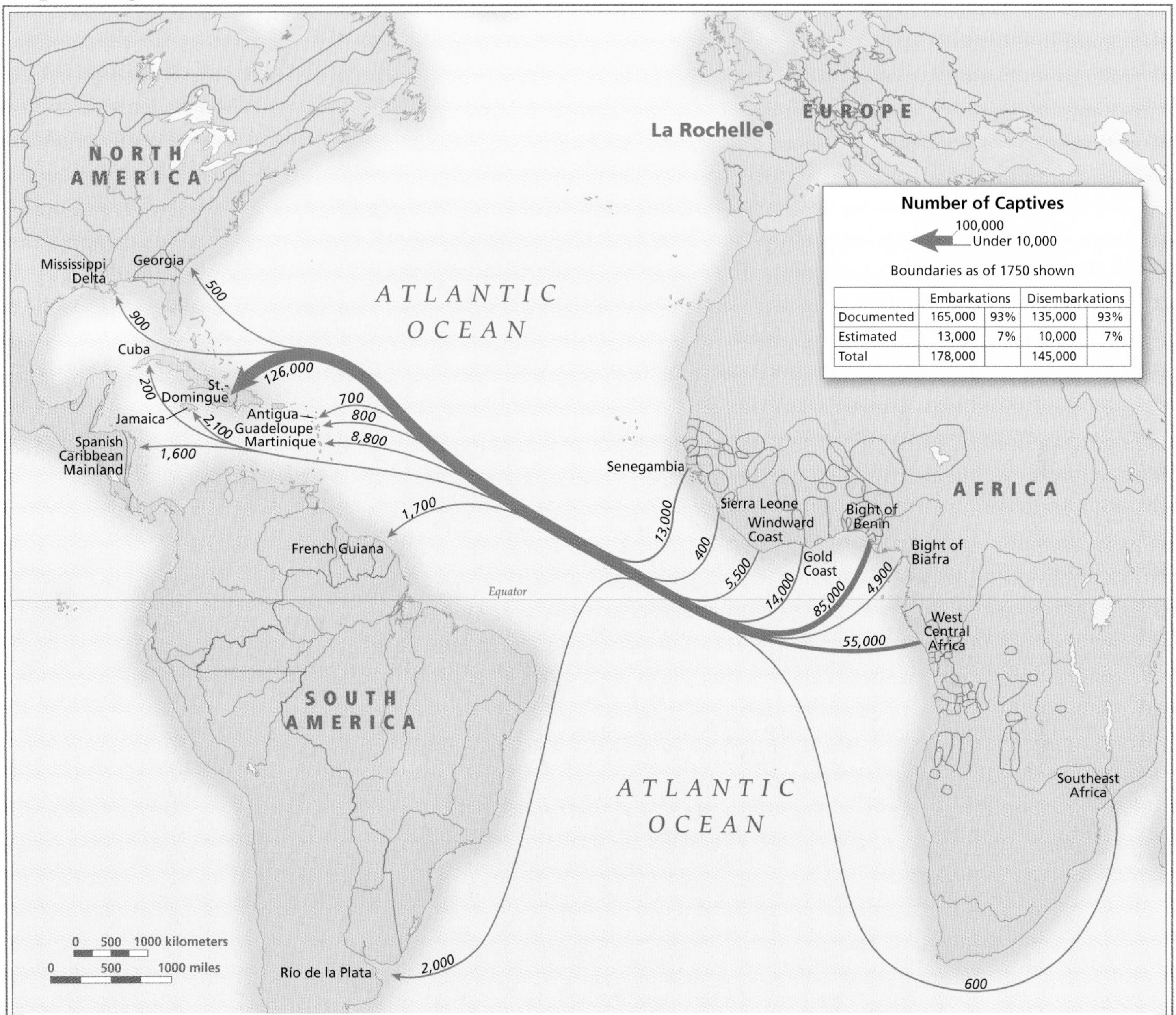

Number of Captives

100,000

Under 10,000

Boundaries as of 1750 shown

	Embarkations		Disembarkations	
Documented	165,000	93%	135,000	93%
Estimated	13,000	7%	10,000	7%
Total	178,000		145,000	

La Rochelle was the second most important slaving port in France, and its location on the Atlantic allowed merchants to organize relatively short triangular voyages. The port's slave traffic declined after 1788, although the French traffic in slaves was still expanding, and it took little part in the illegal nineteenth-century slave trade. La Rochelle's slave merchants drew heavily on just two African ports for slaves, Ouidah and Malembo (see maps 79, 80, and 101), and competed with and lost out to Le Havre for the markets in St.-Domingue.

Du 4 [septembre 1775]

       Rade de Juda, il nous est mort
Un homme captif marqué au poitrail droit *LSM*,
les soins réitérés et suivis du premier chirurgien
qui s'est trouvé à bord lui ont prolongé la vie de
quelques jours, mais cette surprenante maladie
dont les causes nous sont encore inconnues, dans
l'étonnement, où elle nous laisse ne permet pas
d'administrer de remède, puisque au moment
même qu'elle se déclare, la dissolution du sang est
faite que le malade meurt subitement vu qu'une
dyarré violente l'emporte dans les 24 heures, le
sang s'échapant par les pores de toute part.

4 [September 1775]

       Juda [Ouidah] Road, there died
A captive man branded with *LSM* on his right
chest, the leading surgeon on board took constant
care to prolong his life over a few days, but to our
astonishment this uncontrollable sickness, the
causes of which remain unknown, did not allow
us any remedy from the time that it manifested
itself, the loss of blood was such that the sick man
was carried away suddenly within 24 hours by a
violent diarrhea, blood escaping from every pore.

Du 8 [septembre 1775]

       Rade de Juda, il nous est mort
Un homme, marqué au bras droit *LSM* de la petite
vérole, malade depuis huit jours et qui nous avoit
donnez bonne espérance jusqu'à hier au soir qu'il
survint sans doute une révolution qui l'a aportez
en peu de tems

8 [September 1775]

       Juda Road[,] there died
A man, branded with *LSM* on his right arm[,] of
smallpox, [who had been] sick for eight days but
who until yesterday evening gave us hope that he
might survive [but] doubtless a relapse carried
him off in a short time

Du 15 septembre 1775
   Rade de Juda il nous est mort
Une négritte marquée au bras droit *LSM* qui étoit
attaquée du scorbut depuis quelque jours

15 September 1775
   Juda Road[,] there died
A Negro girl branded with *LSM* on the right arm
who went down with scurvy a few days ago

Du 13 octobre
   Rade de Juda il nous est mort
Une femme à la cargaison marquée au bras droit
LSM, elle est morte d'inanition et de scorbut et a
passé assez vite

13 October
   Juda Road[,] there died
A woman of the cargo branded with *LSM* on the
right arm, she died of lethargy and scurvy and
passed away quickly enough.

Excerpt from Journal de Traitte commencée à la Rivière
de Saint-André le 26 février 1775, à l'usage du Navire
La Susanne Marguerite, Cap. Le Sieur André Begaud
de la Rochelle [Journal of Trade of the Ship *La Susanne
Marguerite*, Captain Le Sieur André Begaud, of La Rochelle,
begun 26 February 1775 at the River St. Andrews], Archives
Muncipales de la Rochelle, E 280, partially reproduced in
Alain Yacou, *Journaux de bord et la traite de Joseph Crassous
de Médeuil* (Paris: Karthala, 2001), pp. 257–259. Reprinted by
permission of Karthala. Translated by Filipa da Silva Ribeiro
and David Richardson.

Map 31: Regions of Trade for Slave Voyages Outfitted in Le Havre, 1670–1802

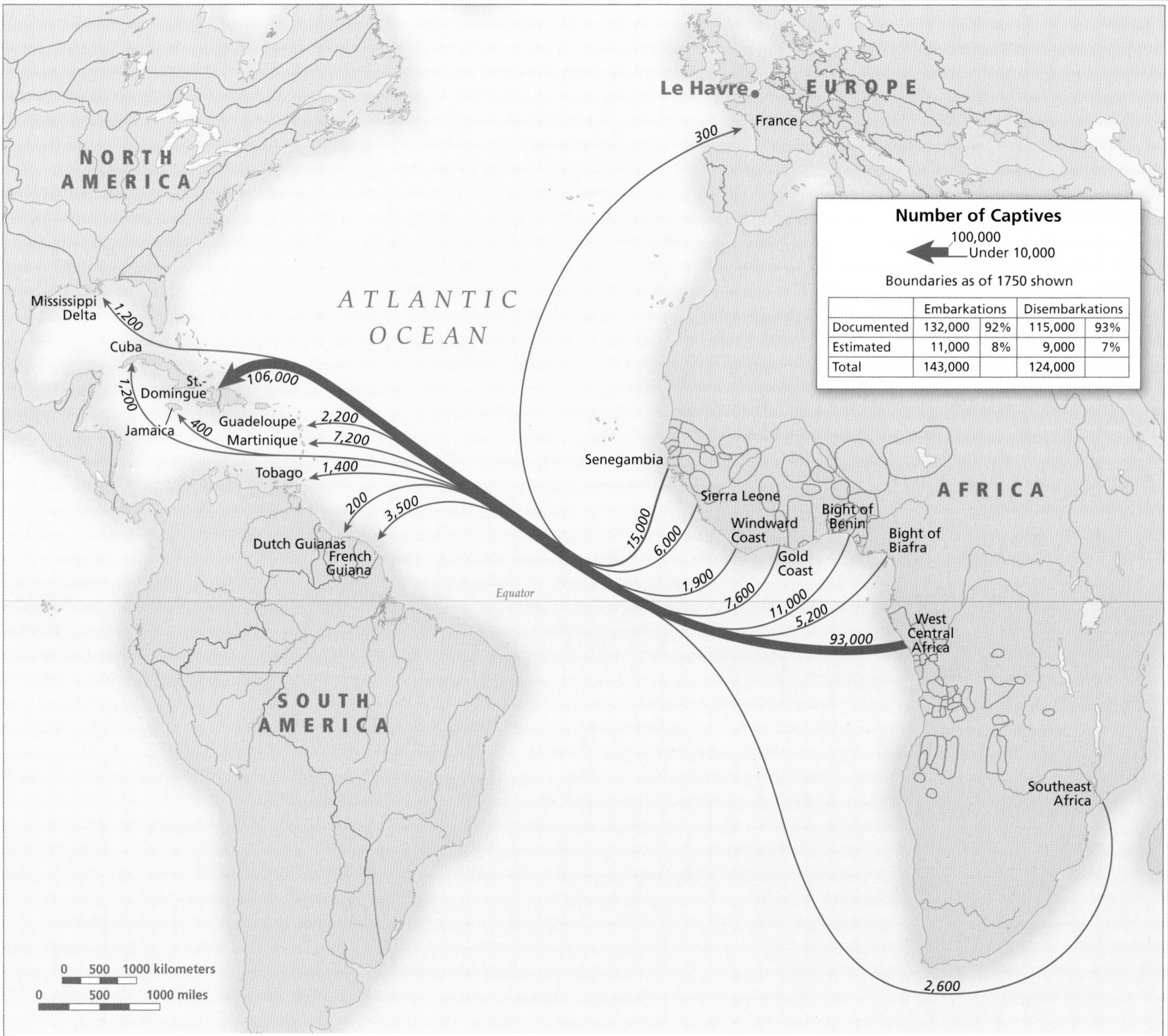

Le Havre

France

300

NORTH
AMERICA

EUROPE

ATLANTIC
OCEAN

Number of Captives

100,000
Under 10,000

Boundaries as of 1750 shown

	Embarkations		Disembarkations	
Documented	132,000	92%	115,000	93%
Estimated	11,000	8%	9,000	7%
Total	143,000		124,000	

Mississippi
Delta

1,200

Cuba

1,200

St.-
Domingue

106,000

Jamaica

400

Guadeloupe

2,200

Martinique

7,200

Tobago

1,400

200

3,500

Dutch Guianas
French
Guiana

Senegambia

Sierra Leone

Windward
Coast

Gold
Coast

Bight of
Benin

Bight of
Biafra

AFRICA

15,000

6,000

1,900

7,600

11,000

5,200

93,000

West
Central
Africa

Equator

SOUTH
AMERICA

Southeast
Africa

0   500   1000 kilometers

0   500   1000 miles

2,600

Le Havre was the first slave-trading port of significance in France and one of the last to quit the traffic, and yet almost 40 percent of its traffic occurred between 1784 and 1792. In the eighteenth century its merchants developed strong ties with Malembo, on the northern West Central African coast (see map 101), and sold over half their captives in St.-Domingue (see map 164).

Map 32: Regions of Trade for Slave Voyages Outfitted in Bordeaux, 1686–1804

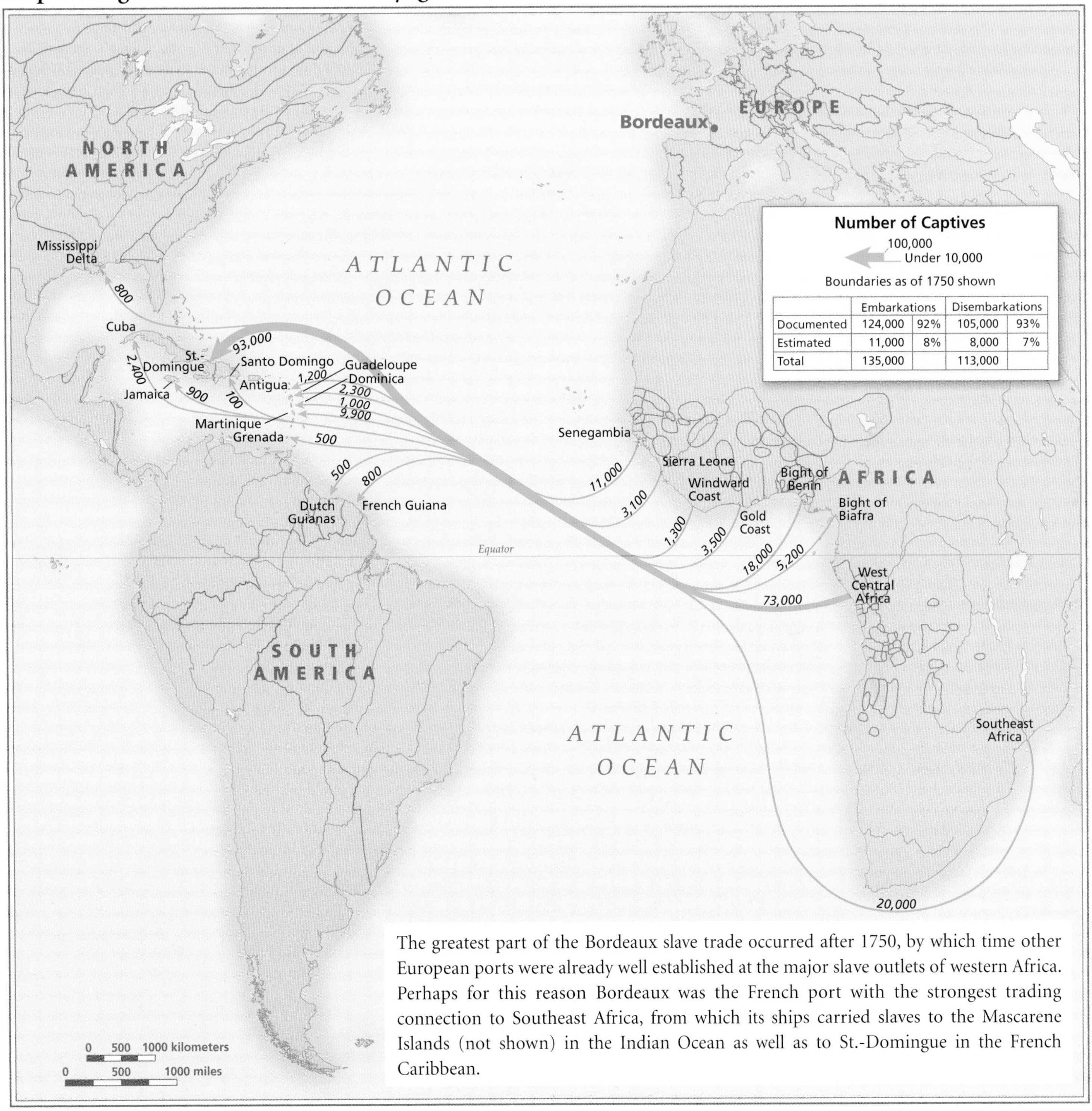

NORTH AMERICA

EUROPE

Bordeaux

ATLANTIC OCEAN

Mississippi Delta

800

Cuba

93,000

St.-Domingue

2,400

Jamaica

900

100

Santo Domingo

Guadeloupe

Dominica

1,200

Antigua

2,300

1,000

9,900

Martinique

Grenada

500

Senegambia

Number of Captives

100,000

Under 10,000

Boundaries as of 1750 shown

	Embarkations		Disembarkations	
Documented	124,000	92%	105,000	93%
Estimated	11,000	8%	8,000	7%
Total	135,000		113,000	

500

800

Dutch Guianas

French Guiana

Equator

Sierra Leone

Windward Coast

Bight of Benin

AFRICA

Bight of Biafra

Gold Coast

11,000

3,100

1,300

3,500

18,000

5,200

73,000

West Central Africa

SOUTH AMERICA

ATLANTIC OCEAN

Southeast Africa

20,000

0   500   1000 kilometers

0   500   1000 miles

The greatest part of the Bordeaux slave trade occurred after 1750, by which time other European ports were already well established at the major slave outlets of western Africa. Perhaps for this reason Bordeaux was the French port with the strongest trading connection to Southeast Africa, from which its ships carried slaves to the Mascarene Islands (not shown) in the Indian Ocean as well as to St.-Domingue in the French Caribbean.

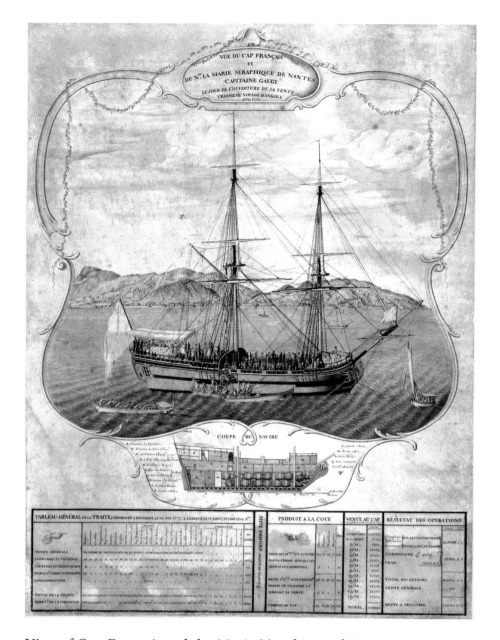

View of Cap-Français and the *Marie Séraphique* of Nantes, 1773

Vue du Cap Français et du n[avi]re la Marie Séraphique de Nantes, Capitaine Gaugy, le jour de l'ouverture de sa vente, troisième voyage d'Angole, 1772, 1773. Watercolor by an unknown artist. Cliché ville de Nantes—Musée d'histoire de Nantes—Château des ducs de Bretagne.

Voyages linking Nantes (France), West Central Africa (Angola), and St.-Domingue (modern-day Haiti) were at the heart of the French slave trade at its peak in the later eighteenth century. This vibrant watercolor depicts the opening of the sale of 340 captives delivered by the *Marie Séraphique* from Angola to Cap-Français, St.-Domingue, in January 1773 (voyage id 30968). On sale were twice as many males as females, a not uncommon ratio at the time. The small boats are ferrying potential buyers to the ship at anchor; other buyers wait under a canopy on board to bid for the captives gathered on the other side of the barrier dividing the deck. Tables at the bottom of the painting provide summary statistics of the ship's transactions, including the trade goods exchanged in Africa and at Cap-Français.

Map 33: Regions of Trade for Slave Voyages Outfitted in Nantes, 1697–1803

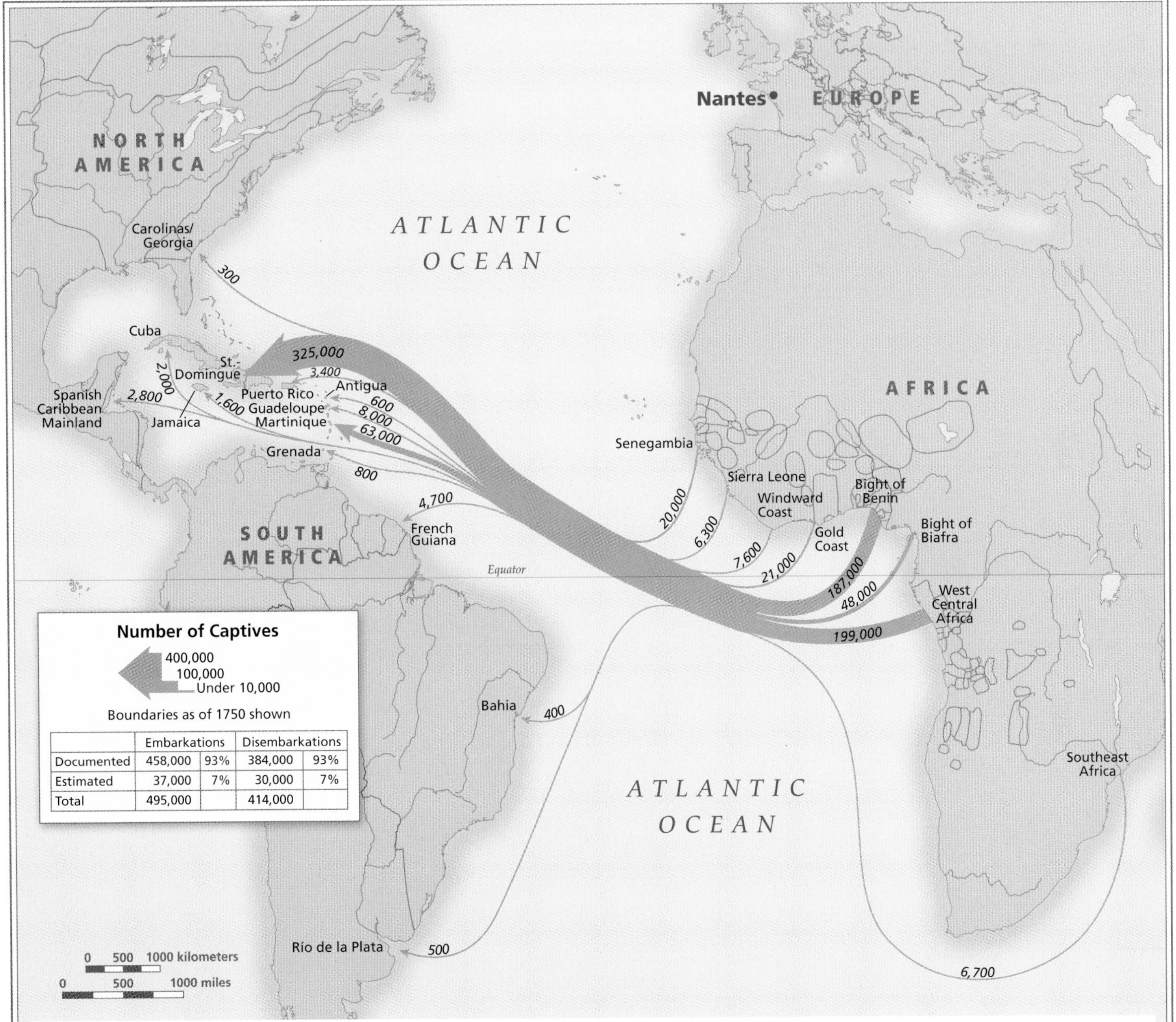

Nantes• EUROPE

NORTH AMERICA

ATLANTIC OCEAN

Carolinas/ Georgia

300

Cuba

St. Domingue

325,000

3,400

Antigua

600

Spanish Caribbean Mainland

2,800

2,000

Puerto Rico

1,600

Guadeloupe

8,000

Jamaica

Martinique

63,000

Grenada

800

French Guiana

4,700

SOUTH AMERICA

Equator

AFRICA

Senegambia

Sierra Leone

Windward Coast

Bight of Benin

20,000

6,300

Gold Coast

7,600

21,000

Bight of Biafra

187,000

48,000

West Central Africa

199,000

Southeast Africa

Number of Captives

400,000
100,000
Under 10,000

Boundaries as of 1750 shown

	Embarkations		Disembarkations	
Documented	458,000	93%	384,000	93%
Estimated	37,000	7%	30,000	7%
Total	495,000		414,000	

Bahia

400

ATLANTIC OCEAN

0   500   1000 kilometers
0   500   1000 miles

Río de la Plata

500

6,700

After the early eighteenth century, Nantes quickly became the premier port for the organization of French slaving voyages, a pre-eminence that lasted until war closed down the French slave trade in 1793. Its vessels supplied all parts of the French plantation Americas. Its merchants were dominant in two of the largest slave-trading centers in Africa – Loango (see map 99) and Ouidah (see maps 79–80). Nantes was also one of the few French ports to trade significantly in the British-dominated Bight of Biafra.

Map 34: Regions of Trade for Slave Voyages Leaving Texel, 1642–1794

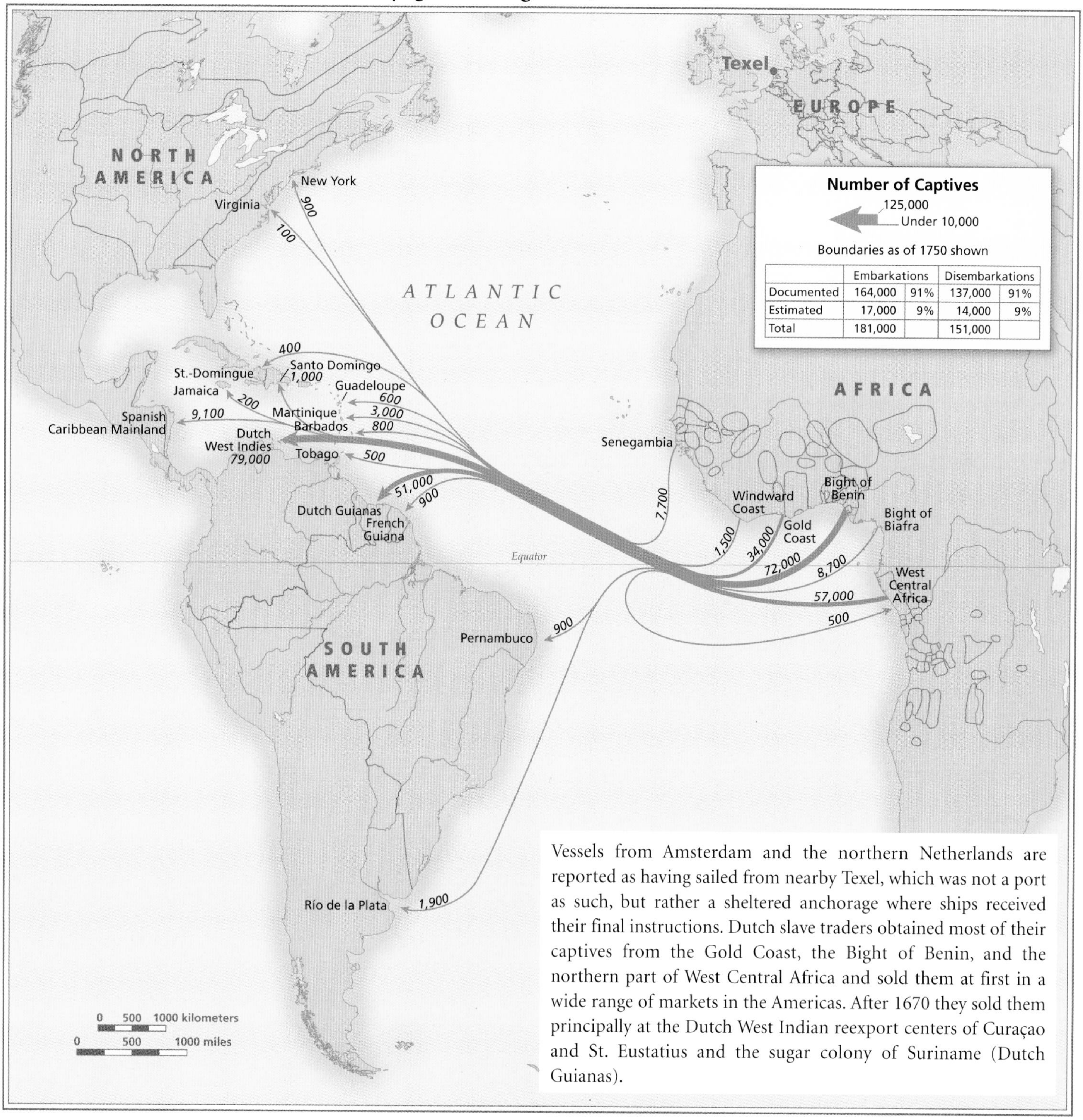

NORTH AMERICA

New York

Virginia

900

100

ATLANTIC OCEAN

Number of Captives

125,000

Under 10,000

Boundaries as of 1750 shown

	Embarkations		Disembarkations	
Documented	164,000	91%	137,000	91%
Estimated	17,000	9%	14,000	9%
Total	181,000		151,000	

Texel

EUROPE

400

St.-Domingue

Santo Domingo
1,000

Guadeloupe
600

Jamaica

200

Martinique

3,000

Spanish
Caribbean Mainland

9,100

Barbados

800

Dutch
West Indies
79,000

Tobago

500

51,000

900

Dutch Guianas
French
Guiana

AFRICA

Senegambia

7,700

Windward
Coast

Bight of
Benin

Bight of
Biafra

Gold
Coast

1,500

34,000

72,000

8,700

West
Central
Africa

57,000

500

Equator

SOUTH
AMERICA

Pernambuco

900

Río de la Plata

1,900

0   500   1000 kilometers

0   500   1000 miles

Vessels from Amsterdam and the northern Netherlands are reported as having sailed from nearby Texel, which was not a port as such, but rather a sheltered anchorage where ships received their final instructions. Dutch slave traders obtained most of their captives from the Gold Coast, the Bight of Benin, and the northern part of West Central Africa and sold them at first in a wide range of markets in the Americas. After 1670 they sold them principally at the Dutch West Indian reexport centers of Curaçao and St. Eustatius and the sugar colony of Suriname (Dutch Guianas).

Map 35: Regions of Trade for Slave Voyages Outfitted in Lisbon, 1642–1807

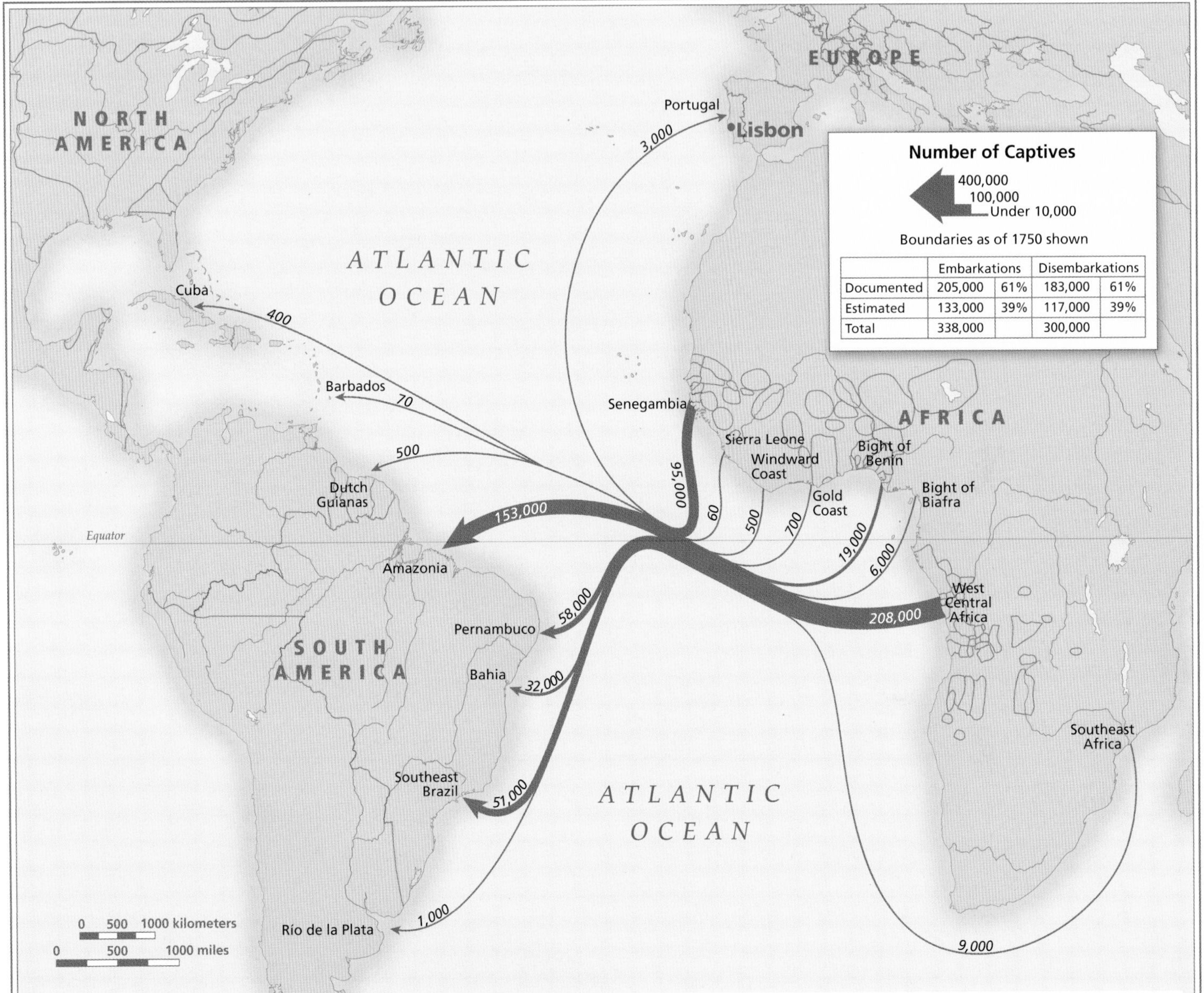

Number of Captives

400,000
100,000
Under 10,000

Boundaries as of 1750 shown

	Embarkations		Disembarkations	
Documented	205,000	61%	183,000	61%
Estimated	133,000	39%	117,000	39%
Total	338,000		300,000	

NORTH AMERICA

EUROPE

Portugal
•Lisbon
3,000

ATLANTIC OCEAN

Cuba
400

Barbados
70

500

Dutch Guianas

153,000

Equator

Amazonia

Senegambia
95,000

AFRICA

Sierra Leone
Windward Coast

Bight of Benin

Gold Coast

Bight of Biafra

60
500
700
19,000
6,000

West Central Africa
208,000

58,000

SOUTH AMERICA

Pernambuco

Bahia
32,000

Southeast Brazil
51,000

Southeast Africa

ATLANTIC OCEAN

0   500   1000 kilometers
0   500   1000 miles

Río de la Plata
1,000

9,000

After 1641 the Lisbon slave trade declined because the separation of the Portuguese and Spanish monarchy closed markets in Spanish America to Portuguese slave merchants. Lisbon maintained a small but steady slave trade with various regions of Brazil, but after 1750 it focused on a new triangular trade that linked it with Senegambia in Africa and Amazonia in South America.

Before a factor buys a slave, his black servants must examine the slave carefully to see if the individual has any injury, is ill, or has lost any teeth. The Negroes know how much the Factor pays, and at what price each Black is valued. It is usually in accordance with the Christiansborg's current price in 1749, for a male slave, 6 ounces of gold or 96 rixdaler. Therefore, we [may] pay [in a mix of goods]:

2 muskets @ 6 rixdaler	=	12	rixdaler
40 lb gunpowder	=	16	"
1 anker Danish brandy	=	7	"
1 piece of cotton cloth [calico]	=	10	"
1 piece [Indian] "Callowaypoos" [cotton]	=	6	"
1 piece [Indian] "Salempuris" [cotton]	=	10	"
2 pieces gingham	=	10	"
2 iron bars	=	4	"
1 copper bar	=	1	"
4 pieces "plattilias" [silesia or linen cloth]	=	8	"
1 "cabes" beads	=	2	"
1 pewter basin	=	2	"
20 lbs cowrie shells	=	8	"
Total		96	rixdaler

If the slave is missing a tooth you deduct four rixdaler from that sum; if two teeth are missing, eight rixdaler.

Excerpt from Ludevig Ferdinand Rømer, *Tilforladelig Efterretning om Kysten Guinea* (Copenhagen, 1760), published in English translation as Ludewig Ferdinand Rømer, *A Reliable Account of the Coast of Guinea (1760)*, ed. and trans. Selena Axelrod Winsnes (Oxford: Oxford University Press for The British Academy, 2000), pp. 225–226. Published with permission of The British Academy. Some minor changes to Winsnes's translation are included.

Map 36: Regions of Trade for Slave Voyages Outfitted in Copenhagen, 1642–1806

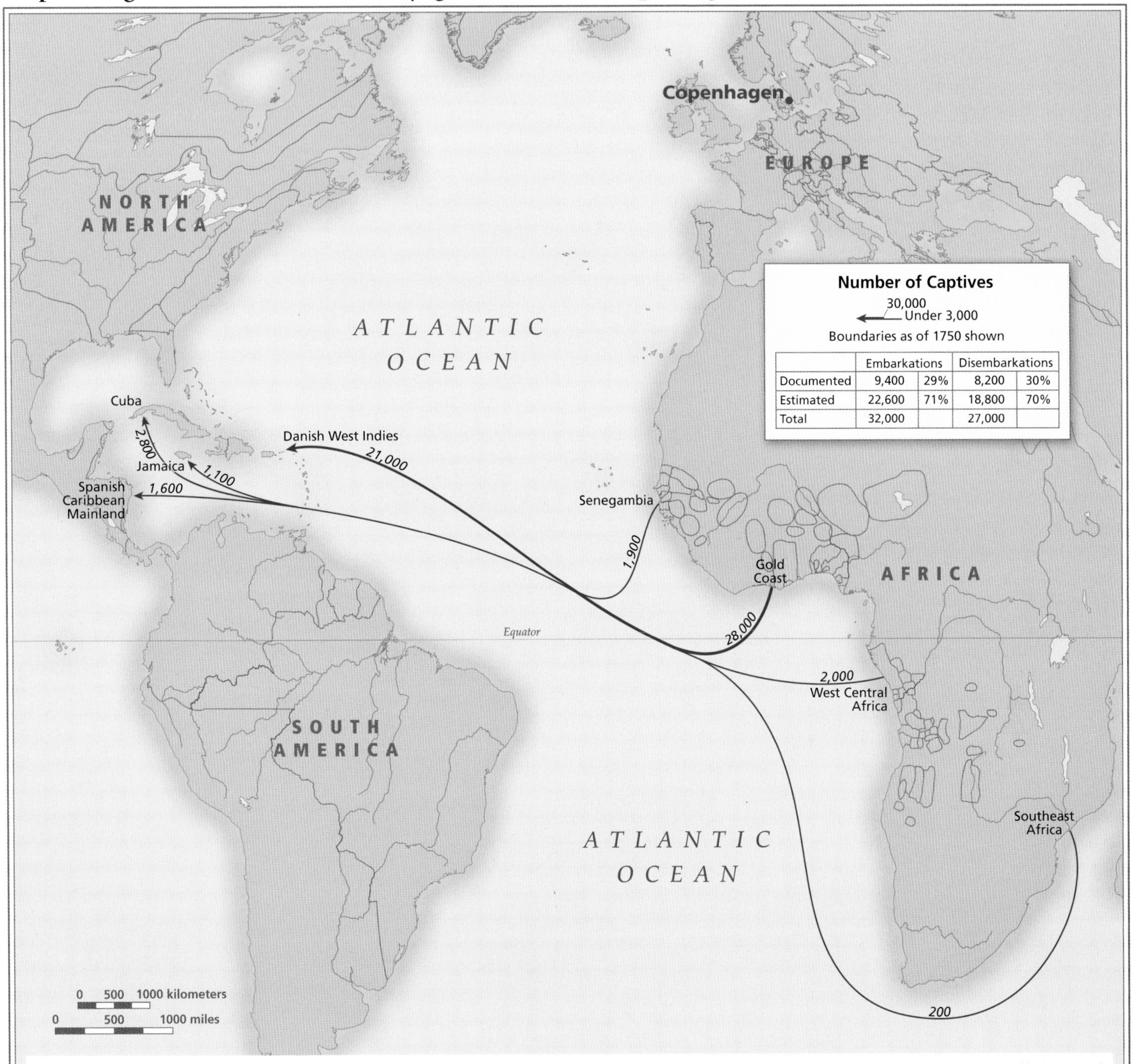

Number of Captives

30,000
⟵ Under 3,000

Boundaries as of 1750 shown

	Embarkations		Disembarkations	
Documented	9,400	29%	8,200	30%
Estimated	22,600	71%	18,800	70%
Total	32,000		27,000	

NORTH AMERICA

Copenhagen

EUROPE

ATLANTIC OCEAN

Cuba

Danish West Indies 21,000

2,800

Jamaica 1,100

Spanish Caribbean Mainland 1,600

Senegambia

1,900

Gold Coast

AFRICA

28,000

2,000 West Central Africa

Equator

SOUTH AMERICA

Southeast Africa

ATLANTIC OCEAN

200

0 500 1000 kilometers

0 500 1000 miles

Copenhagen, the home port of the Danish West Indies Company, was the principal organizational center of slave trafficking of countries bordering the Baltic Sea, although north German ports and ports in the Danish West Indies also outfitted many slave voyages in the late eighteenth and early nineteenth centuries. Danish ships traded mostly at one fort on the Gold Coast, Christiansborg, and two small islands in the Danish West Indies, St. Thomas and St. Croix, both important slave reexport centers.

Map 37: Ports in the Americas Where Slave Voyages Were Outfitted, 1642–1807

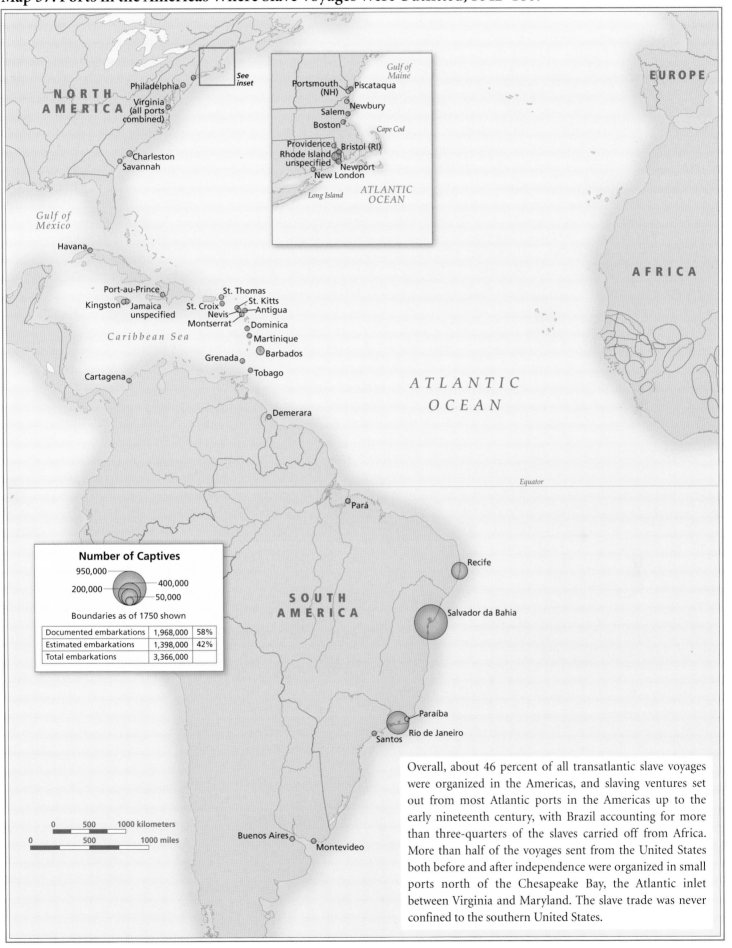

EUROPE

NORTH AMERICA

Philadelphia

Virginia (all ports combined)

See inset

Charleston
Savannah

Gulf of Mexico

Havana

Port-au-Prince
Kingston Jamaica unspecified
St. Croix
Nevis
Montserrat

St. Thomas
St. Kitts
Antigua
Dominica
Martinique

Caribbean Sea

Grenada
Tobago

Barbados

Cartagena

Demerara

Inset — Gulf of Maine

Portsmouth (NH) Piscataqua
Newbury
Salem
Boston
Providence Bristol (RI)
Rhode Island unspecified
Newport
New London
Long Island

Cape Cod

ATLANTIC OCEAN

AFRICA

ATLANTIC OCEAN

Equator

Pará

Recife

SOUTH AMERICA

Salvador da Bahia

Paraíba

Santos Rio de Janeiro

Buenos Aires
Montevideo

Number of Captives

950,000
200,000
400,000
50,000

Boundaries as of 1750 shown

Documented embarkations	1,968,000	58%
Estimated embarkations	1,398,000	42%
Total embarkations	3,366,000	

0   500   1000 kilometers
0   500   1000 miles

Overall, about 46 percent of all transatlantic slave voyages were organized in the Americas, and slaving ventures set out from most Atlantic ports in the Americas up to the early nineteenth century, with Brazil accounting for more than three-quarters of the slaves carried off from Africa. More than half of the voyages sent from the United States both before and after independence were organized in small ports north of the Chesapeake Bay, the Atlantic inlet between Virginia and Maryland. The slave trade was never confined to the southern United States.

Map 38: Regions of Trade for Slave Voyages Outfitted in Recife, 1642–1807

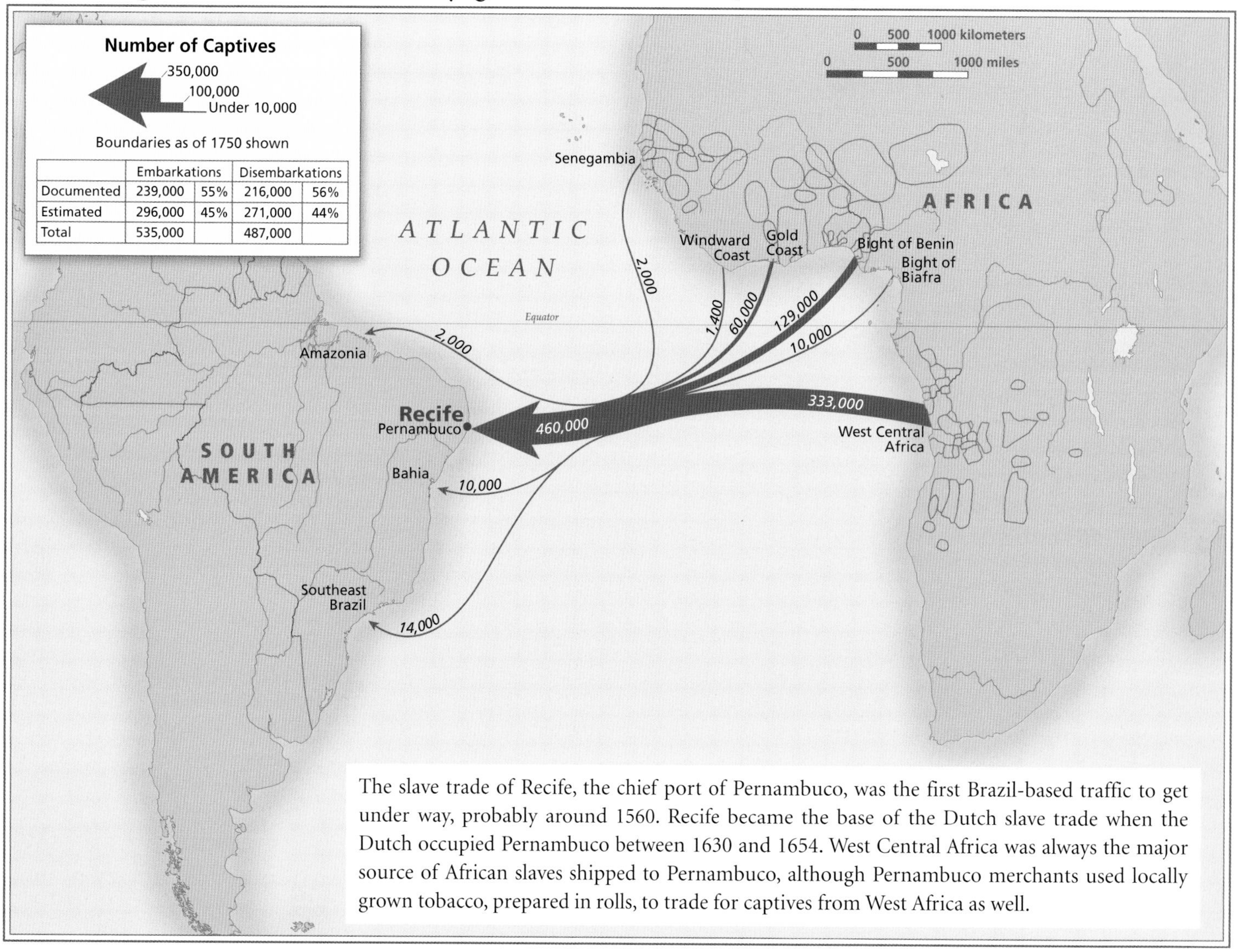

Number of Captives

350,000
100,000
Under 10,000

Boundaries as of 1750 shown

	Embarkations		Disembarkations	
Documented	239,000	55%	216,000	56%
Estimated	296,000	45%	271,000	44%
Total	535,000		487,000	

0   500   1000 kilometers
0   500   1000 miles

Senegambia

ATLANTIC
OCEAN

AFRICA

Windward
Coast
Gold
Coast
Bight of Benin
Bight of
Biafra

2,000
1,400
60,000
129,000
10,000

Equator

Amazonia
2,000

Recife
Pernambuco
460,000

333,000

West Central
Africa

SOUTH
AMERICA

Bahia
10,000

Southeast
Brazil
14,000

The slave trade of Recife, the chief port of Pernambuco, was the first Brazil-based traffic to get under way, probably around 1560. Recife became the base of the Dutch slave trade when the Dutch occupied Pernambuco between 1630 and 1654. West Central Africa was always the major source of African slaves shipped to Pernambuco, although Pernambuco merchants used locally grown tobacco, prepared in rolls, to trade for captives from West Africa as well.

Map 39: Regions of Trade for Slave Voyages Outfitted in Salvador da Bahia, 1642–1807

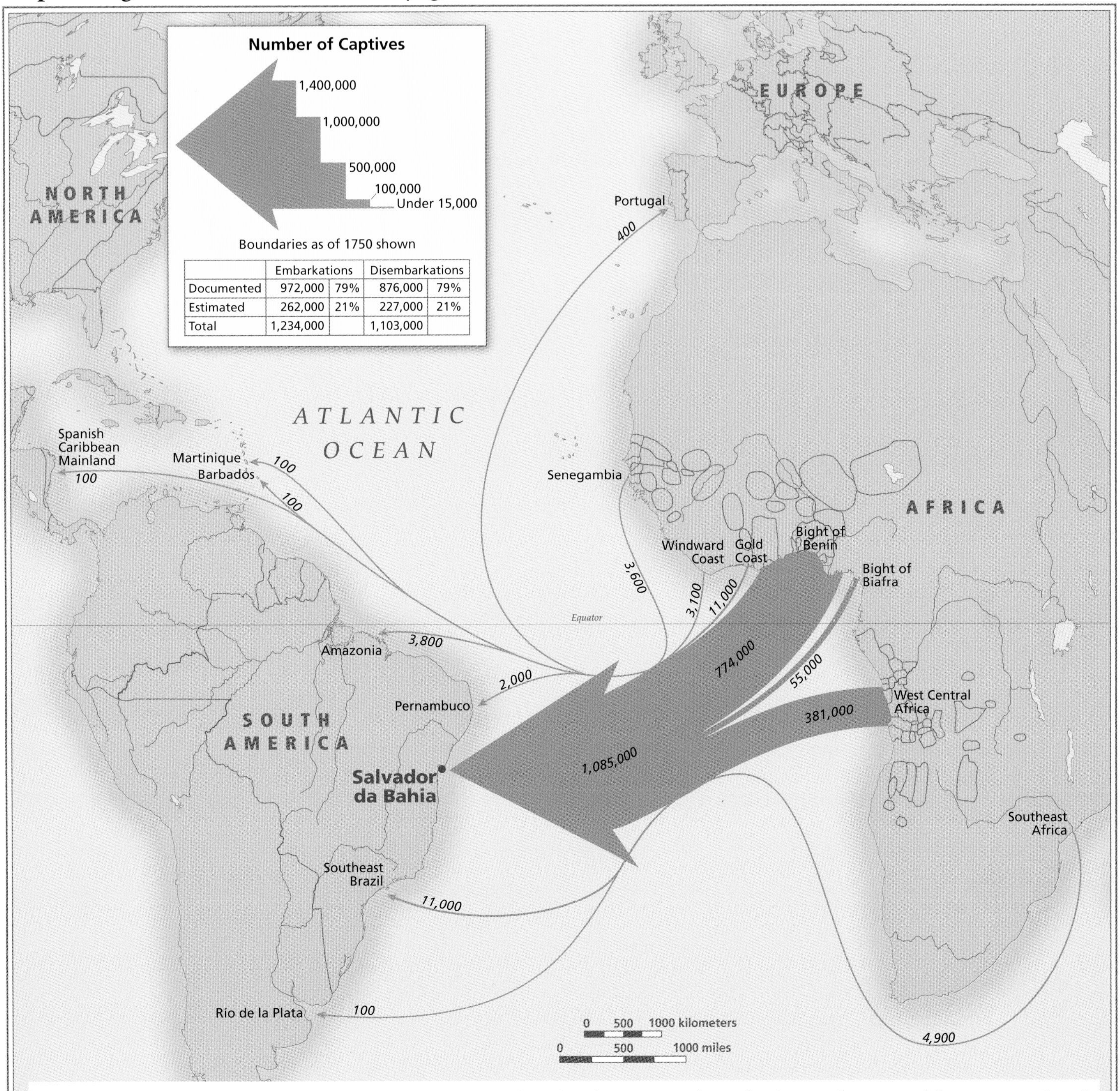

Number of Captives

1,400,000

1,000,000

500,000

100,000

Under 15,000

Boundaries as of 1750 shown

	Embarkations		Disembarkations	
Documented	972,000	79%	876,000	79%
Estimated	262,000	21%	227,000	21%
Total	1,234,000		1,103,000	

EUROPE

NORTH AMERICA

Portugal

400

ATLANTIC OCEAN

Spanish Caribbean Mainland

100

Martinique
Barbados

100

100

Senegambia

AFRICA

Windward Coast

Gold Coast

Bight of Benin

Bight of Biafra

3,600

3,100

11,000

Equator

Amazonia

3,800

774,000

55,000

2,000

Pernambuco

West Central Africa

381,000

SOUTH AMERICA

Salvador da Bahia

1,085,000

Southeast Africa

Southeast Brazil

11,000

Río de la Plata

100

0   500   1000 kilometers

0   500   1000 miles

4,900

More slave voyages were organized at the port of Salvador da Bahia than at any other Atlantic port for most of the seventeenth and eighteenth centuries. Salvador da Bahia established a strong link with the Bight of Benin, a link that took advantage of the two main Atlantic current systems, as Africans in the region developed a taste for Brazilian tobacco coated in molasses. Many captives brought into Bahia after 1695 were sold on to the gold-producing regions south and west, far in the Brazilian interior.

It is my earnest desire that you dispose of at all places upon the Coast of Africa as many Goods as you can of your Cargo for Gold and likewise to sell the Portugueze and others what Negroes you can vend to them for Gold, being well informed that the Portugueze chiefly bring Gold from Brazil to purchase their Negroes with, and have given from 5 to 6 Ounces per head for Windward Negroes and 7 to 8 Ounces per Head for Whydah and Jacqueen [Jakin] Negroes, in those Roads, as I am in hopes you will not miss of any opportunity to get rid of your Negroes you may purchase, which are a perishable Commodity, when you have an oppertunity to dispose of them for Gold, for I should be very glad to have you turn your whole Cargoe of Goods and Negroes into Gold, and so proceed home directly to London, as Capt. Snelgrave did in my Katherine Gally, and put what Goods you may have left and Negroes that remaine unsold aboard my Katherine Gally Capt. Blincko, as Capt. Snelgrave did aboard my Portugall Gally Capt. More.

Instructions of Hum[phry] Morice to Capt. Thomas Hill, of Ship Anne Gally, London, 30th Septem[be]r: 1730, Humphry Morice Papers, Bank of England Archives, London, M 7/12. Published with permission of the Bank of England.

Map 40: Regions of Trade for Slave Voyages Outfitted in Rio de Janeiro, 1642–1807

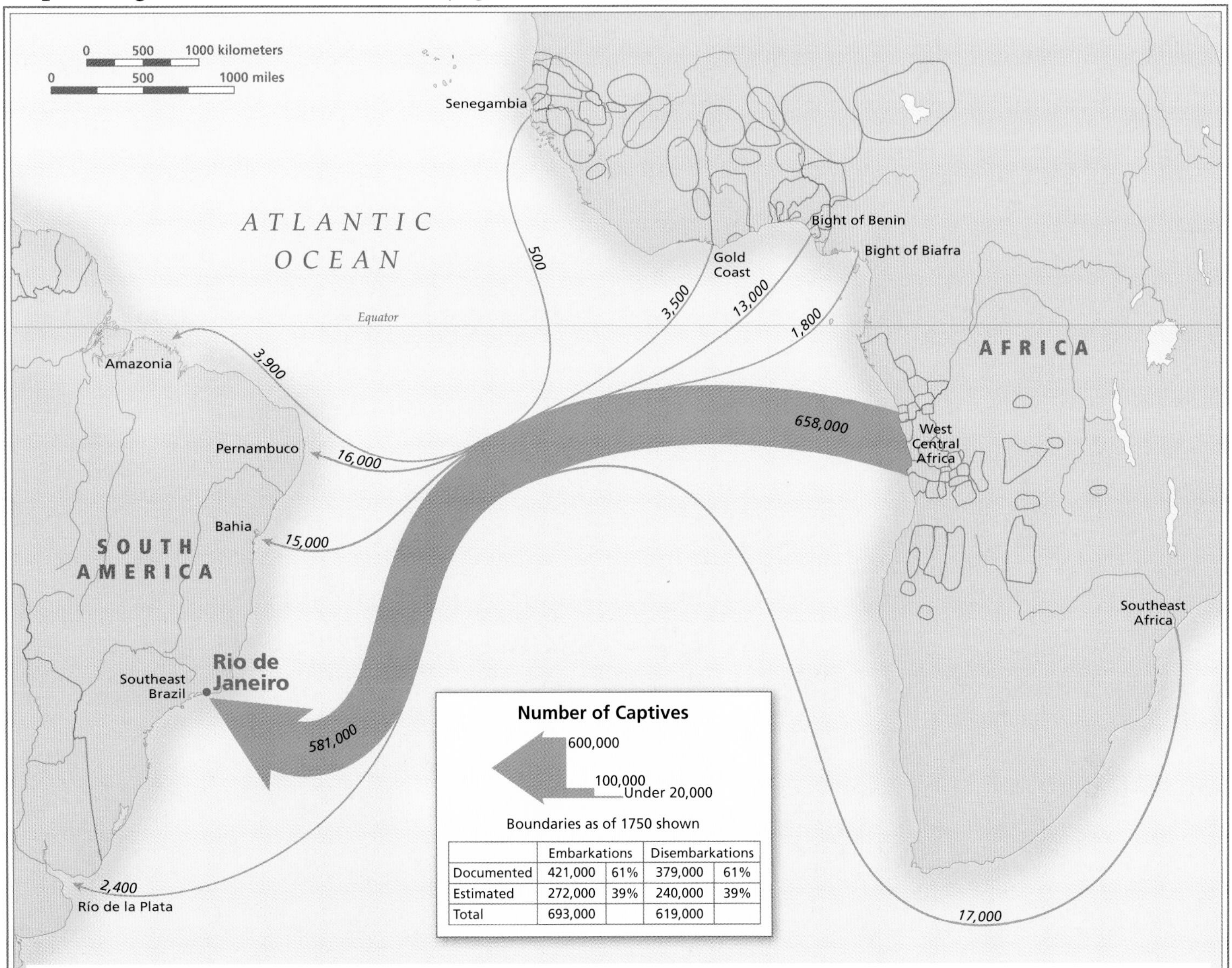

0   500   1000 kilometers
0   500   1000 miles

Senegambia

ATLANTIC OCEAN

Equator

AFRICA

Amazonia

500

3,500

13,000

1,800

Gold Coast

Bight of Benin

Bight of Biafra

3,900

Pernambuco

16,000

658,000

West Central Africa

Bahia

15,000

SOUTH AMERICA

Southeast Africa

Rio de Janeiro

Southeast Brazil

581,000

Number of Captives

600,000
100,000
Under 20,000

Boundaries as of 1750 shown

2,400
Río de la Plata

17,000

	Embarkations		Disembarkations	
Documented	421,000	61%	379,000	61%
Estimated	272,000	39%	240,000	39%
Total	693,000		619,000	

Vessels for the very large slave trade in Rio de Janeiro, as in other major Brazilian ports, were locally owned, financed, and fitted out. The merchandise their captains exchanged for slaves was produced in Brazil or imported from Asia, not Europe. By the early nineteenth century, Rio de Janeiro was the major outfitting center in the Americas for slave voyages.

Map 41: Regions of Trade for Slave Voyages Outfitted in the British Caribbean, 1642–1807

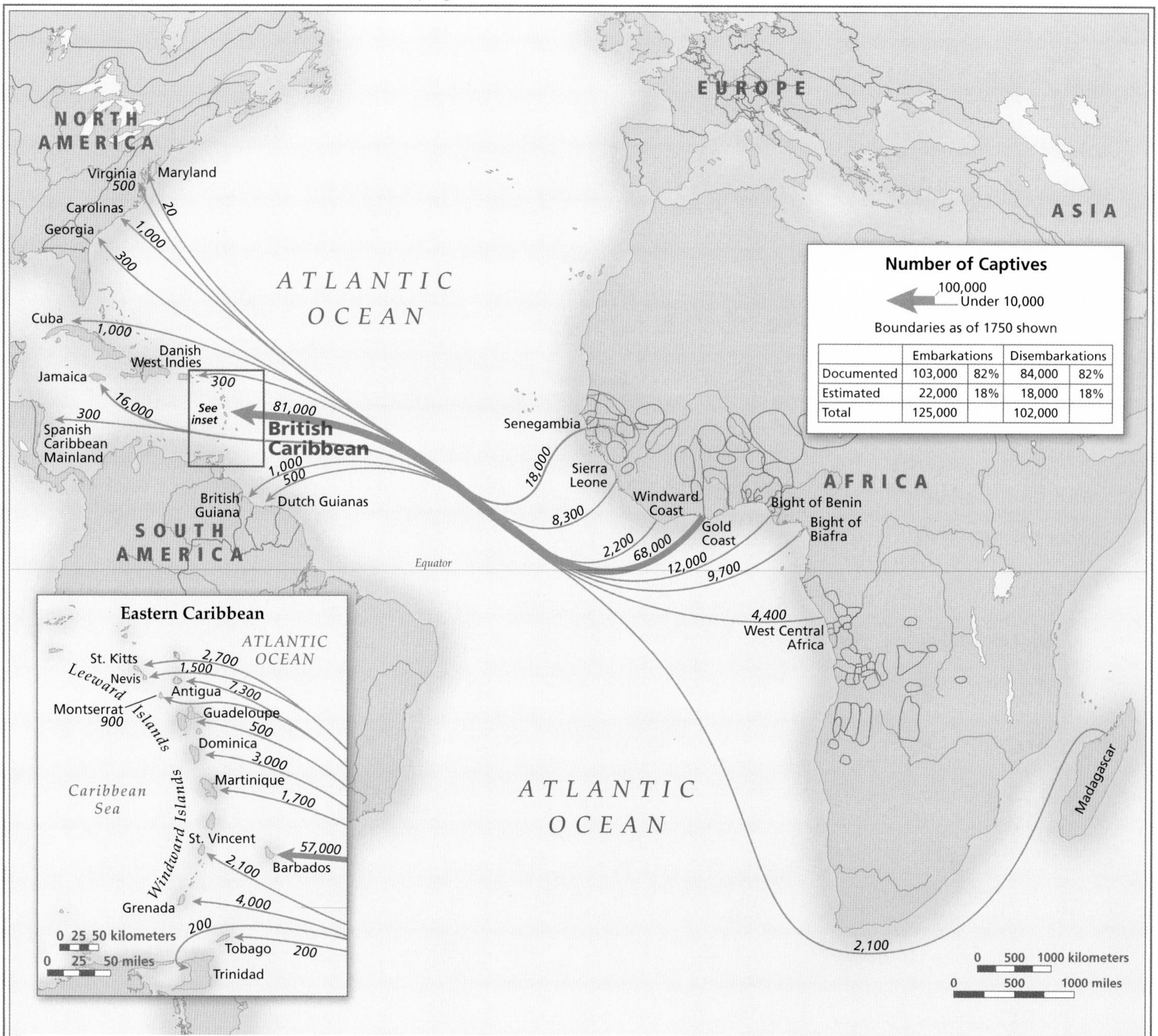

NORTH AMERICA

Virginia 500
Maryland
20
Carolinas
1,000
Georgia
300

ATLANTIC OCEAN

EUROPE

ASIA

Cuba 1,000
Danish West Indies
Jamaica 300
16,000
300
Spanish Caribbean Mainland
See inset
81,000
British Caribbean
1,000
500
British Guiana
Dutch Guianas

SOUTH AMERICA

Equator

Senegambia
18,000
Sierra Leone
8,300
Windward Coast
2,200
68,000
Gold Coast
12,000
9,700

AFRICA

Bight of Benin
Bight of Biafra

4,400
West Central Africa

Number of Captives

100,000
Under 10,000

Boundaries as of 1750 shown

	Embarkations		Disembarkations	
Documented	103,000	82%	84,000	82%
Estimated	22,000	18%	18,000	18%
Total	125,000		102,000	

ATLANTIC OCEAN

Madagascar

2,100

0 500 1000 kilometers

0 500 1000 miles

Eastern Caribbean

ATLANTIC OCEAN

St. Kitts
2,700
Nevis
1,500
Leeward Islands
Antigua
7,300
Montserrat 900
Guadeloupe
500
Dominica
3,000
Martinique
1,700
Caribbean Sea
St. Vincent
57,000
Windward Islands
2,100
Barbados
Grenada
4,000
200
Tobago
200
Trinidad

0 25 50 kilometers

0 25 50 miles

From 1696 to 1705, Barbados was the second-largest point of departure for slaving voyages in the British Empire (after London). Of all the Caribbean colonies in the seventeenth and eighteenth centuries, only the British islands outfitted significant numbers of slaving voyages. The ship captains bought most of their captives on the Gold Coast with Caribbean-produced rum.

Map 42: Regions of Trade for Slave Voyages Outfitted in Rhode Island, 1642–1807

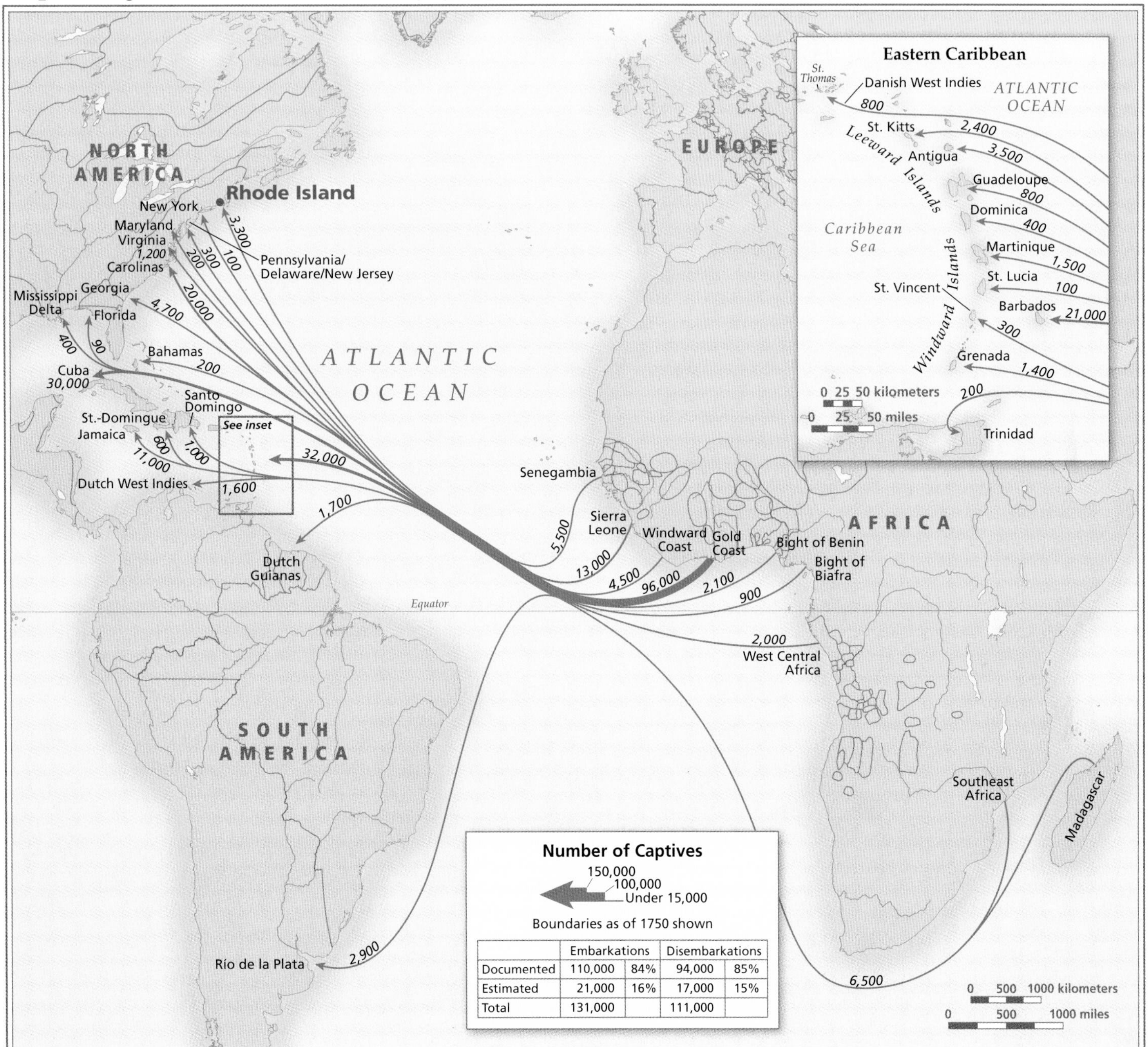

Eastern Caribbean

St. Thomas — Danish West Indies — ATLANTIC OCEAN
800
Leeward Islands
St. Kitts — 2,400
Antigua — 3,500
Guadeloupe — 800
Dominica — 400
Caribbean Sea
Martinique — 1,500
St. Lucia — 100
St. Vincent
Barbados — 21,000
300
Windward Islands
Grenada — 1,400
200
Trinidad

0   25   50 kilometers
0   25   50 miles

NORTH AMERICA

Rhode Island

New York
Maryland
Virginia — 1,200
Carolinas — 3,300
Pennsylvania/Delaware/New Jersey — 100
300
200
Georgia
Florida — 4,700
20,000
Mississippi Delta — 400
90
Bahamas — 200
Cuba — 30,000
Santo Domingo
St.-Domingue
Jamaica — 800
11,000
1,000
Dutch West Indies — 1,600
See inset
32,000

ATLANTIC OCEAN

Dutch Guianas
1,700

Senegambia
5,500
Sierra Leone — 13,000
Windward Coast — 4,500
Gold Coast — 96,000
Bight of Benin — 2,100
Bight of Biafra — 900
AFRICA

Equator

West Central Africa — 2,000

SOUTH AMERICA

Southeast Africa
Madagascar
6,500

Río de la Plata — 2,900

Number of Captives

150,000
100,000
Under 15,000

Boundaries as of 1750 shown

	Embarkations		Disembarkations	
Documented	110,000	84%	94,000	85%
Estimated	21,000	16%	17,000	15%
Total	131,000		111,000	

0   500   1000 kilometers
0   500   1000 miles

A few ports in Rhode Island, initially Newport and later Bristol and Providence, accounted for about half of all voyages from the North American mainland from the 1720s to 1807. The vessels sent out were much smaller than was usual in the slave trade and carried mainly rum. The captains obtained most of their slaves at the forts of Anomabu and Cape Coast Castle on the Gold Coast (see maps 77 and 81). Rhode Islanders sold their slaves throughout British America before 1776 and throughout the Atlantic world after 1783.

Map 43: European Ports Where Slave Voyages Were Outfitted, 1808–1865

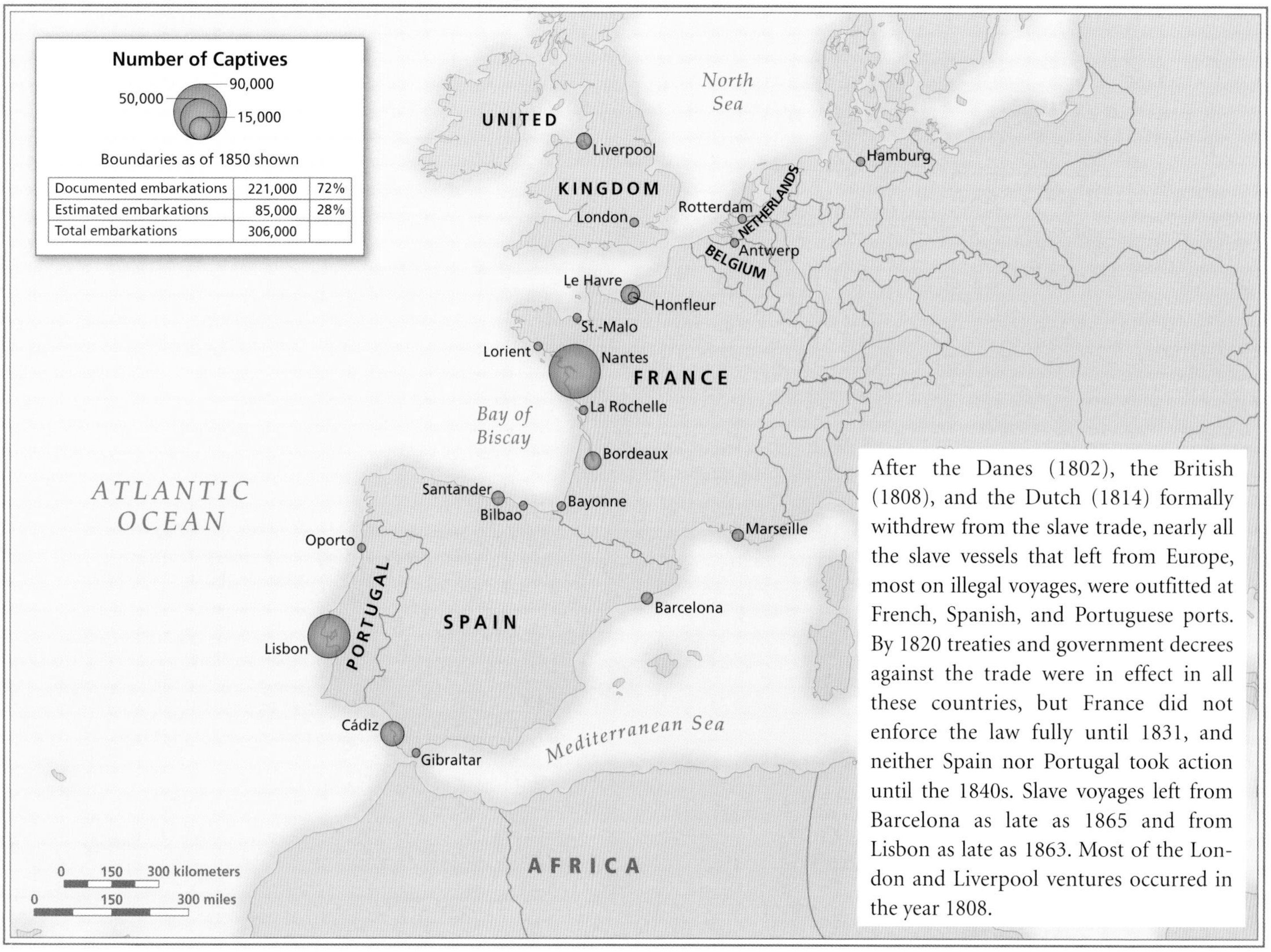

Number of Captives

90,000
50,000
15,000

Boundaries as of 1850 shown

Documented embarkations	221,000	72%
Estimated embarkations	85,000	28%
Total embarkations	306,000	

North Sea

UNITED

Liverpool

Hamburg

KINGDOM

Rotterdam

London

NETHERLANDS

Antwerp

BELGIUM

Le Havre

Honfleur

St.-Malo

Lorient

Nantes

FRANCE

Bay of Biscay

La Rochelle

Bordeaux

ATLANTIC OCEAN

Santander

Bayonne

Bilbao

Marseille

Oporto

PORTUGAL

SPAIN

Barcelona

Lisbon

Cádiz

Gibraltar

Mediterranean Sea

AFRICA

0	150	300 kilometers
0	150	300 miles

After the Danes (1802), the British (1808), and the Dutch (1814) formally withdrew from the slave trade, nearly all the slave vessels that left from Europe, most on illegal voyages, were outfitted at French, Spanish, and Portuguese ports. By 1820 treaties and government decrees against the trade were in effect in all these countries, but France did not enforce the law fully until 1831, and neither Spain nor Portugal took action until the 1840s. Slave voyages left from Barcelona as late as 1865 and from Lisbon as late as 1863. Most of the London and Liverpool ventures occurred in the year 1808.

Map 44: Regions of Trade for Slave Voyages Outfitted in Bordeaux, 1808–1837

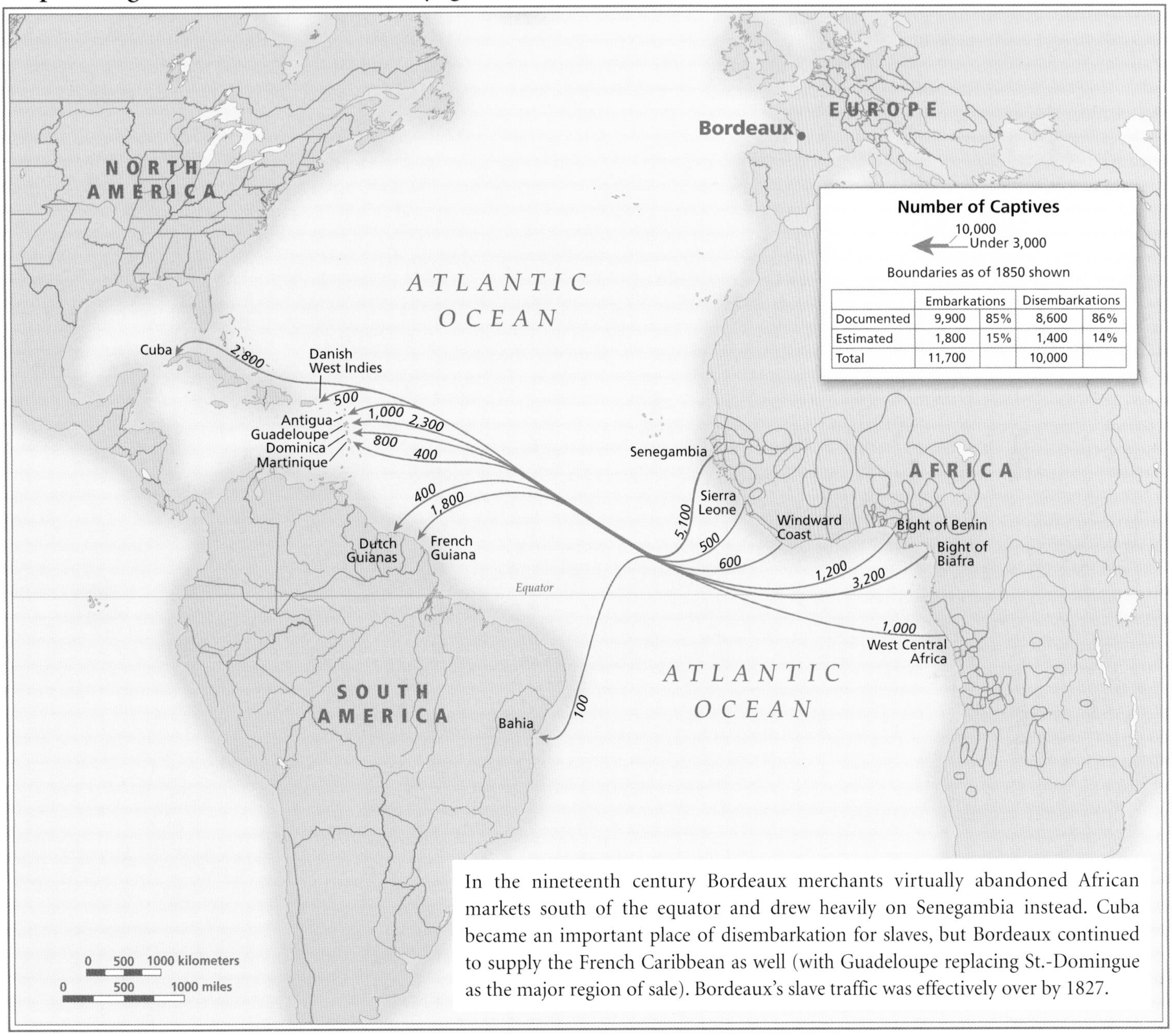

NORTH AMERICA

EUROPE

Bordeaux

ATLANTIC OCEAN

Number of Captives

10,000
Under 3,000

Boundaries as of 1850 shown

	Embarkations		Disembarkations	
Documented	9,900	85%	8,600	86%
Estimated	1,800	15%	1,400	14%
Total	11,700		10,000	

Cuba

2,800

Danish West Indies

500

Antigua
Guadeloupe
Dominica
Martinique

1,000 2,300
800 400

Senegambia

AFRICA

Sierra Leone

Windward Coast

Bight of Benin

Bight of Biafra

400
1,800

Dutch Guianas

French Guiana

5,100
500
600
1,200
3,200

Equator

1,000
West Central Africa

SOUTH AMERICA

Bahia

100

ATLANTIC OCEAN

In the nineteenth century Bordeaux merchants virtually abandoned African markets south of the equator and drew heavily on Senegambia instead. Cuba became an important place of disembarkation for slaves, but Bordeaux continued to supply the French Caribbean as well (with Guadeloupe replacing St.-Domingue as the major region of sale). Bordeaux's slave traffic was effectively over by 1827.

0 500 1000 kilometers

0 500 1000 miles

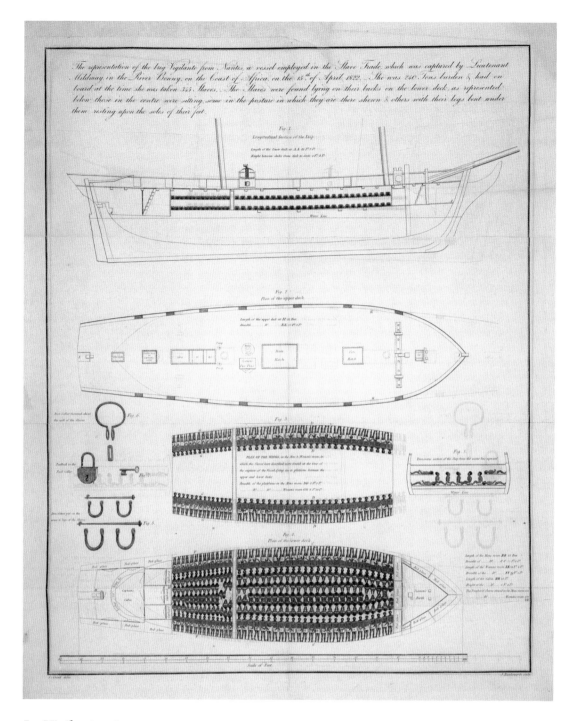

La Vigilante, 1823

Engraving of the captured French slave ship *La Vigilante* from the abolitionist tract
La Vigilante, batiment negrier de Nantes (1823). Beinecke Rare Book and Manuscript Library, Yale
University.

The French slave ship *La Vigilante* (voyage id 2734) was seized at Bonny in 1822 with 345 captives on
board. When approached by a British naval cruiser seeking to verify its papers, the crew had fired,
killing several of the British ship's crew. The French vessel was taken first to Sierra Leone, where
the captives were released, and then to Plymouth, England, where the captain of the British cruiser
anticipated bringing murder charges against the French. Abolitionists made drawings of the ship
while it was at Plymouth, and the ship plans were published in London and Paris. The image here,
which includes drawings of locks and shackles, comes from a French abolitionist tract. Such images
became an important component of the international abolitionist movement against the slave trade
from the late 1780s, as revealed in the images of a slave ship in 1789 (page 164) and the *Feloz* (or *Veloz*)
in 1829 (page 266).

Map 45: Regions of Trade for Slave Voyages Outfitted in Nantes, 1813–1841

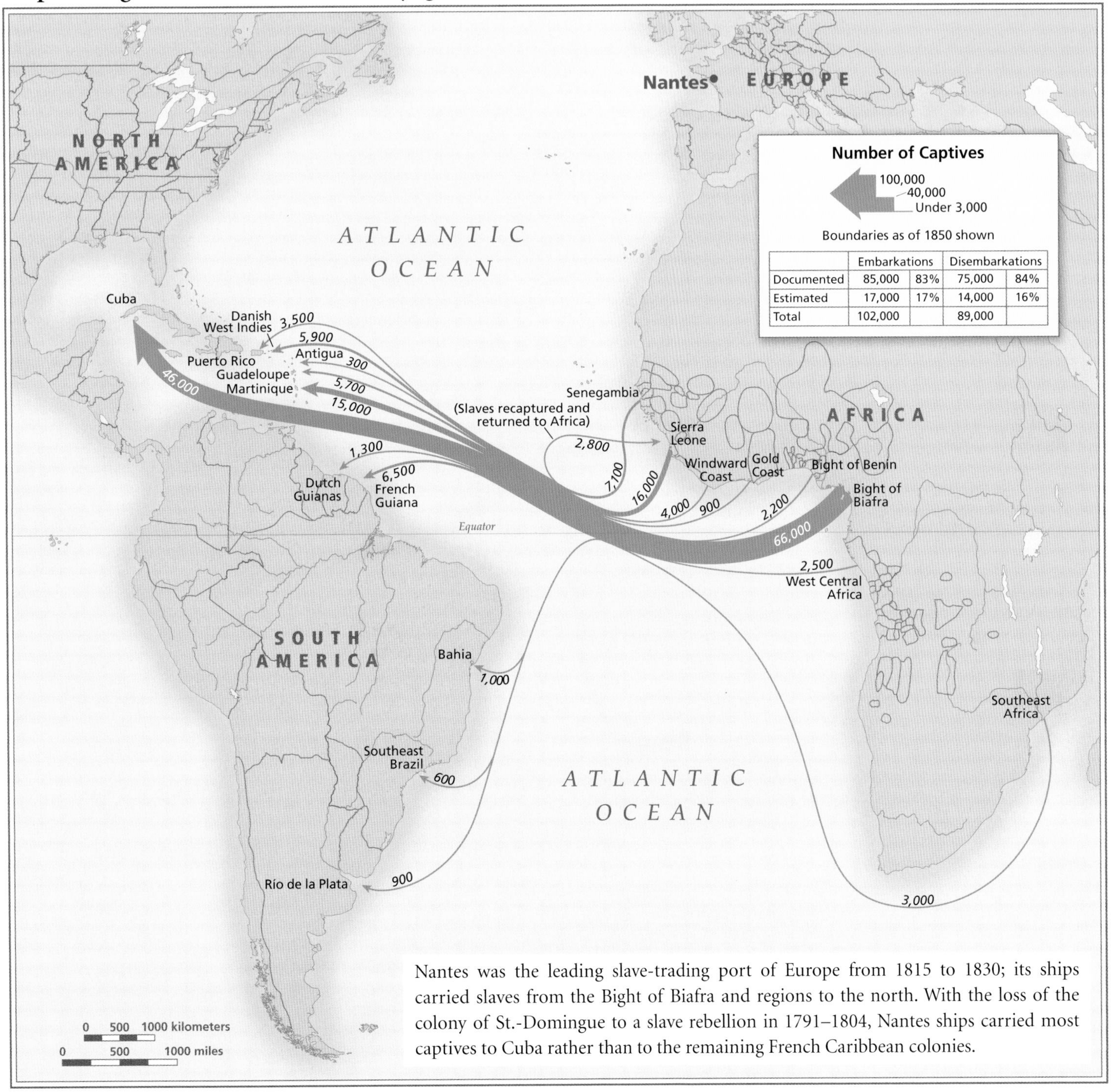

Nantes● EUROPE

NORTH AMERICA

ATLANTIC OCEAN

Number of Captives

100,000
40,000
Under 3,000

Boundaries as of 1850 shown

	Embarkations		Disembarkations	
Documented	85,000	83%	75,000	84%
Estimated	17,000	17%	14,000	16%
Total	102,000		89,000	

Cuba

Danish West Indies 3,500
5,900
Antigua 300
Puerto Rico
Guadeloupe 5,700
Martinique 15,000
46,000

Senegambia
(Slaves recaptured and returned to Africa)
2,800

AFRICA

Sierra Leone

1,300
6,500
Dutch Guianas
French Guiana

Windward Coast Gold Coast Bight of Benin

Bight of Biafra

7,100
16,000
4,000 900 2,200
66,000

Equator

2,500
West Central Africa

SOUTH AMERICA

Bahia
1,000

Southeast Africa

Southeast Brazil
600

ATLANTIC OCEAN

Río de la Plata 900

3,000

0   500   1000 kilometers
0   500   1000 miles

Nantes was the leading slave-trading port of Europe from 1815 to 1830; its ships carried slaves from the Bight of Biafra and regions to the north. With the loss of the colony of St.-Domingue to a slave rebellion in 1791–1804, Nantes ships carried most captives to Cuba rather than to the remaining French Caribbean colonies.

Map 46: Regions of Trade for Slave Voyages Outfitted in Lisbon, 1808–1863

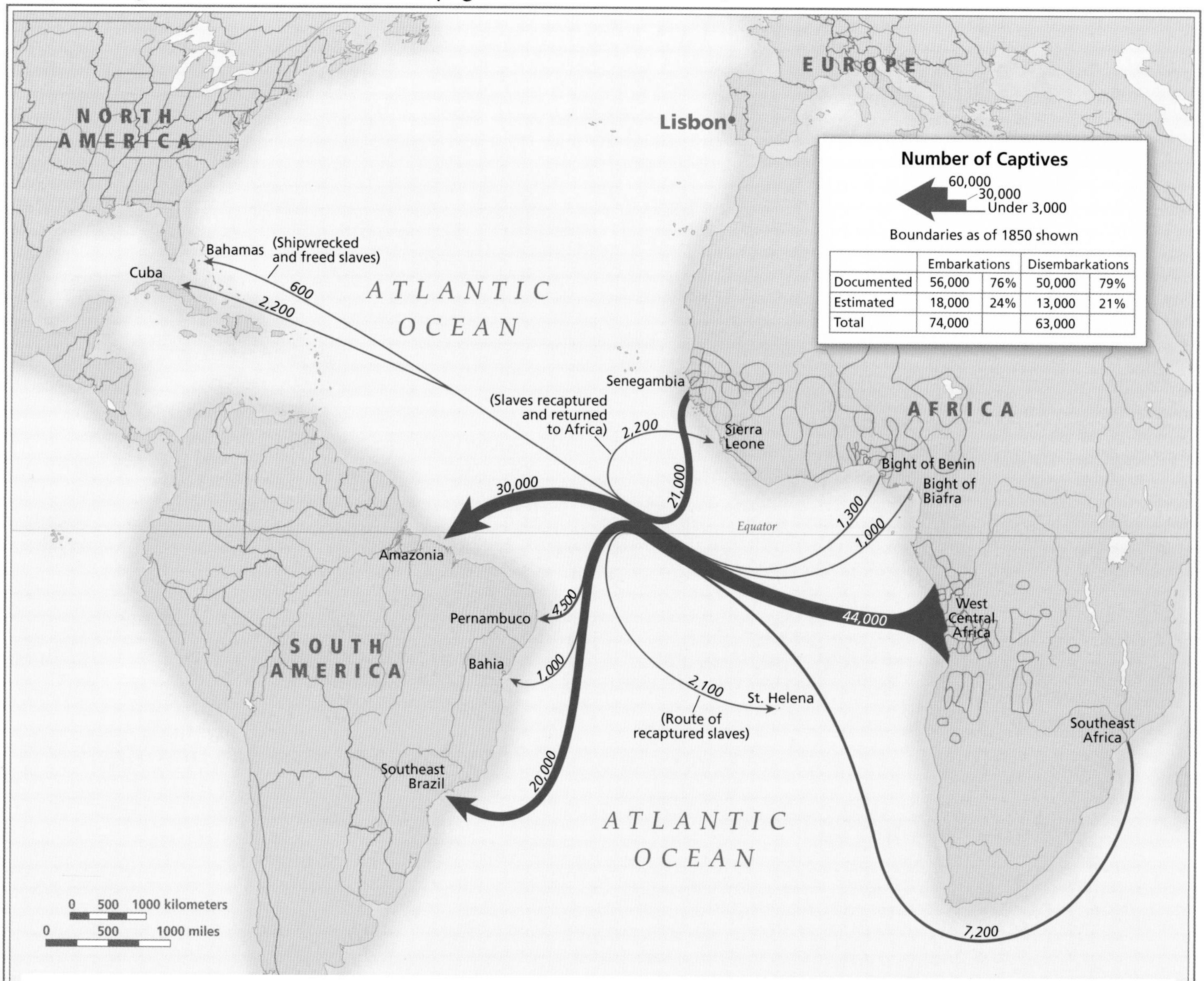

Number of Captives

60,000
30,000
Under 3,000

Boundaries as of 1850 shown

	Embarkations		Disembarkations	
Documented	56,000	76%	50,000	79%
Estimated	18,000	24%	13,000	21%
Total	74,000		63,000	

EUROPE

Lisbon•

NORTH AMERICA

Bahamas
(Shipwrecked and freed slaves)
Cuba
600
2,200

ATLANTIC OCEAN

Senegambia
(Slaves recaptured and returned to Africa)
2,200
Sierra Leone
AFRICA
Bight of Benin
Bight of Biafra
1,300
1,000
21,000
30,000
Equator
Amazonia
4,500
Pernambuco
West Central Africa
44,000
Bahia
1,000
SOUTH AMERICA
2,100
St. Helena
(Route of recaptured slaves)
Southeast Africa
Southeast Brazil
20,000

ATLANTIC OCEAN

7,200

0 500 1000 kilometers
0 500 1000 miles

In the nineteenth century Lisbon merchants continued to carry captives from Senegambia and West Central Africa to Amazonia and Southeast Brazil. They also supplied small numbers to other markets in Brazil and, to a much lesser extent, in the Caribbean. Efforts to suppress the slave trade explain the arrival of nearly 5,000 liberated captives in the Bahamas, St. Helena, and Sierra Leone.

The Slave Deck of the Bark *Wildfire,* Brought into Key West on 30 April 1860

Engraving from a daguerreotype published in *Harper's Weekly,* 2 June 1860. Image courtesy of the Division of Rare and Manuscript Collections, Cornell University Libraries.

The *Wildfire,* sailing out of New York (voyage id 4362), was captured off Cuba by the U.S. Navy ship *Mohawk*. The 510 African captives on board were sent to Key West, Florida, on 30 April 1860. They were the survivors of the 650 who had left the Congo River on board the *Wildfire* thirty-six days earlier. Engravings from daguerreotype photographs published in *Harper's Weekly* showed the naked survivors, males separated from females, huddled together on deck, the ones in front looking emaciated. The U.S. authorities ordered the liberated Africans to be sent to Liberia, which meant a second unwanted and perilous Atlantic crossing to an unfamiliar destination.

Map 47: Ports in the Americas Where Slave Voyages Were Outfitted, 1808–1867

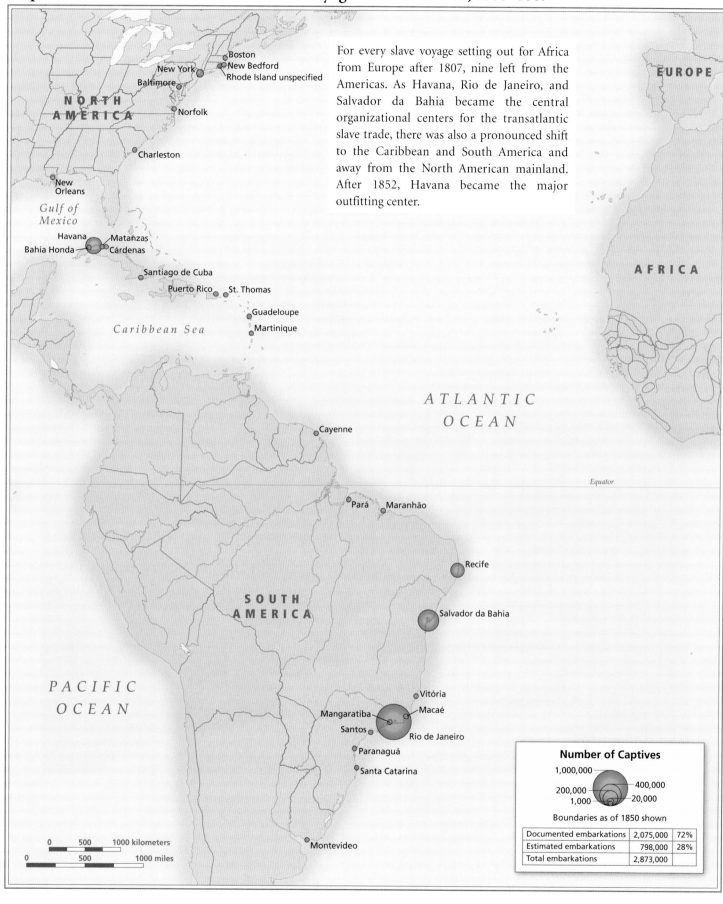

For every slave voyage setting out for Africa from Europe after 1807, nine left from the Americas. As Havana, Rio de Janeiro, and Salvador da Bahia became the central organizational centers for the transatlantic slave trade, there was also a pronounced shift to the Caribbean and South America and away from the North American mainland. After 1852, Havana became the major outfitting center.

Number of Captives

Documented embarkations	2,075,000	72%
Estimated embarkations	798,000	28%
Total embarkations	2,873,000	

Boundaries as of 1850 shown

The only food we had during the voyage was corn soaked and boiled. I cannot tell how long we were thus confined, but it seemed a very long while. We suffered much for want of water, but was denied all we needed. A pint a day was all that was allowed, and no more; and a great many slaves died upon the passage. . . . We arrived at Pernambuco, South America, early in the morning, and the vessel played about during the day, without coming to an anchor. All that day we neither ate or drank anything, and we were given to understand that we were to remain perfectly silent, and not to make any out-cry, otherwise our lives were in danger. But when "night threw her sable mantle on the earth and sea," the anchor dropped, and we were permitted to go on deck to be viewed and handled by our future masters, who had come aboard from the city. We landed a few miles from the city, at a farmer's house, which was used as a kind of slave market . . . I remained in this slave market but a day or two, before I was again sold to a slave dealer in the city, who again sold me to a man in the country, who was a baker, and resided not a great distance from Pernambuco.

When a slaver comes in, the news spreads like wild-fire, and down come all those that are interested in the arrival of the vessel with its cargo of living merchandize, who select from the stock those most suited to their different purposes, and purchase the slaves in the same way that oxen or horses would be purchased in a market. . . . Great numbers make quite a business of this buying and selling human flesh, and do nothing else for a living, depending entirely upon this kind of traffic.

Excerpt from Mahommah G. Baquaqua and Samuel Moore, *Biography of Mahommah G. Baquaqua, a Native of Zoogoo in the Interior of Africa* (Detroit: Geo. E. Pomeroy & Co., 1854). The voyage took place in the 1840s.

Map 48: Regions of Trade for Slave Voyages Outfitted in Recife, 1808–1851

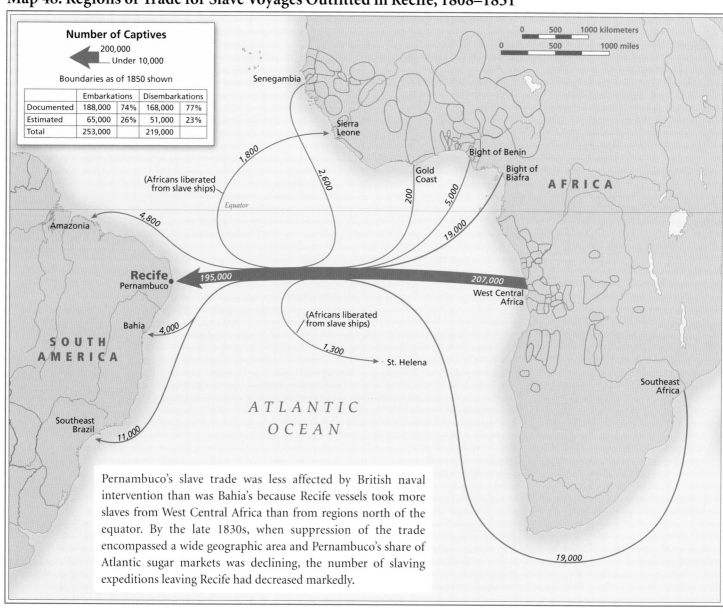

Number of Captives

200,000

Under 10,000

Boundaries as of 1850 shown

	Embarkations		Disembarkations	
Documented	188,000	74%	168,000	77%
Estimated	65,000	26%	51,000	23%
Total	253,000		219,000	

Senegambia

Sierra Leone

1,800

(Africans liberated from slave ships)

2,600

Equator

Gold Coast

Bight of Benin

Bight of Biafra

AFRICA

200

5,000

19,000

Amazonia

4,800

Recife
Pernambuco

195,000

207,000

West Central Africa

Bahia

4,000

(Africans liberated from slave ships)

1,300

St. Helena

SOUTH AMERICA

Southeast Africa

ATLANTIC

OCEAN

Southeast Brazil

11,000

19,000

Pernambuco's slave trade was less affected by British naval intervention than was Bahia's because Recife vessels took more slaves from West Central Africa than from regions north of the equator. By the late 1830s, when suppression of the trade encompassed a wide geographic area and Pernambuco's share of Atlantic sugar markets was declining, the number of slaving expeditions leaving Recife had decreased markedly.

0   500   1000 kilometers

0   500   1000 miles

Gate and Slave Market at Pernambuco, 1823

Hand-colored aquatint by James Sowerby, from John Mawe, *Travels in the Interior of Brazil, particularly in the gold and diamond districts of that country* (London: Longman, Hurst, Rees, Orme and Brown, 1823), frontispiece. Courtesy of the John Carter Brown Library at Brown University.

Recife, also called Pernambuco, after the region it served, was at the center of the early sugar industry in Brazil. The first major Brazilian slave-trading port, it developed a bilateral trade with Africa; ships were outfitted at Recife, and the slaves they returned with were sold there. Recife remained a major slave-trafficking center until well into the nineteenth century. Here we see the slave market of Recife as it existed around 1823. Even when other Brazilian ports, such as Salvador da Bahia and Rio de Janeiro, had eclipsed Recife as slave-trading venues, slavery was still important to the local economy.

Map 49: Regions of Trade for Slave Voyages Outfitted in Salvador da Bahia, 1808–1851

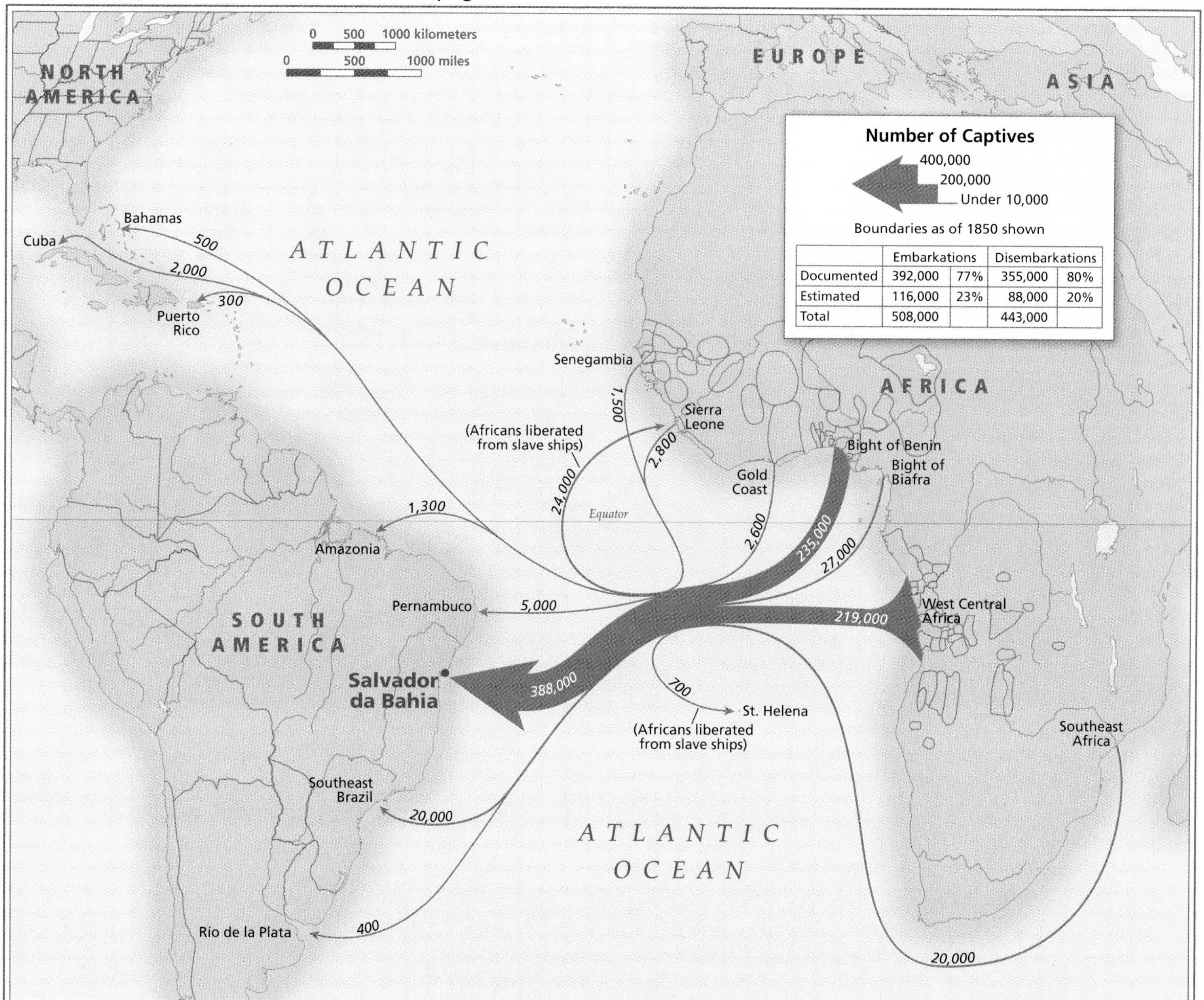

NORTH AMERICA

EUROPE

ASIA

0   500   1000 kilometers

0   500   1000 miles

Number of Captives

400,000
200,000
Under 10,000

Boundaries as of 1850 shown

	Embarkations		Disembarkations	
Documented	392,000	77%	355,000	80%
Estimated	116,000	23%	88,000	20%
Total	508,000		443,000	

ATLANTIC OCEAN

Bahamas

Cuba

500

2,000

300

Puerto Rico

Senegambia

AFRICA

1,500

Sierra Leone

(Africans liberated from slave ships)

2,800

Bight of Benin

Bight of Biafra

Gold Coast

24,000

Equator

1,300

2,600

235,000

27,000

Amazonia

West Central Africa

Pernambuco

5,000

219,000

SOUTH AMERICA

Salvador da Bahia

388,000

700

St. Helena

(Africans liberated from slave ships)

Southeast Africa

Southeast Brazil

20,000

ATLANTIC OCEAN

Río de la Plata

400

20,000

Attempts to suppress the slave trade began in Salvador da Bahia as early as 1810 as a result of an Anglo-Portuguese treaty that the British interpreted as forbidding the Portuguese slave trade north of the equator. The traditional links between Bahia and the Bight of Benin (which lay north of the equator) were thus threatened, and Bahian slave traders and captains began to claim, falsely, that they were buying all their captives in West Central Africa (south of the equator).

Map 50: Regions of Trade for Slave Voyages Outfitted in Rio de Janeiro, 1808–1856

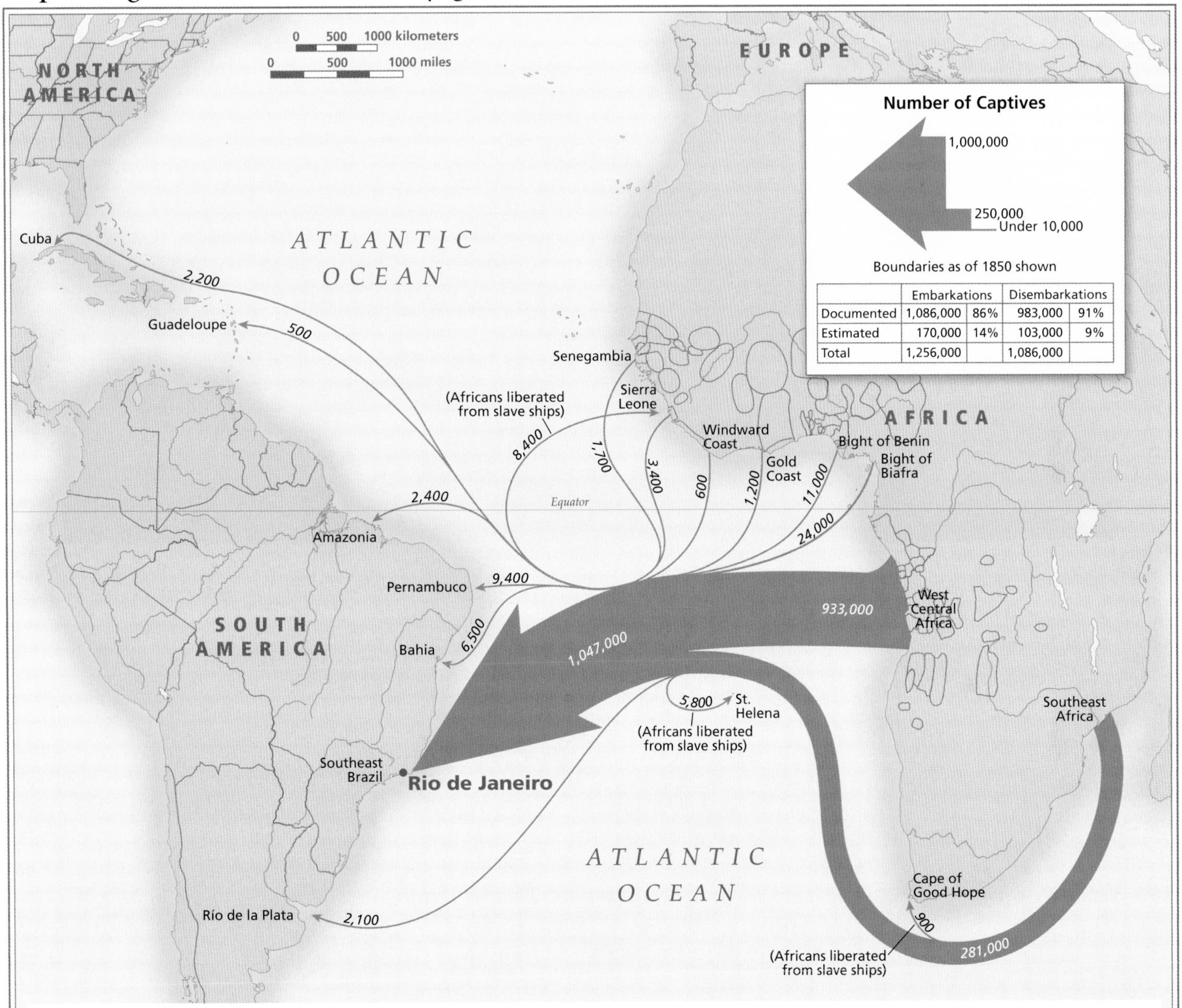

0   500   1000 kilometers

0   500   1000 miles

NORTH AMERICA

EUROPE

ATLANTIC OCEAN

Number of Captives

1,000,000

250,000

Under 10,000

Boundaries as of 1850 shown

	Embarkations		Disembarkations	
Documented	1,086,000	86%	983,000	91%
Estimated	170,000	14%	103,000	9%
Total	1,256,000		1,086,000	

Cuba

2,200

Guadeloupe

500

(Africans liberated from slave ships)

Senegambia

Sierra Leone

8,400

1,700

3,400

600

Windward Coast

Gold Coast

1,200

11,000

AFRICA

Bight of Benin

Bight of Biafra

24,000

2,400

Equator

Amazonia

Pernambuco

9,400

933,000

West Central Africa

SOUTH AMERICA

Bahia

6,500

1,047,000

5,800

St. Helena

(Africans liberated from slave ships)

Southeast Brazil

Rio de Janeiro

Southeast Africa

ATLANTIC OCEAN

Cape of Good Hope

Río de la Plata

2,100

900

281,000

(Africans liberated from slave ships)

Increasing demand for coffee and sugar beginning in the late eighteenth century sustained the Brazilian slave trade close to peak levels until the mid-nineteenth century. In the 1830s, the slave trade from Rio de Janeiro became subject to Portuguese, Brazilian, and especially British attempts at suppression – represented in part on the map by the return loops of Africans liberated from slave vessels and taken to Sierra Leone and St. Helena. After 1838, slave vessels from Rio de Janeiro obtained their slaves from more remote parts of the West Central African coast, instead of the traditional centers of Luanda and Benguela, and also drew heavily from Southeast Africa.

Palace and Great Square in Rio de Janeiro, 1823

Lithograph by C. Shoosmith from a sketch by James Henderson, from James Henderson,
A History of the Brazil (London: Longman, Hurst, Rees, Orme and Brown, 1821). Courtesy
of the John Carter Brown Library at Brown University.

Custom House Negroes, Rio de Janeiro, 1821

Hand-colored aquatint by James Sowerby, from John
Mawe, *Travels in the Interior of Brazil, particularly in
the gold and diamond districts of that country* (London:
Longman, Hurst, Rees, Orme and Brown, 1823). Courtesy
of the John Carter Brown Library at Brown University.

Rio de Janeiro was the Atlantic Ocean's largest single
outfitting port for slave ships, as well as the single most
important disembarkation point in the Americas for African
captives. Slave trading played a vital role in the growth of
the city's wealth and population, allowing its merchants and
church and city leaders to invest in the public spaces and
buildings depicted here. Most Africans entering the port
were sold on to work in sugar, coffee, and, especially in the
eighteenth century, gold production in Minas Gerais and
other provinces. But some remained in Rio de Janeiro itself,
providing labor for urban crafts and household and other
services, including work at the customs house of the city, as
shown in the second image here.

Map 51: Regions of Trade for Slave Voyages Outfitted in Havana, 1808–1867

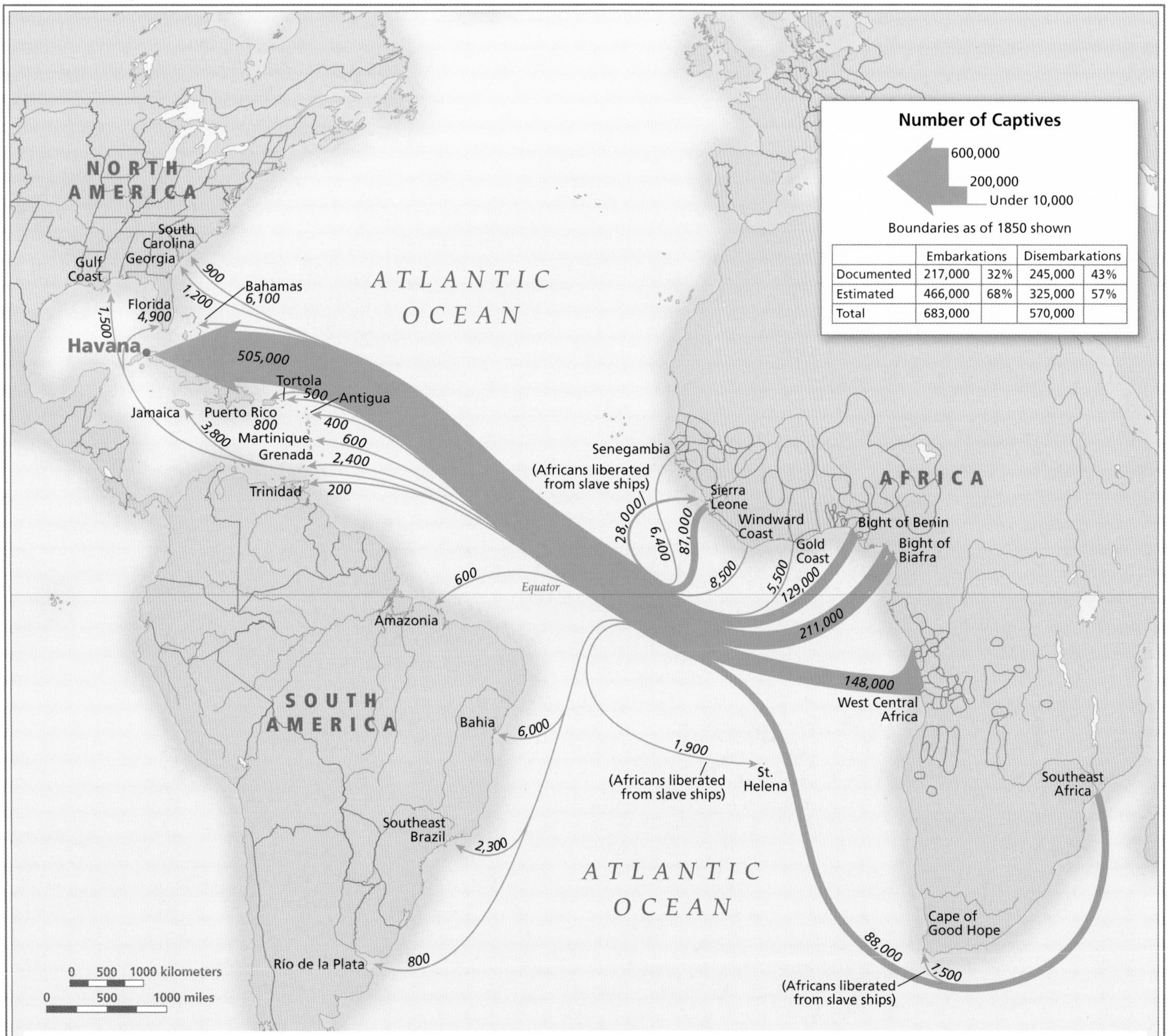

Number of Captives

600,000
200,000
Under 10,000

Boundaries as of 1850 shown

	Embarkations		Disembarkations	
Documented	217,000	32%	245,000	43%
Estimated	466,000	68%	325,000	57%
Total	683,000		570,000	

NORTH AMERICA

South Carolina
Georgia
Gulf Coast
Florida 4,900
Havana
900
1,200
1,500
Bahamas 6,100
ATLANTIC OCEAN
505,000
Tortola 500
Antigua
Jamaica
Puerto Rico 800
Martinique 400
Grenada 600
3,800
Trinidad 2,400
200

Senegambia (Africans liberated from slave ships)
28,000
6,400
7,000
Sierra Leone
Windward Coast
Gold Coast
8,500
5,500
AFRICA
Bight of Benin
Bight of Biafra
129,000
211,000
148,000
West Central Africa

600
Equator
Amazonia

SOUTH AMERICA
Bahia 6,000
1,900
(Africans liberated from slave ships)
St. Helena
Southeast Brazil 2,300
Southeast Africa

ATLANTIC OCEAN

Cape of Good Hope
88,000
1,500
(Africans liberated from slave ships)

Río de la Plata 800

0 500 1000 kilometers
0 500 1000 miles

Havana, a larger center for the slave trade than any nineteenth-century port in Europe, was always the main organizational center for the traffic arriving in Cuba, although expeditions from France sold many captives in eastern Cuba between 1815 and 1830. After 1835, Havana merchants unloaded their slaves away from the regular port facilities, sometimes in remote parts of the island, to avoid detection. Ship capture and shipwreck meant that many survivors on Cuba-bound ships disembarked in British-held territories in both Africa and the West Indies.

Map 52: Regions of Trade for Slave Voyages Outfitted in Martinique and Guadeloupe, 1817–1832

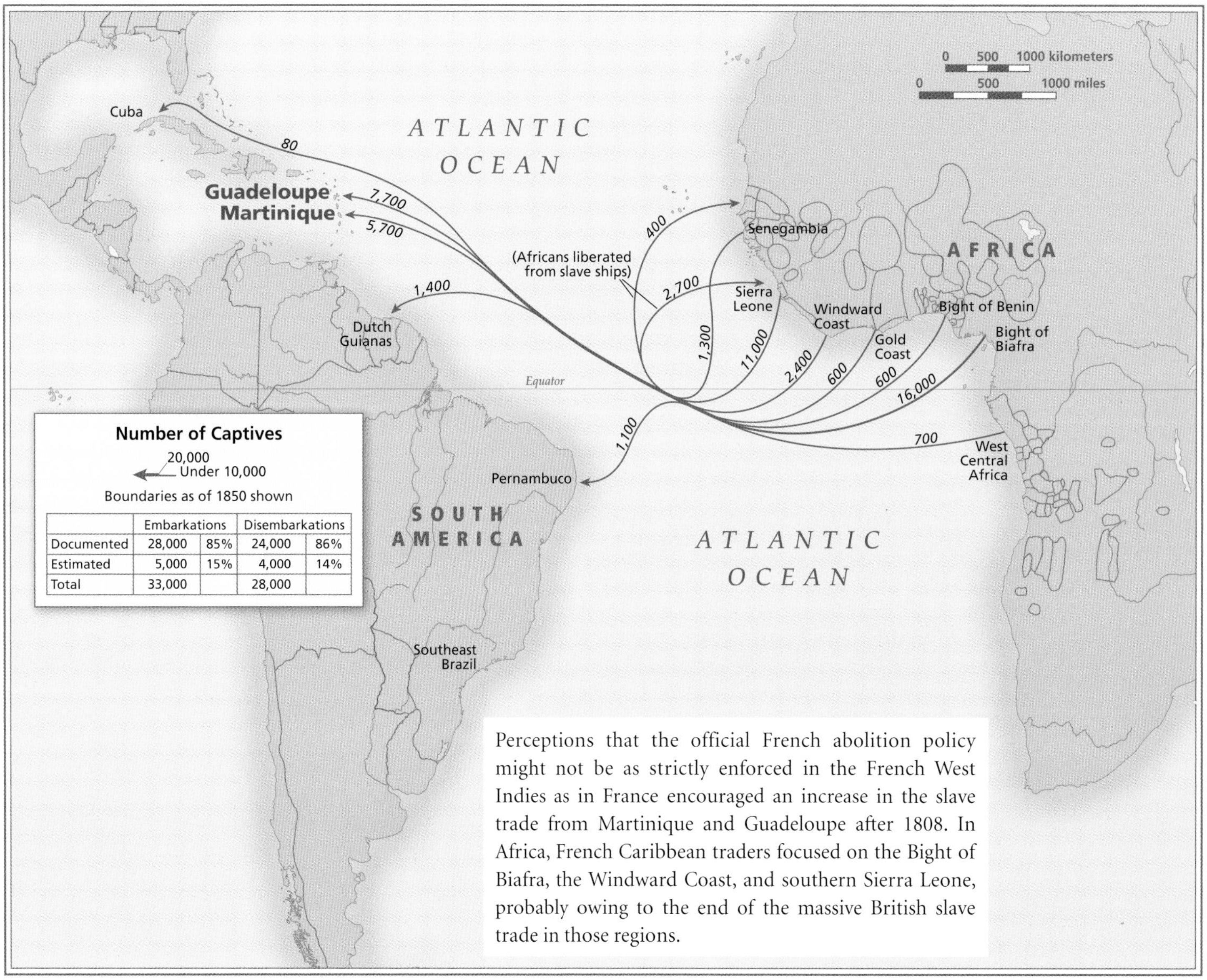

ATLANTIC OCEAN

Cuba

80

Guadeloupe
Martinique

7,700

5,700

1,400

Dutch
Guianas

(Africans liberated
from slave ships)

400

2,700

1,300

11,000

2,400

600

600

16,000

700

Senegambia

Sierra
Leone

Windward
Coast

Gold
Coast

Bight of Benin

Bight of
Biafra

AFRICA

West
Central
Africa

Equator

1,100

Pernambuco

SOUTH
AMERICA

Southeast
Brazil

ATLANTIC OCEAN

0   500   1000 kilometers
0   500   1000 miles

Number of Captives

20,000
Under 10,000

Boundaries as of 1850 shown

	Embarkations		Disembarkations	
Documented	28,000	85%	24,000	86%
Estimated	5,000	15%	4,000	14%
Total	33,000		28,000	

Perceptions that the official French abolition policy might not be as strictly enforced in the French West Indies as in France encouraged an increase in the slave trade from Martinique and Guadeloupe after 1808. In Africa, French Caribbean traders focused on the Bight of Biafra, the Windward Coast, and southern Sierra Leone, probably owing to the end of the massive British slave trade in those regions.

Part III

The African Coastal Origins of Slaves and the Links between Africa and the Atlantic World

Information on the sources of African captives entering the Atlantic slave trade is limited, as is information on the circumstances in which they were enslaved and moved to the coast for the voyage to the plantations and mines of the Americas. Some came from several hundred miles inland and took months to reach the African coast. Many, if not most, came from places much closer to the coast. Some captives from Senegambia and West Central Africa were victims of drought and famine. Others found themselves enslaved because of debt. But the largest single source of captives was violence, including warfare, state-sponsored raiding, and kidnapping. As the scale of the Atlantic slave trade grew, the circles of violence in Africa linked to transatlantic slavery intensified and widened.

We have much fuller information about the captives' places of sale and embarkation. The links between African trading venues and markets for captives in the Americas are also on record. The embarkation points for captives are commonly grouped into regions: Upper Guinea (Senegambia, Sierra Leone, and the Windward Coast), the Gold Coast, the Bights of Benin and Biafra, West Central Africa (much of the trade there is centered on Angola), and Southeast Africa. Historians have charted both the longevity of West Central Africa and Senegambia as slaving venues and the varying trajectories of involvement of these and the four other Atlantic coastal regions in supplying slaves from 1650 as the transatlantic slave trade began a rapid expansion with the entry of northern European nations. Table 4 displays the relative importance of these regions over time. Research on slaving voyages also allows historians to track the specific ports at which captives were sold and boarded ship. There are hundreds of such venues, ranging from inlets on the Windward Coast to cities such as Luanda, where sizable Portuguese and mulatto populations resided. Such trading venues were commonly islands or enclaves of cross-cultural exchange embedded within African coastal communities. The enclaves largely established the rules of commercial engagement with the purchasers of captives.

More than four out of every five captives passed through just twenty of the many ports of trade that dotted the African seaboard, as table 5 shows. Ten of these embarkation points collectively supplied almost two-thirds of the captives entering the Atlantic slave trade whose places of embarkation have been documented. All ten ports were located south of the Windward Coast. The principal ones included Anomabu (on the Gold Coast); Ouidah (Bight of Benin); Bonny and Old Calabar (Bight of Biafra); Luanda, Benguela, Cabinda, Malembo, and Loango (West Central Africa), and Quilimane (Southeast Africa). Each had its own particular mix of local ecological, political, and social attributes that help to explain its importance in the slave-export trade. Each offered a bridgehead between inland suppliers and European and American carriers of captives and thus played a vital part in the ongoing integration of sub-Saharan Africa into the emergent Atlantic world. Each, too, established concentrations of exchange with particular shippers that underscored the value of networking and local knowledge in forging commercial relationships in coastal Africa and had wider implications for the cultural history of the Atlantic world.

The South Atlantic wheel of winds and currents allowed Portuguese and Brazilian traders to monopolize trade at Luanda and Benguela. Although Brazilian traders from Salvador da Bahia failed to establish a similar monopoly, they took large numbers of captives from Ouidah and adjacent ports. British traders consistently dominated trade at Anomabu, Bonny, and Old Calabar through 1807. French traders took unusually high proportions of their captives from Ouidah, Loango, and Cabinda. Similar concentrations of trading activity by national or even subnational carriers are found outside the major African trading venues, with French traders dominating Senegal, British traders Gambia, and Liverpool traders in particular the surge of captives exported from Sierra Leone and the Windward Coast beginning in 1750. The carriers' concentrations of activity north of the Congo River reflected in part early European trading companies' investments in physical infrastructure along sections of Atlantic Africa. But certain carriers also tended to draw slaves from the same ports as accumulated local knowledge and connections generated commercial advantages.

Whatever the factors involved, patterns of concentration of trade by national carriers ensured that the distribution of African captives by ethnic characteristics around the Atlantic world was far from random. African captives of Bantu origin (south of the Congo) overwhelmingly ended up in Brazil. Most Igbo captives leaving the Bight of Biafra before 1807 went to British America, as did many captives of various ethnic groups leaving Gambia, Sierra Leone, the Windward Coast, and the Gold Coast. High proportions of Aje-Fon and Yoruba (from the Bight of Benin) disembarked in Bahia (Brazil) as well as French St.-Domingue (now Haiti). The implications of such ethnic patterns among arriving African captives for the cultural history of the Americas are the source of much debate among historians. Whatever the outcome of the debate, the cultural history of the Atlantic world is clearly inseparable from the commercial and economic forces that shaped patterns of cross-cultural exchange along the African coast.

Table 4   Estimated Number of Slaves Carried on Vessels Leaving Major Coastal Regions of Africa, 1501–1867

	Upper Guinea*	Gold Coast	Bight of Benin	Bight of Biafra	West Central Africa	Southeast Africa	Total[†]
1501–1525	13,000	0	0	0	600	0	13,600
1526–1550	44,000	0	0	2,100	4,200	0	50,300
1551–1575	49,000	0	0	3,400	8,100	0	60,500
1576–1600	44,000	0	0	3,000	105,000	0	152,000
1601–1625	24,000	70	3,500	2,900	322,000	300	352,770
1626–1650	32,000	2,400	6,100	34,000	241,000	0	315,500
1651–1675	29,000	31,000	53,000	81,000	278,000	17,000	489,000
1676–1700	60,000	75,000	207,000	69,000	293,000	15,000	719,000
1701–1725	71,000	229,000	378,000	67,000	331,000	12,000	1,088,000
1726–1750	141,000	231,000	357,000	182,000	557,000	3,200	1,471,200
1751–1775	388,000	268,000	289,000	320,000	655,000	5,300	1,925,300
1776–1800	254,000	286,000	261,000	336,000	822,000	50,000	2,009,000
1801–1825	218,000	81,000	201,000	265,000	930,000	182,000	1,877,000
1826–1850	108,000	5,200	210,000	230,000	990,000	228,000	1,771,200
1851–1867	4,800	0	34,000	0	157,000	30,000	225,800
Total[†]	1,479,800	1,208,670	1,999,600	1,595,400	5,693,900	542,800	12,520,170

Source: Voyages Web site, http://www.slavevoyages.org/tast/assessment/estimates.faces?yearFrom=1501&yearTo=1866; set columns = "Embarkation regions."

* Senegambia, Sierra Leone, and the Windward Coast.

[†] The column and row totals in this table differ slightly from the data on the *Voyages* Web site because of the rounding rules used throughout this volume and explained in "About This Atlas."

Table 5 Estimated Number of Slaves Carried on Vessels Leaving the Largest Twenty Ports of Embarkation in Africa, 1501–1867

Embarkation Points	Number of Slaves Who Embarked
Luanda	2,826,000
Ouidah	1,004,000
Benguela	764,000
Cabinda	753,000
Bonny	672,000
Malembo	549,000
Anomabu	466,000
Loango	418,000
Old Calabar	412,000
Cape Coast Castle	318,000
Mozambique	293,000
Congo River	276,000
Gambia River	258,000
Elmina	255,000
Offra	231,000
Lagos	230,000
Ambriz	206,000
Quilimane	159,000
Sierra Leone Estuary	148,000
St.-Louis, Senegal	145,000
Total	10,383,000
All 140 known slave-trade ports of embarkation combined*	12,520,000

Source: Voyages Web site, http://www.slavevoyages.org/tast/database/search.faces?yearFrom=1514&yearTo=1866&mjbyptimp=60108.60118.60202.60299.60408.60412.60415.60506.60515.60517.60605.60608.60703.60707.60711.60717.60724.60725.60734.60820.60822: go to the tables tab and create the table of "embarkation ports" and "sum of embarked slaves." The ratios derived from the numbers of embarked slaves for each port are applied to the regional totals from http://www.slavevoyages.org/tast/assessment/estimates.faces to obtain estimates for the major ports.

* These are ports where the major portion of the human cargo of at least one slave ship was purchased. Slaves also embarked at many additional points. The codebook for the *Voyages* database lists 192 separate African places of trade.

Metal Branding Irons with Owners' Initials

From Isabelle Aguet, *A Pictorial History of the Slave Trade* (Geneva: Éditions Minerva, 1971), plate 33, p. 45.

Branding African captives, whether upon purchase at the African coast or at the time of resale in the Americas, was commonplace. The branding irons shown here each bear the initials of an owner. Brands were typically applied to the arms or torso. They were sometimes used to identify captives who died during the Atlantic crossing. The British abolitionist Thomas Clarkson and others focused on branding to condemn slavery as brutal.

Maps 53, 54, and 55: Slaves Leaving African Coastal Regions for the Americas, 1501–1867

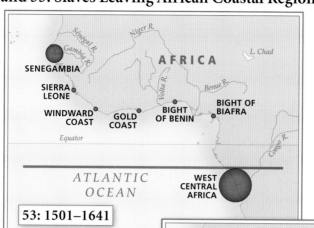

53: 1501–1641

	1501–1641		1642–1807		1808–1867	
Documented embarkations	233,000	28%	5,632,000	66%	2,057,000	64%
Estimated embarkations	601,000	72%	2,851,000	34%	1,148,000	36%
Total embarkations	834,000		8,483,000		3,205,000	

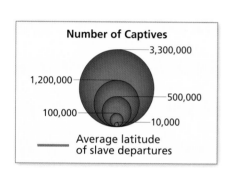

Number of Captives

3,300,000

1,200,000

500,000

100,000

10,000

Average latitude of slave departures

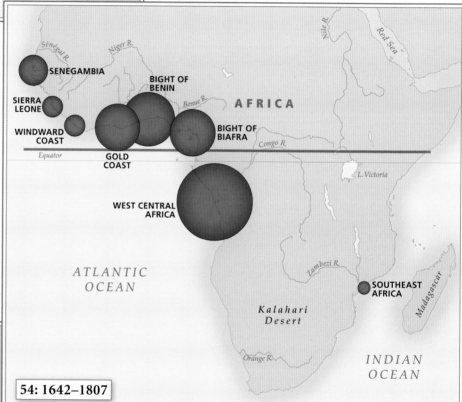

54: 1642–1807

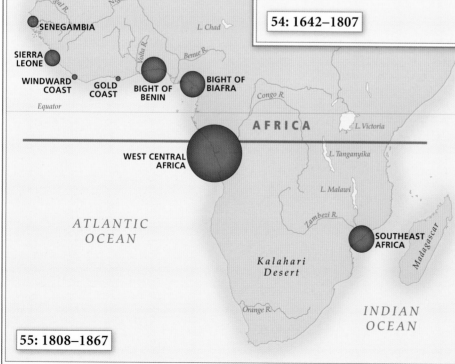

55: 1808–1867

The center of gravity of the oceanic traffic in African peoples moved north between the sixteenth and the eighteenth centuries and almost as far south again in the late eighteenth century and into the nineteenth. West Central Africa was always the largest source of captives, but as the transatlantic traffic expanded after 1640, West Africa (sub-Saharan Africa north of West Central Africa) became more prominent than it had been. Abolition of the slave trade initially had least effect in West Central Africa. The Gold Coast and Senegambia dropped out of the traffic first. By contrast, Southeast Africa became relatively more important. The blue line in the three maps is an average of the midpoint latitudes of each African coastal region weighted according to the volume of slave departures from each region.

The general Rule is, that the Merchant, with
the Captain, surveys the Ship, to see how many
[slaves] may be carried properly—the Merchant
then makes an assorted Cargo, to purchase
as near that Number as he can. . . . If a Ship is
properly constructed for the Trade, with sufficient
Height between Decks, and does not exceed 220
or 240 Tons, I have found from the Windward
Coast and Bonny, that she carried more than
Two to a Ton—sometimes more, depending on
the Number of small Slaves—I have also found,
on Enquiry, that the Slaves, with that Number,
have not been at all crowded for Room—they have
not been obliged to interfere in the disposing of
them when they go to Rest—that they have had
Room enough; and the Captains have frequently
told me, there has been considerable Spaces,
and they could have carried more. . . . . I have
never experienced One instance of any Captain
purchasing more than he was sent for—but, in
general, they have fallen short of the Number they
have gone for. . . . When a Captain purchases less
than he is sent for, it arises from a Competition
on that Part of the Coast; and, in general, I have
found the Slaves have not been so healthy as when
they have purchased their full Cargo, because
they have been longer on the Coast.

Excerpt from the Evidence of James Jones, slave merchant
of Bristol, England, 1788, to House of Commons, in Sheila
Lambert, ed., *Eighteenth Century House of Commons
Sessional Papers,* 145 vols. (Wilmington, Del.: Scholarly
Resources, 1975), vol. 68, *Reports & Papers, 1788 and 1789,*
pp. 43–44.

Maps 56, 57, and 58: Political and Ethnolinguistic Boundaries of Upper Guinea, 1650, 1750, and 1850

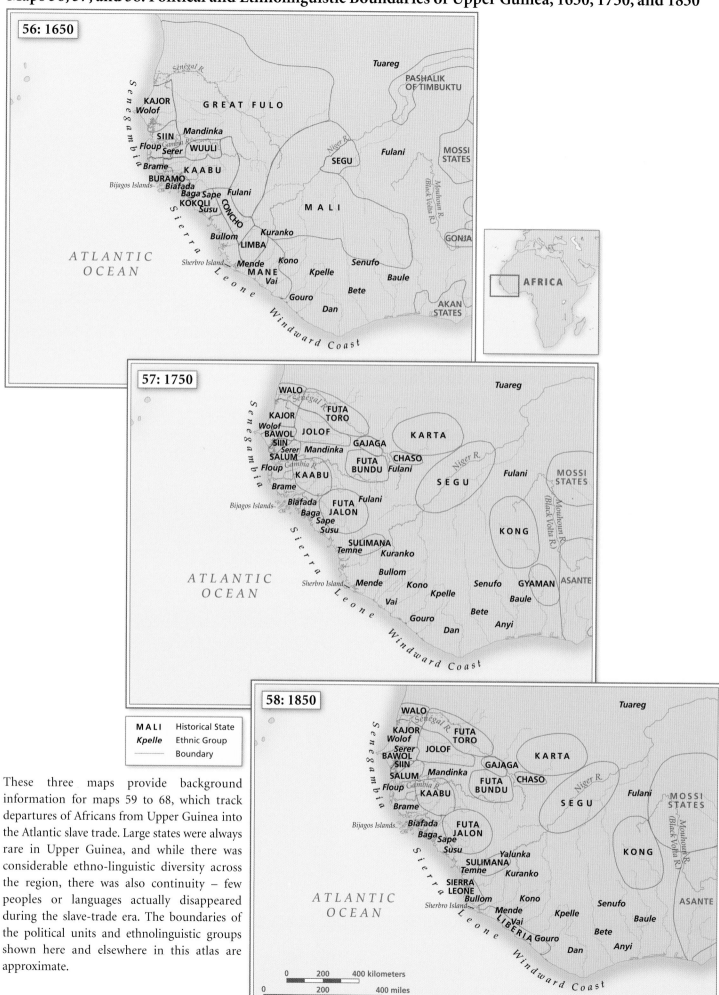

56: 1650

Senegal R.
Senegambia
KAJOR
Wolof
GREAT FULO
Tuareg
PASHALIK OF TIMBUKTU
Mandinka
SIIN
Floup Gambia R.
Serer
WUULI
Niger R.
Fulani
MOSSI STATES
Brame
KAABU
SEGU
BURAMO
Biafada
Bijagos Islands
Baga Sape Fulani
KOKOLI
Susu CONCHO
MALI
Bullom Kuranko
LIMBA
Kono
GONJA
Sherbro Island Mende
Kono
Senufo
ATLANTIC OCEAN
MANE Vai
Kpelle
Baule
Bete
Gouro
Dan
AKAN STATES
Sierra Leone
Windward Coast

AFRICA

57: 1750

WALO
Senegal R.
Tuareg
KAJOR
Wolof
FUTA TORO
BAWOL JOLOF
KARTA
SIIN GAJAGA
Serer Mandinka
SALUM
Floup Gambia R. FUTA BUNDU CHASO
KAABU Fulani
Senegambia
Brame
Niger R.
Biafada Fulani
Bijagos Islands
Baga FUTA JALON
Sape SEGU
Susu
Fulani
MOSSI STATES
KONG
SULIMANA
Temne Kuranko
Bullom
Sherbro Island Mende
Kono
Senufo GYAMAN
ATLANTIC OCEAN
Vai Kpelle
Baule ASANTE
Gouro Bete
Dan Anyi
Sierra Leone
Windward Coast

MALI	Historical State
Kpelle	Ethnic Group
—	Boundary

These three maps provide background information for maps 59 to 68, which track departures of Africans from Upper Guinea into the Atlantic slave trade. Large states were always rare in Upper Guinea, and while there was considerable ethno-linguistic diversity across the region, there was also continuity – few peoples or languages actually disappeared during the slave-trade era. The boundaries of the political units and ethnolinguistic groups shown here and elsewhere in this atlas are approximate.

58: 1850

WALO
Senegal R.
Tuareg
KAJOR
Wolof
FUTA TORO
Serer
BAWOL JOLOF
SIIN
KARTA
SALUM
Mandinka GAJAGA
Floup Gambia R. FUTA CHASO
KAABU BUNDU
Senegambia
Brame
Niger R.
Biafada FUTA
Baga JALON
Bijagos Islands
Sape
Susu
Fulani
MOSSI STATES
Yalunka
SULIMANA KONG
Temne Kuranko
SIERRA LEONE
Bullom Kono
Sherbro Island Mende
Senufo
ATLANTIC OCEAN
Vai Kpelle
Baule
LIBERIA Gouro
Bete ASANTE
Dan Anyi
Sierra Leone
Windward Coast

0   200   400 kilometers
0   200   400 miles

A Group of Slaves, Being Led to the West African Coast by Traders, 1780s

Chaîne d'esclaves venant de l'intérieur. Color engraving by an unknown artist of the French School (19th century), from R. Geoffroy, *L'Afrique, ou histoire, moeurs, usages et coutumes des africains: Le Sénégal,* 4 vols. (Paris: Nepveu, 1814), vol. 4. Bibliothèque de L'Arsenal, Paris, France / Archives Charmet / The Bridgeman Art Library.

The slave coffle in which Africans were marched from points of capture to places of sale and embarkation on the Atlantic coast was frequently described in slave narratives. In some coffles the slaves were chained together or yoked in pairs. Here we see six naked captives, all apparently adult males, bound together by a neck harness and escorted by two captors carrying spears; the one in front also holds the harness lead. The image comes from a book by René Claude Geoffroy de Villeneuve, who spent about two years in Senegal in the 1780s and produced illustrations to document the history and culture of the local people. The distances that captives were made to travel to the coast varied, but their journeys contributed to high levels of injury and death.

Maps 59–60: Slaves Leaving Locations in Upper Guinea, 1501–1740

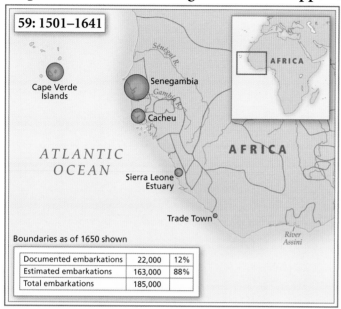

59: 1501–1641

Cape Verde Islands

Senegambia

Cacheu

ATLANTIC OCEAN

Sierra Leone Estuary

AFRICA

Trade Town

River Assini

Boundaries as of 1650 shown

Documented embarkations	22,000	12%
Estimated embarkations	163,000	88%
Total embarkations	185,000	

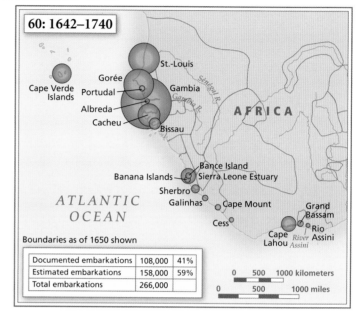

60: 1642–1740

Cape Verde Islands

St.-Louis

Gorée

Portudal

Gambia

Albreda

Cacheu

Bissau

AFRICA

Bance Island

Banana Islands

Sierra Leone Estuary

Sherbro

Galinhas

ATLANTIC OCEAN

Cape Mount

Grand Bassam

Cess

Rio Assini

Cape Lahou

River Assini

Boundaries as of 1650 shown

Documented embarkations	108,000	41%
Estimated embarkations	158,000	59%
Total embarkations	266,000	

0   500   1000 kilometers

0   500   1000 miles

Upper Guinea is a large area that includes the modern countries of Senegal, Gambia, Guinea-Bissau, Guinea, Sierra Leone, and Liberia and part of Côte d'Ivoire. Upper Guinea was the first part of Africa to be pulled into the Atlantic slave trade, and slaves went to Europe initially. Sixteenth-century records mostly specify the Cape Verde Islands as the source of captives, but the Portuguese gathered slaves there from many parts of Upper Guinea.

The slave traffic from Upper Guinea grew after 1642, largely due to the entry of English and French chartered companies into the trade between 1660 and 1700 and their subsequent replacement by independent traders. The English concentrated on the Gambia River, the French on the Sénégal River.

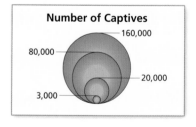

Number of Captives

160,000

80,000

20,000

3,000

Maps 61–62: Slaves Leaving Locations in Upper Guinea, 1741–1856

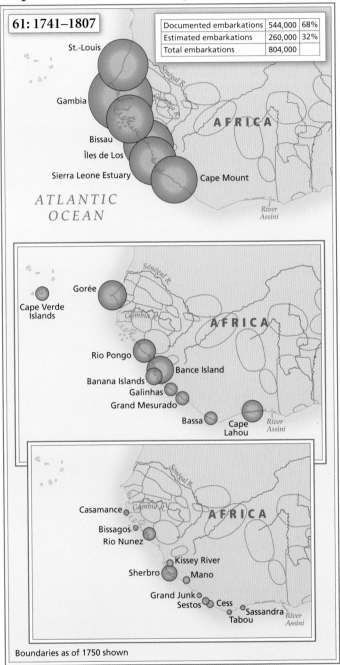

61: 1741–1807

Documented embarkations	544,000	68%
Estimated embarkations	260,000	32%
Total embarkations	804,000	

Boundaries as of 1750 shown

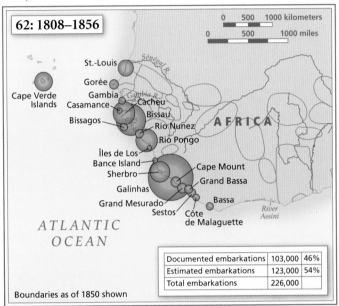

62: 1808–1856

Documented embarkations	103,000	46%
Estimated embarkations	123,000	54%
Total embarkations	226,000	

Boundaries as of 1850 shown

The withdrawal of the Dutch and the British and later the Americans and the French from slaving accelerated a general decline in transatlantic trafficking from Upper Guinea between the 1780s and the late 1820s. The main exception was Galinhas, previously almost unknown as a slave-trading venue but site of an illegal trade in slaves to mid-century.

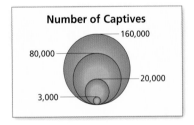

Number of Captives

160,000
80,000
20,000
3,000

Shipments of captives from Upper Guinea reached their historic peak in 1750–1780. Portuguese chartered companies expanded the area from which they shipped slaves to Brazil (see map 66). Large, medium, and small embarkation points are shown in the three maps above.

	bars [local currency]
547 Gallns of Brandy	410
1999 Pounds of Virginia Tobacco	333
75 Dyed Garrolds Blue [cloth]	450
60 Chints Patna 12 yds	300
68 Chillaes Blue	408
60 Bejutapauts Blue	360
60 Cherryderryes Blue	240
60 Cushtaes Blue	240
62 Romalls Blue	248
120 Necaneese Blue	480
10 Bandanaes Yellow	60
12 1/2 Mallabarr Hkfs [handkerchiefs] (Say) Romalls	50
58 Shawls cotton	58
1 Dozen Husling [?] Hkfs	6
588 Yards Callicoes Printed	249
538 Yards Chet [sheet]	202
120 Brass Kettles	209
60 Brass Panns	60
180 Pounds Pewter in different sized basins	45
240 French & Danish Guns	1200
410 kegs Gunpowder	820
710 Pieces Earthenware assorted	177
137 Barrs Iron	137
720 Worsted Capps	180
360 Trade Hatts	240
491 Yards Irish Linen	245
180 Dozen Knives	120
380 Bunches Barley Corn Beads	126
12 Pounds Thread	12
4 Swivells Guns Wt [weight] 1 cwt. 2 q[tr] Pack [Each]	48
4 Carriages for do. [ditto]	24
1 Swivell Gun without Carriage	6
2 Dozen Clasp Knives	6
Part of one box of Pipes	13
	7762

Against	2 Tons Rice	200
	49 Prime Slaves @ 145 [bars]	7105
	4 Slaves Under Measure	457
		7762

Account of Richard Rogers of Bristol with James Cleveland [a local trader] at Windward Coast 1786–7, dated 19 February 1787, bundle, Sloop Fly to Africa 1787, C 107/1, The National Archives, Kew, London. Published with permission of The National Archives, Kew, London.

Bance Island, River Sierra Leone, Coast of Africa, c. 1805

Watercolor by Joseph Corry. © National Maritime Museum, Greenwich, London.

Europeans built castles, forts, and trading factories on some parts of the African coast to facilitate trade. Bance (or Bunce) Island, in the Sierra Leone River, became the site of a trading factory. Less than fourteen acres in area, Bance Island was, from 1672, a base where the English Royal African Company traded for produce and provisioned slave ships. Abandoned by the company by 1730, it was taken over by Grant, Oswald & Company of London and then by John and Alexander Anderson of the same city, who successively developed the island as a base for slave trafficking until British abolition in 1807. Joseph Corry painted the Bance Island trading factory and included the watercolor in his travelogue *Observations on the Windward Coast of Africa,* published in 1807 (London: W. Bulmer & Co.). His painting depicts the island at the height of its involvement in the slave trade from the Sierra Leone River.

Map 63: Sierra Leone Estuary:
Destinations of Slaves and Home Ports of Vessels Carrying Them, 1563–1808

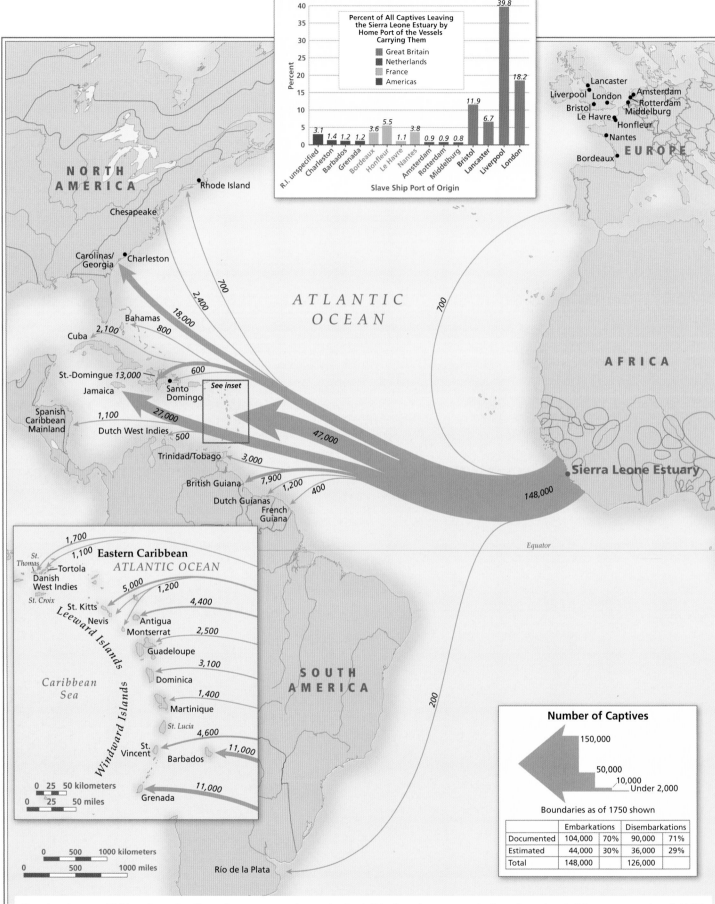

Percent of All Captives Leaving the Sierra Leone Estuary by Home Port of the Vessels Carrying Them

- Great Britain
- Netherlands
- France
- Americas

Slave Ship Port of Origin	Percent
R.I. unspecified	3.1
Charleston	1.4
Barbados	1.2
Grenada	1.2
Bordeaux	3.6
Honfleur	5.5
Le Havre	1.1
Nantes	3.8
Amsterdam	0.9
Rotterdam	0.9
Middelburg	0.8
Bristol	11.9
Lancaster	6.7
Liverpool	39.8
London	18.2

Number of Captives
150,000
50,000
10,000
Under 2,000

Boundaries as of 1750 shown

	Embarkations		Disembarkations	
Documented	104,000	70%	90,000	71%
Estimated	44,000	30%	36,000	29%
Total	148,000		126,000	

Regular slave trafficking from the Sierra Leone estuary began in the 1680s, but the great majority of captives left between 1750 and 1807, mainly on British ships. The major trading site was Bance (Bunce) Island (see page 99), located about twenty miles from the ocean. British abolition and Sierra Leone's new status as a British colony after 1807 triggered a rapid decline in slave shipments from the estuary. After 1808 the colony's capital, Freetown, became a base from which Britain attempted to suppress the slave trade.

On Being Brought from Africa to America

'Twas mercy brought me from my *Pagan* land,
Taught my benighted soul to understand
That there's a God, that there's a *Saviour* too:
Once I redemption neither sought nor knew.
Some view our sable race with scornful eye,
"Their colour is a diabolic die."
Remember, *Christians, Negros,* black as *Cain,*
May be refin'd, and join th' angelic train.

From Phillis Wheatley, *Poems on Various Subjects,
Religious and Moral* (London: Printed for A. Bell,
bookseller, Aldgate, 1773), p. 18.

Map 64: Gambia: Destinations of Slaves and Home Ports of Vessels Carrying Them, 1644–1816

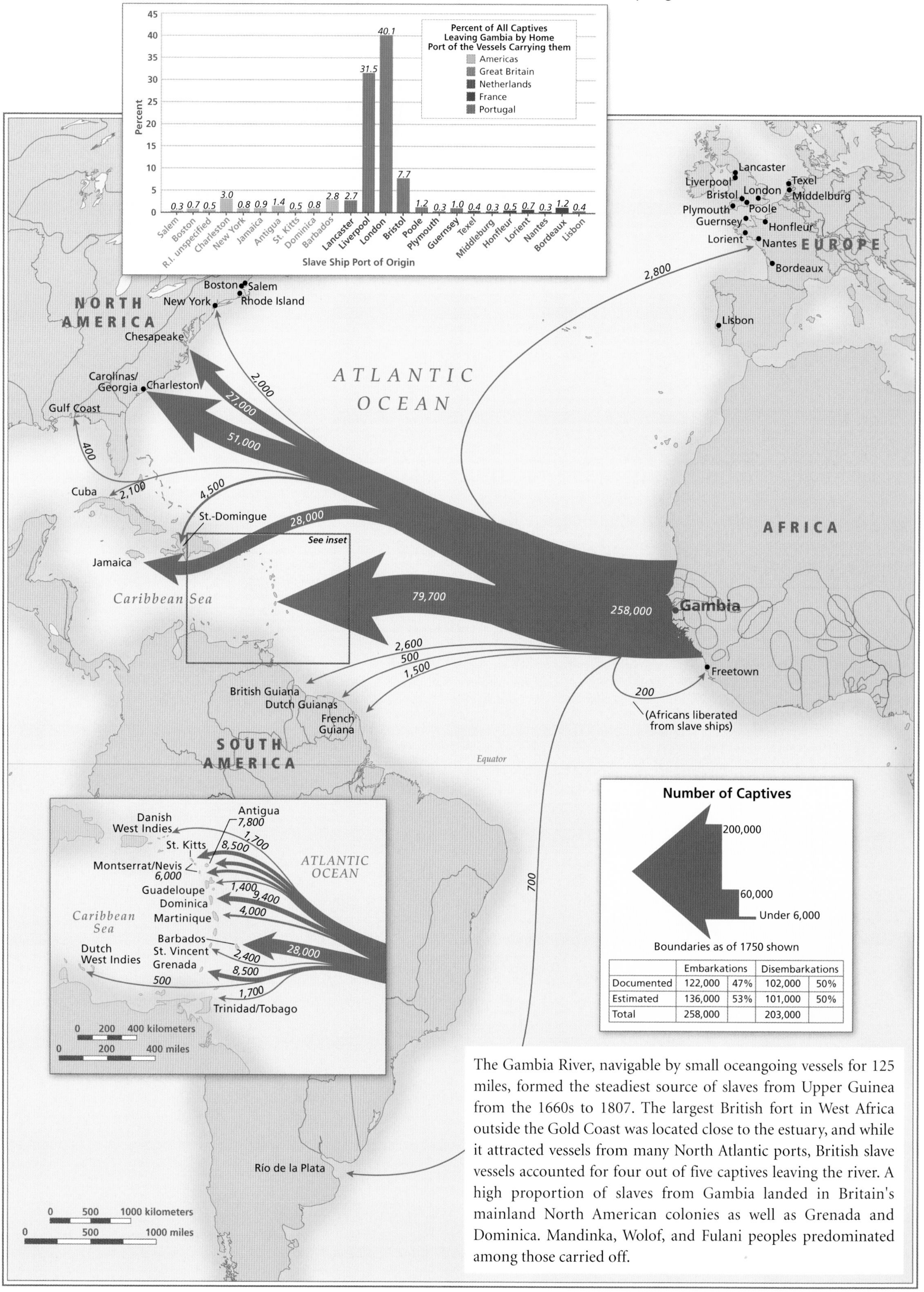

Percent of All Captives Leaving Gambia by Home Port of the Vessels Carrying them
Americas
Great Britain
Netherlands
France
Portugal
Percent
Slave Ship Port of Origin
Salem 0.3
Boston 0.7
R.I. unspecified 0.5
Charleston 3.0
New York 0.8
Jamaica 0.9
Antigua 1.4
St. Kitts 0.5
Dominica 0.8
Barbados 2.8
Lancaster 2.7
Liverpool 31.5
London 40.1
Bristol 7.7
Poole 1.2
Plymouth 0.3
Guernsey 1.0
Texel 0.4
Middleburg 0.3
Honfleur 0.5
Lorient 0.7
Nantes 0.3
Bordeaux 1.2
Lisbon 0.4
NORTH AMERICA
Boston
Salem
New York
Rhode Island
Chesapeake
Carolinas/ Georgia
Charleston
Gulf Coast
Cuba
St.-Domingue
Jamaica
Caribbean Sea
ATLANTIC OCEAN
EUROPE
Lancaster
Liverpool
Bristol
London
Texel
Middelburg
Plymouth
Poole
Guernsey
Honfleur
Lorient
Nantes
Bordeaux
Lisbon
AFRICA
Gambia
Freetown
(Africans liberated from slave ships)
British Guiana
Dutch Guianas
French Guiana
SOUTH AMERICA
Equator
Río de la Plata
2,800
2,000
27,000
51,000
400
2,100
4,500
28,000
79,700
258,000
2,600
500
1,500
200
700
See inset
Danish West Indies
Antigua 7,800
1,700
St. Kitts
8,500
Montserrat/Nevis 6,000
Guadeloupe
1,400
9,400
Dominica
Martinique
4,000
Barbados
St. Vincent
2,400
Grenada
8,500
28,000
Dutch West Indies
500
1,700
Trinidad/Tobago
0 200 400 kilometers
0 200 400 miles
0 500 1000 kilometers
0 500 1000 miles
Number of Captives
200,000
60,000
Under 6,000
Boundaries as of 1750 shown

	Embarkations		Disembarkations	
Documented	122,000	47%	102,000	50%
Estimated	136,000	53%	101,000	50%
Total	258,000		203,000	

The Gambia River, navigable by small oceangoing vessels for 125 miles, formed the steadiest source of slaves from Upper Guinea from the 1660s to 1807. The largest British fort in West Africa outside the Gold Coast was located close to the estuary, and while it attracted vessels from many North Atlantic ports, British slave vessels accounted for four out of five captives leaving the river. A high proportion of slaves from Gambia landed in Britain's mainland North American colonies as well as Grenada and Dominica. Mandinka, Wolof, and Fulani peoples predominated among those carried off.

At 10 AM Our Carpenter Went Down into the Mens
Room to Put up a Stantion to Prevent the Slaves from
Breaking the Main Gratings and having allmost
finished, the Men Slaves rose on him and took the
Sledge Maul from him not withstanding a Centinal
being Placed over the Mens Gratings with a Loaded
Pistol in his Hand to Protect the Carpenter in his
Duty, at the same time about Seventy Men Slaves being
in the Room Double Iron with three Chains Rose
thro' the bolts at the same time the Slaves Violently
Breaking their Irons and Chains by the Assistance of
the Maul by which time the other Vessels in the River
was Alarmed and Came to our Assistance having
at the same time only Seven White Men & Boys on
board belonging to the Ship we was Oblig'd to fire our
Small Arms among them thro' the Ports & down the
Gratings Permiscousely without any purpose they still
persisting and trying to break the Bulk Head down but
could not on which they repaired to the fore scuttle
which they Forced and went below and Haul'd up
several spare Sails and Barracaded the Ports with, the
Slaves still Endeavour'g to Break thro' the fore Peak
Bulk Head into the Hold, At this time having no other
Means to save the Ship we was oblig'd to throw Powder
in a Mong them and blow several of them up they still
Persisting to break into the Hold and say'd they would
not give out as Long as any One was Living among
them After a Long parley we was Oblig'd to Blow them
up the Second time, they still Refusing to give it up We
then sent Six of the Natives down with Cutlasses on
which they surrender'd And we Immediately got them
on Deck and found about Thirty Burnt & Wounded,
drest their Wounds and Secured the Whole below.

Protest of Captain Edward at Bristol, England, 29 August 1793,
regarding an insurrection on the ship Mermaid in the River
Gambia, 27 August 1792, C 107/13, box no. 2, bundle no. 3, The
National Archives, Kew, London. Published with permission
of The National Archives, Kew, London. It was reported that
nineteen "Burnt" captives subsequently died of their wounds,
between 28 August and 24 September 1792.

Map 65: St.-Louis, Senegal: Destinations of Slaves and Home Ports of Vessels Carrying Them, 1668–1829

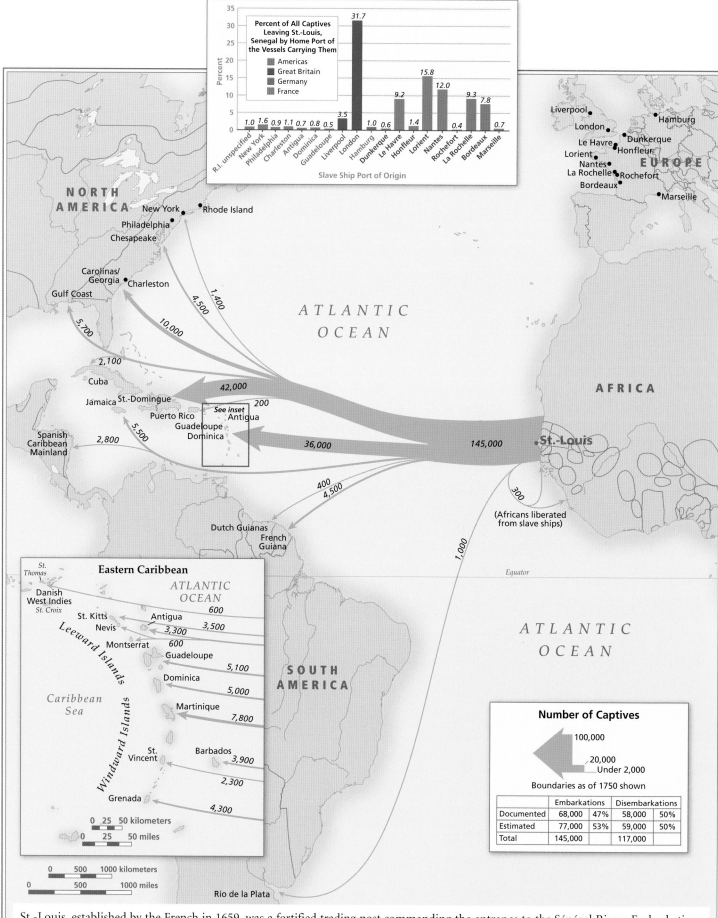

Percent of All Captives Leaving St.-Louis, Senegal by Home Port of the Vessels Carrying Them

- Americas
- Great Britain
- Germany
- France

Slave Ship Port of Origin

Number of Captives

100,000
20,000
Under 2,000

Boundaries as of 1750 shown

	Embarkations		Disembarkations	
Documented	68,000	47%	58,000	50%
Estimated	77,000	53%	59,000	50%
Total	145,000		117,000	

St.-Louis, established by the French in 1659, was a fortified trading post commanding the entrance to the Sénégal River. Embarkations of slaves from the fort began in the 1680s and continued through the 1820s. The French were usually the main carriers, and most captives went to French America, especially St.-Domingue. The French loss of their fort to the British in 1759 allowed vessels from London to establish a major British presence in Senegal in 1759–1779. After the French regained their settlement in 1779, American slave vessels began to trade at St.-Louis.

Map 66: Bissau: Destinations of Slaves and Home Ports of Vessels Carrying Them, 1686–1843

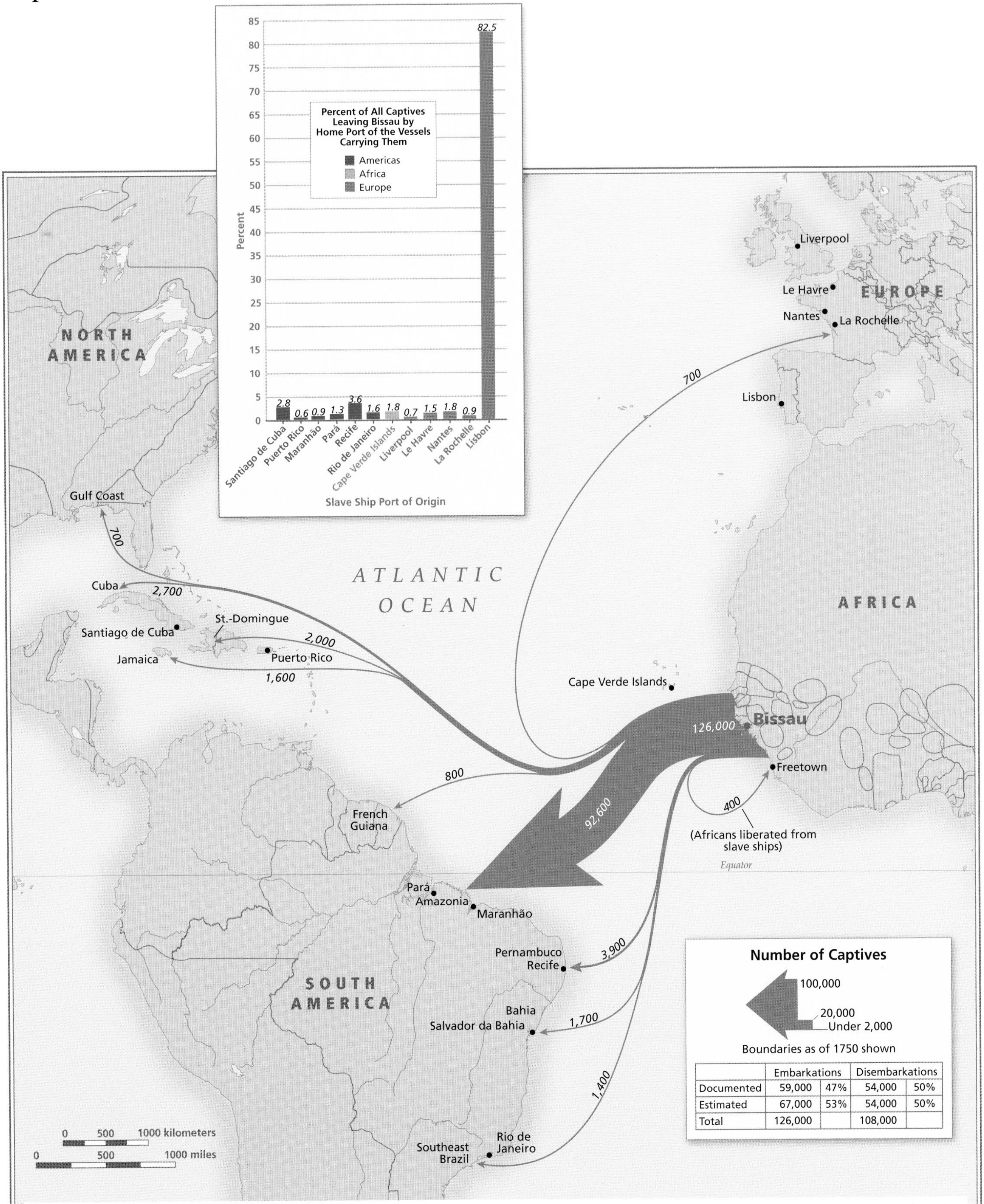

Percent of All Captives Leaving Bissau by Home Port of the Vessels Carrying Them

- Americas
- Africa
- Europe

Percent (y-axis: 0 to 85)

Slave Ship Port of Origin:
- Santiago de Cuba: 2.8
- Puerto Rico: 0.6
- Maranhão: 0.9
- Pará: 1.3
- Recife: 3.6
- Rio de Janeiro: 1.6
- Cape Verde Islands: 1.8
- Liverpool: 0.7
- Le Havre: 1.5
- Nantes: 1.8
- La Rochelle: 0.9
- Lisbon: 82.5

NORTH AMERICA

EUROPE

Liverpool
Le Havre
Nantes • La Rochelle
Lisbon

Gulf Coast — 700

Cuba — 2,700

Santiago de Cuba
St.-Domingue
Jamaica
Puerto Rico — 2,000
— 1,600

ATLANTIC OCEAN

700

Cape Verde Islands

AFRICA

126,000 • Bissau

• Freetown

400

(Africans liberated from slave ships)

800

French Guiana

92,600

Equator

Pará
Amazonia
Maranhão

Pernambuco
Recife — 3,900

SOUTH AMERICA

Bahia
Salvador da Bahia — 1,700

1,400

Rio de Janeiro
Southeast Brazil

0   500   1000 kilometers
0   500   1000 miles

Number of Captives

100,000
20,000
Under 2,000

Boundaries as of 1750 shown

	Embarkations		Disembarkations	
Documented	59,000	47%	54,000	50%
Estimated	67,000	53%	54,000	50%
Total	126,000		108,000	

Slaves were traded locally from Bissau in the sixteenth century and perhaps earlier. Between 1760 and 1814 most captives for the Americas embarked on vessels owned in and operated from Lisbon, initially as part of attempts to develop Amazonia. A treaty between Britain and Portugal in 1815 was intended to end the Portuguese slave trade north of the equator, but the traffic nevertheless continued from Bissau at reduced levels into the 1840s.

Map 67: Galinhas: Destinations of Slaves and Home Ports of Vessels Carrying Them, 1731–1856

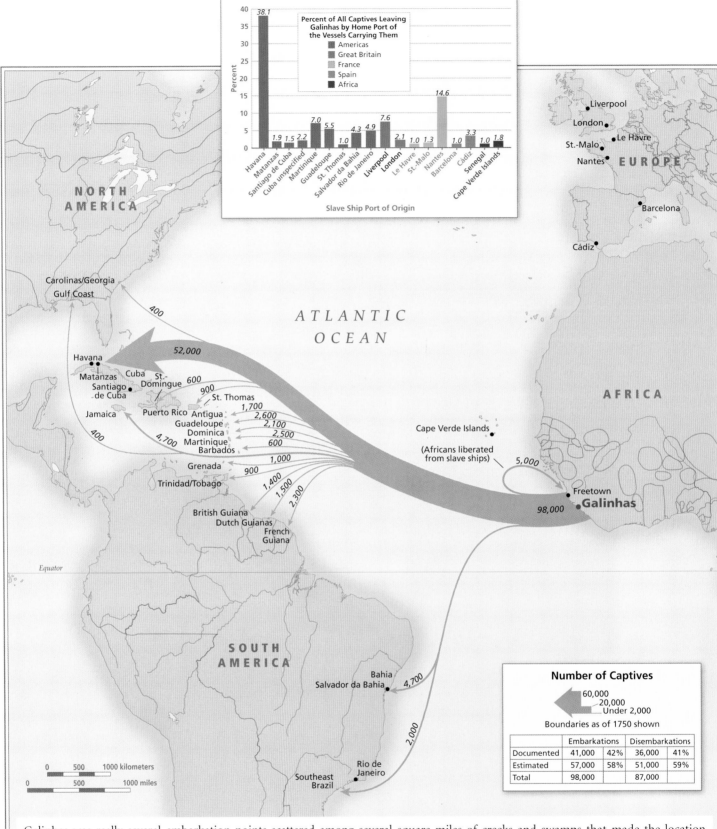

Galinhas was really several embarkation points scattered among several square miles of creeks and swamps that made the location particularly suitable for the illegal slave trade in the nineteenth century. From 1819 it became the major venue for slaving activities in Upper Guinea, notably for vessels from Havana, but also from other ports in the Spanish and (until 1831) the French Caribbean. Galinhas continued to be a source of slaves until at least 1856. Half of those embarking at Galinhas were landed in Cuba, but about one in twenty were recaptured and returned to Africa.

Slaves on the West Coast of Africa, c. 1833

By François Auguste Biard (1798–1882), oil on canvas. © Wilberforce House, Hull City Museums and Art Galleries, UK / The Bridgeman Art Library.

With the rise of abolitionism various artists undertook to portray the inhumanity of slave transactions on the African coast. Among the earliest depictions was George Morland's *Execrable Human Traffick; or the Affectionate Slaves,* shown at the Royal Academy, London, in 1788. John Raphael Samuel published it in 1791 as *The Slave Trade* and reissued it as a mezzotint in 1814. The painting shown here, also called *The Slave Trade,* is a perhaps even more famous image of a similar scene. Painted by François Auguste Biard around 1833 and set at an unknown location on the African coast, it catalogues horrors of the slave trade: the routine personal inspection of a man being sold; the branding of a woman; the whipping of a second man. The whole scene is casually witnessed by an African trader with a European bookkeeper and a small child. Presented to the British abolitionist Thomas Fowell Buxton, Biard's painting provided ammunition for those seeking to encourage other nations to follow Britain in ending slavery and the transatlantic slave trade.

Map 68: Îles de Los: Destinations of Slaves and Home Ports of Vessels Carrying Them, 1759–1820

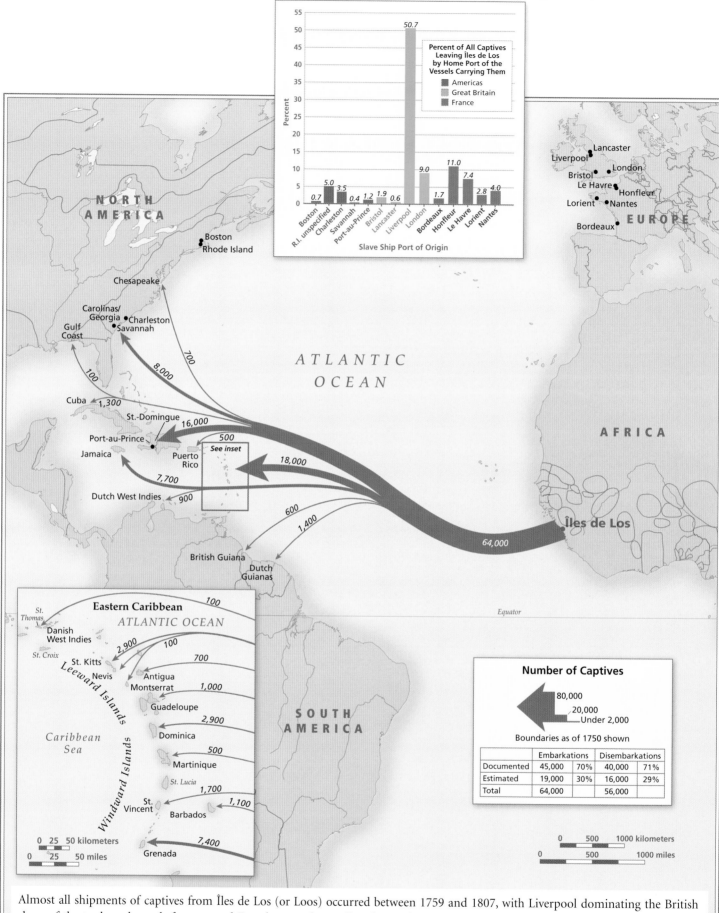

Percent of All Captives Leaving Îles de Los by Home Port of the Vessels Carrying Them
- Americas
- Great Britain
- France

Number of Captives

	Embarkations		Disembarkations	
Documented	45,000	70%	40,000	71%
Estimated	19,000	30%	16,000	29%
Total	64,000		56,000	

Boundaries as of 1750 shown

Almost all shipments of captives from Îles de Los (or Loos) occurred between 1759 and 1807, with Liverpool dominating the British share of the trade and vessels from several French ports also trading there. The British landed an unusually large number of slaves at Grenada and Dominica; French vessels almost always went to St.-Domingue. Vessels from the United States began trading at Îles de Los in the 1790s.

A late writer, who was well acquainted with Africa, from his long residence there, has pointed out the very different circumstances of Europe and Africa, with regard to the advantages and disadvantages attending the propagation of the species in each. What numbers of both sexes, says he, are there in the European world, who grow up and die, without ever having children! The increase of luxury has always been an enemy to matrimony; and accordingly, we find many decline it from choice, and many from necessity. The vain are deterred from it, from an unwillingness to abridge any part of the splendor of their appearance; and the indigent, from a certainty of multiplying their necessities. . . . In Africa none of these impediments prevail: there we find desire, unchecked by the dread of want, taking its full scope . . . and here are no impediments against pursuing the dictates of natural inclination. Polygamy is universally practised in Africa, and contributes greatly to its populousness. . . . . Hence it is, that Africa can not only continue supplying all the demands that offer for her surplus inhabitants, in the quantities it has hitherto done, but, if necessity required it, could spare thousands, nay millions more, to the end of time, all of whom may be considered as rescued by this means from that certain death, which awaited them in their own country. . . .

    Yet this trade, so highly beneficial to the adventurers, and important to the state; a trade sanctioned by the clergy, supported by the judges, and authorized by the laws, has lately been condemned both in principle and practice. By the law and usage of parliament, the most trivial right of the most inconsiderable subject is never taken away, even for the public good itself, without a manifest necessity, and a full compensation. Yet an attempt has been made, and measures are unremittingly pursued, to deprive the British planters, merchants and manufacturers, of the advantage of this important traffic; and under a pretence of regulation, restrictions have already been proposed, which strike at its existence: but though the liberty of Negroes seems now to be the favourite idea, the liberty of Britons to pursue their lawful occupations should not be forgotten.

Excerpt from Robert Norris, *Memoirs of the Reign of Bossa Ahadee, King of Dahomy, an Inland Country of Guiney, to which are added, the Author's Journey to Abomey, the Capital: and A Short Account of the African Slave Trade* (London: W. Lowndes, 1789).

Maps 69, 70, and 71: Political and Ethnolinguistic Boundaries along the Gold Coast and the Bight of Benin, 1650, 1750, and 1850

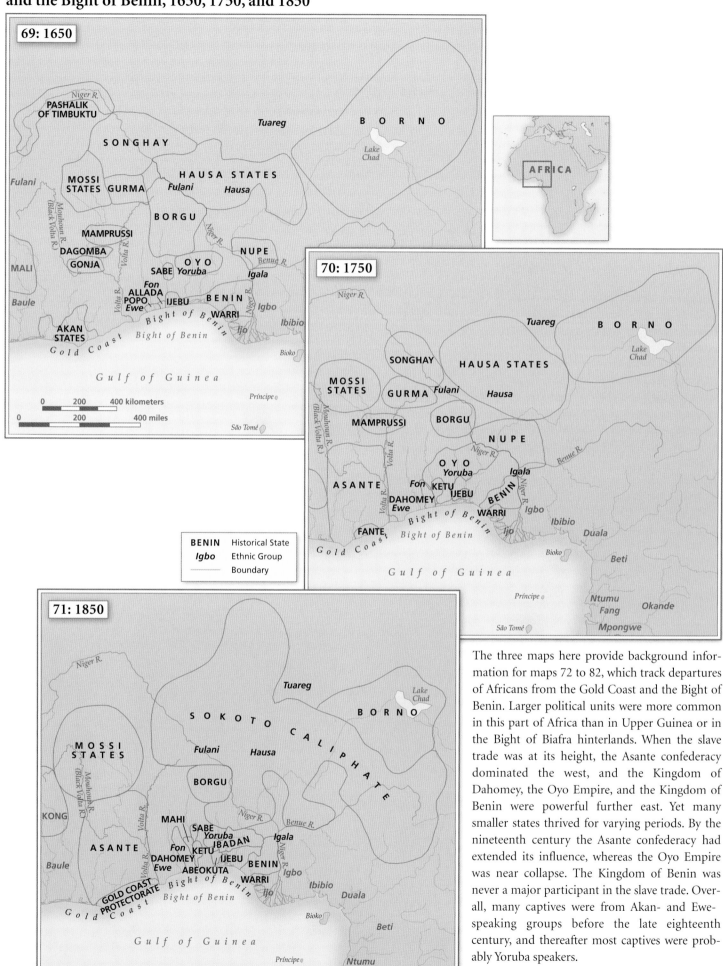

69: 1650

PASHALIK OF TIMBUKTU

Niger R.

Tuareg

B O R N O

Lake Chad

S O N G H A Y

Fulani

MOSSI STATES GURMA

H A U S A S T A T E S

Fulani *Hausa*

Mouhoun R. (Black Volta R.)

B O R G U

MAMPRUSSI

Niger R.

DAGOMBA

MALI

GONJA

Volta R.

NUPE

Benue R.

O Y O

SABE *Yoruba*

Igala

Baule

Fon
ALLADA
POPO IJEBU
Ewe

BENIN

WARRI

Igbo

AKAN STATES

Bight of Benin

Ijo

Ibibio

Gold Coast *Bight of Benin*

Bioko

Gulf of Guinea

| 0 | 200 | 400 kilometers |
| 0 | 200 | 400 miles |

Príncipe

São Tomé

70: 1750

Niger R.

Tuareg

B O R N O

Lake Chad

SONGHAY

H A U S A S T A T E S

MOSSI STATES

GURMA *Fulani*

Hausa

Mouhoun R. (Black Volta R.)

MAMPRUSSI

BORGU

N U P E

Niger R.

Benue R.

O Y O
Yoruba

Igala

ASANTE

Fon KETU
IJEBU

BENIN

DAHOMEY
Ewe

WARRI

Igbo

Ibibio

Duala

FANTE

Bight of Benin

Ijo

Gold Coast *Bight of Benin*

Bioko

Beti

Gulf of Guinea

Príncipe

Ntumu Fang *Okande*

São Tomé

Mpongwe

BENIN	Historical State
Igbo	Ethnic Group
	Boundary

71: 1850

Niger R.

Tuareg

Lake Chad

S O K O T O C A L I P H A T E

B O R N O

MOSSI STATES

Fulani *Hausa*

Mouhoun R. (Black Volta R.)

BORGU

KONG

Volta R.

Niger R.

Benue R.

MAHI

SABE
Yoruba IBADAN

Igala

ASANTE

Fon KETU
DAHOMEY IJEBU
Ewe ABEOKUTA

BENIN

Baule

WARRI

Igbo

GOLD COAST PROTECTORATE

Bight of Benin

Ijo

Ibibio

Duala

Gold Coast *Bight of Benin*

Bioko

Beti

Gulf of Guinea

Príncipe

Ntumu Fang

AFRICA

The three maps here provide background information for maps 72 to 82, which track departures of Africans from the Gold Coast and the Bight of Benin. Larger political units were more common in this part of Africa than in Upper Guinea or in the Bight of Biafra hinterlands. When the slave trade was at its height, the Asante confederacy dominated the west, and the Kingdom of Dahomey, the Oyo Empire, and the Kingdom of Benin were powerful further east. Yet many smaller states thrived for varying periods. By the nineteenth century the Asante confederacy had extended its influence, whereas the Oyo Empire was near collapse. The Kingdom of Benin was never a major participant in the slave trade. Overall, many captives were from Akan- and Ewe-speaking groups before the late eighteenth century, and thereafter most captives were probably Yoruba speakers.

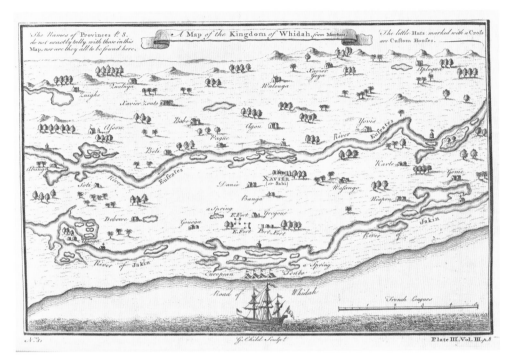

A Map of the Kingdom of Whidah, 1727

Engraving from Thomas Astley, *A New General Collection of Voyages and Travels,* 4 vols. (London: Thomas Astley, 1745–1747), vol. 2, p. 394, plate 184, no. 105. Rare Books Division, The New York Public Library, Astor, Lenox and Tilden Foundations.

Gezo, King of Dahomey, 1849

Aquatint from Frederick E. Forbes, *Dahomey and the Dahomans: Being the Journal of Two Missions to the King of Dahomey, and His Residence in the Capital in 1849 and 1850,* 2 vols. (London: Longman, Brown, Green and Longmans, 1851), vol. 1, frontispiece. General Research and Reference Division, Schomburg Center for Research in Black Culture, The New York Public Library, Astor, Lenox and Tilden Foundations.

Ouidah (Whidah), on the Bight of Benin, was the largest single embarkation point for captives shipped from West Africa. Its emergence as a slave port dates from the late seventeenth century, but the Kingdom of Dahomey conquered it in 1725–1727 and ruled it until the late nineteenth century. Slave trafficking at Ouidah, as at most other African ports, though open to private traders, was subject to state oversight. The British missionary Frederick Forbes drew King Gezo of Dahomey in 1849. Gezo ruled Dahomey from 1818 to 1868. Forbes described him as "about 48 years of age, good looking . . . his appearance commanding." During Gezo's reign, slave trafficking through Ouidah continued, but suppression of the transatlantic slave trade diminished the port's long-term commercial position and encouraged Dahomey (modern-day Benin) to develop other export trades.

Maps 72, 73, and 74: Slaves Leaving Locations on the Gold Coast and the Bight of Benin, 1616–1863

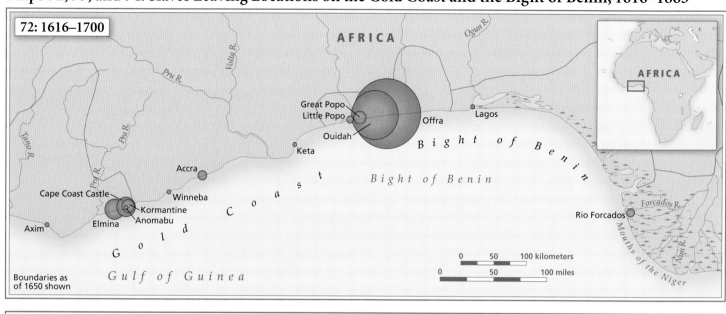

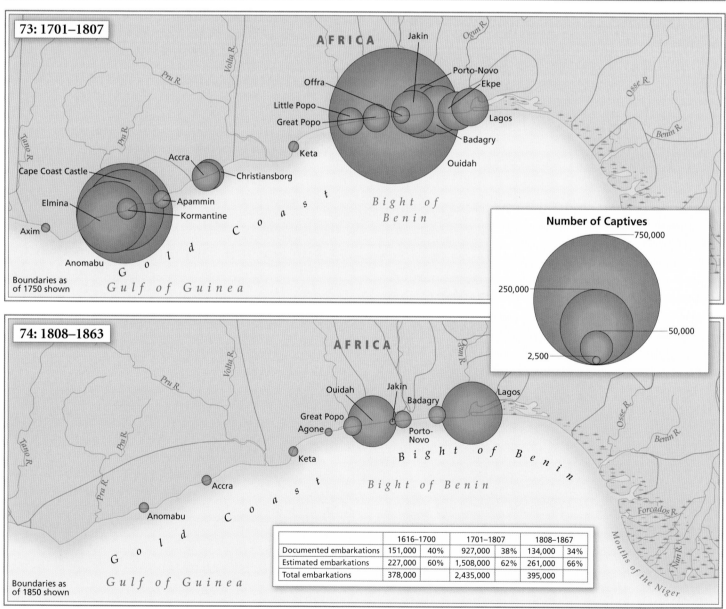

	1616–1700		1701–1807		1808–1867	
Documented embarkations	151,000	40%	927,000	38%	134,000	34%
Estimated embarkations	227,000	60%	1,508,000	62%	261,000	66%
Total embarkations	378,000		2,435,000		395,000	

The Bight of Benin (modern eastern Ghana to western Nigeria) was known as the Slave Coast in the late seventeenth and most of the eighteenth centuries. The Gold Coast (modern Ghana), by contrast, was not involved in the transatlantic slave trade until later, and the value of slaves carried off from the region lagged behind the value of gold exports until about 1700. Together, the Bight of Benin and the Gold Coast supplied about one-quarter of the slaves in the transatlantic slave trade. Ports such as Anomabu, Ouidah, and later Lagos were among the very largest sources of captives anywhere on the African coast. The Gold Coast trade in slaves was shut down by the early 1820s.

After I was ordered out, the horrors I soon saw
and felt, cannot be well described; I saw many
of my miserable countrymen chained two and
two, some hand-cuffed, and some with their
hands tied behind. We were conducted along by a
guard, and when we arrived at the castle, I asked
my guide what I was brought there for, he told
me to learn the ways of the browsow, that is the
white faced people. I saw him take a gun, a piece
of cloth, and some lead for me, and then he told
me that he must now leave me there, and went
off. This made me cry bitterly, but I was soon
conducted to a prison, for three days, where I
heard the groans and cries of many, and saw some
of my fellow-captives. But when a vessel arrived to
conduct us away to the ship, it was a most horrible
scene; there was nothing to be heard but rattling
of chains, smacking of whips, and the groans and
cries of our fellow-men. Some would not stir from
the ground, when they were lashed and beat in
the most horrible manner.

Excerpt from Quobna Ottobah Cugoano, *Thoughts and
Sentiments on the Evil and Wicked Traffic of the Slavery and
Commerce of the Human Species* (London: Mr. Hall and Mr.
Phillips, 1787).

Map 75: Offra: Destinations of Slaves and Home Ports of Vessels Carrying Them, 1616–1787

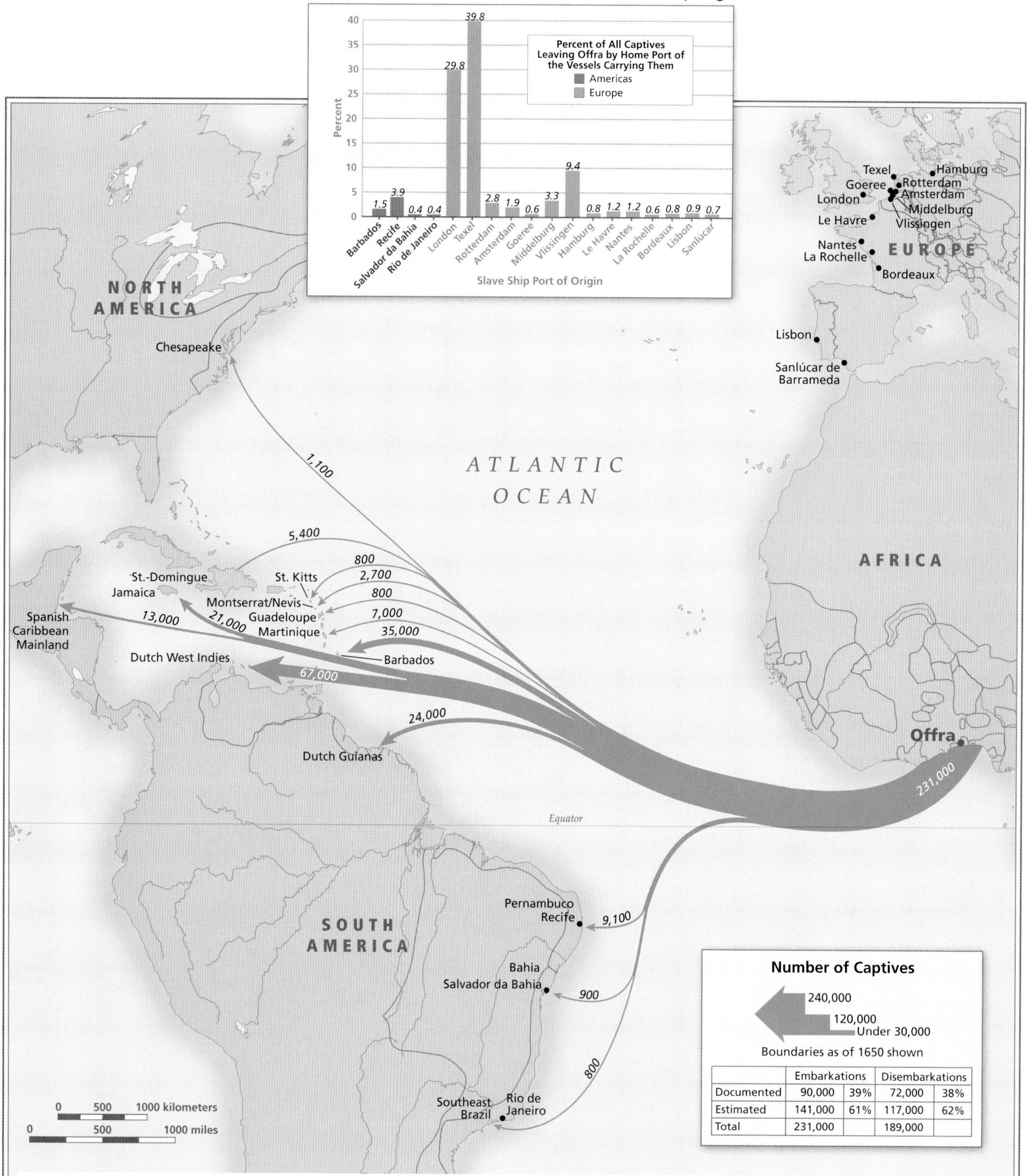

Percent of All Captives Leaving Offra by Home Port of the Vessels Carrying Them
- Americas
- Europe

Chart (Percent vs Slave Ship Port of Origin):
- Barbados: 1.5
- Recife: 3.9
- Salvador da Bahia: 0.4
- Rio de Janeiro: 0.4
- London: 29.8
- Texel: 39.8
- Rotterdam: 2.8
- Amsterdam: 1.9
- Goeree: 0.6
- Middelburg: 3.3
- Vlissingen: 9.4
- Hamburg: 0.8
- Le Havre: 1.2
- Nantes: 1.2
- La Rochelle: 0.6
- Bordeaux: 0.8
- Lisbon: 0.9
- Sanlúcar: 0.7

NORTH AMERICA

EUROPE

Texel · Hamburg
Goeree · Rotterdam · Amsterdam
London · Middelburg · Vlissingen
Le Havre
Nantes
La Rochelle · Bordeaux

Lisbon
Sanlúcar de Barrameda

AFRICA

ATLANTIC OCEAN

Chesapeake — 1,100

St.-Domingue
Jamaica
Spanish Caribbean Mainland — 13,000
Montserrat/Nevis — 21,000
Guadeloupe
Martinique
Dutch West Indies
St. Kitts — 5,400
800
2,700
800
7,000
35,000
Barbados
67,000
24,000

Dutch Guianas

Offra — 231,000

Equator

SOUTH AMERICA

Pernambuco Recife — 9,100
Bahia
Salvador da Bahia — 900
Southeast Brazil
Rio de Janeiro — 800

0   500   1000 kilometers
0   500   1000 miles

Number of Captives

240,000
120,000
Under 30,000

Boundaries as of 1650 shown

	Embarkations		Disembarkations	
Documented	90,000	39%	72,000	38%
Estimated	141,000	61%	117,000	62%
Total	231,000		189,000	

Offra became a trading venue for English and Dutch chartered trading companies in the last third of the seventeenth century. Located in what is now the state of Benin, it was the outlet for the Atlantic trade of the African kingdom of Allada. Offra was destroyed in a local war in 1690, after which few slave vessels traded there. Most slaves taken from Offra landed in the British or Dutch Caribbean.

[To Royal African Company Chief Agents
at Cape Coast Castle from] John Thorne

Ophra [Offra] in Arda, 4 Dec. 1681

A note of what goods is vendible you will find inclosed
herein. Wee have great occasion for a canoe or two and
some padles. The great canoe was stav'd upon the breakers
and the 7 hand canoe broke away from the stern of
Captain Low's ship in a turnadoe, soe that wee have great
need of canoes and you had as good send noe ships as
noe canoes. For canoemen I have 13 here, and if you send
downe any more pray lett them be pawnes [i.e., laborers
in debt bondage], for those that came with Captain Low
proved rogues. For the last three dayes when there was
most occasion for them, could not gett them to carry off
the slaves, to Captain Lowes great damage, but was forced
to hyre others. . . .

[Inclosure]

An account of what goods are fitt to purchase slaves att
Ophra in Arda:
Booges [cowries], all sorts of brass bassons great and
small, and satin, all sorts of flowered and stripd silks,
red cuttanees, ginghams, chercolees, sallampores, all
sorts of linnen, longcloth, Holland, muslins, white baftes,
pintados, chints, linnens printed, beads of all sorts,
chiefly yallow, lamon and greene, rangoes [beads], cases
of spirrits, brandy, musketts 200, powder 20 barrells, lead
barrs 400, what linnens you send let it all be white.

John Thorne.

From *The English in West Africa, 1681–1683: The Local Correspondence
of the Royal African Company of England, 1681–1699, Part 1*, ed. Robin
Law, Fontes Historiae Africanae, New Series, Sources of African
History (Published for The British Academy by Oxford University
Press, Oxford, 1997), pp. 223–225. Reprinted with permission of The
British Academy.

Map 76: Elmina: Destinations of Slaves and Home Ports of Vessels Carrying Them, 1650–1814

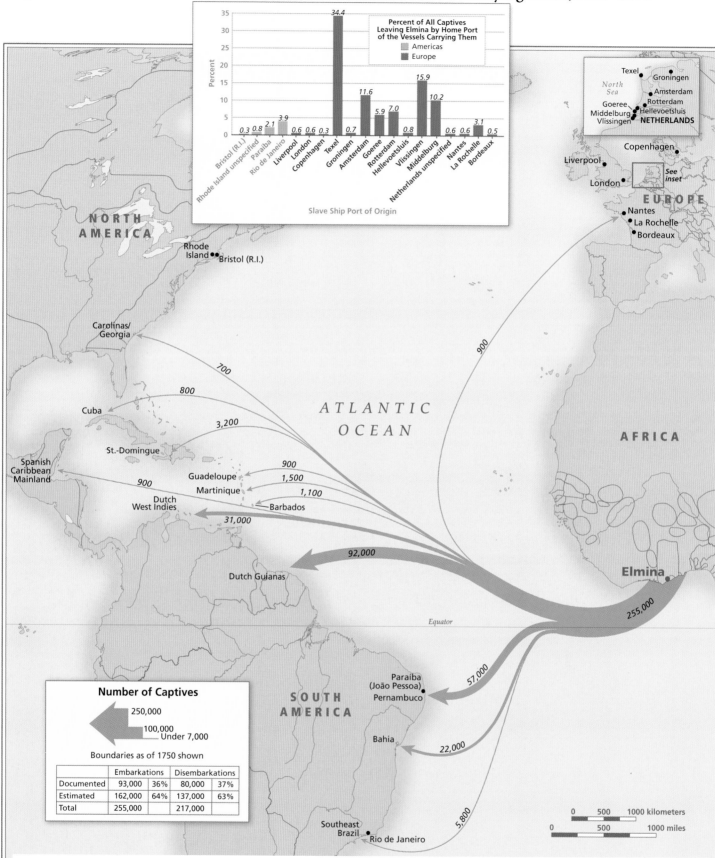

Number of Captives

250,000
100,000
Under 7,000

Boundaries as of 1750 shown

	Embarkations		Disembarkations	
Documented	93,000	36%	80,000	37%
Estimated	162,000	64%	137,000	63%
Total	255,000		217,000	

Built in 1482 by the Portuguese, Elmina Castle was captured by the Dutch in 1637 and became the headquarters of Dutch trading activity on the Gold Coast. The scale of slave shipments from Elmina to Brazil is probably exaggerated because under a treaty signed in 1678 the Portuguese agreed to pay dues at Dutch Elmina en route to trading places farther east. The principal destination of captives leaving Elmina shifted during the eighteenth century, from the Dutch West Indies (where most slaves were passed on to Spanish America) to the Dutch Guianas, because the French (in 1701) and then the English (in 1713) took over the *asiento* (the exclusive contract to supply captives to Spanish possessions in the New World).

Elmina Village Showing Elmina Castle and Fort St. Jago, 1731

Pen and ink drawing by Robert Durand from his *Journal de bord d'un negrier* (1731). Beinecke Rare Book and Manuscript Library, Yale University.

Europeans established more trading forts and castles on the Gold Coast than any other part of the Atlantic seaboard of Africa in the seventeenth century. Robert Durand, first lieutenant on the French slave ship *Diligent,* drew Elmina Castle and its locality as the *Diligent* sailed past en route to the Bight of Benin, where it took on captives for Martinique. Elmina Castle, then the center of Dutch trading activity on the Gold Coast, appears in the foreground of the drawing, with Fort St. Jago on the hill behind it.

Map 77: Anomabu: Destinations of Slaves and Home Ports of Vessels Carrying Them, 1652–1839

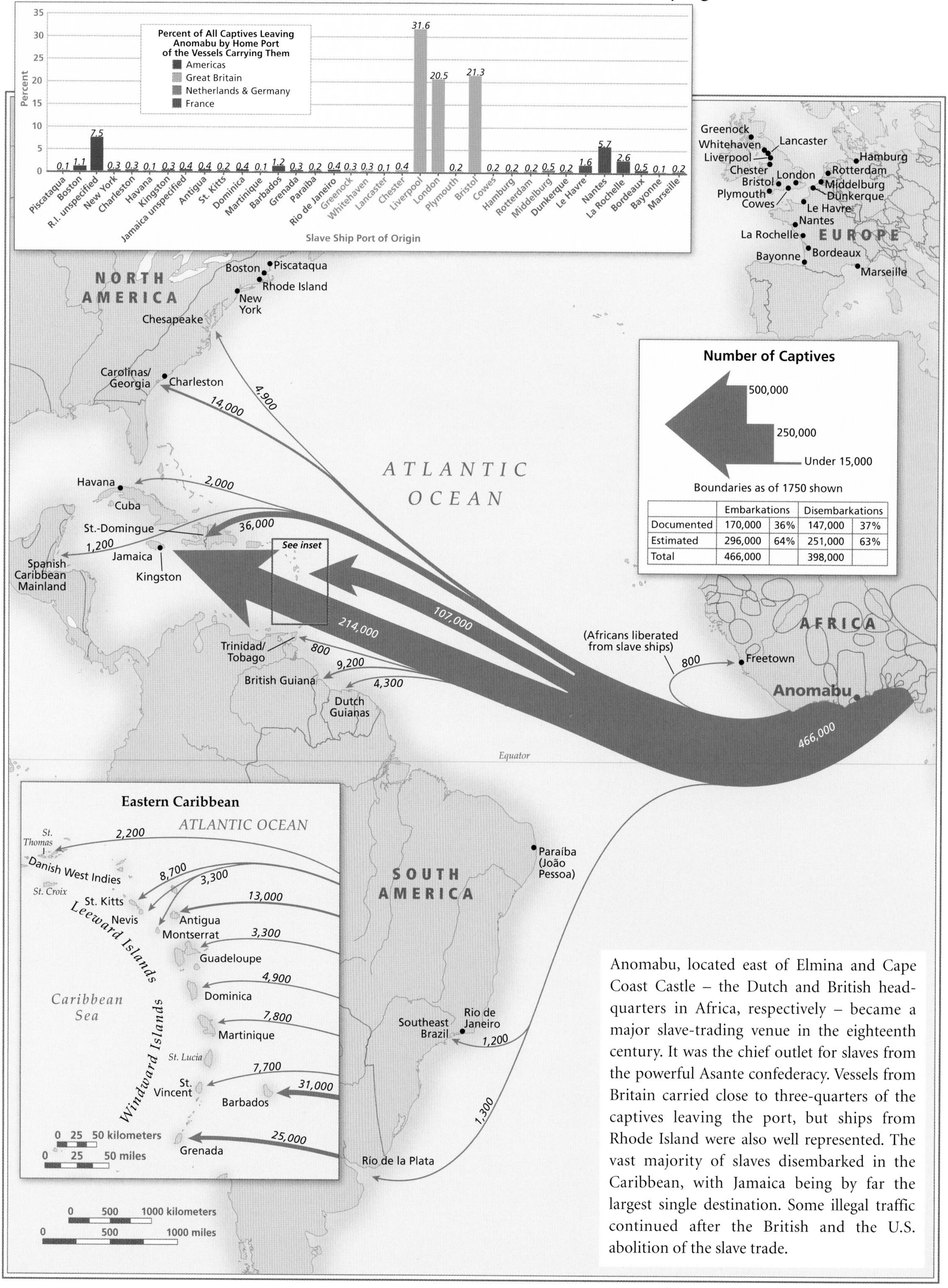

Percent of All Captives Leaving Anomabu by Home Port of the Vessels Carrying Them

Americas ▪
Great Britain ▪
Netherlands & Germany ▪
France ▪

Percent (y-axis)

Slave Ship Port of Origin (x-axis):
Piscataqua 0.1, Boston 1.1, R.I. unspecified 7.5, New York 0.3, Charleston 0.3, Havana 0.1, Kingston 0.3, Jamaica unspecified 0.4, Antigua 0.4, St. Kitts 0.2, Dominica 0.4, Martinique 0.1, Barbados 1.2, Grenada 0.3, Paraíba 0.2, Rio de Janeiro 0.4, Greenock 0.3, Whitehaven 0.3, Lancaster 0.1, Chester 0.4, Liverpool 31.6, London 20.5, Plymouth 0.2, Bristol 21.3, Cowes 0.2, Hamburg 0.2, Rotterdam 0.2, Middelburg 0.5, Dunkerque 0.2, Le Havre 1.6, Nantes 5.7, La Rochelle 2.6, Bordeaux 0.5, Bayonne 0.1, Marseille 0.2

NORTH AMERICA

Boston • Piscataqua
Rhode Island
New York
Chesapeake

Carolinas/Georgia • Charleston

4,900

14,000

Havana • Cuba
2,000

St.-Domingue
1,200
Jamaica • Kingston
Spanish Caribbean Mainland

36,000

See inset

214,000

107,000

Trinidad/Tobago 800
9,200
British Guiana
4,300
Dutch Guianas

ATLANTIC OCEAN

EUROPE

Greenock
Whitehaven
Liverpool
Chester
Bristol
Plymouth
Cowes
London
Hamburg
Rotterdam
Middelburg
Dunkerque
Le Havre
Nantes
La Rochelle
Bayonne
Bordeaux
Marseille

Number of Captives

500,000
250,000
Under 15,000

Boundaries as of 1750 shown

	Embarkations		Disembarkations	
Documented	170,000	36%	147,000	37%
Estimated	296,000	64%	251,000	63%
Total	466,000		398,000	

AFRICA

(Africans liberated from slave ships)
800 → • Freetown

Anomabu

466,000

Equator

Eastern Caribbean

ATLANTIC OCEAN

St. Thomas
2,200
Danish West Indies
St. Croix

8,700
3,300
St. Kitts
Nevis
13,000
Antigua
Montserrat
3,300
Guadeloupe
4,900
Dominica
7,800
Martinique
St. Lucia
7,700
St. Vincent
31,000
Barbados
25,000
Grenada

Leeward Islands
Windward Islands
Caribbean Sea

0 25 50 kilometers
0 25 50 miles

SOUTH AMERICA

Paraíba (João Pessoa)

Rio de Janeiro
Southeast Brazil
1,200

1,300

Río de la Plata

0 500 1000 kilometers
0 500 1000 miles

Anomabu, located east of Elmina and Cape Coast Castle – the Dutch and British head-quarters in Africa, respectively – became a major slave-trading venue in the eighteenth century. It was the chief outlet for slaves from the powerful Asante confederacy. Vessels from Britain carried close to three-quarters of the captives leaving the port, but ships from Rhode Island were also well represented. The vast majority of slaves disembarked in the Caribbean, with Jamaica being by far the largest single destination. Some illegal traffic continued after the British and the U.S. abolition of the slave trade.

The invaders . . . pinioned the prisoners of all
ages and sexes indiscriminately, took their flocks
and all their effects, and moved on their way
towards the sea. On the march the prisoners were
treated with clemency, on account of their being
submissive and humble. Having come to the
next tribe, the enemy laid siege and immediately
took men, women, children, flocks, and all their
valuable effects. They then went on to the next
district which was contiguous to the sea, called
in Africa, Anamaboo. The enemies' provisions
were then almost spent, as well as their strength.
The inhabitants knowing what conduct they had
pursued, and what were their present intentions,
improved the favorable opportunity, attacked
them, and took enemy, prisoners, flocks and all
their effects. I was then taken a second time. All
of us were then put into the castle, and kept for
market. On a certain time I and other prisoners
were put on board a canoe, under our master, and
rowed away to a vessel belonging to Rhode Island,
commanded by Captain Collingwood, and the
mate Thomas Mumford. While we were going to
the vessel, our master told us all to appear to the
best possible advantage for sale. I was bought on
board by one Robertson Mumford, steward of
said vessel, for four gallons of rum, and a piece
of calico, and called VENTURE, on account of
his having purchased me with his own private
venture. Thus I came by my name. All the slaves
that were bought for that vessel's cargo, were two
hundred and sixty.

Excerpt from Venture Smith, *A Narrative of the Life and
Adventures of Venture, a Native of Africa: but Resident Above
Sixty Years in the United States of America* (New London,
Conn.: C. Holt, 1798).

Map 78: Lagos: Destinations of Slaves and Home Ports of Vessels Carrying Them, 1652–1851

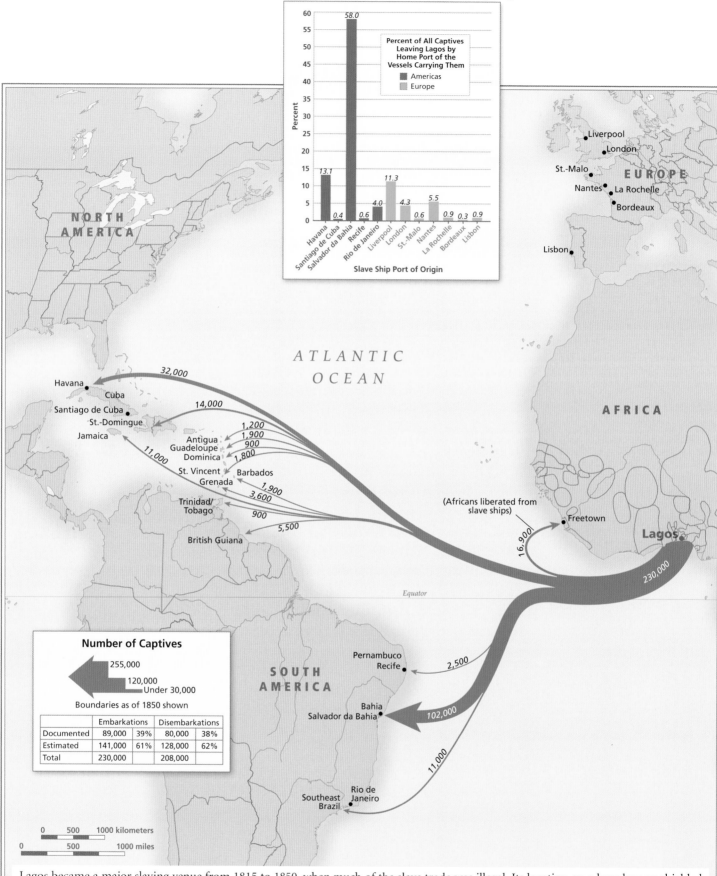

Percent of All Captives Leaving Lagos by Home Port of the Vessels Carrying Them

- Americas
- Europe

	Havana	Santiago de Cuba	Salvador da Bahia	Recife	Rio de Janeiro	Liverpool	London	St.-Malo	Nantes	La Rochelle	Bordeaux	Lisbon
Percent	13.1	0.4	58.0	0.6	4.0	11.3	4.3	0.6	5.5	0.9	0.3	0.9

Slave Ship Port of Origin

Number of Captives

255,000
120,000
Under 30,000

Boundaries as of 1850 shown

	Embarkations		Disembarkations	
Documented	89,000	39%	80,000	38%
Estimated	141,000	61%	128,000	62%
Total	230,000		208,000	

0   500   1000 kilometers
0   500   1000 miles

Lagos became a major slaving venue from 1815 to 1850, when much of the slave trade was illegal. Its location on a long lagoon shielded the embarkation of slaves from the attention of naval cruisers on the watch for illegal traders. Over 7,000 captives a year went from Lagos to the Americas, and for a time the port was more important than Ouidah. After 1807 over three-quarters of the slaves embarking at Lagos left on vessels outfitted at ports in the Americas. A relatively large number of captives leaving Lagos were recaptured, almost all after 1808 by British anti-slave-trade cruisers, and taken to Freetown, Sierra Leone.

Map 79: Ouidah: Destinations of Slaves and Home Ports of Vessels Carrying Them, 1659–1726

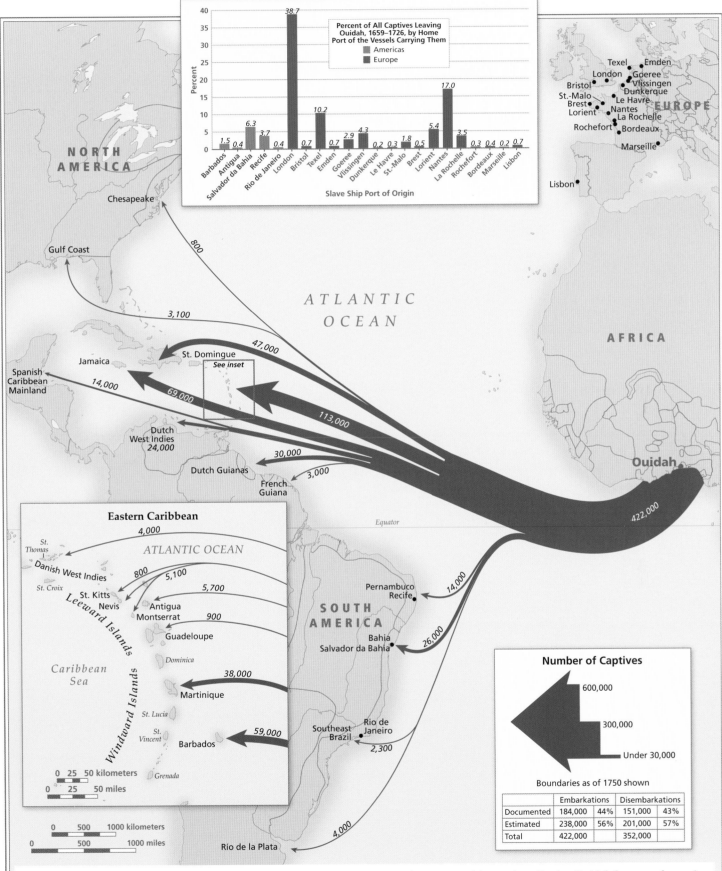

Ouidah's history of involvement in the slave trade is shown in maps 79 and 80. Located in modern Benin, Ouidah became the major slave port in West Africa by the end of the seventeenth century. Slave traders from European nations and Brazil bought captives there, even when their nations were at war with each other. After 1727, when Ouidah was incorporated into the Kingdom of Dahomey, the number of slaves dispatched from the port diminished, never again to reach the heights achieved when Ouidah was independent. For the vessels that visited the port, the British and the Dutch Caribbean were the chief destinations, but the British and the Dutch lost ground to their French and Brazilian rivals in the 1720s, and St.-Domingue, Bahia, and eventually Cuba received the most captives from Ouidah thereafter. Initially slaves would have been mainly Ewe peoples, but late in the eighteenth century, Yoruba speakers became dominant.

Map 80: Ouidah: Destinations of Slaves and Home Ports of Vessels Carrying Them, 1727–1863

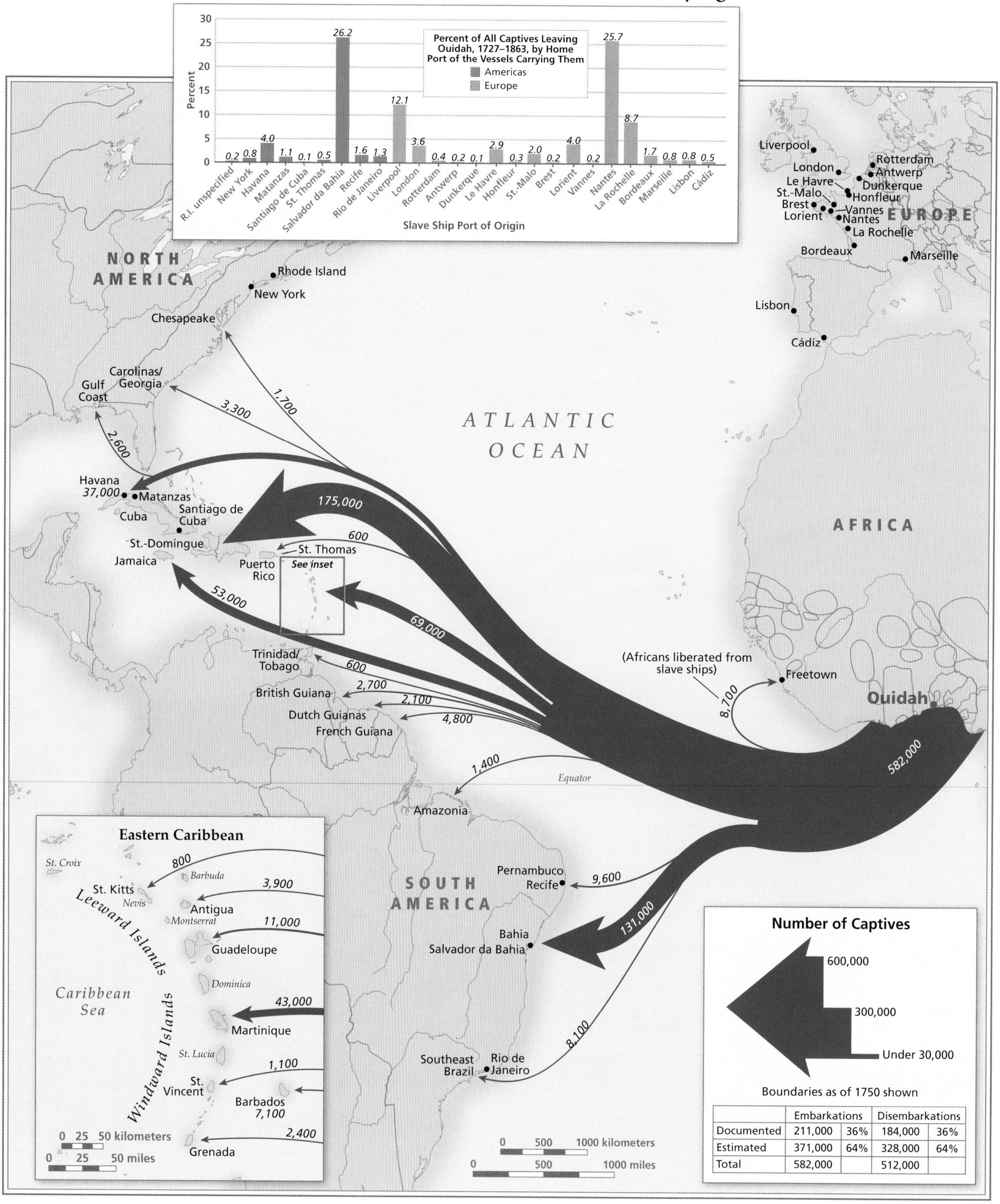

Percent of All Captives Leaving Ouidah, 1727–1863, by Home Port of the Vessels Carrying Them

- Americas
- Europe

Percent (y-axis): 0, 5, 10, 15, 20, 25, 30

Slave Ship Port of Origin (x-axis):
R.I. unspecified 0.2, New York 0.8, Havana 4.0, Matanzas 1.1, Santiago de Cuba 0.1, St. Thomas 0.5, Salvador da Bahia 26.2, Recife 1.6, Rio de Janeiro 1.3, Liverpool 12.1, London 3.6, Rotterdam 0.4, Antwerp 0.2, Dunkerque 0.1, Le Havre 2.9, Honfleur 0.3, St.-Malo 2.0, Brest 0.2, Lorient 4.0, Vannes 0.2, Nantes 25.7, La Rochelle 8.7, Bordeaux 1.7, Marseille 0.8, Lisbon 0.8, Cádiz 0.5

NORTH AMERICA

Liverpool, London, Le Havre, St.-Malo, Brest, Lorient, Rotterdam, Antwerp, Dunkerque, Honfleur, Vannes, Nantes, La Rochelle, Bordeaux, Marseille, EUROPE

Lisbon

Cádiz

Rhode Island
New York
Chesapeake
Carolinas/Georgia
Gulf Coast

1,700

3,300

2,600

ATLANTIC OCEAN

Havana 37,000
Matanzas
Cuba
Santiago de Cuba
St.-Domingue
Jamaica
Puerto Rico
St. Thomas
See inset

175,000

600

53,000

69,000

600

Trinidad/Tobago
British Guiana 2,700
Dutch Guianas 2,100
French Guiana 4,800

AFRICA

(Africans liberated from slave ships)
Freetown
8,700

Quidah

582,000

1,400

Amazonia

Equator

SOUTH AMERICA

Pernambuco Recife 9,600

131,000

Bahia
Salvador da Bahia

8,100

Southeast Brazil

Rio de Janeiro

Eastern Caribbean

St. Croix
Barbuda
St. Kitts
Nevis
Leeward Islands
Antigua
Montserrat
Guadeloupe
Dominica
Caribbean Sea
Windward Islands
Martinique
St. Lucia
St. Vincent
Barbados 7,100
Grenada

800
3,900
11,000
43,000
1,100
2,400

0 25 50 kilometers
0 25 50 miles

0   500   1000 kilometers
0   500   1000 miles

Number of Captives

600,000
300,000
Under 30,000

Boundaries as of 1750 shown

	Embarkations		Disembarkations	
Documented	211,000	36%	184,000	36%
Estimated	371,000	64%	328,000	64%
Total	582,000		512,000	

Map 81: Cape Coast Castle: Destinations of Slaves and Home Ports of Vessels Carrying Them, 1674–1807

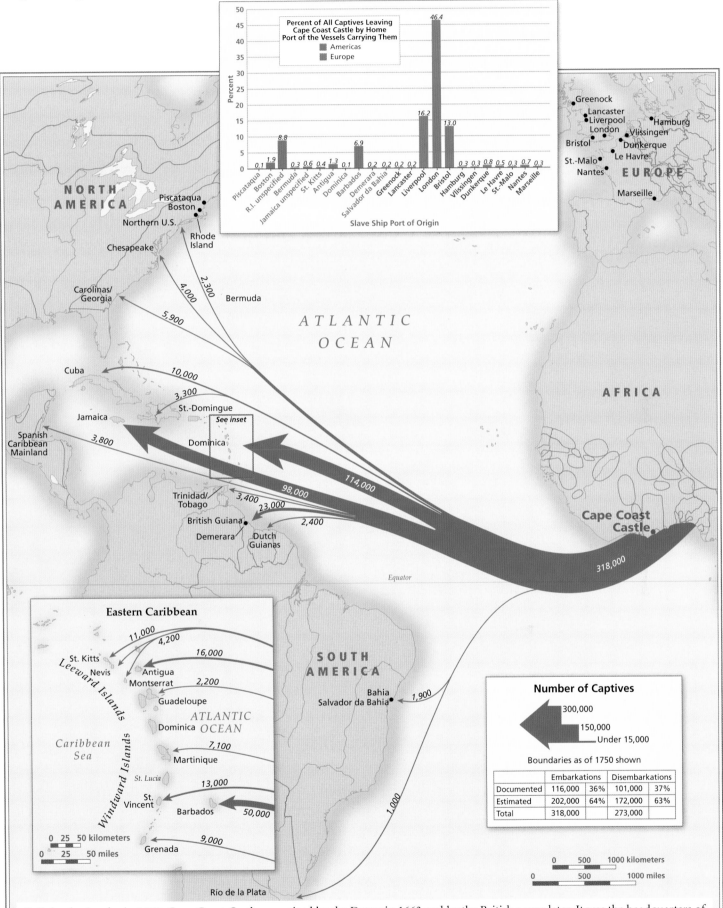

Percent of All Captives Leaving Cape Coast Castle by Home Port of the Vessels Carrying Them

Americas
Europe

Slave Ship Port of Origin

	Embarkations		Disembarkations	
Documented	116,000	36%	101,000	37%
Estimated	202,000	64%	172,000	63%
Total	318,000		273,000	

Number of Captives

300,000
150,000
Under 15,000

Boundaries as of 1750 shown

Built by the Swedes in 1653, Cape Coast Castle was seized by the Danes in 1663 and by the British a year later. It was the headquarters of the English Royal African Company, which for several decades held an English monopoly on slave trading in West Africa, and subsequently became a trading venue for British and other independent traders, mainly ones based in London. Slaves taken from Cape Coast Castle often had first been traded along the coast from other forts; most went to Barbados and Jamaica. Slave trading at Cape Coast Castle ended in 1808, after the British abolished their slave trade. Cape Coast Castle is now one of Ghana's major tourist attractions.

Map 82: Porto-Novo: Destinations of Slaves and Home Ports of Vessels Carrying Them, 1760–1850

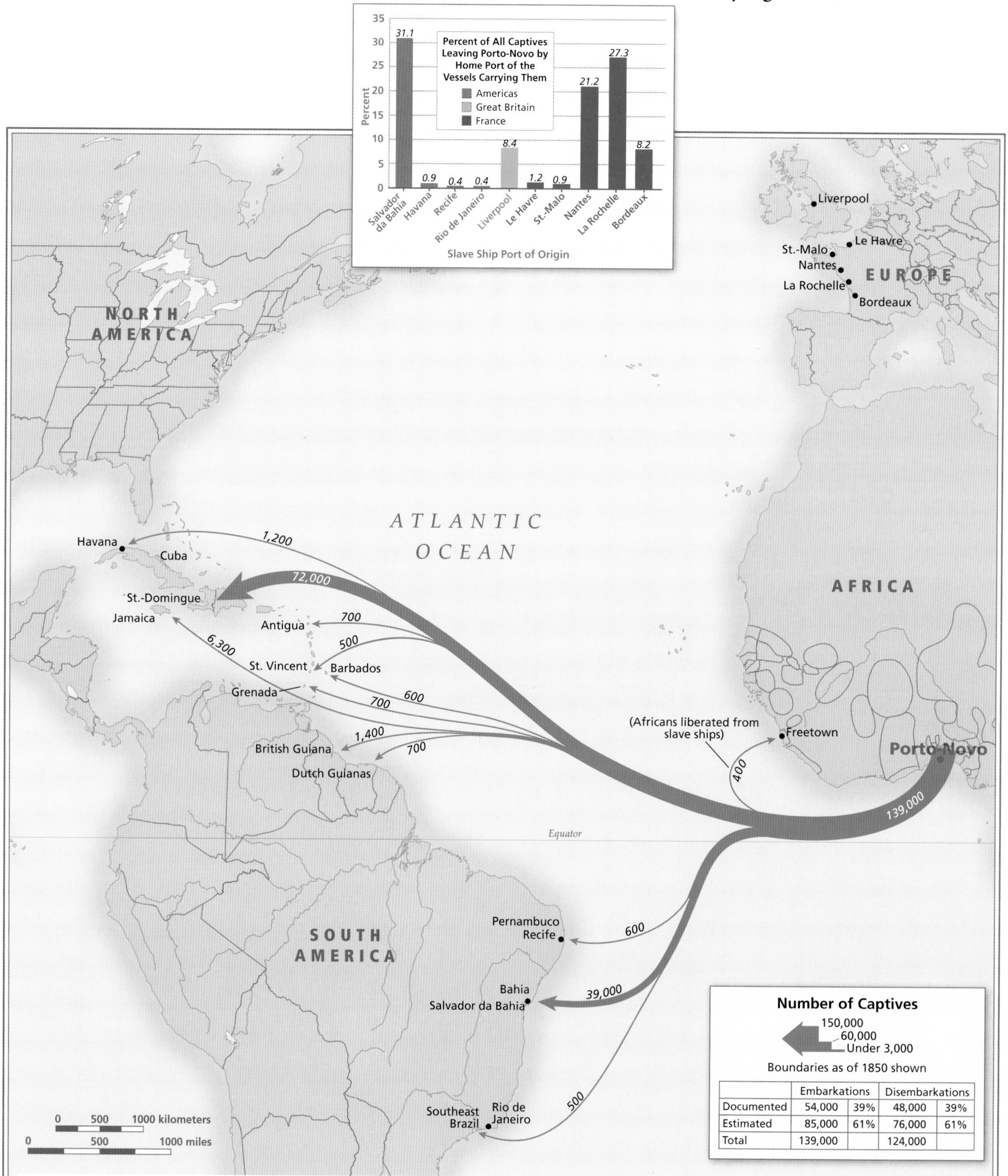

Percent of All Captives Leaving Porto-Novo by Home Port of the Vessels Carrying Them

- Americas
- Great Britain
- France

Salvador da Bahia 31.1 · Havana 0.9 · Recife 0.4 · Rio de Janeiro 0.4 · Liverpool 8.4 · Le Havre 1.2 · St.-Malo 0.9 · Nantes 21.2 · La Rochelle 27.3 · Bordeaux 8.2

Slave Ship Port of Origin

ATLANTIC OCEAN

NORTH AMERICA

EUROPE

Liverpool · St.-Malo · Le Havre · Nantes · La Rochelle · Bordeaux

AFRICA

Havana · Cuba
St.-Domingue
Jamaica
1,200
72,000
6,300
Antigua — 700
St. Vincent · Barbados — 500
Grenada — 700 · 600
British Guiana — 1,400 · 700
Dutch Guianas

(Africans liberated from slave ships) — Freetown · 400

Porto-Novo — 139,000

Equator

Pernambuco Recife — 600

SOUTH AMERICA

Bahia
Salvador da Bahia — 39,000

Southeast Brazil · Rio de Janeiro — 500

Number of Captives

150,000
60,000
Under 3,000

Boundaries as of 1850 shown

	Embarkations		Disembarkations	
Documented	54,000	39%	48,000	39%
Estimated	85,000	61%	76,000	61%
Total	139,000		124,000	

0 500 1000 kilometers
0 500 1000 miles

Porto-Novo was a significant embarkation point for captives only in the last third of the eighteenth century, although it became important again briefly in the mid-nineteenth century. It competed for a time with Ouidah to the west, then Lagos to the east. The great majority of slaves left in vessels originating in Salvador da Bahia, in Brazil, or in French ports, notably Nantes and La Rochelle. Bahia and St.-Domingue, the largest French slave colony, received most of the captives.

Map 83: Political and Ethnolinguistic Boundaries along the Bight of Biafra during the Slave-Trade Era

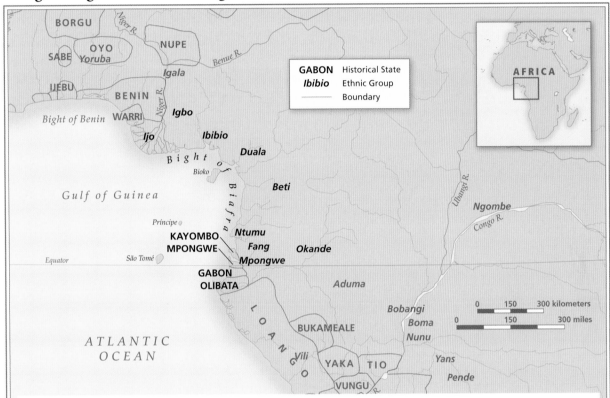

BORGU

Niger R.

OYO
SABE Yoruba

NUPE

Benue R.

Igala

IJEBU

BENIN

Niger R.

Bight of Benin WARRI Igbo

Ijo Ibibio

Bight

Duala

Bioko

GABON	Historical State
Ibibio	Ethnic Group
———	Boundary

AFRICA

Gulf of Guinea

of Biafra

Beti

Ubangi R.

Ngombe

Congo R.

Príncipe

KAYOMBO Ntumu
MPONGWE

Equator São Tomé Fang Okande

Mpongwe

GABON
OLIBATA

Aduma

Bobangi

0   150   300 kilometers

Boma

0   150   300 miles

BUKAMEALE

Nunu

ATLANTIC
OCEAN

L O A N G O

Vili

YAKA TIO

Yans

Pende

VUNGU

For the Bight of Biafra, whose involvement in the slave trade is depicted in maps 84 to 91, only this one map is necessary for the identification of political units and ethnolinguistic labels. The Bight of Biafra hinterland contained no major state formations during the slave-trade era, and there was no major shift in the distribution of languages or peoples in the precolonial period, as far as historians know. The major development in the region was the emergence of the Aro network, a quasi-political unit that exercised some of the powers of a state (particularly judicial) and that helped generate captives for sale and became increasingly influential in the eighteenth century.

Map 84: Slaves Leaving Locations on the Bight of Biafra, 1525–1750

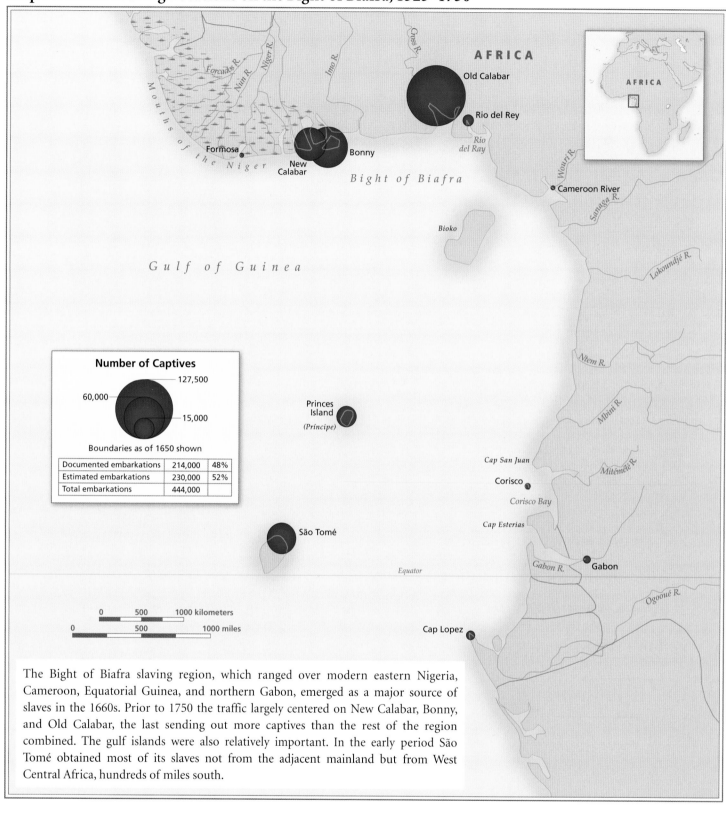

Number of Captives

127,500
60,000
15,000

Boundaries as of 1650 shown

Documented embarkations	214,000	48%
Estimated embarkations	230,000	52%
Total embarkations	444,000	

0   500   1000 kilometers
0   500   1000 miles

The Bight of Biafra slaving region, which ranged over modern eastern Nigeria, Cameroon, Equatorial Guinea, and northern Gabon, emerged as a major source of slaves in the 1660s. Prior to 1750 the traffic largely centered on New Calabar, Bonny, and Old Calabar, the last sending out more captives than the rest of the region combined. The gulf islands were also relatively important. In the early period São Tomé obtained most of its slaves not from the adjacent mainland but from West Central Africa, hundreds of miles south.

Map 85: Slaves Leaving Locations on the Bight of Biafra, 1751–1843

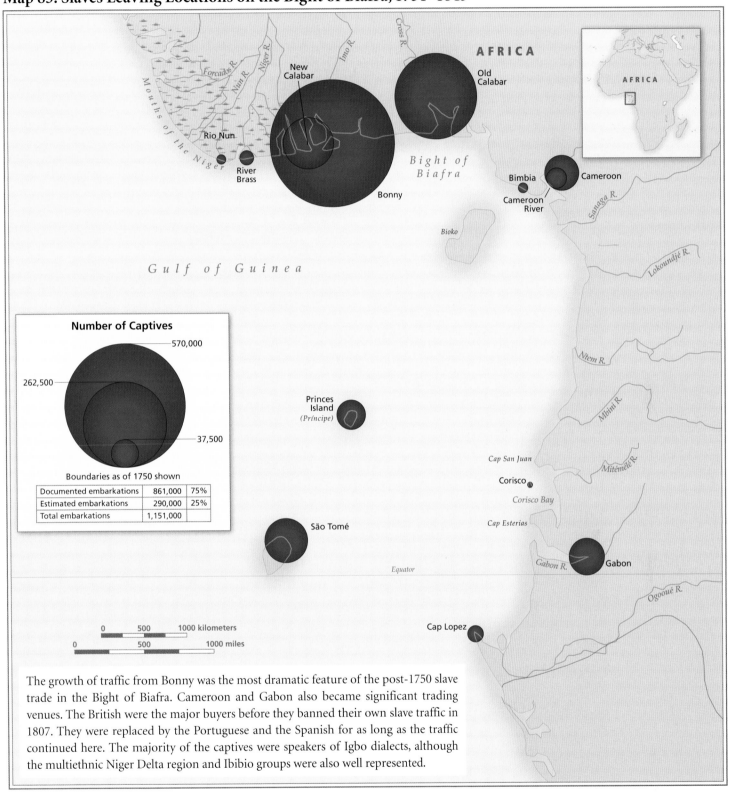

The growth of traffic from Bonny was the most dramatic feature of the post-1750 slave trade in the Bight of Biafra. Cameroon and Gabon also became significant trading venues. The British were the major buyers before they banned their own slave traffic in 1807. They were replaced by the Portuguese and the Spanish for as long as the traffic continued here. The majority of the captives were speakers of Igbo dialects, although the multiethnic Niger Delta region and Ibibio groups were also well represented.

December 22 the 1785
about 6 am in aqua Landing with fine morning so wee have Esin go down
for hughes so I Did send 2 canow for 1500 yams for 150 copper to pay Captin
hughes his so Captin William go Down Captin William carry 169 slave
Captin Hughes carry 480 slave

December 22, 1785
About 6 a.m. at Aqua Landing, a fine morning. Esien went down to
Hughes's ship. I sent 2 canoes with 1,500 yams for 150 coppers to pay Captain
Hughes. Captain Williams went down the river. Captain Williams carried
169 slaves. Captain Hughes carried 480 slaves.

December 23 the 1785
. . . Captin Hughes his go way with 484 slave   Captin William go his way
with 160 slave so I & Esin go on bord Cooper for brek Book for 4 slave
arshbong Duk son com hom for Orroup with slave

December 23, 1785
. . . Captain Hughes went away with 484 slaves. Captain Williams went away
with 160 slaves. I and Esien went on board Cooper's ship to "break book" for
4 slaves. Archibong Duke's son came home from Orroup with slaves.

December 25 the 1785
about 6 am in aqua Landing with fog morning so I go Down with Drehst
man and Captin Fairwether Drehst & Bring his Dinner from Esin   so all
wee to Esin new house Captin Fairwether & Tom Cooper Captin Potter
Duke Ephrim & Coffee Duk & Egbo Young & Esim & I & Eshen Ambo Eyo
Willy Honesty & Ebitim to Dinner for new year and Drink all Day befor
night

December 25, 1785
About 6 a.m. at Aqua Landing, a foggy morning. I went down after dressing
and Captain Fairweather dressed and brought his dinner from Esien. We
all went to Esien [Duke's] new house—Captain Fairweather, Tom Cooper,
Captain Potter, Duke Ephraim, Coffee Duke, Egbo Young [Ofiong], Esien
and I, Esien Ambo, Eyo Willy Honesty, and Ebitim—for New Year's dinner,
and we drank all day until night.

Excerpt from Stephen D. Behrendt, A. J. H. Latham, and David Northrup, *The Diary of
Antera Duke: An Eighteenth-Century African Slave Trader* (Oxford: Oxford University Press,
with the assistance of the International African Institute, 2010), pp. 170–171. Published with
permission of Oxford University Press, Inc. "Coppers" refers to the local unit of account. To
"break book" is to negotiate a trade.

Map 86: Old Calabar: Destinations of Slaves and Home Ports of Vessels Carrying Them, 1622–1807

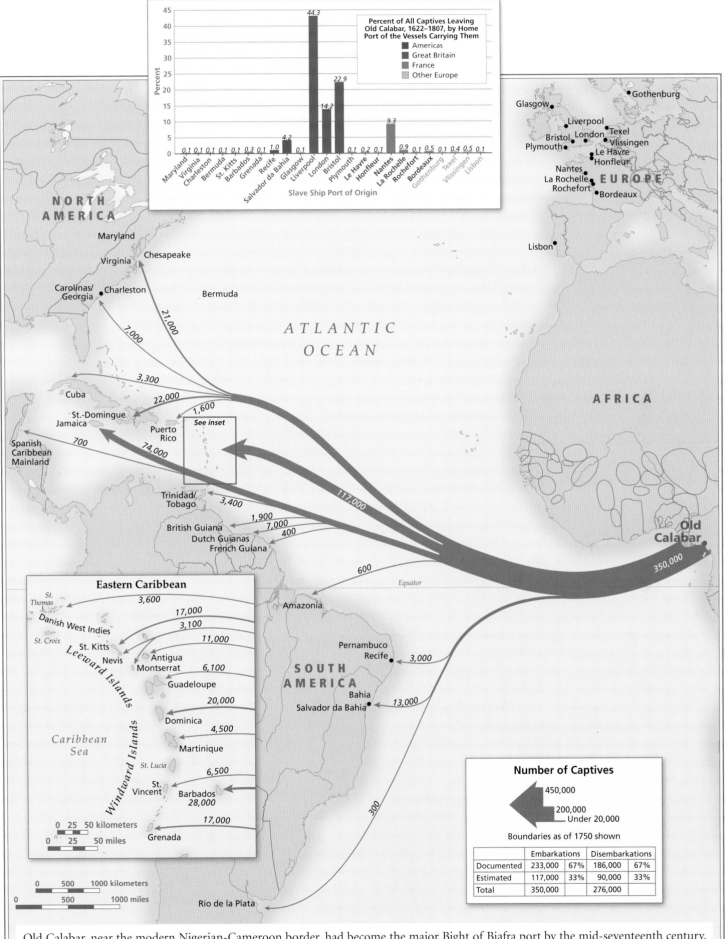

Old Calabar, near the modern Nigerian-Cameroon border, had become the major Bight of Biafra port by the mid-seventeenth century. Major trading houses controlled by African Efik traders dominated this port. Ships from British ports (first London, then Bristol, and then Liverpool) carried the most slaves from Old Calabar before 1808, just as they did from Bonny (see map 90), ensuring that the vast majority of enslaved Africans leaving the Bight of Biafra disembarked in British America.

Map 87: Old Calabar: Destinations of Slaves and Home Ports of Vessels Carrying Them, 1808–1843

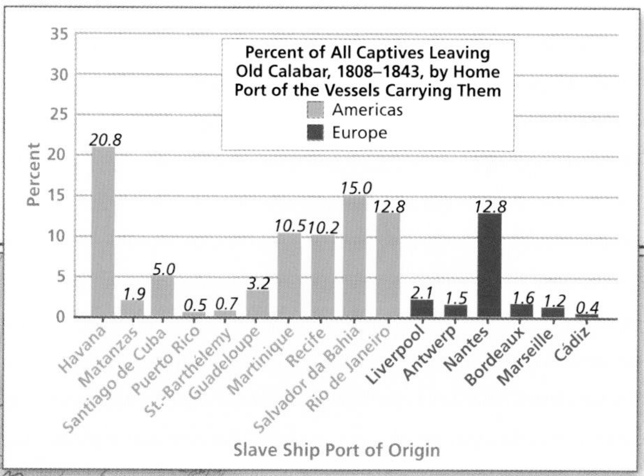

Percent of All Captives Leaving Old Calabar, 1808–1843, by Home Port of the Vessels Carrying Them

Americas: Havana 20.8, Matanzas 1.9, Santiago de Cuba 5.0, Puerto Rico 0.5, St-Barthélemy 0.7, Guadeloupe 3.2, Martinique 10.5, Recife 10.2, Salvador da Bahia 15.0, Rio de Janeiro 12.8

Europe: Liverpool 2.1, Antwerp 1.5, Nantes 12.8, Bordeaux 1.6, Marseille 1.2, Cádiz 0.4

Slave Ship Port of Origin

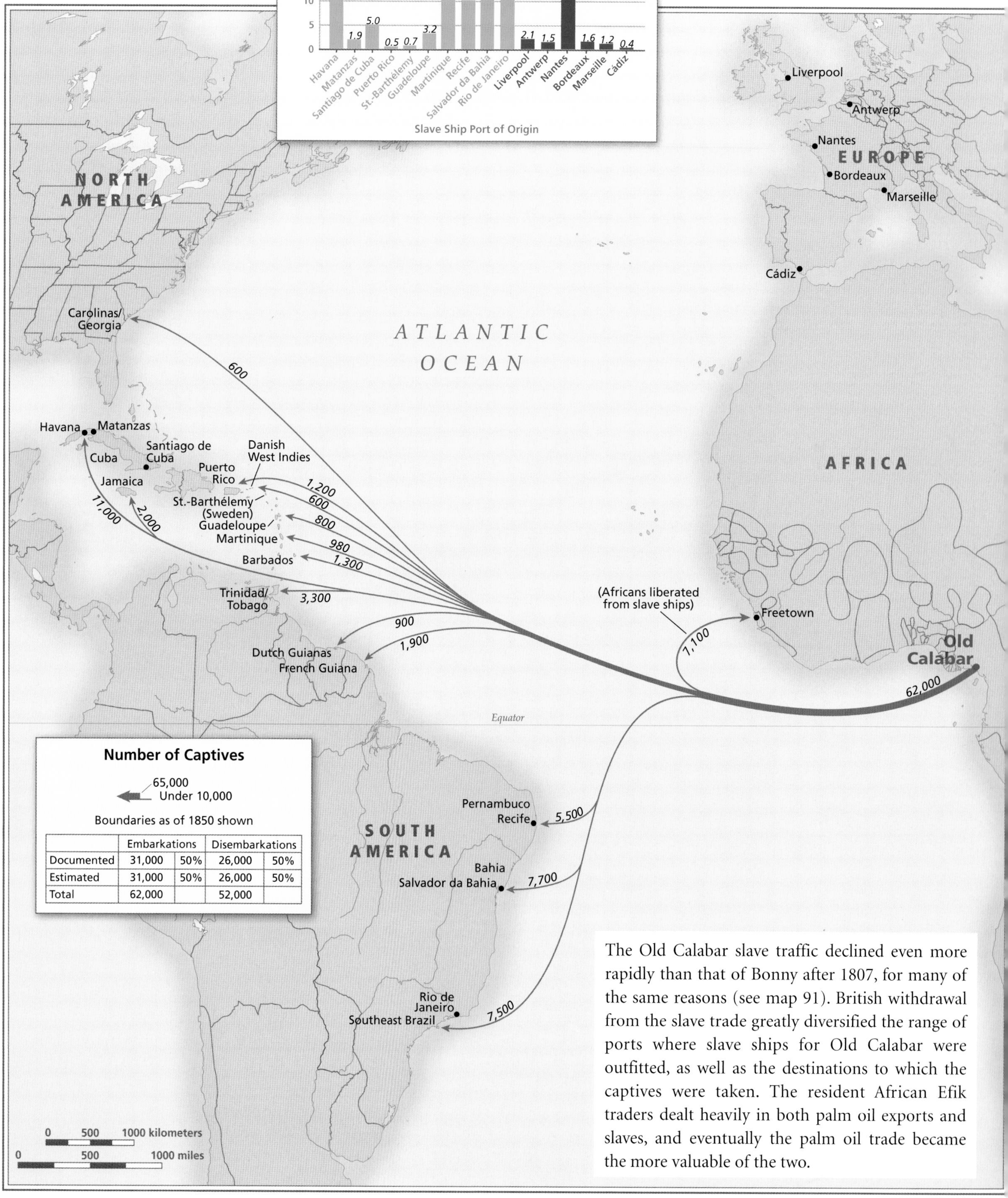

Number of Captives

65,000 → Under 10,000

Boundaries as of 1850 shown

	Embarkations		Disembarkations	
Documented	31,000	50%	26,000	50%
Estimated	31,000	50%	26,000	50%
Total	62,000		52,000	

The Old Calabar slave traffic declined even more rapidly than that of Bonny after 1807, for many of the same reasons (see map 91). British withdrawal from the slave trade greatly diversified the range of ports where slave ships for Old Calabar were outfitted, as well as the destinations to which the captives were taken. The resident African Efik traders dealt heavily in both palm oil exports and slaves, and eventually the palm oil trade became the more valuable of the two.

Map 88: New Calabar: Destinations of Slaves and Home Ports of Vessels Carrying Them, 1652–1851

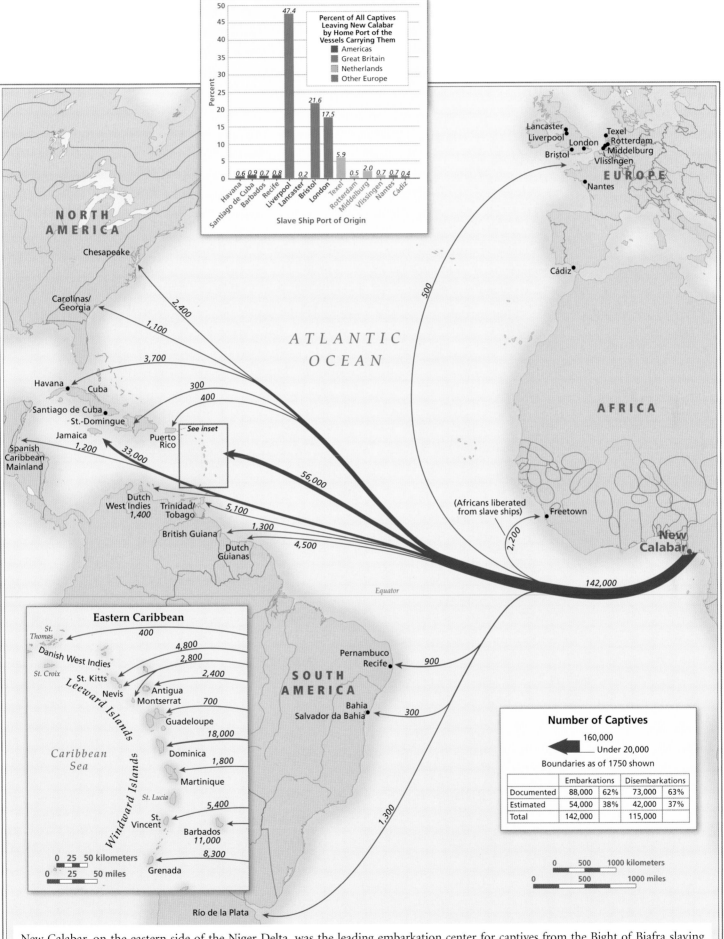

New Calabar, on the eastern side of the Niger Delta, was the leading embarkation center for captives from the Bight of Biafra slaving region before 1700, but it was thereafter eclipsed by Old Calabar and Bonny (see maps 86–87, 90–91). British vessels dominated the slave traffic from the port, and a large proportion of slaves from New Calabar disembarked in the Caribbean islands coming under British rule between 1763 and 1807. New Calabar's trade declined rapidly after British withdrawal from the slave trade.

Map 89: Cameroon: Destinations of Slaves and Home Ports of Vessels Carrying Them, 1658–1838

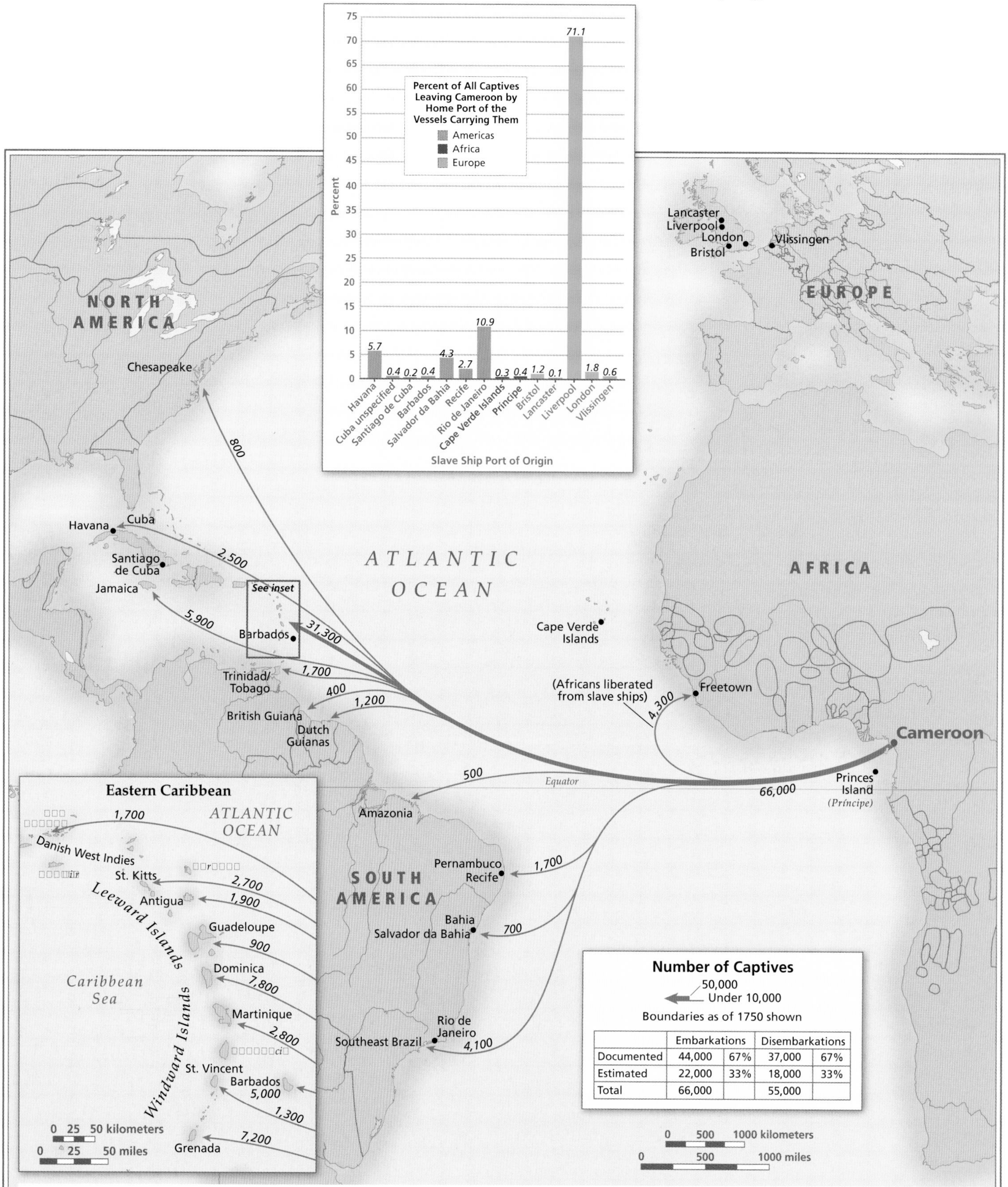

Percent of All Captives Leaving Cameroon by Home Port of the Vessels Carrying Them

- Americas
- Africa
- Europe

Slave Ship Port of Origin

Number of Captives

50,000
Under 10,000

Boundaries as of 1750 shown

	Embarkations		Disembarkations	
Documented	44,000	67%	37,000	67%
Estimated	22,000	33%	18,000	33%
Total	66,000		55,000	

Cameroon was the smallest of the major embarkation points in the Bight of Biafra and the last to engage in the slave trade in a significant fashion. Apart from a single voyage recorded in 1658, departures did not begin until the 1760s, when the overall slave traffic was approaching its peak, and while departures of slaves continued into the nineteenth century, the highest volumes – about 2,000 slaves a year – were recorded in the early 1770s. British slave traders predominated before 1808 and Brazilians thereafter. In the later period at least, most captives originated in the Cameroon Highlands (see map 133).

By capt. Wright of the Endeavour, from the Coast of Guinea, we had the following account of the loss of the Marlborough, capt. Codd, of Bristol, by an insurrection of the Negroes the beginning of October last [1752]. Capt. Codd having indulged 28 Gold-coast Negroes with their liberty on deck to assist in navigating the ship, they behaved for some time in a very tractable, civil manner. But on the 3d day after he sailed from the bar of Bonny, while most of the crew were below cleaning the rooms, and none but the captain and two white men, armed with cutlasses, left above to take care of the ship, all of a sudden the Negroes on deck snatched the arms from them, wounded the captain, and forced him up the fore-shrouds, where they shot him dead. The rest of the Negroes securing the quarter deck and small arms, became soon masters of the ship, and spent the rest of the day in most cruelly butchering the crew (who were in number 35) except the boatswain and cabin-boy, whom they saved to conduct the ship back again; which they did after 8 days and came to an anchor within the bar of Bonny. About the same time the Hawk, capt. Jones, of Bristol, arrived at that place, and hearing of the affair, bore down on her, with an intent to re-take her; but the Negroes were so expert at the great guns and small-arms, that they soon repelled him. After putting the Bite Negroes ashore that chose it, in number 270, the remainder, consisting of 150, weighed anchor, set their sails, and stood to sea, with intent, as is supposed, to go to their own country, tho' the undertaking was extremely hazardous, as they had no one to navigate the ship, the boatswain having jumped overboard the night before they sailed, and got to the hawk; and it is supposed, that on his escape, the poor cabin-boy fell a sacrifice to their revenge.

The London Magazine: or, Gentleman's Monthly Intelligencer [commonly known as *Gentleman's Magazine*], vol. 22 (February 1753): 91.

Map 90: Bonny: Destinations of Slaves and Home Ports of Vessels Carrying Them, 1659–1807

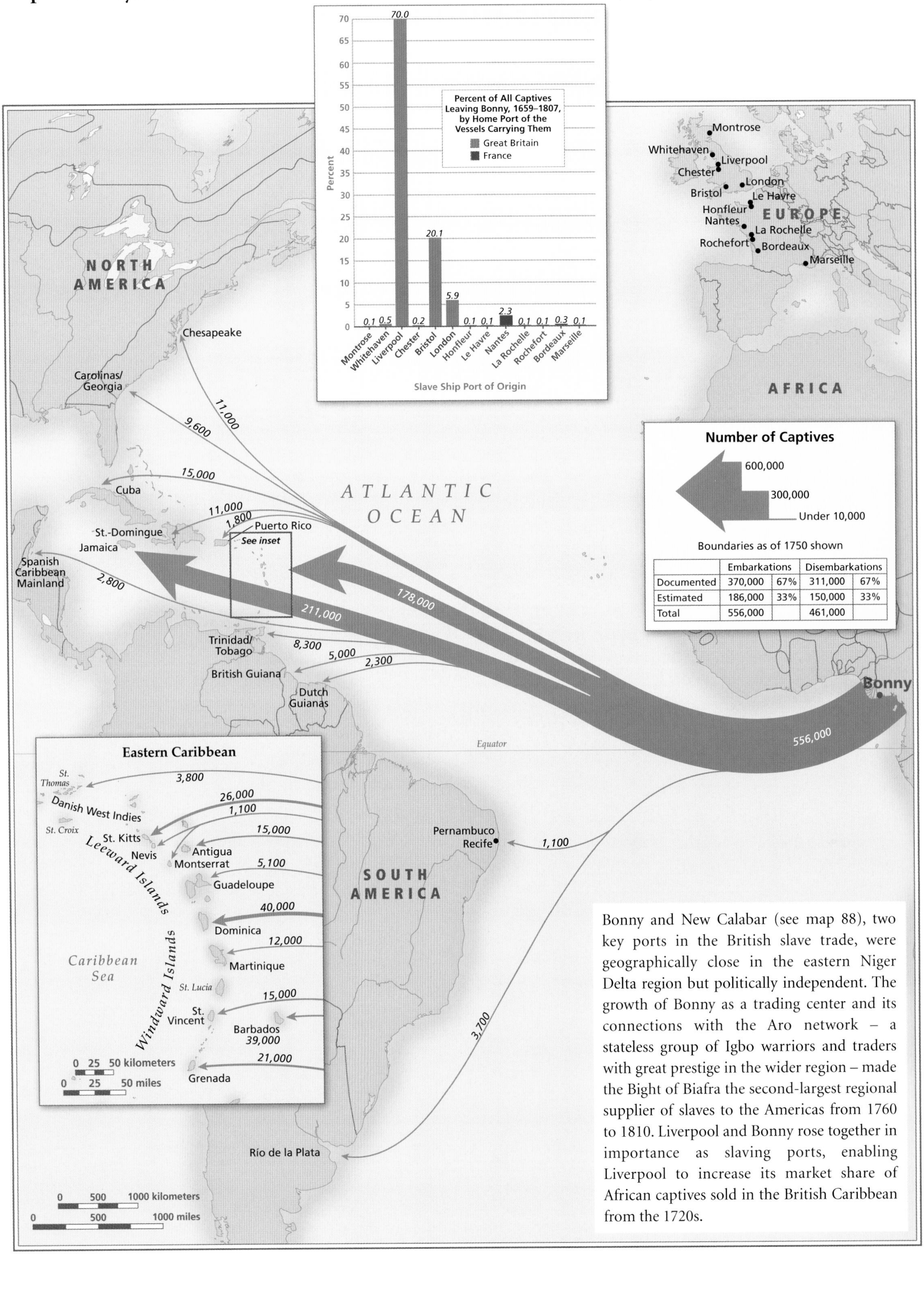

Percent of All Captives Leaving Bonny, 1659–1807, by Home Port of the Vessels Carrying Them
- Great Britain
- France

Percent (y-axis)

Values by port:
- Montrose 0.1
- Whitehaven 0.5
- Liverpool 70.0
- Chester 0.2
- Bristol 20.1
- London 5.9
- Honfleur 0.1
- Le Havre 0.1
- Nantes 2.3
- La Rochelle 0.1
- Rochefort 0.1
- Bordeaux 0.3
- Marseille 0.1

Slave Ship Port of Origin

NORTH AMERICA

EUROPE

Montrose
Whitehaven
Liverpool
Chester
London
Bristol
Le Havre
Honfleur
Nantes
La Rochelle
Rochefort
Bordeaux
Marseille

AFRICA

ATLANTIC OCEAN

Number of Captives

600,000
300,000
Under 10,000

Boundaries as of 1750 shown

	Embarkations		Disembarkations	
Documented	370,000	67%	311,000	67%
Estimated	186,000	33%	150,000	33%
Total	556,000		461,000	

Chesapeake
Carolinas/Georgia 11,000
9,600
Cuba 15,000
11,000
St.-Domingue 1,800
Puerto Rico
See inset
Jamaica
Spanish Caribbean Mainland 2,800
211,000
178,000
Trinidad/Tobago 8,300
British Guiana 5,000
Dutch Guianas 2,300

Bonny
556,000

Equator

Pernambuco Recife 1,100

SOUTH AMERICA

Eastern Caribbean

St. Thomas 3,800
Danish West Indies 26,000
St. Croix 1,100
St. Kitts 15,000
Nevis
Antigua
Montserrat 5,100
Guadeloupe 40,000
Dominica 12,000
Martinique
St. Lucia 15,000
St. Vincent
Barbados 39,000
Grenada 21,000

Leeward Islands
Windward Islands
Caribbean Sea

0 25 50 kilometers
0 25 50 miles

3,700

Río de la Plata

0 500 1000 kilometers
0 500 1000 miles

Bonny and New Calabar (see map 88), two key ports in the British slave trade, were geographically close in the eastern Niger Delta region but politically independent. The growth of Bonny as a trading center and its connections with the Aro network – a stateless group of Igbo warriors and traders with great prestige in the wider region – made the Bight of Biafra the second-largest regional supplier of slaves to the Americas from 1760 to 1810. Liverpool and Bonny rose together in importance as slaving ports, enabling Liverpool to increase its market share of African captives sold in the British Caribbean from the 1720s.

Map 91: Bonny: Destinations of Slaves and Home Ports of Vessels Carrying Them, 1808–1838

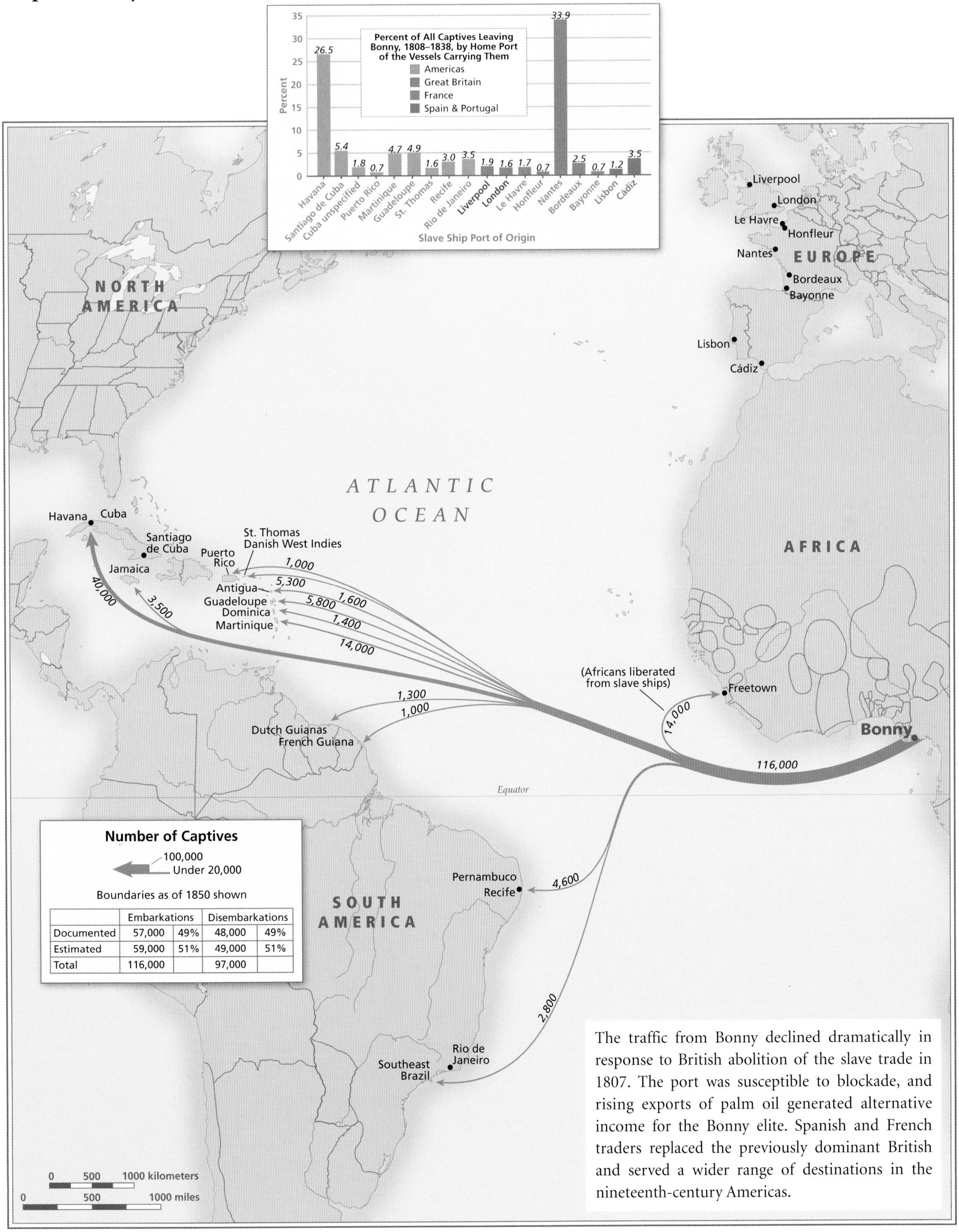

Percent of All Captives Leaving Bonny, 1808–1838, by Home Port of the Vessels Carrying Them

- Americas
- Great Britain
- France
- Spain & Portugal

(Bar chart, Percent vs. Slave Ship Port of Origin)

Port	Percent
Havana	26.5
Santiago de Cuba	5.4
Cuba unspecified	1.8
Puerto Rico	0.7
Martinique	4.7
Guadeloupe	4.9
St. Thomas	1.6
Recife	3.0
Rio de Janeiro	3.5
Liverpool	1.9
London	1.6
Le Havre	1.7
Honfleur	0.7
Nantes	33.9
Bordeaux	2.5
Bayonne	0.7
Lisbon	1.2
Cádiz	3.5

NORTH AMERICA

ATLANTIC OCEAN

EUROPE
Liverpool
London
Le Havre
Honfleur
Nantes
Bordeaux
Bayonne
Lisbon
Cádiz

AFRICA

Havana — Cuba
Santiago de Cuba
Puerto Rico
Jamaica
St. Thomas Danish West Indies
Antigua
Guadeloupe
Dominica
Martinique

40,000
3,500
1,000
5,300
1,600
5,800
1,400
14,000
1,300
1,000

Dutch Guianas
French Guiana

(Africans liberated from slave ships)
14,000
Freetown

Bonny
116,000

Equator

Number of Captives

← 100,000
Under 20,000

Boundaries as of 1850 shown

	Embarkations		Disembarkations	
Documented	57,000	49%	48,000	49%
Estimated	59,000	51%	49,000	51%
Total	116,000		97,000	

SOUTH AMERICA

Pernambuco
Recife
4,600

2,800

Rio de Janeiro
Southeast Brazil

0   500   1000 kilometers
0   500   1000 miles

The traffic from Bonny declined dramatically in response to British abolition of the slave trade in 1807. The port was susceptible to blockade, and rising exports of palm oil generated alternative income for the Bonny elite. Spanish and French traders replaced the previously dominant British and served a wider range of destinations in the nineteenth-century Americas.

Maps 92, 93, and 94: Political and Ethnolinguistic Boundaries of West Central Africa, 1526–1867

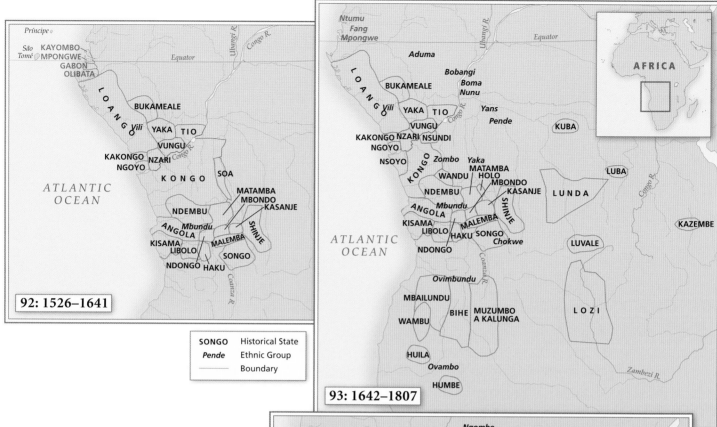

92: 1526–1641

SONGO	Historical State
Pende	Ethnic Group
——	Boundary

93: 1642–1807

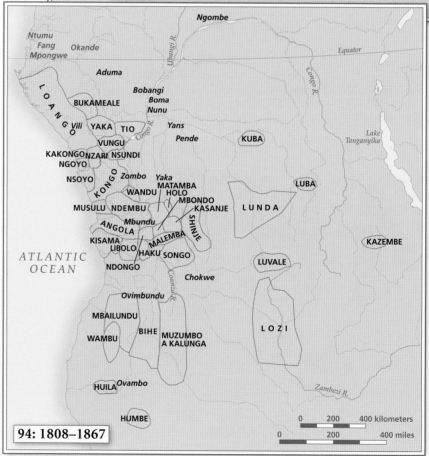

94: 1808–1867

These three maps provide background information for maps 95 to 106. West Central Africa contained some significant state formations and was thus more like the Bight of Benin than the rest of western Africa. The first captives to be sent overseas came from the Kingdom of Kongo in the early sixteenth century. Kongo captives were joined later in the sixteenth century by Ngolas (named for the Ngola or Ndongo Kingdom of the Coanza River, which enters the Atlantic near Luanda). The Vili kingdoms north of the Congo River, the most important of which was Loango, emerged as major slave-trading centers in the eighteenth century; the source of the slaves was undoubtedly the vast Congo River basin. Further south, the Portuguese, who had a continuous political presence in the area, drew many of their captives from marauding trading chiefs whose ultimate sources were often the Ovimbundu people or those living in the Lunda Confederacy. So many slaves came from West Central Africa that slaves were mostly just called Congos in the Americas, but they were in fact drawn from a wide range of ethnolinguistic groups.

Map 95: Slaves Leaving Locations in West Central Africa, 1526–1641

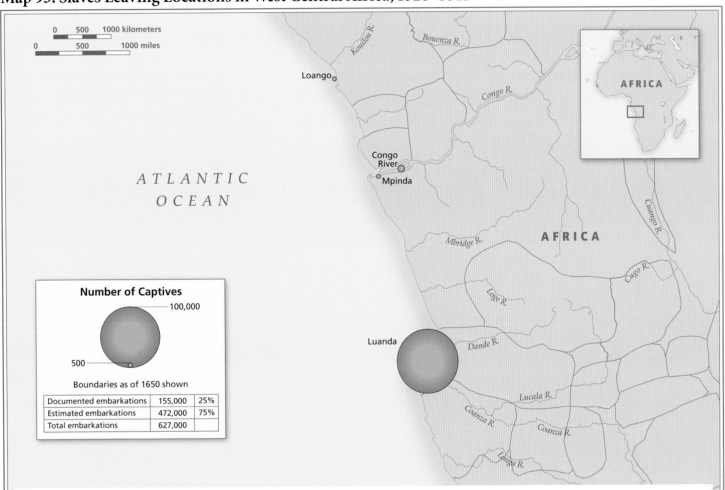

Number of Captives		
Documented embarkations	155,000	25%
Estimated embarkations	472,000	75%
Total embarkations	627,000	

Boundaries as of 1650 shown

Almost all the slaves from West Central Africa left from ports located in modern Angola and the Democratic Republic of the Congo. In the sixteenth century, captives were taken first to São Tomé (see maps 3 and 84) before being transshipped to the Americas. The first vessels sailing directly for the Americas left from the Congo River region, but a decade or so after the founding of Luanda in 1575, this new Portuguese settlement south of the Congo had come to almost monopolize traffic from the region.

Map 96: Slaves Leaving Locations in West Central Africa, 1642–1807

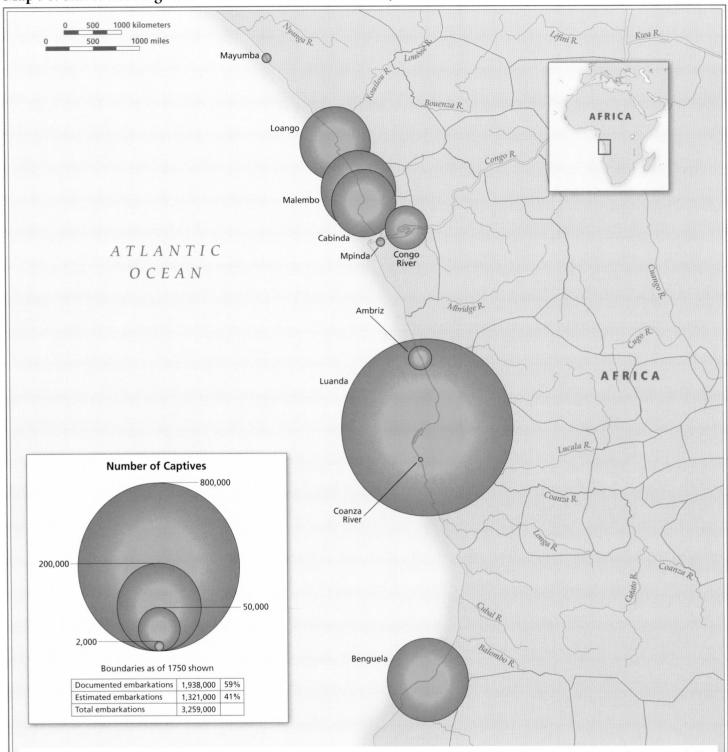

Number of Captives

800,000
200,000
50,000
2,000

Boundaries as of 1750 shown

Documented embarkations	1,938,000	59%
Estimated embarkations	1,321,000	41%
Total embarkations	3,259,000	

Although the slave trade expanded sevenfold overall between the 1640s and 1800 as regions outside West Central Africa entered the business, West Central Africa's dominance in supplying slaves to the Americas eroded only slightly. Trading volume increased at Luanda, but new ports north of the Congo River became significant in the 1670s, and Benguela, to the south, grew rapidly after 1700. The Portuguese controlled Luanda and Benguela, but points north of Luanda remained under African control and were open to slave traders of all nationalities.

Map 97: Slaves Leaving Locations in West Central Africa, 1808–1867

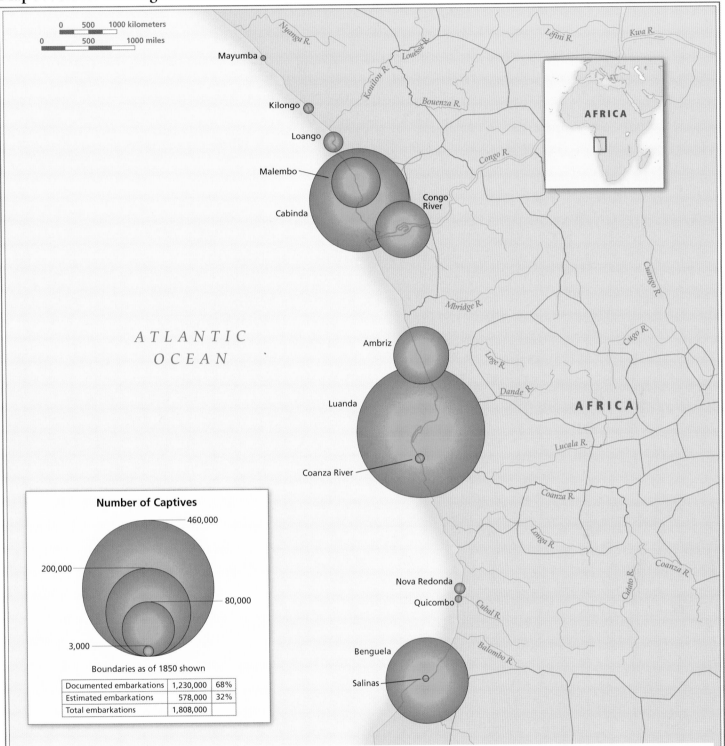

Number of Captives

460,000
200,000
80,000
3,000

Boundaries as of 1850 shown

Documented embarkations	1,230,000	68%
Estimated embarkations	578,000	32%
Total embarkations	1,808,000	

Luanda remained the leading embarkation center for captives shipped from West Central Africa in the first half of the nineteenth century as slave departures from the region continued at high levels. But ports near the mouth of the Congo River, notably Cabinda, eventually displaced Luanda. After 1835, when the Portuguese began to enforce restrictions, the slave trade was carried on less openly in Luanda, although Luanda merchants continued to organize and finance voyages that took on slaves at other locations.

[T]he slaves lie in two rows, one above the other, and as close together as they can be crouded. . . .

The planks, or deals, contract some dampness more or less, either from the deck being so often wash'd to keep it clean and sweet, or from the rain that gets in now and then through the scuttles or other openings, and even from the very sweat of the slaves; which being so crouded in a low place, is perpetual, and occasions many distempers, or at best great inconveniences dangerous to their health. . . .

It has been observ'd before, that some slaves fancy they are carry'd to be eaten, which make them desperate; and others are so on account of their captivity: so that if care be not taken, they will mutiny and destroy the ship's crue in hopes to get away.

To prevent such misfortunes, we used to visit them daily, narrowly searching every corner between decks, to see whether they have not found means, to gather any pieces of iron, or wood, or knives, about the ship, notwithstanding the great care we take not to leave any tools or nails, or other things in the way: which, however cannot be always so exactly observ'd, where so many people are in the narrow compass of a ship.

We cause as many of our men as is convenient to lie in the quarter-deck and gun-room, and our principal officers in the great cabin, where we keep all our small arms in a readiness, with sentinels constantly at the doors and avenues to it; being thus ready to disappoint any attempts our slaves might make on a sudden.

These precautions contribute very much to keep them in awe; and if all those who carry slaves duly observ'd them, we should not hear of so many revolts as have happen'd.

Excerpt from Jean Barbot, *An Abstract of a Voyage to Congo River, or the Zair, and to Cabinde, in the Year 1700,* in Awnsham Churchill and John Churchill, eds., *A Collection of Voyages and Travels,* 6 vols. (London: Henry Linton and John Osborn, 1746), vol. 5, pp. 367–370.

Map 98: The Congo River: Destinations of Slaves and Home Ports of Vessels Carrying Them, 1534–1862

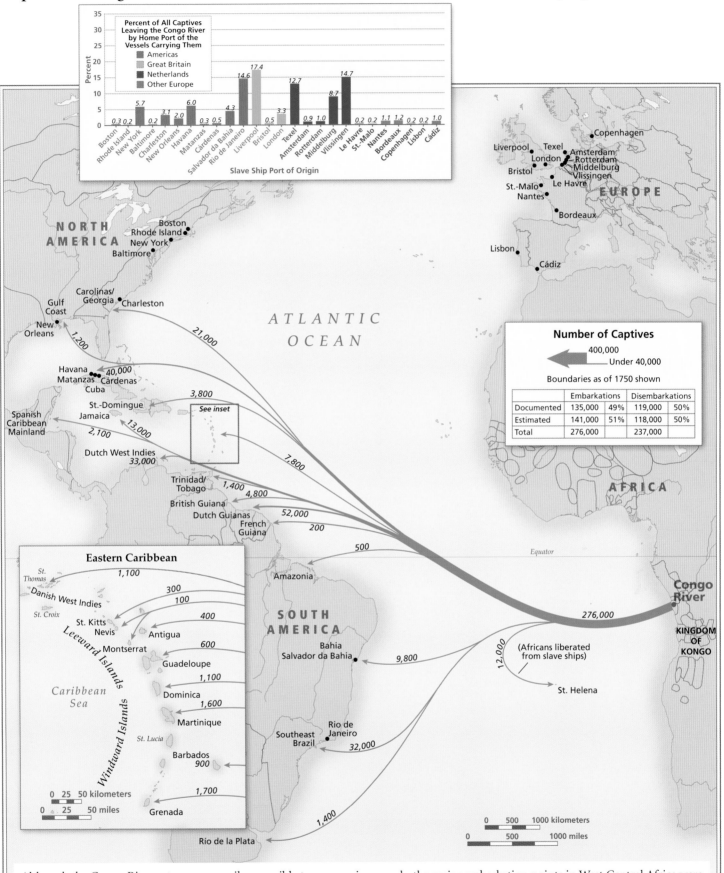

Percent of All Captives Leaving the Congo River by Home Port of the Vessels Carrying Them

- Americas
- Great Britain
- Netherlands
- Other Europe

Boston 0.3, Rhode Island 0.2, New York 5.7, Baltimore 0.2, Charleston 3.1, New Orleans 2.0, Havana 6.0, Matanzas 0.3, Cárdenas 0.5, Salvador da Bahia 4.3, Rio de Janeiro 14.6, Liverpool 17.4, Bristol 0.5, London 3.3, Texel 12.7, Amsterdam 0.9, Rotterdam 1.0, Middelburg 8.7, Vlissingen 14.7, Le Havre 0.2, St.-Malo 0.2, Nantes 1.1, Bordeaux 1.2, Copenhagen 0.2, Lisbon 0.2, Cádiz 1.0

Slave Ship Port of Origin

Number of Captives

400,000
Under 40,000

Boundaries as of 1750 shown

	Embarkations		Disembarkations	
Documented	135,000	49%	119,000	50%
Estimated	141,000	51%	118,000	50%
Total	276,000		237,000	

Eastern Caribbean

Although the Congo River estuary was easily accessible to oceangoing vessels, the major embarkation points in West Central Africa were usually located north and south of the river. The relative importance of this area in the transatlantic slave trade was greatest at the beginning and at the very end of the slave-trade era. Slaves from the powerful African Kingdom of Kongo embarked on the southern bank of the lower Congo in the sixteenth century. The Portuguese were the only slave traders initially, but Dutch and British traders developed trading ties with the Congo River region in the mid and late eighteenth century. Thereafter, traders based in the United States, Brazil, and Cuba helped sustain a steady flow of slaves until the trade ended.

Map 99: Loango: Destinations of Slaves and Home Ports of Vessels Carrying Them, 1556–1807

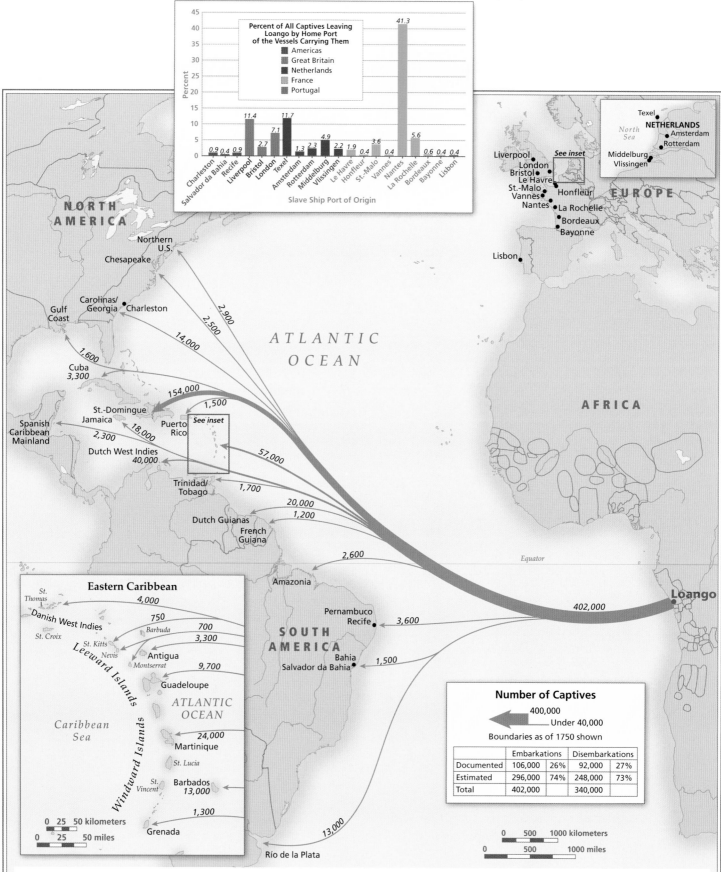

Records of a continuing trade from Loango date from the 1660s. The port was controlled by Vili traders. As with many coastal groups involved in the slave trade, Vili traders acted as brokers between the European slave vessels and the suppliers of captives. Almost all slave vessels trading in Loango originated in British, Dutch, and French ports, with the Dutch by far the major traders in the seventeenth century, and the French the dominant traders after 1750. Although slaves from Loango disembarked in the Caribbean colonies of all three nations, St.-Domingue was the largest single destination. Loango was heavily affected by the withdrawal of Britain from the slave trade; very few captives left from the port after 1807.

Map 100: Luanda: Destinations of Slaves and Home Ports of Vessels Carrying Them, 1582–1850

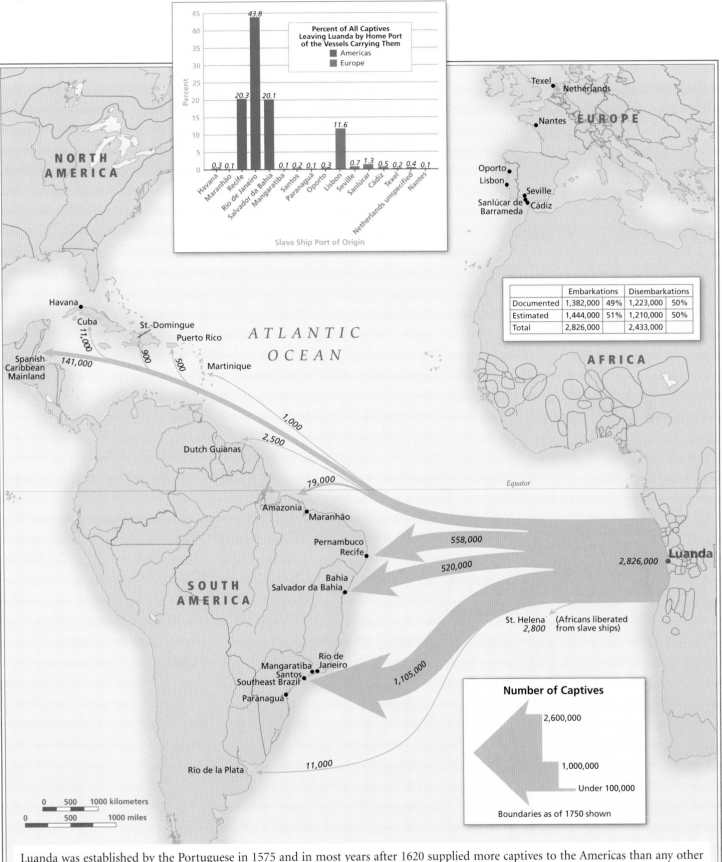

Percent of All Captives Leaving Luanda by Home Port of the Vessels Carrying Them
- Americas
- Europe

Percent — Slave Ship Port of Origin

Port	Percent
Havana	0.3
Maranhão	0.1
Recife	43.8
Rio de Janeiro	20.3
Salvador da Bahia	20.1
Mangaratiba	0.1
Santos	0.2
Paranaguá	0.1
Oporto	0.3
Lisbon	11.6
Seville	0.7
Sanlúcar	1.3
Cádiz	0.5
Texel	0.2
Netherlands unspecified	0.4
Nantes	0.1

	Embarkations		Disembarkations	
Documented	1,382,000	49%	1,223,000	50%
Estimated	1,444,000	51%	1,210,000	50%
Total	2,826,000		2,433,000	

Number of Captives
- 2,600,000
- 1,000,000
- Under 100,000

Boundaries as of 1750 shown

Luanda was established by the Portuguese in 1575 and in most years after 1620 supplied more captives to the Americas than any other location in sub-Saharan Africa. Yet in Luanda, unlike in other major slaving ports, the basic pattern of traffic did not change much over three centuries. Except during a very short Dutch occupation in the 1640s, Portuguese (and, later, Brazilian) vessels had exclusive access to the port, and until 1640 almost all slaves went to Brazil or Spanish America. Vessels from Lisbon dominated the slave trade from Luanda at first, but by the early seventeenth century Recife, then Salvador da Bahia, and ultimately Rio de Janeiro accounted for the great majority of captives shipped from the port. The Bantu-speaking Lunda Empire, east of Luanda, is thought to have been central to the supply of slaves since it doubled in size by way of conquest between 1650 and 1850.

1 February 1759 at Malemba from the merchant Banse 3 male slaves @ 15 pieces [local currency] per slave

	Pieces	Guilders		
6 8lbs Barrels of Gunpowder @ 4 fl[orins] [guilders]	6	24,		
3 pcs Soldiers guns @ 3, 13	3	10,	19	
3 pcs Blue Guinea stuffs @ 11, 5	9	33,	15	
1 pc Large Cavalry Chelloes @ 8, 15	2.5	8,	15	
2 pcs Long English nicanes @ 9, 10	4	19,		
1 pc "Compy" [i.e., Dutch company] nicanese @ 6, 7, 8	2	6,	7,	8
3 pcs East India Tapseils @ 9	6	27,		
2 pcs Blue Bejutapauts @ 9, 5	5	18,	10	
3 [pieces?]/17 ells Blue Bays @ 48.5 [stuivers]	1	2,	8,	8
5/16 ells Blue Cloth @ 48 [stuivers]	0.5		15	
2 "kelder" [cauldrons?] 5–6 kan [quarts or jugs] malt @ 2, 15	2	5,	10	
Packages iron knives, 6 doz[en] @ 14 [stuivers per dozen]	1.5	4,	4	
6 [dozen?] Glass Tankards @ 6 [stuivers]	1	1,	16	
1 [dozen?] Earthenware Pots @ 8 [stuivers], 8 [penningen]	1.5	1,	5,	8
	45	164,	5,	8

Excerpt from Journal of Daily Trade Negotiations by Captain David Mulders, on behalf of Ship Vrouw Johanna Cores, 1759, Middelburgshe Commercie Compagnie, item 1224, Middelburg Archives, The Netherlands. Translated by Filipa da Silva Ribeiro and Stacey Sommerdyk. In the table the price "6, 7, 8" means 6 guilders, 7 stuivers, and 8 penningen. There are 20 stuivers per guilder and 16 penningen per stuiver. Many of the products—Guinea stuffs, chelloes, nicanese, tapseils, bejutapauts, and bays—are textiles, mostly from the East Indies. The ell is a unit of length; it varied even within the Netherlands but was equivalent to around twenty-seven inches. A jug was equivalent to a quart (a quarter gallon).

Map 101: Malembo: Destinations of Slaves and Home Ports of Vessels Carrying Them, 1660–1807

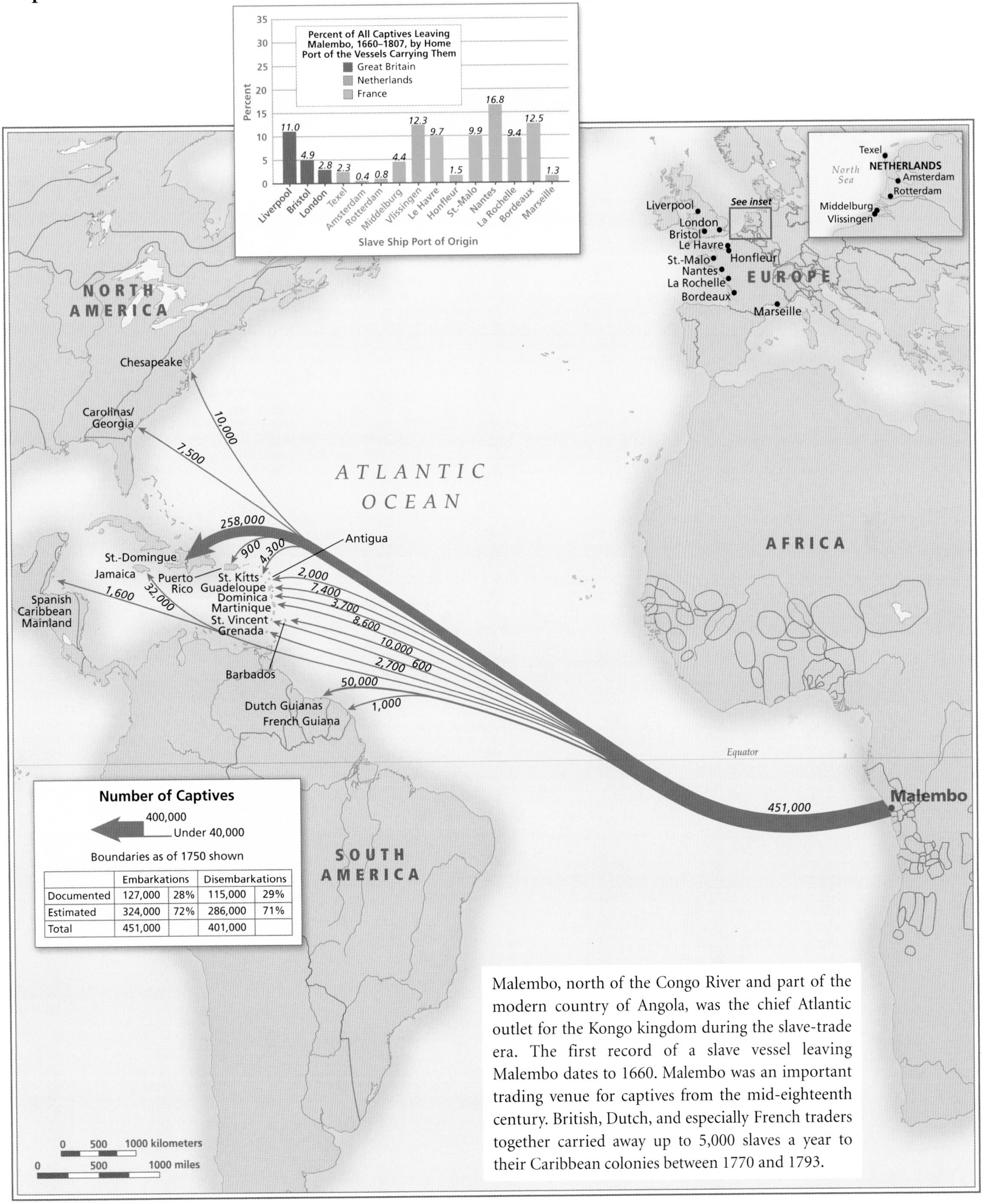

Percent of All Captives Leaving Malembo, 1660–1807, by Home Port of the Vessels Carrying Them
- Great Britain
- Netherlands
- France

Liverpool 11.0, Bristol 4.9, London 2.8, Texel 2.3, Amsterdam 0.4, Rotterdam 0.8, Middelburg 4.4, Vlissingen 12.3, Le Havre 9.7, Honfleur 1.5, St.-Malo 9.9, Nantes 16.8, La Rochelle 9.4, Bordeaux 12.5, Marseille 1.3

Slave Ship Port of Origin

Number of Captives

400,000 — Under 40,000

Boundaries as of 1750 shown

	Embarkations		Disembarkations	
Documented	127,000	28%	115,000	29%
Estimated	324,000	72%	286,000	71%
Total	451,000		401,000	

Malembo, north of the Congo River and part of the modern country of Angola, was the chief Atlantic outlet for the Kongo kingdom during the slave-trade era. The first record of a slave vessel leaving Malembo dates to 1660. Malembo was an important trading venue for captives from the mid-eighteenth century. British, Dutch, and especially French traders together carried away up to 5,000 slaves a year to their Caribbean colonies between 1770 and 1793.

Map 102: Malembo: Destinations of Slaves and Home Ports of Vessels Carrying Them, 1808–1861

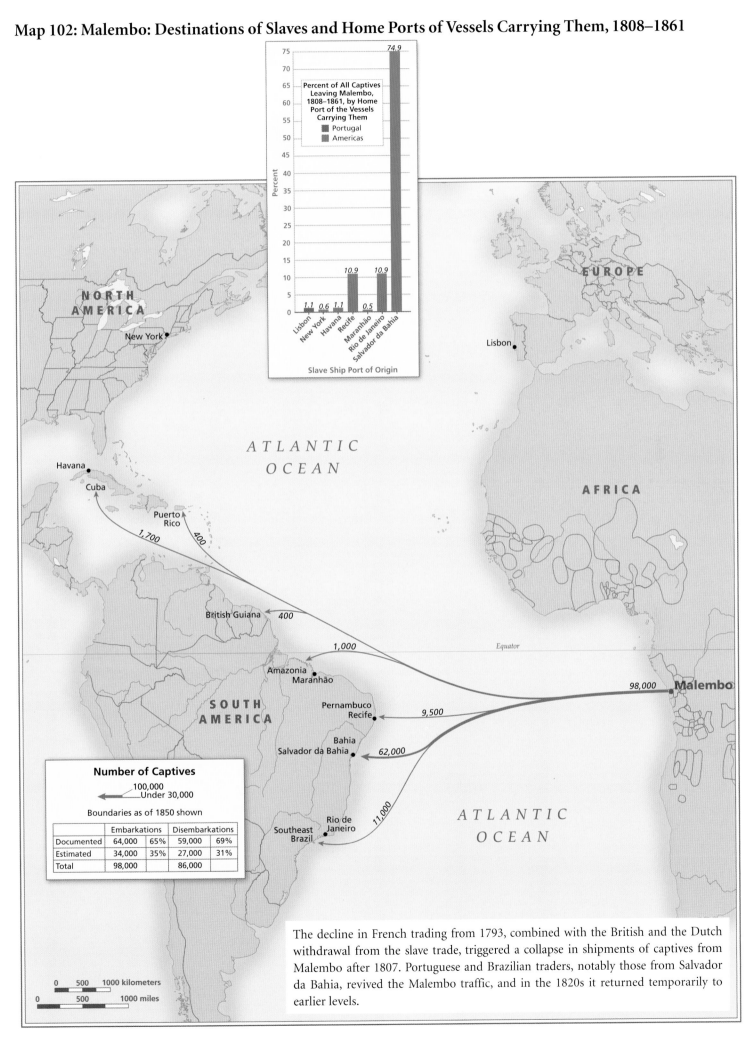

Percent of All Captives Leaving Malembo, 1808–1861, by Home Port of the Vessels Carrying Them

■ Portugal
■ Americas

Slave Ship Port of Origin

Number of Captives

100,000
Under 30,000

Boundaries as of 1850 shown

	Embarkations		Disembarkations	
Documented	64,000	65%	59,000	69%
Estimated	34,000	35%	27,000	31%
Total	98,000		86,000	

The decline in French trading from 1793, combined with the British and the Dutch withdrawal from the slave trade, triggered a collapse in shipments of captives from Malembo after 1807. Portuguese and Brazilian traders, notably those from Salvador da Bahia, revived the Malembo traffic, and in the 1820s it returned temporarily to earlier levels.

Map 103: Cabinda: Destinations of Slaves and Home Ports of Vessels Carrying Them, 1681–1807

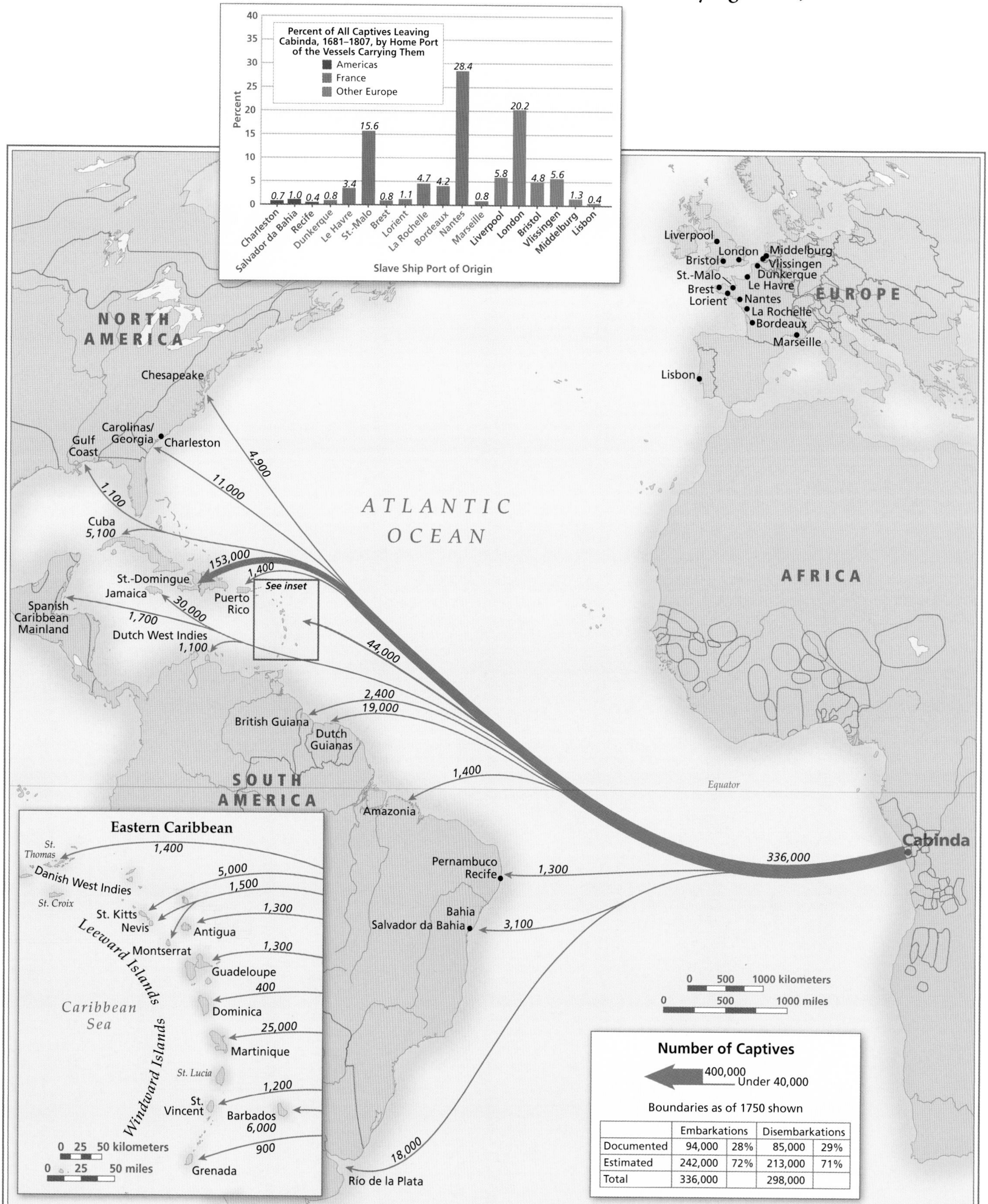

Percent of All Captives Leaving Cabinda, 1681–1807, by Home Port of the Vessels Carrying Them

- Americas
- France
- Other Europe

Chart values by Slave Ship Port of Origin (Percent):
Charleston 0.7, Salvador da Bahia 1.0, Recife 0.4, Dunkerque 0.8, Le Havre 3.4, St.-Malo 15.6, Brest 0.8, Lorient 1.1, La Rochelle 4.7, Bordeaux 4.2, Nantes 28.4, Marseille 0.8, Liverpool 5.8, London 20.2, Bristol 4.8, Vlissingen 5.6, Middelburg 1.3, Lisbon 0.4

Number of Captives

400,000 — Under 40,000

Boundaries as of 1750 shown

	Embarkations		Disembarkations	
Documented	94,000	28%	85,000	29%
Estimated	242,000	72%	213,000	71%
Total	336,000		298,000	

Map destinations and values:
Chesapeake 4,900; Carolinas/Georgia; Gulf Coast 1,100; Charleston 11,000; Cuba 5,100; St.-Domingue 153,000; Jamaica 30,000; Spanish Caribbean Mainland 1,700; Puerto Rico 1,400; Dutch West Indies 1,100; British Guiana 2,400; Dutch Guianas 19,000; Amazonia 1,400; Pernambuco Recife 1,300; Bahia Salvador da Bahia 3,100; Río de la Plata 18,000; 44,000; 336,000

Eastern Caribbean

St. Thomas; Danish West Indies 1,400; St. Croix 5,000; St. Kitts 1,500; Nevis; Antigua 1,300; Montserrat 1,300; Guadeloupe 400; Dominica 25,000; Martinique; St. Lucia 1,200; St. Vincent; Barbados 6,000; Grenada 900

Europe ports: Liverpool, Bristol, St.-Malo, Brest, Lorient, London, Middelburg, Vlissingen, Dunkerque, Le Havre, Nantes, La Rochelle, Bordeaux, Marseille, Lisbon

Cabinda, a port some thirty miles north of the Congo River and now part of modern Angola, became an embarkation center for African slaves in the eighteenth century as British and French traders sought new sources of captives. Cabinda was the Atlantic outlet for the Kingdom of Ngoyo and shared a language with and had laws, customs, and government structures similar to those in Loango (see map 99) and Malembo (see maps 101 and 102). These states were competitors, but until 1808 Cabinda was the least successful of the trio. Europeans tried at various times to establish a monopoly north of the Congo River, but all three ports remained open to all comers and under African jurisdiction.

Map 104: Cabinda: Destinations of Slaves and Home Ports of Vessels Carrying Them, 1808–1863

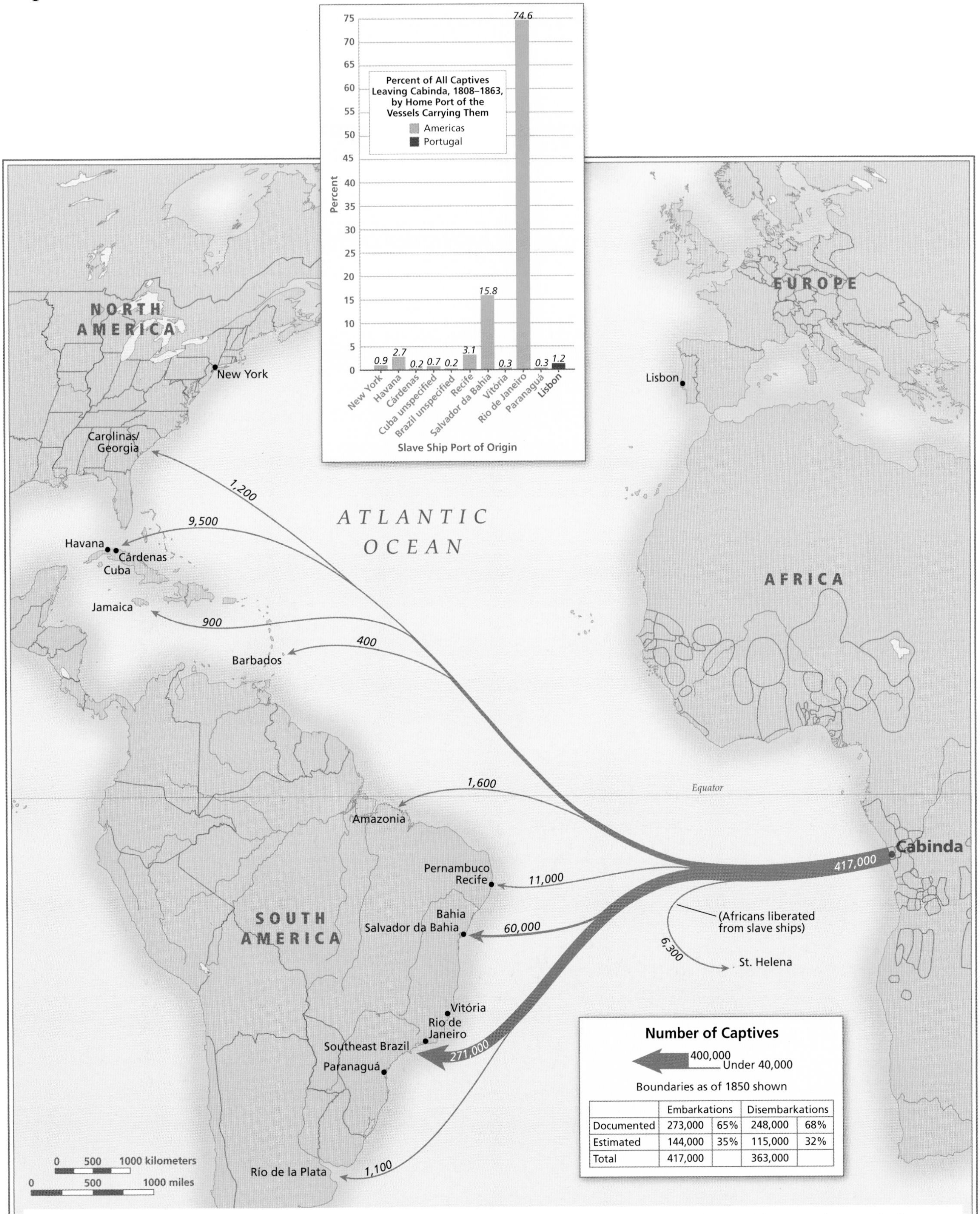

Percent of All Captives Leaving Cabinda, 1808–1863, by Home Port of the Vessels Carrying Them

Americas
Portugal

Percent

75
70
65
60
55
50
45
40
35
30
25
20
15
10
5
0

New York 0.9
Havana 2.7
Cárdenas 0.2
Cuba unspecified 0.7
Brazil unspecified 0.2
Recife 3.1
Salvador da Bahia 15.8
Vitória 74.6
Rio de Janeiro 0.3
Paranaguá 0.3
Lisbon 1.2

Slave Ship Port of Origin

ATLANTIC OCEAN

NORTH AMERICA

EUROPE

AFRICA

SOUTH AMERICA

New York

Carolinas/Georgia

1,200

9,500

Havana
Cárdenas
Cuba

Jamaica

900

Barbados

400

Lisbon

Equator

1,600

Amazonia

Pernambuco
Recife

11,000

Bahia
Salvador da Bahia

60,000

(Africans liberated from slave ships)

6,300

St. Helena

417,000

Cabinda

Vitória
Rio de Janeiro

Southeast Brazil

Paranaguá

271,000

Río de la Plata

1,100

Number of Captives

400,000
Under 40,000

Boundaries as of 1850 shown

	Embarkations		Disembarkations	
Documented	273,000	65%	248,000	68%
Estimated	144,000	35%	115,000	32%
Total	417,000		363,000	

0   500   1000 kilometers
0   500   1000 miles

War in Europe forced French withdrawal from slaving in 1793. This, together with British abolition of its own slave trade in 1807, allowed Portuguese and Brazilian traders to substantially increase their own shipping of slaves from Cabinda. Three-quarters of those leaving Cabinda after 1807 were taken on vessels originating in and returning to Rio de Janeiro. A creek that connected Cabinda to the Congo River allowed illicit slave traders to take their captives to the Atlantic, bypassing naval patrols attempting to suppress the trade.

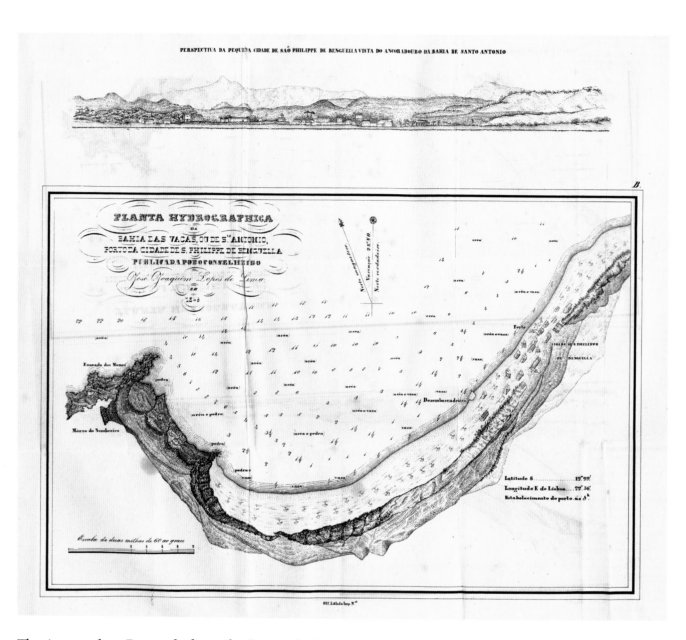

The Approach to Benguela from the Sea, c. 1846

Planta Hydrographica da Bahia das Vacas, from José Joaquim Lopes de Lima, *Ensaios sobre a statistica das possessões portuguezas,* 6 vols. (Lisbon, 1844–1862), vol. 3, part 2, between pp. 26 and 27. Manuscript, Archives, and Rare Book Library, Emory University.

Although Luanda was the principal slave port south of the Congo River, Benguela emerged as a major southern outpost for the traffic in humans from Atlantic Africa and remained a key embarkation point for captives from the 1720s, eclipsing even Luanda in the 1840s. The map shown here originates in a report on Portuguese overseas possessions compiled by José Joaquim Lopes de Lima. The map provides navigational instructions for entering the Bay of Santo Antonio, on which Benguela stands, as well as a view of the port from the bay.

Map 105: Benguela: Destinations of Slaves and Home Ports of Vessels Carrying Them, 1688–1864

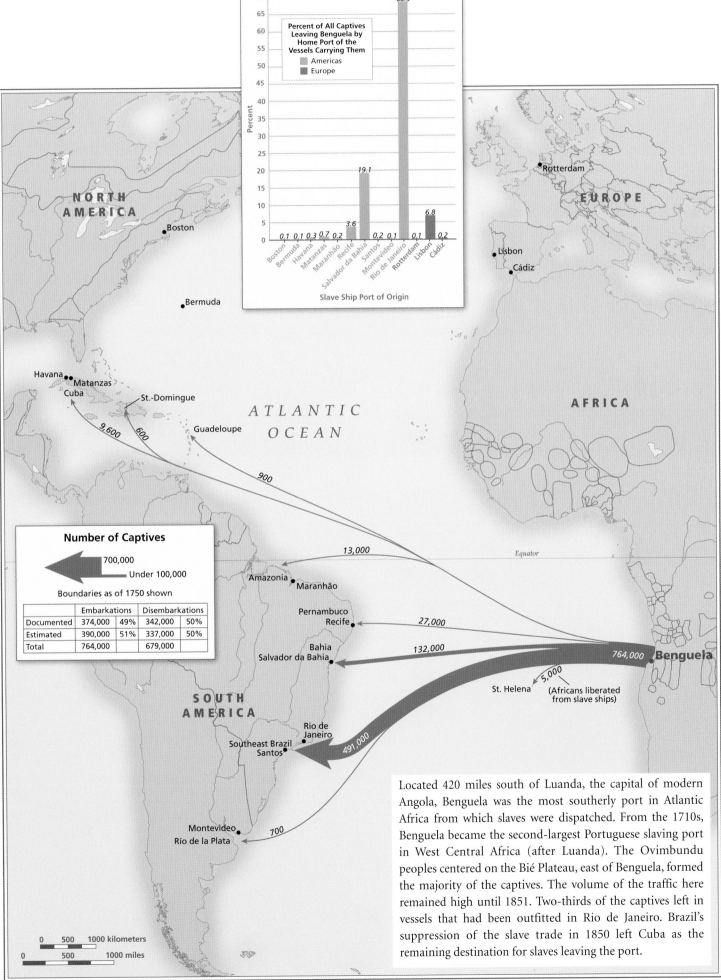

Percent of All Captives Leaving Benguela by Home Port of the Vessels Carrying Them

- Americas
- Europe

Percent

Boston 0.1, Bermuda 0.1, Havana 0.3, Matanzas 0.7, Maranhão 0.2, Recife 3.6, Salvador da Bahia 19.1, Santos 0.2, Montevideo 0.1, Rio de Janeiro 68.5, Rotterdam 0.1, Lisbon 6.8, Cádiz 0.2

Slave Ship Port of Origin

Number of Captives

700,000

Under 100,000

Boundaries as of 1750 shown

	Embarkations		Disembarkations	
Documented	374,000	49%	342,000	50%
Estimated	390,000	51%	337,000	50%
Total	764,000		679,000	

9,600

600

900

13,000

27,000

132,000

491,000

5,000

(Africans liberated from slave ships)

700

764,000 Benguela

Located 420 miles south of Luanda, the capital of modern Angola, Benguela was the most southerly port in Atlantic Africa from which slaves were dispatched. From the 1710s, Benguela became the second-largest Portuguese slaving port in West Central Africa (after Luanda). The Ovimbundu peoples centered on the Bié Plateau, east of Benguela, formed the majority of the captives. The volume of the traffic here remained high until 1851. Two-thirds of the captives left in vessels that had been outfitted in Rio de Janeiro. Brazil's suppression of the slave trade in 1850 left Cuba as the remaining destination for slaves leaving the port.

I do further declare that this vessel measured as
follows

	Feet	Inches
Extreme length	36	6
Extreme breadth	10	4
Extreme depth of hold	5	7

and that she contained only 15 Casks of Water of
about 40 Gallons each, some more some less, that
the height of the space left for the Stowage of Slaves
was only one foot 2 inches, that one half were
obliged always to be on deck, where they were so
confined that every foot of the Deck was occupied,
while the remainder below were squeezed to excess
all the Slaves being obliged to lay flat down [so]
that there was no room whatever for the Master
and Crew, who were obliged to live entirely upon
Deck and that I consider the smoothness of the
sea up to the moment of my falling in with her the
cause of her slaves having kept so healthy.

Admiralty to Aberdeen, 15 September 1842 (enc. Proceedings
of the trial of the Minerva), Foreign Office, FO 84/441, The
National Archives, Kew, London. Published with permission
of The National Archives, Kew, London. The voyage id is 3175.

Map 106: Ambriz: Destinations of Slaves and Home Ports of Vessels Carrying Them, 1786–1863

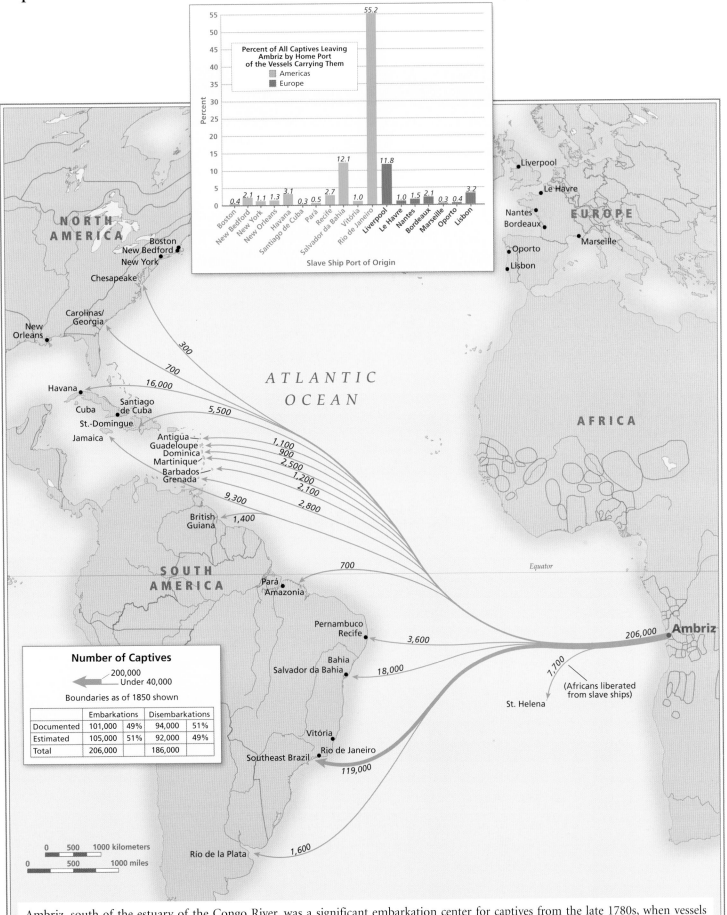

Percent of All Captives Leaving Ambriz by Home Port of the Vessels Carrying Them

Americas
Europe

Chart values (Percent) by Slave Ship Port of Origin:
- Boston: 0.4
- New Bedford: 2.1
- New York: 1.1
- New Orleans: 1.3
- Havana: 3.1
- Santiago de Cuba: 0.3
- Pará: 0.5
- Recife: 2.7
- Salvador da Bahia: 12.1
- Vitória: 1.0
- Rio de Janeiro: 55.2
- Liverpool: 11.8
- Le Havre: 1.0
- Nantes: 1.5
- Bordeaux: 2.1
- Marseille: 0.3
- Oporto: 0.4
- Lisbon: 3.2

Number of Captives

200,000
Under 40,000

Boundaries as of 1850 shown

	Embarkations		Disembarkations	
Documented	101,000	49%	94,000	51%
Estimated	105,000	51%	92,000	49%
Total	206,000		186,000	

Map labels: NORTH AMERICA, Boston, New Bedford, New York, Chesapeake, Carolinas/Georgia, New Orleans, Havana, Cuba, Santiago de Cuba, St.-Domingue, Jamaica, Antigua, Guadeloupe, Dominica, Martinique, Barbados, Grenada, British Guiana, SOUTH AMERICA, Pará, Amazonia, Pernambuco Recife, Bahia Salvador da Bahia, Vitória, Southeast Brazil, Rio de Janeiro, Río de la Plata, ATLANTIC OCEAN, AFRICA, Equator, St. Helena, Ambriz, EUROPE, Liverpool, Le Havre, Nantes, Bordeaux, Marseille, Oporto, Lisbon

Flow values: 300, 700, 16,000, 5,500, 1,100, 900, 2,500, 1,200, 2,100, 2,800, 9,300, 1,400, 700, 3,600, 18,000, 119,000, 1,600, 206,000, 1,700 (Africans liberated from slave ships)

Scale: 0 500 1000 kilometers / 0 500 1000 miles

Ambriz, south of the estuary of the Congo River, was a significant embarkation center for captives from the late 1780s, when vessels from Europe began trading there, to 1807. Embarkations, now on vessels from the Americas, revived in the early 1820s and reached unprecedented levels in the late 1820s. The slave trade from Arabia continued unevenly through 1863. After 1807, when the British pulled out of the trade, slaves went mainly to Brazil; before, they had been taken to European colonies in the Caribbean. Many leaving from north and south of the Congo estuary started their journey to the Americas many miles inland.

Map 107: Political and Ethnolinguistic Boundaries of Southeast Africa, 1750 and 1850

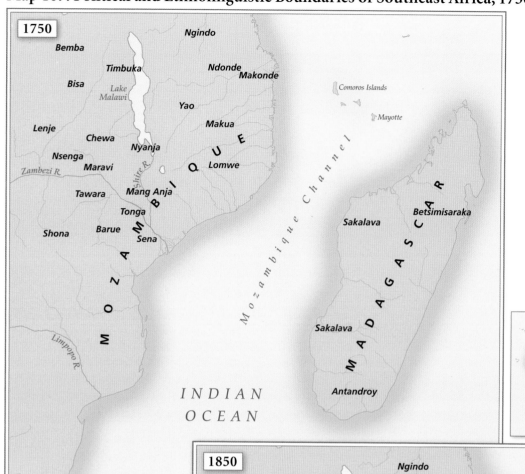

MOZAMBIQUE	Historical Region
Tawara	Ethnic Group

These two maps provide background for maps 108 to 111. Almost all captives sent from Southeast Africa to the Americas before 1750 came from Madagascar, where, in the north of the island, the Sakalava kingdom, emerging in the seventeenth century, made slaves available to purchasers from many parts of the Indian Ocean world as well as to Europeans. When mainland Africa became the main source of captives after 1750, there were few comparable state formations there. Small chieftancies, not shown in the maps, generated slaves, who before 1810 were drawn heavily from Makua peoples and after 1810 were overwhelmingly Yao.

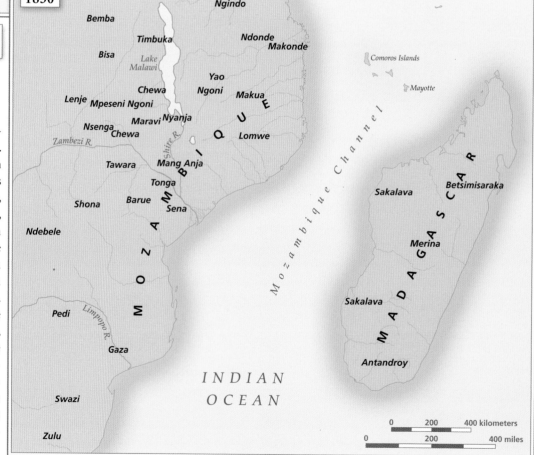

Maps 108 and 109: Slaves Leaving Locations in Southeast Africa, 1624–1860

Southeast Africa was the slave-trading region farthest away from the Americas, and more captives died on voyages from there than from anywhere else. This part of Africa provided only a few hundred African slaves a year for the Americas before 1781, although it had supplied Africans to Indian Ocean and Arabian markets for many centuries and to the Dutch Cape Province (South Africa) from the late seventeenth century. Prior to the mid-eighteenth century the island of Madagascar was the dominant source of captives for sale, but the tiny Portuguese colony at Mozambique Island became significant in the transatlantic traffic late in this period.

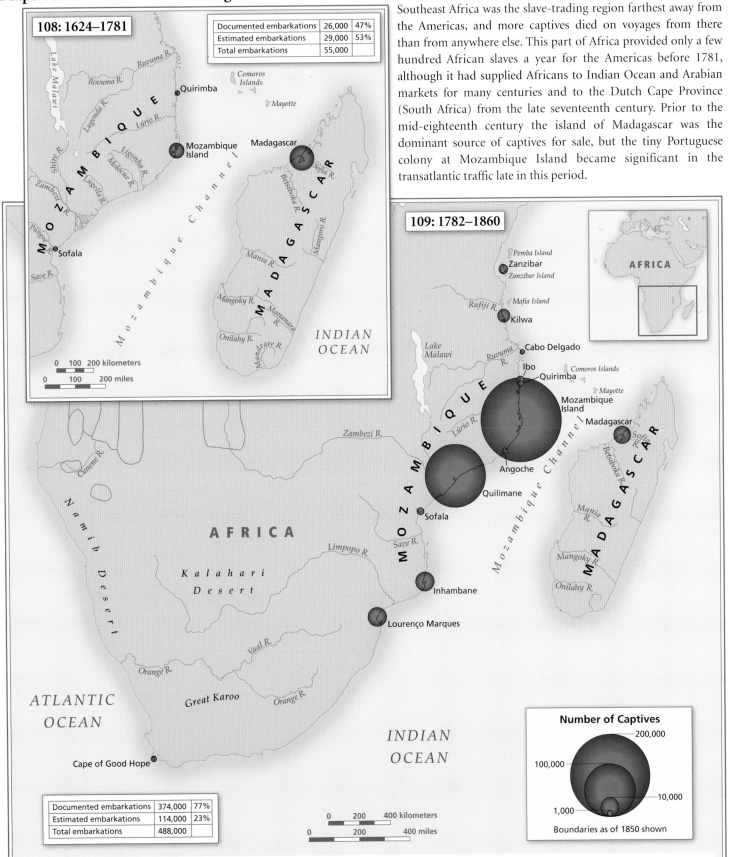

108: 1624–1781

Documented embarkations	26,000	47%
Estimated embarkations	29,000	53%
Total embarkations	55,000	

109: 1782–1860

Boundaries as of 1850 shown

Number of Captives

200,000
100,000
10,000
1,000

Documented embarkations	374,000	77%
Estimated embarkations	114,000	23%
Total embarkations	488,000	

After 1781, slave departures from Southeast Africa grew rapidly. By the 1830s the region had become the largest supplier of slaves to the Americas after West Central Africa, probably owing to the expansion of plantation agriculture in Brazil, increased French subsidies for slave trading after 1783, and British-led efforts in the Atlantic to suppress slaving activities north of the equator after 1815. Slaves now embarked from the African mainland rather than the island of Madagascar, and new embarkation points multiplied. Many of them, such as Quilimane and Lourenço Marques (now Maputo), were Portuguese trading outposts.

Map 110: Mozambique Island:
Destinations of Slaves and Home Ports of Vessels Carrying Them, 1664–1859

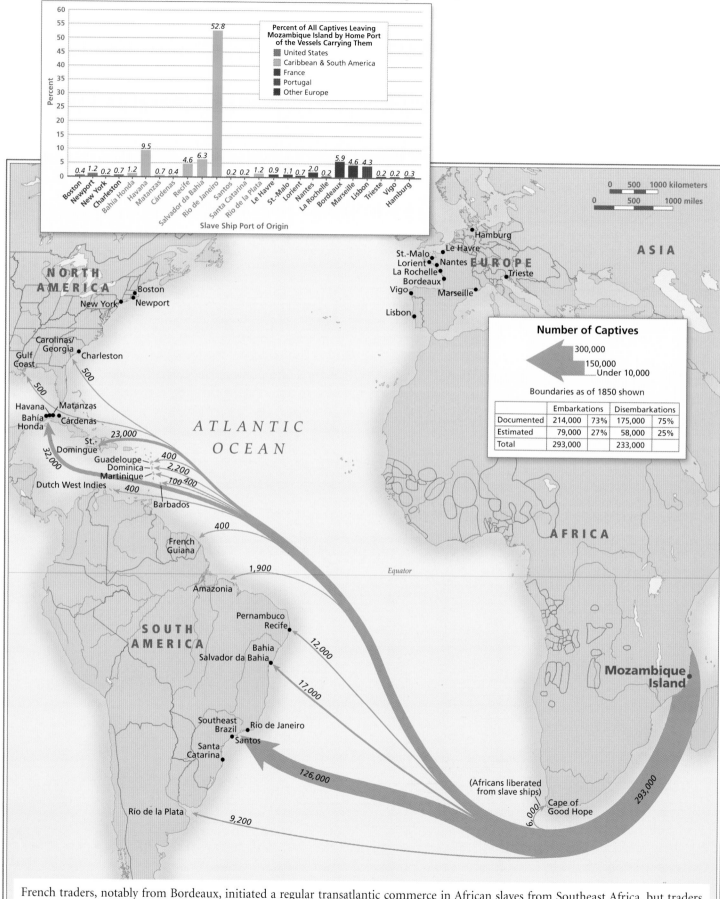

Percent of All Captives Leaving Mozambique Island by Home Port of the Vessels Carrying Them

- United States
- Caribbean & South America
- France
- Portugal
- Other Europe

Percent

Slave Ship Port of Origin

Boston 0.4, Newport 1.2, New York 0.2, Charleston 0.7, Bahia Honda 1.2, Havana 9.5, Matanzas 0.7, Cárdenas 0.4, Recife 4.6, Salvador da Bahia 6.3, Rio de Janeiro 52.8, Santos 0.2, Santa Catarina 0.2, Rio de la Plata 1.2, Le Havre 0.9, St.-Malo 1.1, Lorient 0.7, Nantes 2.0, La Rochelle 0.2, Bordeaux 5.9, Marseille 4.6, Lisbon 4.3, Trieste 0.2, Vigo 0.2, Hamburg 0.3

Number of Captives

300,000
150,000
Under 10,000

Boundaries as of 1850 shown

	Embarkations		Disembarkations	
Documented	214,000	73%	175,000	75%
Estimated	79,000	27%	58,000	25%
Total	293,000		233,000	

ATLANTIC OCEAN

NORTH AMERICA

Boston · New York · Newport · Carolinas/Georgia · Charleston · Gulf Coast · Havana · Matanzas · Bahía Honda · Cárdenas · St.-Domingue · Guadeloupe · Dominica · Martinique · Dutch West Indies · Barbados

500 · 500 · 23,000 · 32,000 · 400 · 2,200 · 400 · 100 · 400 · 400

French Guiana

400

1,900

Equator

Amazonia

SOUTH AMERICA

Pernambuco · Recife · Bahia · Salvador da Bahia · Southeast Brazil · Rio de Janeiro · Santos · Santa Catarina · Río de la Plata

12,000 · 17,000 · 126,000 · 9,200

ASIA

EUROPE

Hamburg · Le Havre · St.-Malo · Nantes · Lorient · La Rochelle · Bordeaux · Trieste · Vigo · Marseille · Lisbon

AFRICA

Mozambique Island

(Africans liberated from slave ships) · Cape of Good Hope

6,000 · 293,000

0 500 1000 kilometers
0 500 1000 miles

French traders, notably from Bordeaux, initiated a regular transatlantic commerce in African slaves from Southeast Africa, but traders from Rio de Janeiro ultimately dominated the traffic. Portuguese traders sometimes used the designation Mozambique to refer to anywhere in Southeast Africa, not always meaning specifically Mozambique Island, the original Portuguese settlement in the region. Slaves shipped from Mozambique and other mainland sites were enslaved as far north as the great lakes region of the African interior. Major trade routes funneled captives and ivory to the coast. The captives were mostly Yao and Makua peoples.

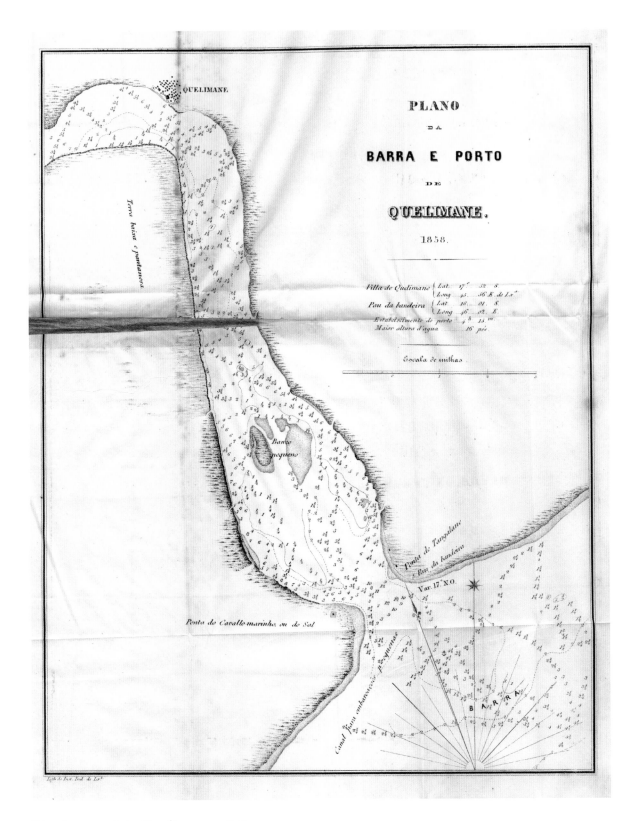

The Approach to Quelimane, 1858

Plano da barra e porto de Quelimane, from José Joaquim Lopes de Lima, *Ensaios sobre a statistica das possessões portuguezas,* 6 vols. (Lisbon, 1844–1862), vol. 4, at end of volume. Manuscript, Archives, and Rare Book Library, Emory University.

Founded as a Portuguese trading station on the Indian Ocean in the sixteenth century, Quilimane (also spelled Quelimane) emerged as a major slave port for Americas-bound African captives after 1815. The map shows the location of the city and the port, indicates the names of the principal coastal points of the channel linking the sea and the port, and gives the channel's depth. Francisco Maria Bordalo, who was charged with completing the report on Portuguese overseas possessions begun by José Joaquim Lopes de Lima, published the map in 1858.

Map 111: Quilimane: Destinations of Slaves and Home Ports of Vessels Carrying Them, 1797–1852

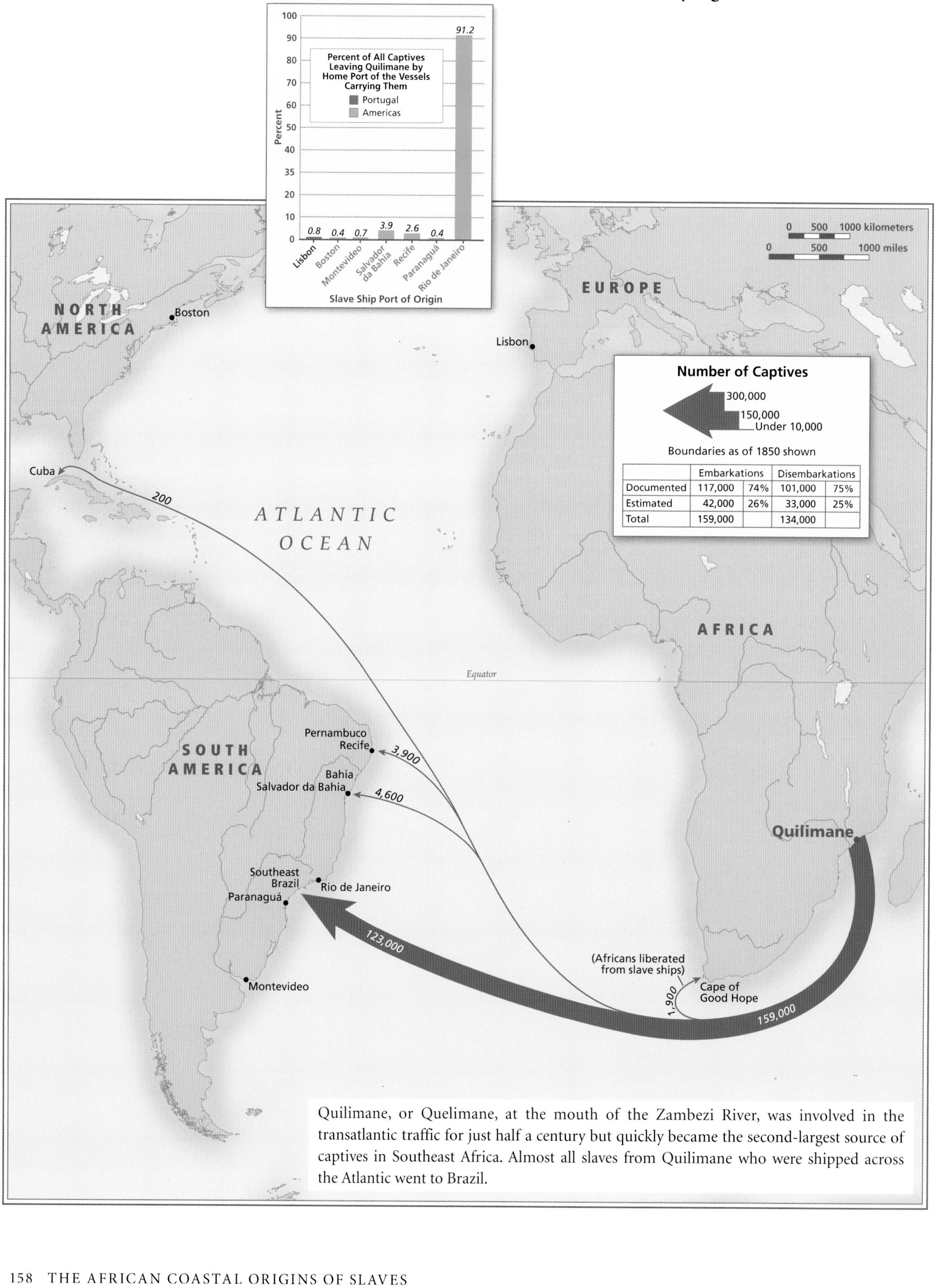

Percent of All Captives Leaving Quilimane by Home Port of the Vessels Carrying Them

- Portugal
- Americas

Percent (y-axis)

Lisbon	Boston	Montevideo	Salvador da Bahia	Recife	Paranaguá	Rio de Janeiro
0.8	0.4	0.7	3.9	2.6	0.4	91.2

Slave Ship Port of Origin

NORTH AMERICA

Boston

EUROPE

Lisbon

0 500 1000 kilometers
0 500 1000 miles

Cuba

200

ATLANTIC OCEAN

Number of Captives

300,000
150,000
Under 10,000

Boundaries as of 1850 shown

	Embarkations		Disembarkations	
Documented	117,000	74%	101,000	75%
Estimated	42,000	26%	33,000	25%
Total	159,000		134,000	

AFRICA

Equator

Pernambuco
Recife

SOUTH AMERICA

3,900

Bahia
Salvador da Bahia

4,600

Southeast Brazil
Paranaguá

Rio de Janeiro

123,000

Quilimane

Montevideo

(Africans liberated from slave ships)

1,900

Cape of Good Hope

159,000

Quilimane, or Quelimane, at the mouth of the Zambezi River, was involved in the transatlantic traffic for just half a century but quickly became the second-largest source of captives in Southeast Africa. Almost all slaves from Quilimane who were shipped across the Atlantic went to Brazil.

Part IV
The Experience of the Middle Passage

Despair and degradation were inevitable consequences of being herded naked onto small, overcrowded vessels and dispatched to far-off lands from which no return was possible. Although it is impossible to measure psychological trauma in ways that can be represented on maps, it is possible to measure and represent mortality on the Middle Passage. It is also possible to measure two obvious ways in which the slave trade, like any form of migration, restructured the populations of both the society of origin and the society of arrival: by calculating the ratio of males to females and of adults to children, both of which were dependent on the volume of migration relative to the populations at source and destination. The *Voyages* database (www.slavevoyages.org) also makes it possible to analyze patterns of slave resistance, a major element in the experience of those on board transatlantic slave vessels.

Maps 112 to 115 display variations in the gender and age distributions of Africans transported across the Atlantic. Adults are usually defined as those older than thirteen or fourteen years of age or taller than four feet four inches. Traditionally, historians have described the transatlantic slave traffic as dominated by males and adults and have attributed high ratios of males to females to the plantation owners' demand for strong laborers. Modern research shows that, in comparison to almost all other long-distance migrations before 1800, the share of females and children in the traffic was extremely high and that important differences among African regions in the shares of males and children entering the trade cannot be explained by the demands of buyers in the Americas. Given that ship captains obtained captives from African sellers by trade rather than by force, any transaction reflected the wishes of both buyer and seller. African influences over the demographic makeup of the slave trade must have been as important as influences from slave owners in the Americas.

Unfortunately, few data have survived for Brazil, and the data that exist derive from the nineteenth century. More data are available for North America (including the Caribbean), and there, three important patterns emerge. First, the male share of captives leaving the Bight of Biafra was always lower than the female share of captives leaving other regions; females formed the majority of all deportees prior to 1710. Second, adult-to-child ratios varied enormously across African regions. Third, over time, the proportion of males carried off from Africa increased, as did the proportion of children. Historians have as yet no explanation for this pattern, but strikingly, it appears across all African slaving regions at about the same time.

Maps 116 to 130 show the length of the Middle Passage and the number of deaths that occurred during the transatlantic crossing. Voyage length varied according to region of embarkation in Africa and region of disembarkation in the Americas, and some of the changes in the overall average voyage length are explained by the increasing or decreasing use of particular routes at different times. If we hold this factor constant, however, it is clear that voyage length did decline over time, with most of the decline occurring in the nineteenth century. This pattern was certainly associated with improved oceangoing technology; even some steam-powered slave ships operated in the last phase of the slave trade.

Many of the maps in part IV come in pairs, one focusing on the African region of departure, one focusing on the American region of arrival. For some voyages we know the specific point of embarkation in Africa, but for others we know only that the ship came from Africa. The reverse is also true: we know exactly where some ships left Africa but not where in the Americas they arrived. The maps are in pairs, then, because we have different pools of data for the departures and arrivals of the ships, and the maps may span different years even though many voyages are common to both.

The gender and age bar graphs likewise represent different pools of voyages. Thus, in map 112, the Senegambia bars are for all voyages going to the Caribbean and mainland North America from Senegambia. The Chesapeake bars are for all voyages arriving in the Chesapeake from anywhere in Africa, and so on.

In general, vessels that completed the Middle Passage without leaving the wheel of either the North Atlantic or the South Atlantic current experienced the most rapid passages and the lowest shipboard mortality (see map 4). Vessels that crossed from one wheel to the other, traversing the equator and the doldrums, had longer passages and more deaths because the calms and the squalls of the doldrums, along the equator, were unpredictable. A ship could sail from West Central Africa to Brazil without leaving the southern wheel, and from Upper Guinea to the Caribbean and the North American mainland without moving outside its northern counterpart. Such a voyage typically lasted six weeks. By contrast, voyages to Brazil from the Gold Coast and the Bight of Benin began in one system and ended in another; they averaged two months in duration (although those going from the southern to the northern wheels—that is from northern West Central Africa to the Caribbean—were shorter). The longest and most lethal voyages were in ships that set out from Southeast Africa or that had to cross between the two Atlantic wheels of currents not once but twice. Thus, ships taking captives to the Caribbean from the Gold Coast, the Bight of Benin, and the Bight of Biafra first dropped south into the southern wheel before turning west to cross the Atlantic. They then had to cross the equator and the doldrums a second time to return to the northern wheel to complete their passage. Such journeys lasted just under three months; nearly one in six captives taken on board died.

While these broad wind-and-current patterns help to explain mortality levels for the Middle Passage, health status before embarkation also played a major role. Long journeys to the coast or lengthy periods of confinement on the coast while more captives were sought had a major impact on shipboard mortality. Slave vessels leaving the Bight of Biafra to anywhere in the Americas experienced higher mortality rates than those leaving any other region. Over the 350-plus years that the slave trade lasted, average voyage length and mortality both declined by over 40 percent. This pattern held for all routes for which data have survived.

Maps 131 and 132 track patterns of resistance. All slave voyages must have experienced acts of resistance, and in some cases resistance manifested itself in the form of open revolt. Although records of revolts exist for only about 600 (or 2 percent) of the voyages in the *Voyages* database, we have estimated in essays in the *Economic History Review* (2001) and the *William and Mary Quarterly* (2001) that about one in ten vessels that took slaves on board either experienced a rebellion or was attacked from the African coast—usually as the result of a dispute between the buyers of slaves on board the vessel and the sellers of slaves on land. Of the 600 violent outbreaks on record, in only 26 did captives manage to return the vessel to Africa. The threat of rebellion had a very real impact on costs, however. Slave captains had to carry more crew and armaments than did their counterparts in other lines of business. Higher costs always meant, in the end, higher prices for slaves in the Americas and hence fewer slaves sold. Even unsuccessful revolts reduced the number of slaves carried off from Africa.

The *Voyages* data show two striking patterns. Rebellions were much more prevalent on board vessels leaving from Upper Guinea than on those leaving from regions of Africa south of the equator. The reason for this is still unclear. A second pattern is that rebellions were much more likely to occur in the eighteenth century than either before or after. What can account for this? Before 1650 or so, as far as we can tell, vessels carried more crew relative to the number of slaves on board, although between 1650 and 1810, the number of slaves per crew member did not vary much. After 1810 a fairly strong shift toward carrying more children occurred, and children were certainly easier to handle than adults. Not surprisingly, the number of slaves per crew member increased substantially.

Maps 133 and 134 shed some light on the origins of the captives who reached the African coast, cultural diversity being a key component of the shipboard experience. The data provide some evidence about the linguistic diversity of captives who embarked from particular regions. For several thousand African captives who set out across the Atlantic between 1819 and 1844 and were subsequently freed from their slave ships by British naval cruisers, sufficient personal information has survived that we are able to estimate their linguistic and thus geographic origins. The freed captives were not from major sources of labor for American plantations. But they may be regarded as samples at either end of a continuum: at one extreme were Cameroon captives, who came from a very concentrated area, and at the other extreme were Sierra Leone captives, who originated from a very large geographic region. It is not yet clear which was the dominant pattern in other regions supplying slaves.

Africans who survived the Middle Passage had dramatically different experiences when they landed, depending on where their voyage took them, as maps 135 and 136 show. Life expectancy and reproductive potential were much poorer in the Caribbean than on the North American mainland. The relationship of the slave trade to the growth of the population of African origin in the two areas was strikingly different. A small inflow of Africans to the mainland led to a large population decades later, whereas a large inflow of Africans to the Caribbean failed to generate similar slave population increases over time. In the last half-century of slavery in the United States, when there was virtually no slave trade with Africa, the slave population tripled. The slave population of the Caribbean doubled between 1780 and 1830, but in the same years the slave trade brought twice the number of people from Africa to the Caribbean than were living there in 1780.

Map 112: Gender and Age of Slaves Carried from African Regions to Mainland North America and the Caribbean, 1545–1864

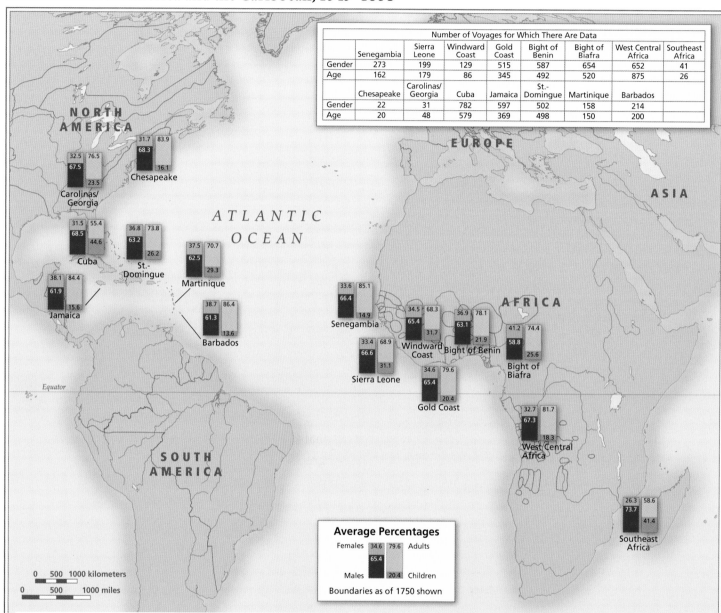

	Senegambia	Sierra Leone	Windward Coast	Gold Coast	Bight of Benin	Bight of Biafra	West Central Africa	Southeast Africa
				Number of Voyages for Which There Are Data				
Gender	273	199	129	515	587	654	652	41
Age	162	179	86	345	492	520	875	26

	Chesapeake	Carolinas/ Georgia	Cuba	Jamaica	St.- Domingue	Martinique	Barbados	
Gender	22	31	782	597	502	158	214	
Age	20	48	579	369	498	150	200	

Average Percentages

Females 34.6 / 79.6 Adults

Males 65.4 / 20.4 Children

Boundaries as of 1750 shown

European and American buyers of captives generally wanted adult males, whereas African sellers typically offered more females and children than transatlantic buyers wanted. The outcome was that males and adults normally formed the majority of those crossing the Atlantic, but far more women and children were involved than was usual in long-distance migrations in the early modern Atlantic world. The share of men and children arriving at any given Caribbean island generally represented a blend of the sex and age distributions in the African regions from which the slaves were drawn, as well as the sellers' and buyers' preferences. For a fuller explanation of the different pools of data, see the introduction to part IV.

Map 113: Gender and Age of Slaves Carried from African Regions to the Caribbean, 1545–1700

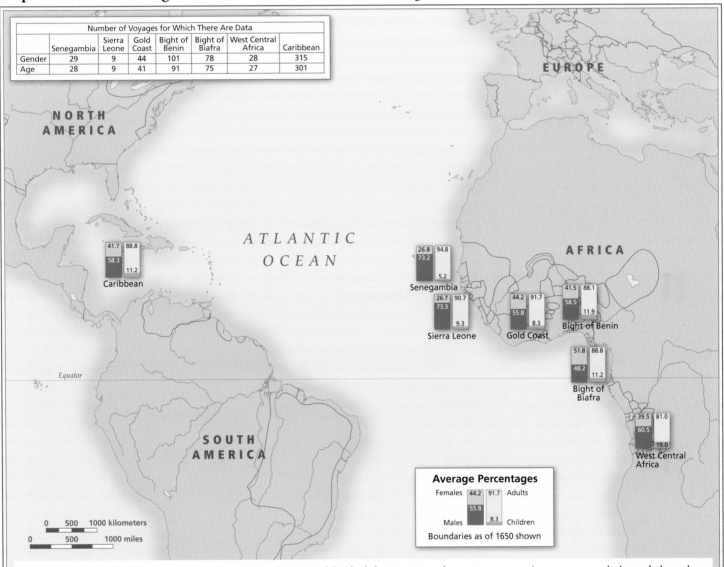

Number of Voyages for Which There Are Data							
	Senegambia	Sierra Leone	Gold Coast	Bight of Benin	Bight of Biafra	West Central Africa	Caribbean
Gender	29	9	44	101	78	28	315
Age	28	9	41	91	75	27	301

NORTH AMERICA

EUROPE

ATLANTIC OCEAN

AFRICA

Caribbean
41.7 | 88.8
58.3 | 11.2

Senegambia
26.8 | 94.8
73.2 | 5.2

Sierra Leone
26.7 | 90.7
73.3 | 9.3

Gold Coast
44.2 | 91.7
55.8 | 8.3

Bight of Benin
41.5 | 88.1
58.5 | 11.9

Bight of Biafra
51.8 | 88.8
48.2 | 11.2

West Central Africa
39.5 | 81.0
60.5 | 19.0

Equator

SOUTH AMERICA

0   500   1000 kilometers
0   500   1000 miles

Average Percentages

Females | 44.2 | 91.7 | Adults
Males | 55.8 | 8.3 | Children

Boundaries as of 1650 shown

In the earliest period for which good data exist, the second half of the seventeenth century, sex ratios were more balanced than they were to become, and there were relatively few children in the traffic. More females than males left the Bight of Biafra before the late seventeenth century, and only slightly more males than females left the Gold Coast. Of the major African regions, only West Central Africa yielded significant numbers of children at this time.

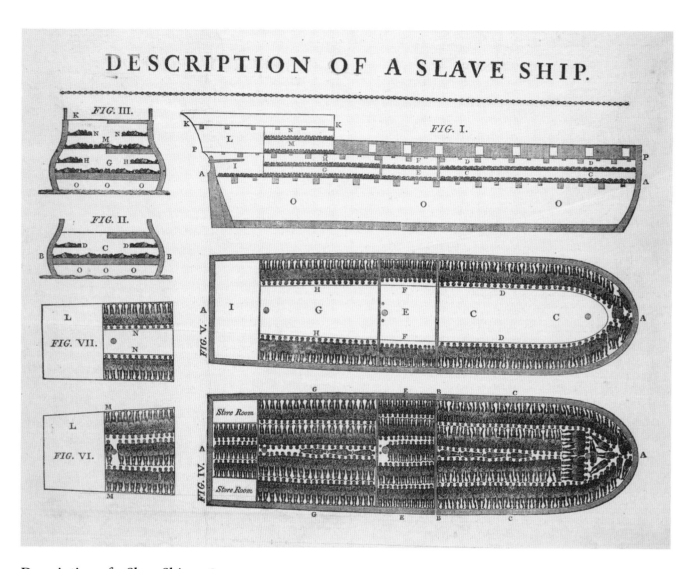

Description of a Slave Ship, 1789

Engraving by James Phillips for the London Committee of the Society for Effecting the Abolition of the Slave Trade. Beinecke Rare Book and Manuscript Library, Yale University.

Description of a Slave Ship, based on the *Brooks,* a Liverpool slave ship, provided one of the earliest images of the methods of stowing African captives on board British slave ships. Showing darkened figures laid out sardinelike on four tiers of shelves in compartments between decks, with adult males separated from women and children, the engraving was distributed widely by the abolitionist sympathizer James Phillips in support of the popular campaign against the British slave trade in 1789–1792. The text accompanying the image provided an explanatory guide to the dimensions of the ship and to slave stowage practices.

Map 114: Gender and Age of Slaves Carried from African Regions to the Caribbean, 1701–1807

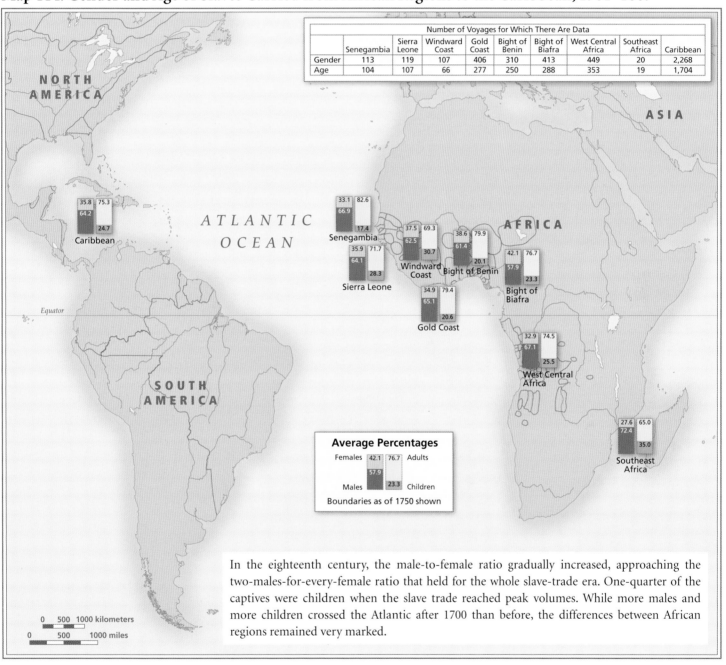

		Number of Voyages for Which There Are Data							
	Senegambia	Sierra Leone	Windward Coast	Gold Coast	Bight of Benin	Bight of Biafra	West Central Africa	Southeast Africa	Caribbean
Gender	113	119	107	406	310	413	449	20	2,268
Age	104	107	66	277	250	288	353	19	1,704

Average Percentages

Females 42.1 | 76.7 Adults
57.9 | 23.3
Males | Children

Boundaries as of 1750 shown

In the eighteenth century, the male-to-female ratio gradually increased, approaching the two-males-for-every-female ratio that held for the whole slave-trade era. One-quarter of the captives were children when the slave trade reached peak volumes. While more males and more children crossed the Atlantic after 1700 than before, the differences between African regions remained very marked.

Map 115: Gender and Age of Slaves Carried from African Regions to the Caribbean, 1808–1864

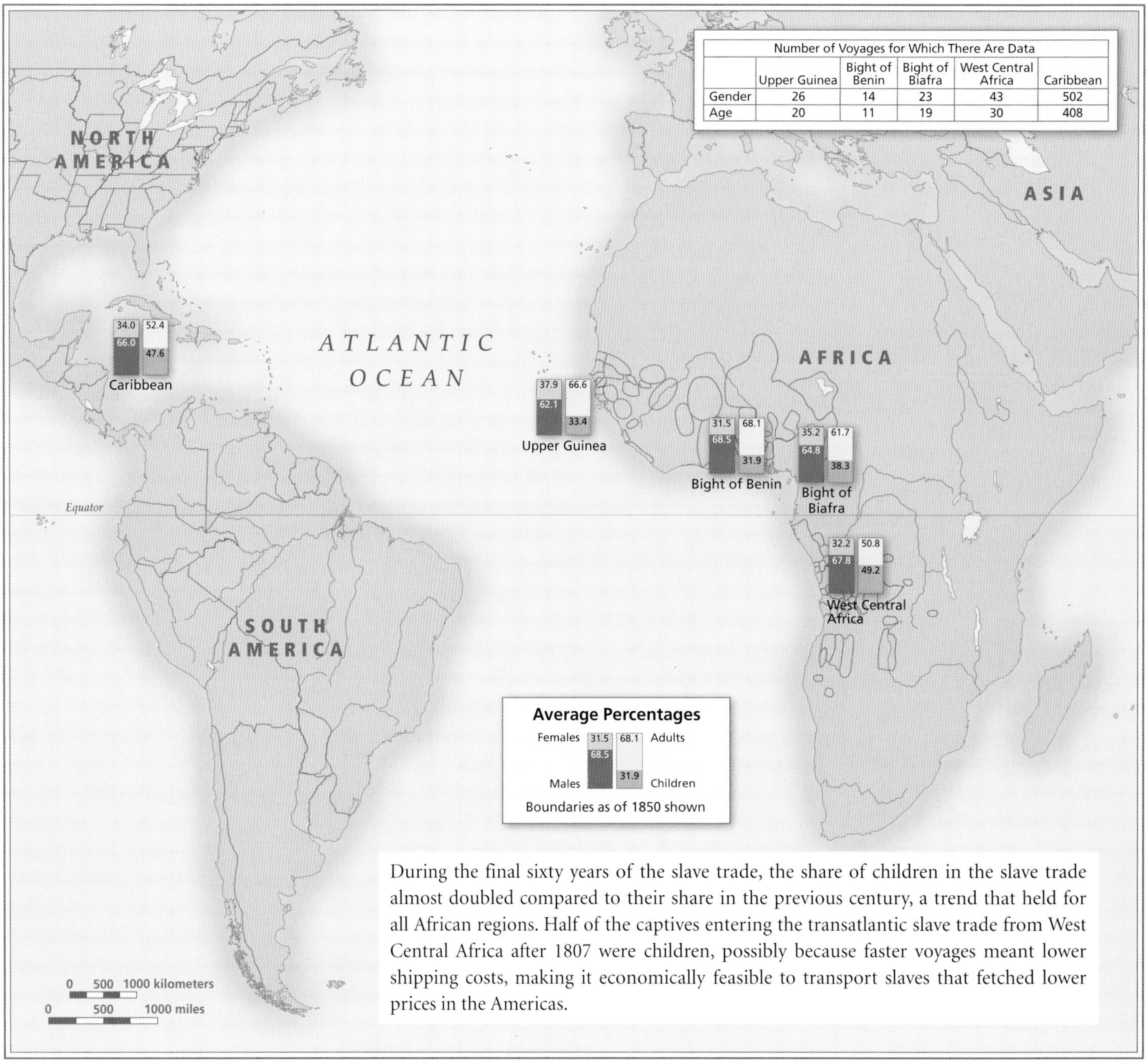

	Number of Voyages for Which There Are Data				
	Upper Guinea	Bight of Benin	Bight of Biafra	West Central Africa	Caribbean
Gender	26	14	23	43	502
Age	20	11	19	30	408

NORTH AMERICA

ASIA

AFRICA

ATLANTIC OCEAN

Caribbean
34.0 / 52.4
66.0
47.6

Upper Guinea
37.9 / 66.6
62.1
33.4

Bight of Benin
31.5 / 68.1
68.5
31.9

Bight of Biafra
35.2 / 61.7
64.8
38.3

West Central Africa
32.2 / 50.8
67.8
49.2

Equator

SOUTH AMERICA

Average Percentages

Females 31.5 | 68.1 Adults
68.5
Males | 31.9 Children

Boundaries as of 1850 shown

0   500   1000 kilometers
0   500   1000 miles

During the final sixty years of the slave trade, the share of children in the slave trade almost doubled compared to their share in the previous century, a trend that held for all African regions. Half of the captives entering the transatlantic slave trade from West Central Africa after 1807 were children, possibly because faster voyages meant lower shipping costs, making it economically feasible to transport slaves that fetched lower prices in the Americas.

Map 116: Slave Mortality and Voyage Length for Slaves Leaving African Regions for Mainland North American Regions, 1663–1860

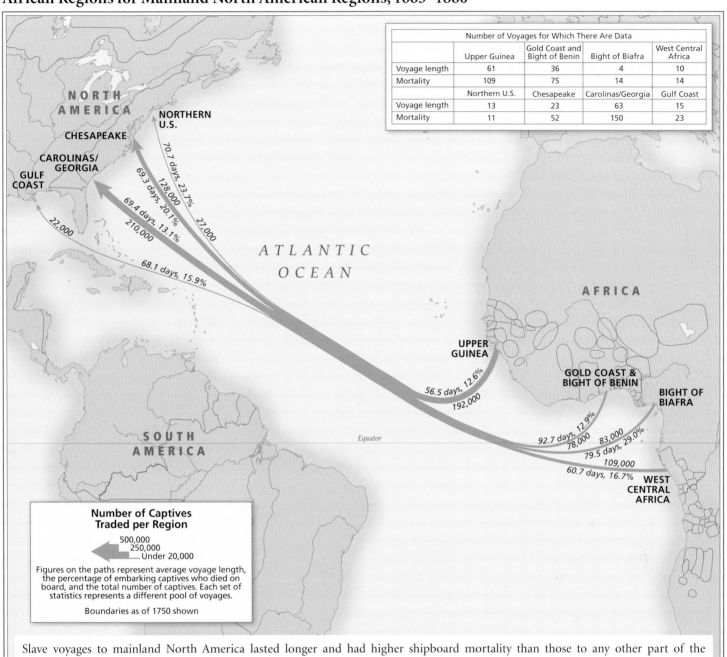

Number of Voyages for Which There Are Data				
	Upper Guinea	Gold Coast and Bight of Benin	Bight of Biafra	West Central Africa
Voyage length	61	36	4	10
Mortality	109	75	14	14
	Northern U.S.	Chesapeake	Carolinas/Georgia	Gulf Coast
Voyage length	13	23	63	15
Mortality	11	52	150	23

Number of Captives Traded per Region

500,000
250,000
Under 20,000

Figures on the paths represent average voyage length, the percentage of embarking captives who died on board, and the total number of captives. Each set of statistics represents a different pool of voyages.

Boundaries as of 1750 shown

Slave voyages to mainland North America lasted longer and had higher shipboard mortality than those to any other part of the Americas. The voyages were longer partly because all vessels sailing from Africa to the North American mainland stopped at ports in the eastern Caribbean for information and provisions and partly because passing from the southern wind-and-current system to the northern took time (see map 4). Nevertheless, as available data on voyages from the Gold Coast show, longer voyages did not automatically mean higher mortality (see map 121). The health of individuals at the point of embarkation was often more important than voyage length in determining their survival of the Middle Passage.

I must speak of the transit of the slaves in the West Indies. This I confess, in my own opinion, is the most wretched part of the whole subject [of slavery]. So much misery condensed in so little room, is more than the human imagination had ever before conceived. I will not accuse the Liverpool merchants: I will allow them, nay, I will believe them to be men of humanity; and I will therefore believe, if it were not for the enormous magnitude and extent of the evil which distracts their attention from individual cases, and makes them think generally, and therefore less feelingly on the subject, they would never have persisted in the trade. I verily believe therefore, if the wretchedness of any one of the many hundred Negroes stowed in each ship could be brought before their view, and remain within the sight of the African Merchant, that there is no one among them whose heart would bear it. Let any one imagine to himself 6 or 700 of these wretches chained two and two, surrounded with every object that is nauseous and disgusting, diseased, and struggling under every kind of wretchedness! How can we bear to think of such a scene as this? One would think it had been determined to heap upon them all the varieties of bodily pain, for the purpose of blunting the feelings of the mind; and yet, in this very point (to show the power of human prejudice) the situation of the slaves has been described by Mr. Norris, one of the Liverpool delegates, in a manner which, I am sure will convince the House how interest can draw a film across the eyes, so thick, that total blindness could do no more; and how it is our duty therefore to trust not to the reasonings of interested men, or to their way of colouring a transaction.

Excerpt from William Wilberforce's speech to Parliament, 12 May 1789, in William Cobbett, *The Parliamentary History of England: From the Norman Conquest in 1066 to the Year 1803*, 36 vols. (London: T. Curson Hansard, 1806–1820), vol. 28, *(1789–91)*, cols. 42–68.

Map 117: Slave Mortality and Voyage Length for Slaves Leaving African Regions for the Caribbean, 1652–1700

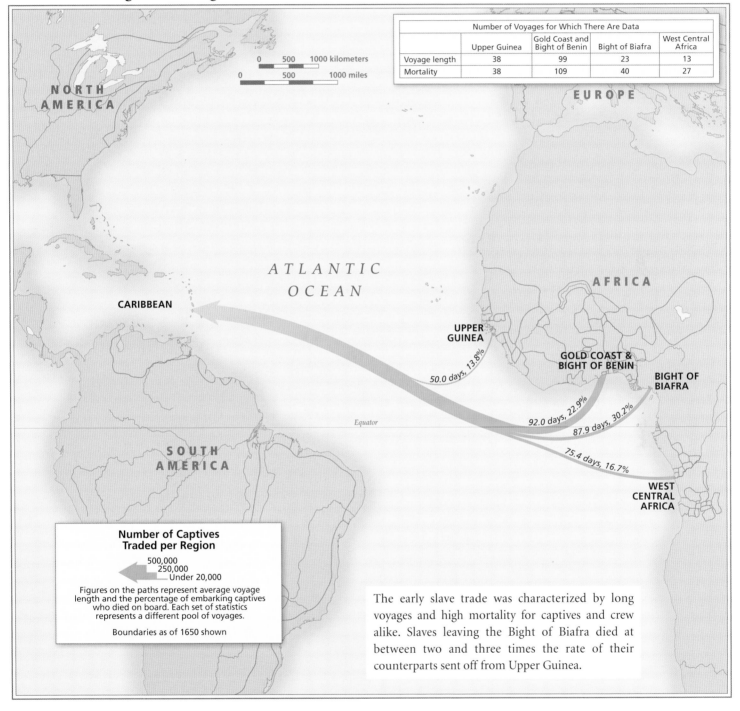

Number of Voyages for Which There Are Data				
	Upper Guinea	Gold Coast and Bight of Benin	Bight of Biafra	West Central Africa
Voyage length	38	99	23	13
Mortality	38	109	40	27

0 500 1000 kilometers
0 500 1000 miles

NORTH AMERICA

EUROPE

ATLANTIC OCEAN

AFRICA

CARIBBEAN

UPPER GUINEA

50.0 days, 13.8%

GOLD COAST & BIGHT OF BENIN

BIGHT OF BIAFRA

92.0 days, 22.9%

87.9 days, 30.2%

75.4 days, 16.7%

Equator

SOUTH AMERICA

WEST CENTRAL AFRICA

Number of Captives Traded per Region

500,000
250,000
Under 20,000

Figures on the paths represent average voyage length and the percentage of embarking captives who died on board. Each set of statistics represents a different pool of voyages.

Boundaries as of 1650 shown

The early slave trade was characterized by long voyages and high mortality for captives and crew alike. Slaves leaving the Bight of Biafra died at between two and three times the rate of their counterparts sent off from Upper Guinea.

Map 118: Slave Mortality and Voyage Length for Slaves Arriving in Caribbean Regions from Africa, 1534–1700

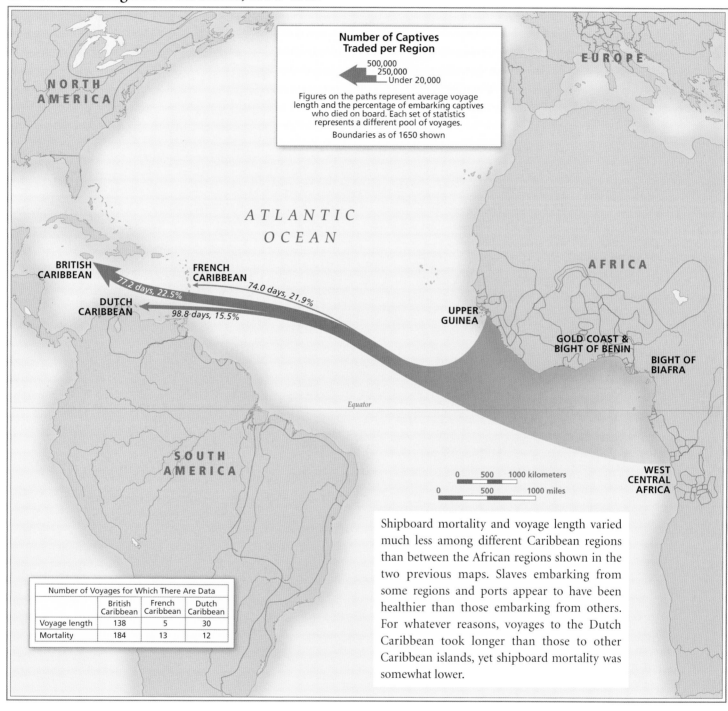

Number of Captives Traded per Region

500,000
250,000
Under 20,000

Figures on the paths represent average voyage length and the percentage of embarking captives who died on board. Each set of statistics represents a different pool of voyages.

Boundaries as of 1650 shown

EUROPE

NORTH AMERICA

ATLANTIC OCEAN

BRITISH CARIBBEAN

FRENCH CARIBBEAN

77.2 days, 22.5%

74.0 days, 21.9%

DUTCH CARIBBEAN

98.8 days, 15.5%

AFRICA

UPPER GUINEA

GOLD COAST & BIGHT OF BENIN

BIGHT OF BIAFRA

Equator

SOUTH AMERICA

WEST CENTRAL AFRICA

| 0 | 500 | 1000 kilometers |
| 0 | 500 | 1000 miles |

Number of Voyages for Which There Are Data			
	British Caribbean	French Caribbean	Dutch Caribbean
Voyage length	138	5	30
Mortality	184	13	12

Shipboard mortality and voyage length varied much less among different Caribbean regions than between the African regions shown in the two previous maps. Slaves embarking from some regions and ports appear to have been healthier than those embarking from others. For whatever reasons, voyages to the Dutch Caribbean took longer than those to other Caribbean islands, yet shipboard mortality was somewhat lower.

The wretched Africans . . . are conveyed to the
plantations, and are put to their respective work.
. . . Calculations are accordingly made upon
their lives. It is conjectured, that if three in four
survive what is called the *seasoning,* the bargain
is highly favourable. This seasoning is said to
expire, when the two first years of their servitude
are completed: it is the time which an African
must take to be so accustomed to the colony,
as to be able to endure the common labour of a
plantation, and to be put into the *gang.* At the end
of this period the calculations become verified,
twenty thousand of those annually imported,
dying before the seasoning is over. This is surely
an horrid and awful consideration; and thus it
does appear, (and let it be remembered, that it is
the lowest calculation that has been ever made
upon the subject) that out of every annual supply
that is shipped from the coast of Africa, *forty-
five thousand lives,* including the number who
perish on the voyage, are regularly expended,
even before it can be said, that there is really any
additional stock for the colonies.

Thomas Clarkson, *An Essay on the Slavery and Commerce
of the Human Species, particularly the African,* 2nd ed.
(London: J. Phillips, 1788), pp. 104–105.

Map 119: Slave Mortality and Voyage Length
for Slaves Leaving African Regions for the Caribbean, 1701–1775

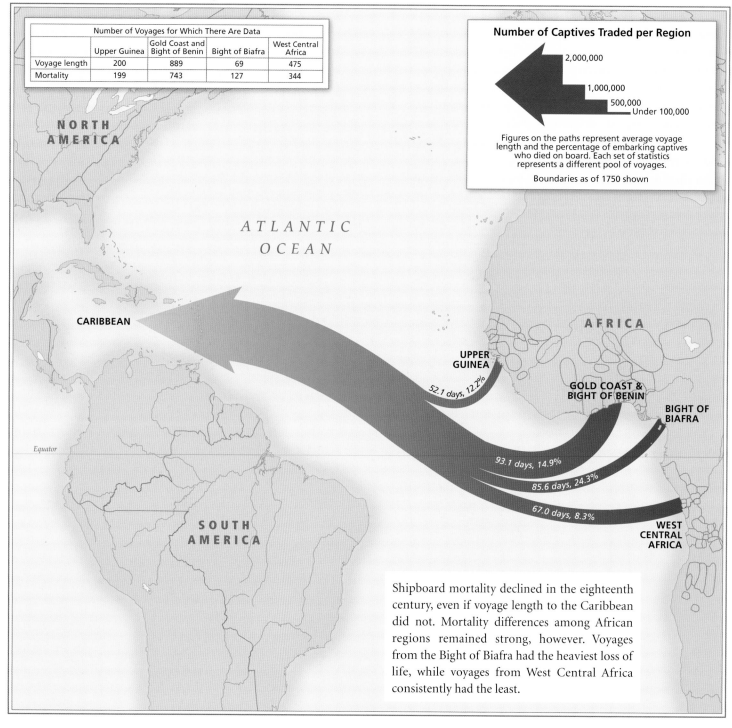

Number of Voyages for Which There Are Data				
	Upper Guinea	Gold Coast and Bight of Benin	Bight of Biafra	West Central Africa
Voyage length	200	889	69	475
Mortality	199	743	127	344

Number of Captives Traded per Region

2,000,000
1,000,000
500,000
Under 100,000

Figures on the paths represent average voyage length and the percentage of embarking captives who died on board. Each set of statistics represents a different pool of voyages.

Boundaries as of 1750 shown

NORTH AMERICA

ATLANTIC OCEAN

CARIBBEAN

AFRICA

UPPER GUINEA

GOLD COAST & BIGHT OF BENIN

BIGHT OF BIAFRA

52.1 days, 12.2%

93.1 days, 14.9%

85.6 days, 24.3%

67.0 days, 8.3%

Equator

SOUTH AMERICA

WEST CENTRAL AFRICA

Shipboard mortality declined in the eighteenth century, even if voyage length to the Caribbean did not. Mortality differences among African regions remained strong, however. Voyages from the Bight of Biafra had the heaviest loss of life, while voyages from West Central Africa consistently had the least.

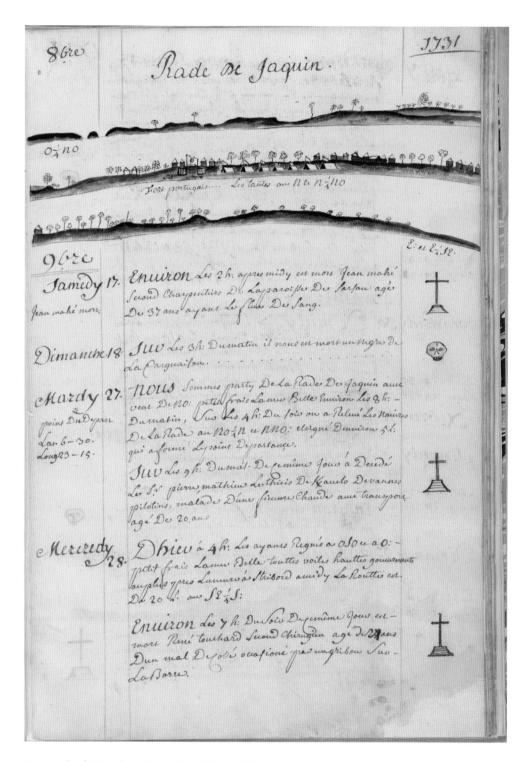

Record of Deaths Aboard a Slave Ship, 1731

Pen and ink drawing by Robert Durand from his *Journal de bord d'un negrier* (1731). Beinecke Rare Book and Manuscript Library, Yale University.

Those involved in managing slave voyages routinely kept a record of the deaths of both crew and Africans in their charge. Methods of recordkeeping varied but often distinguished between deaths of crew and deaths of Africans. On a page from the journal of Robert Durand, first lieutenant on the French ship *Diligent* in 1731 (voyage id 33330), Durand recorded the location of the ship and some other details and in the margin indicated the deaths of crew members and Africans. Crew were identified by a cross, Africans by a skull. Such distinctions continued in burial ceremonies. The bodies of dead African captives were typically thrown unceremoniously overboard, but dead seamen were given some kind of Christian service before being sent to their watery grave.

Map 120: Slave Mortality and Voyage Length for Slaves Arriving in Caribbean Regions from Africa, 1701–1775

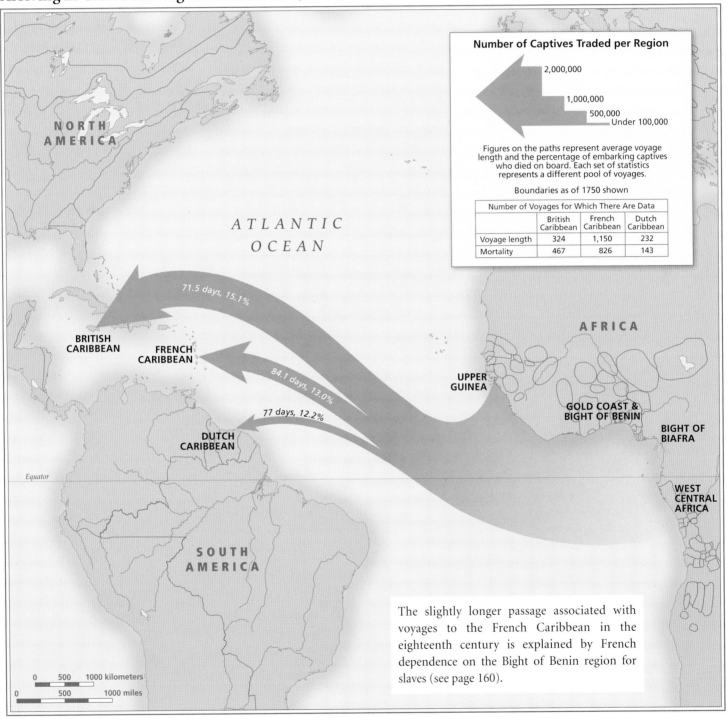

Number of Captives Traded per Region

2,000,000
1,000,000
500,000
Under 100,000

Figures on the paths represent average voyage length and the percentage of embarking captives who died on board. Each set of statistics represents a different pool of voyages.

Boundaries as of 1750 shown

Number of Voyages for Which There Are Data			
	British Caribbean	French Caribbean	Dutch Caribbean
Voyage length	324	1,150	232
Mortality	467	826	143

NORTH AMERICA

ATLANTIC OCEAN

AFRICA

71.5 days, 15.1%

BRITISH CARIBBEAN

FRENCH CARIBBEAN

84.1 days, 13.0%

UPPER GUINEA

GOLD COAST & BIGHT OF BENIN

BIGHT OF BIAFRA

77 days, 12.2%

DUTCH CARIBBEAN

Equator

SOUTH AMERICA

WEST CENTRAL AFRICA

0   500   1000 kilometers
0   500   1000 miles

The slightly longer passage associated with voyages to the French Caribbean in the eighteenth century is explained by French dependence on the Bight of Benin region for slaves (see page 160).

[Europeans] prepared their floating hells manned with fiends, to carry the Africans across a wide ocean, to a new-explored continent, to wit, America. Would to God that Columbus with his exploring schemes had perished in Europe ere he touched the American Isles. . . . Then might Africa [have] been spared the terrible calamity she has suffered. . . .

On ship-board in their passage from Africa, they were treated with the most horrible cruelty that the imagination can conceive of. . . . An infant of ten months old, had taken sulk on board of a slave ship, that is, refused to eat; the savage captain with his knotted cat whipped it until its body and legs had much swollen; he then ordered it in water so hot, that its skin and nails came off; he then bound it in oilcloth; he after a few days whipped it again, swearing he would make it eat or kill it; in a few hours after it expired, he then ordered the mother to throw her murdered infant overboard, she refused, he beat her until she took it up, turned her head aside, and dropped it into the sea. Now tell me my brethren, is there in God's domain other and worse fiends than these?

Excerpt from William Hamilton, "O! Africa," in his *Oration, on the Abolition of the [U.S.] Slave Trade, Delivered in the Episcopal Asbury African Church, in Elizabeth St., New York, January 2, 1815* (New York: C. W. Bunce, for the New York African Society, 1815).

Map 121: Slave Mortality and Voyage Length for Slaves Leaving African Regions for the Caribbean, 1776–1830

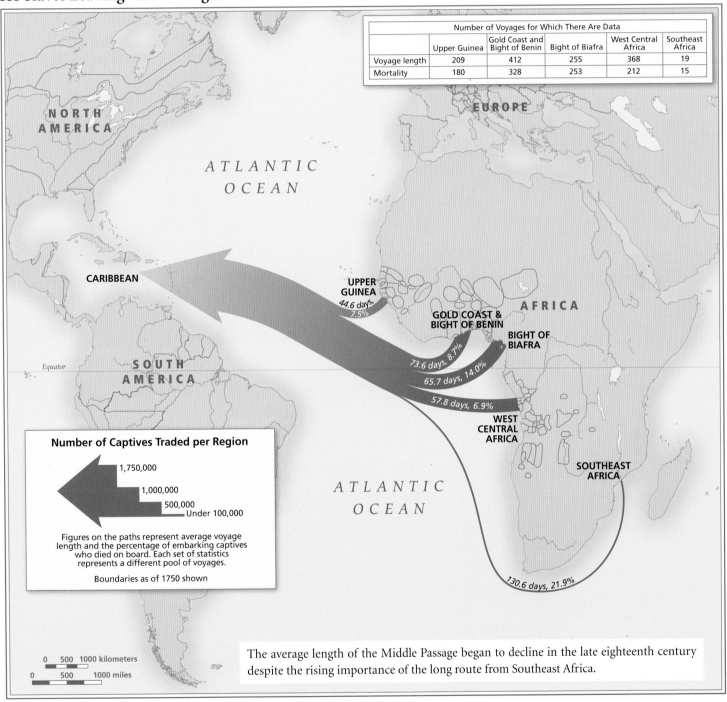

	Number of Voyages for Which There Are Data				
	Upper Guinea	Gold Coast and Bight of Benin	Bight of Biafra	West Central Africa	Southeast Africa
Voyage length	209	412	255	368	19
Mortality	180	328	253	212	15

NORTH AMERICA

EUROPE

ATLANTIC OCEAN

CARIBBEAN

UPPER GUINEA
44.6 days, 7.5%

GOLD COAST & BIGHT OF BENIN

BIGHT OF BIAFRA

AFRICA

Equator

SOUTH AMERICA

73.6 days, 8.7%

65.7 days, 14.0%

57.8 days, 6.9%

WEST CENTRAL AFRICA

SOUTHEAST AFRICA

ATLANTIC OCEAN

130.6 days, 21.9%

Number of Captives Traded per Region

1,750,000
1,000,000
500,000
Under 100,000

Figures on the paths represent average voyage length and the percentage of embarking captives who died on board. Each set of statistics represents a different pool of voyages.

Boundaries as of 1750 shown

0 500 1000 kilometers
0 500 1000 miles

The average length of the Middle Passage began to decline in the late eighteenth century despite the rising importance of the long route from Southeast Africa.

List of sick and dying slaves on board ship Brandenbourg 1791–1792

Date died	Days sick	Description of person	Attributed cause of death
14 Nov 1791	12	Boy	Febris lente [spring fever]
26 Nov 1791	22	Woman	Malum histericum [hysteria]
7 Dec 1791	37	Woman	Effectus pectoris [chest complaint]
22 Jan 1792	20	Man	Anasarca [extreme edema]
8 Apr 1792	60	Girl	Dijsenterie [dysentery]
9 May 1792	—	Woman	Haemoragie uteri [hemorrhage of uterus]
2 Jun 1792	21	Woman	Anasarca
7 Jul 1792	32	Man	Febris lente
7 Jul 1792	2	Man	Febres pudrita [putrid fever]
7 Jul 1792	6	Man	Dijsenterie
12 Jul 1792	39	Woman	Hectica [hectic fever; vel ethica]
21 Jul 1792	9	Man	Dijsenterie
22 Jul 1792	10	Girl	Dijsenterie
27 Jul 1792	15	Boy	Dijsenterie
1 Aug 1792	-	Man	Verdroncken [drowned]
3 Aug 1792	7	Man	Collera [cholera]
10 Aug 1792	13	Woman	Effectus pectoris
12 Aug 1792	33	Woman	Anasarca
12 Aug 1792	31	Man	Anasarca
21 Aug 1792	13	Woman	Scorbut [scurvy]
28 Aug 1792	16	Man	Effectus pectoris
29 Aug 1792	17	Man	Effectus pectoris
31 Aug 1792	19	Woman	Effectus pectoris

In addition to reports of the slaves who died [gystorben or gestorvan], the journal reports that 26 captives recovered [genessen or genesen] from sickness. The journal was signed in Demerara River, 15 November 1792, by the Brandenbourg's chief surgeon, Johannes Andreas Kraus, who reported on 16 November 1792 that expenditure on medicines on the ship totaled 89 guilders.

Journal of the ship *Brandenbourg* commanded by Captein [*sic*] Alexandre Geritzon from 10th August 1791 until the 15th September 1792. Middelburgsche Commercie Compagnie, MCC 292, Middelburg Archives, The Netherlands. Translated and adapted by Simon J. Hogerzeil and David Richardson.

Map 122: Slave Mortality and Voyage Length for Slaves Arriving in Caribbean Regions from Africa, 1776–1830

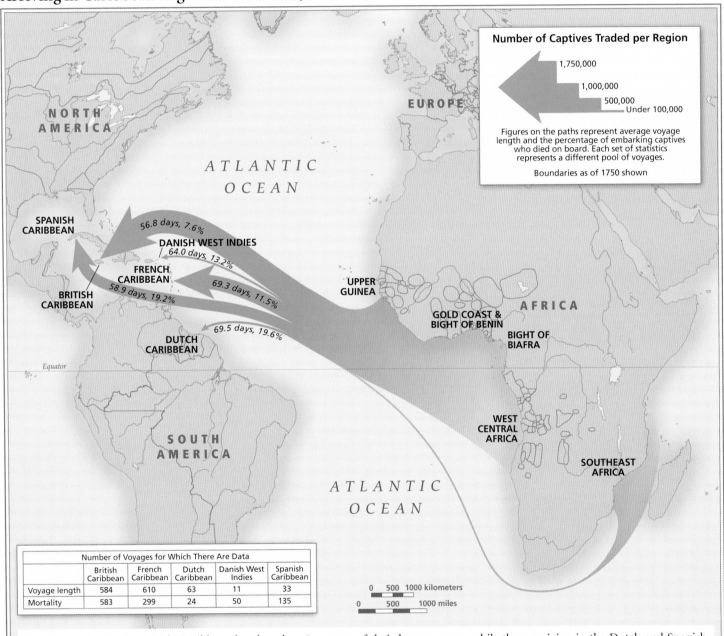

Number of Captives Traded per Region

1,750,000
1,000,000
500,000
Under 100,000

Figures on the paths represent average voyage length and the percentage of embarking captives who died on board. Each set of statistics represents a different pool of voyages.

Boundaries as of 1750 shown

NORTH AMERICA

EUROPE

ATLANTIC OCEAN

SPANISH CARIBBEAN

56.8 days, 7.6%

DANISH WEST INDIES

64.0 days, 13.2%

FRENCH CARIBBEAN

58.9 days, 19.2%

69.3 days, 11.5%

BRITISH CARIBBEAN

DUTCH CARIBBEAN

69.5 days, 19.6%

Equator

UPPER GUINEA

AFRICA

GOLD COAST & BIGHT OF BENIN

BIGHT OF BIAFRA

WEST CENTRAL AFRICA

SOUTHEAST AFRICA

SOUTH AMERICA

ATLANTIC OCEAN

Number of Voyages for Which There Are Data					
	British Caribbean	French Caribbean	Dutch Caribbean	Danish West Indies	Spanish Caribbean
Voyage length	584	610	63	11	33
Mortality	583	299	24	50	135

0   500   1000 kilometers
0   500   1000 miles

Vessels arriving in the British Caribbean lost less than 8 percent of their human cargo, while those arriving in the Dutch and Spanish territories lost nearly 20 percent. The British regulation of their slave trade from 1788 to abolition in 1807 may have reduced mortality. At the other end of the range, traders to the Spanish Caribbean began drawing on African regions associated with higher shipboard mortality rates (the Bight of Biafra and Southeast Africa). Also, after 1820 bringing slaves for sale to the Spanish Caribbean was illegal, and the conditions under which the trade was carried on increased shipboard mortality.

Map 123: Slave Mortality and Voyage Length for Slaves Leaving African Regions for the Caribbean, 1831–1864

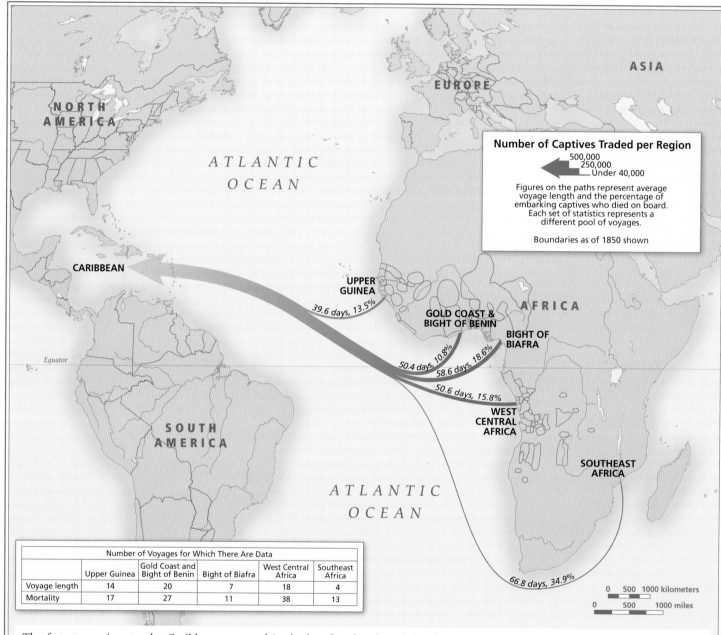

Number of Captives Traded per Region

500,000
250,000
Under 40,000

Figures on the paths represent average voyage length and the percentage of embarking captives who died on board. Each set of statistics represents a different pool of voyages.

Boundaries as of 1850 shown

39.6 days, 13.5%

50.4 days, 10.8%

58.6 days, 18.6%

50.6 days, 15.8%

66.8 days, 34.9%

Number of Voyages for Which There Are Data					
	Upper Guinea	Gold Coast and Bight of Benin	Bight of Biafra	West Central Africa	Southeast Africa
Voyage length	14	20	7	18	4
Mortality	17	27	11	38	13

The fastest crossings to the Caribbean occurred in the last few decades of the slave trade, partly because slave traders began to use yacht-type vessels as well as a few steamships to outrun naval cruisers charged with suppressing the traffic. Despite the increased speed of passage, shipboard mortality increased as a result of efforts to bring the traffic to an end. Naval blockades of known embarkation points in Africa often caused food shortages for captives and long periods of confinement on shore.

Map 124: Slave Mortality and Voyage Length for Slaves Arriving in Caribbean Regions from Africa, 1831–1864

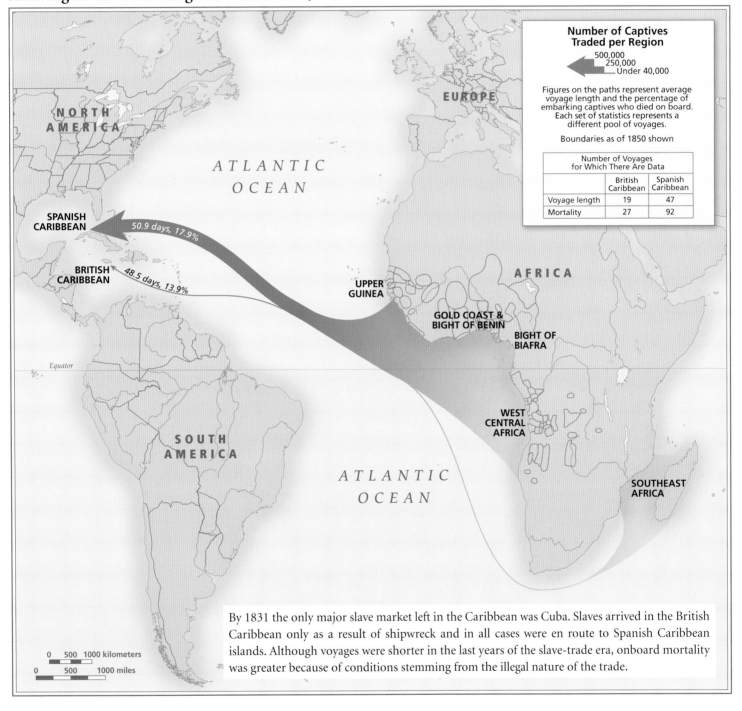

Number of Captives Traded per Region

500,000
250,000
Under 40,000

Figures on the paths represent average voyage length and the percentage of embarking captives who died on board. Each set of statistics represents a different pool of voyages.

Boundaries as of 1850 shown

Number of Voyages for Which There Are Data	British Caribbean	Spanish Caribbean
Voyage length	19	47
Mortality	27	92

EUROPE

NORTH AMERICA

ATLANTIC OCEAN

SPANISH CARIBBEAN

50.9 days, 17.9%

BRITISH CARIBBEAN

48.5 days, 13.9%

AFRICA

UPPER GUINEA

GOLD COAST & BIGHT OF BENIN

BIGHT OF BIAFRA

WEST CENTRAL AFRICA

SOUTHEAST AFRICA

Equator

SOUTH AMERICA

ATLANTIC OCEAN

By 1831 the only major slave market left in the Caribbean was Cuba. Slaves arrived in the British Caribbean only as a result of shipwreck and in all cases were en route to Spanish Caribbean islands. Although voyages were shorter in the last years of the slave-trade era, onboard mortality was greater because of conditions stemming from the illegal nature of the trade.

0 500 1000 kilometers

0 500 1000 miles

Map 125: Slave Mortality for Slaves Leaving African Regions for Brazil, 1638–1775

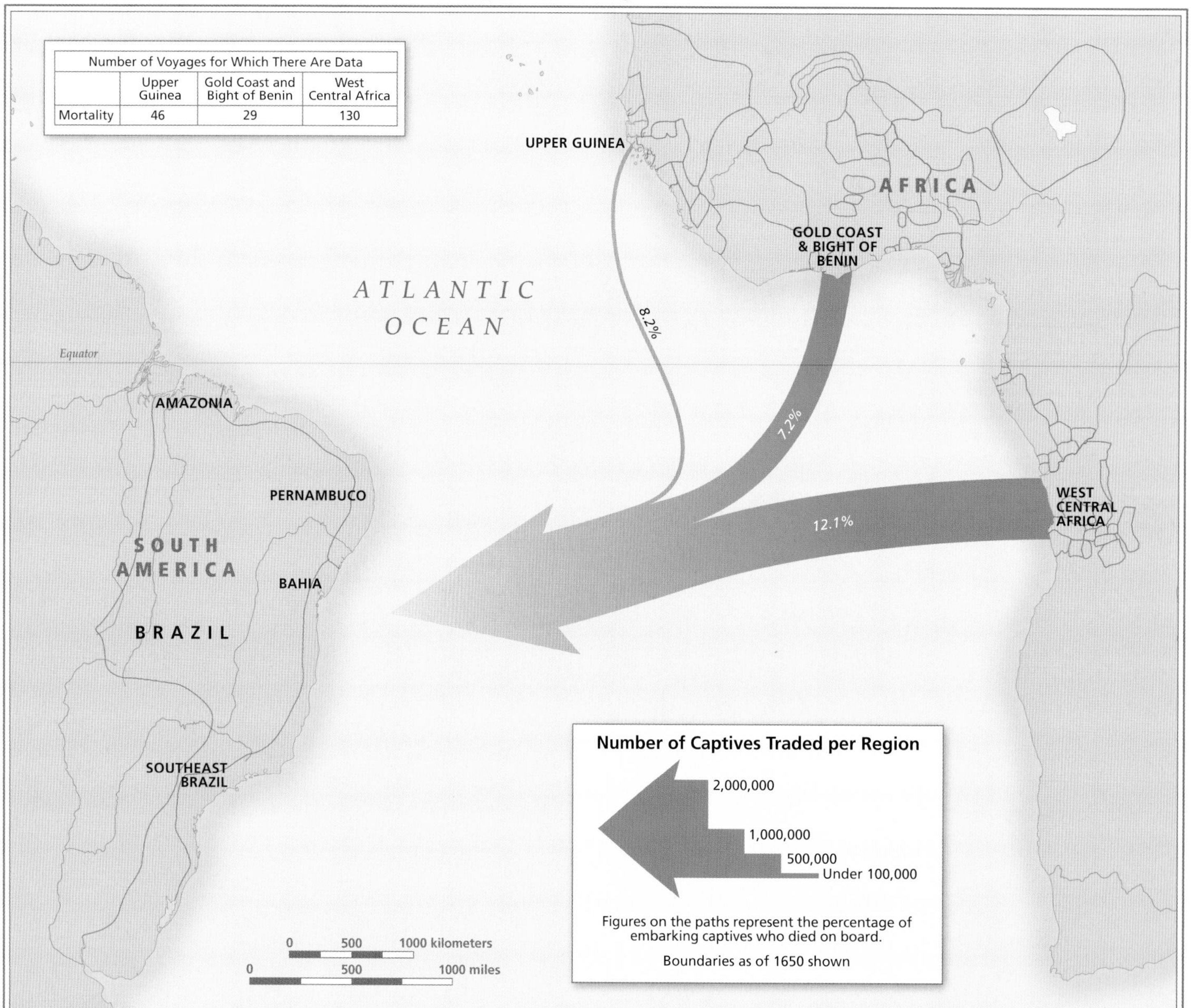

Number of Voyages for Which There Are Data			
	Upper Guinea	Gold Coast and Bight of Benin	West Central Africa
Mortality	46	29	130

UPPER GUINEA

AFRICA

GOLD COAST & BIGHT OF BENIN

ATLANTIC OCEAN

8.2%

Equator

AMAZONIA

7.2%

PERNAMBUCO

12.1%

WEST CENTRAL AFRICA

SOUTH AMERICA

BAHIA

BRAZIL

SOUTHEAST BRAZIL

Number of Captives Traded per Region

2,000,000

1,000,000

500,000

Under 100,000

Figures on the paths represent the percentage of embarking captives who died on board.

Boundaries as of 1650 shown

0   500   1000 kilometers

0   500   1000 miles

Little is known about voyage length in the early Brazilian slave trade; mortality was substantially below that on vessels sailing to the Caribbean in the same period. A larger proportion of West Central African than West African captives died on the crossing to Brazil even though vessels from West Central Africa probably spent less time en route. The pattern is the opposite to the one that appears in the Caribbean traffic (see maps 117, 119, 121, and 123). As this map shows, slavers bound for Brazil did not draw on the Bight of Biafra region, with its high mortality.

Map 126: Slave Mortality for Slaves Arriving in Brazilian Regions from Africa, 1638–1775

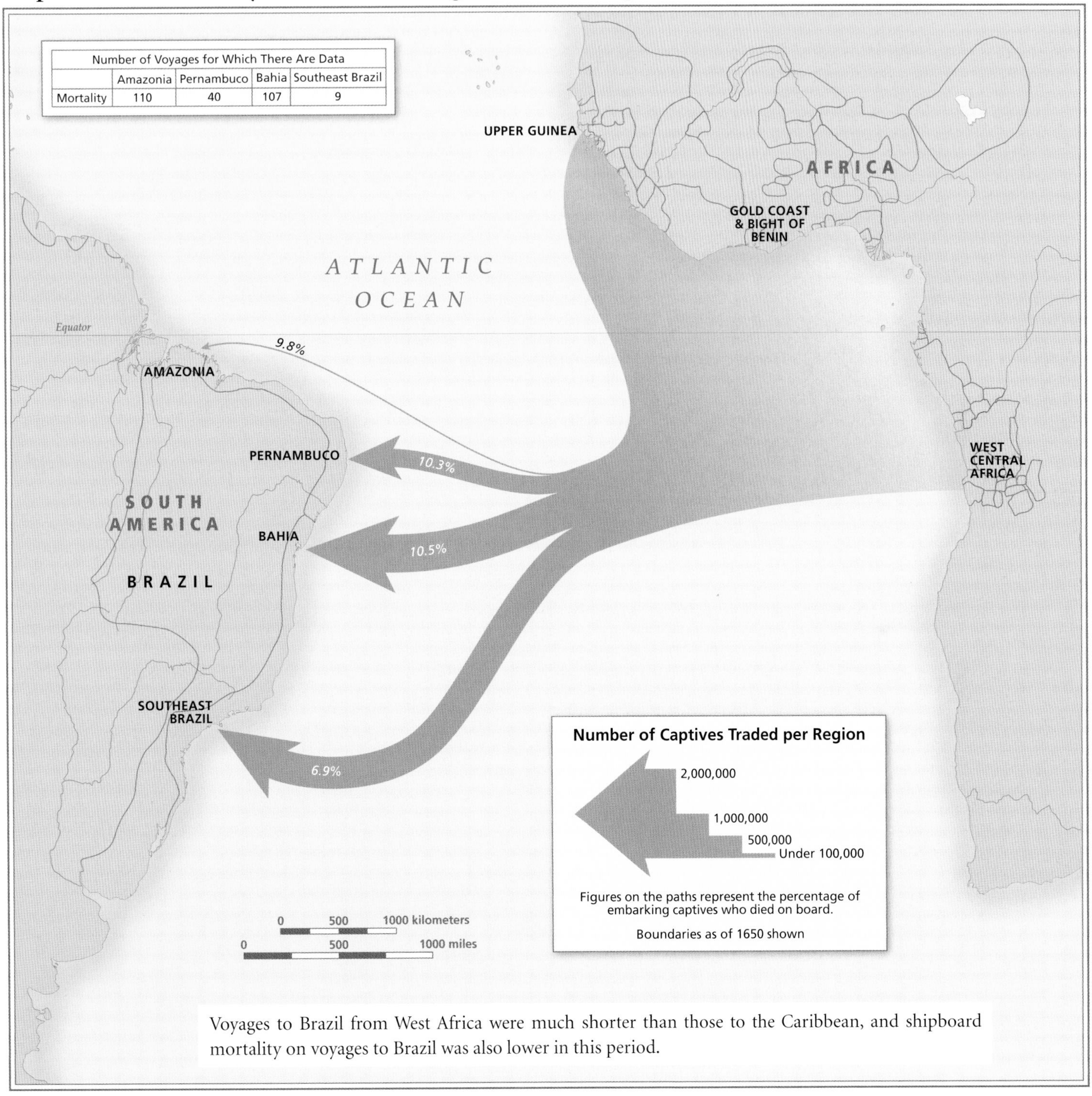

Number of Voyages for Which There Are Data				
	Amazonia	Pernambuco	Bahia	Southeast Brazil
Mortality	110	40	107	9

UPPER GUINEA

AFRICA

GOLD COAST & BIGHT OF BENIN

ATLANTIC OCEAN

Equator

9.8%

AMAZONIA

PERNAMBUCO

10.3%

WEST CENTRAL AFRICA

SOUTH AMERICA

BAHIA

10.5%

BRAZIL

SOUTHEAST BRAZIL

6.9%

Number of Captives Traded per Region

2,000,000

1,000,000

500,000

Under 100,000

Figures on the paths represent the percentage of embarking captives who died on board.

Boundaries as of 1650 shown

0   500   1000 kilometers

0   500   1000 miles

Voyages to Brazil from West Africa were much shorter than those to the Caribbean, and shipboard mortality on voyages to Brazil was also lower in this period.

Map 127: Slave Mortality and Voyage Length for Slaves Leaving African Regions for Brazil, 1776–1830

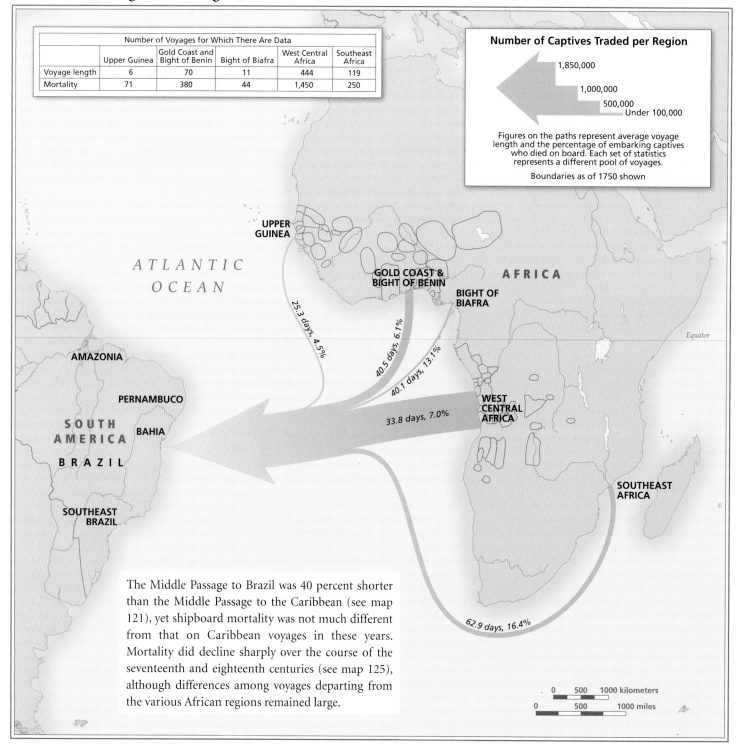

Number of Voyages for Which There Are Data					
	Upper Guinea	Gold Coast and Bight of Benin	Bight of Biafra	West Central Africa	Southeast Africa
Voyage length	6	70	11	444	119
Mortality	71	380	44	1,450	250

Number of Captives Traded per Region

1,850,000

1,000,000

500,000

Under 100,000

Figures on the paths represent average voyage length and the percentage of embarking captives who died on board. Each set of statistics represents a different pool of voyages.

Boundaries as of 1750 shown

ATLANTIC OCEAN

AFRICA

UPPER GUINEA

GOLD COAST & BIGHT OF BENIN

BIGHT OF BIAFRA

WEST CENTRAL AFRICA

SOUTHEAST AFRICA

Equator

AMAZONIA

PERNAMBUCO

SOUTH AMERICA

BAHIA

BRAZIL

SOUTHEAST BRAZIL

25.3 days, 4.5%

40.5 days, 6.1%

40.1 days, 13.1%

33.8 days, 7.0%

62.9 days, 16.4%

The Middle Passage to Brazil was 40 percent shorter than the Middle Passage to the Caribbean (see map 121), yet shipboard mortality was not much different from that on Caribbean voyages in these years. Mortality did decline sharply over the course of the seventeenth and eighteenth centuries (see map 125), although differences among voyages departing from the various African regions remained large.

0   500   1000 kilometers

0   500   1000 miles

Map 128: Slave Mortality and Voyage Length for Slaves Arriving in Brazilian Regions from Africa, 1776–1830

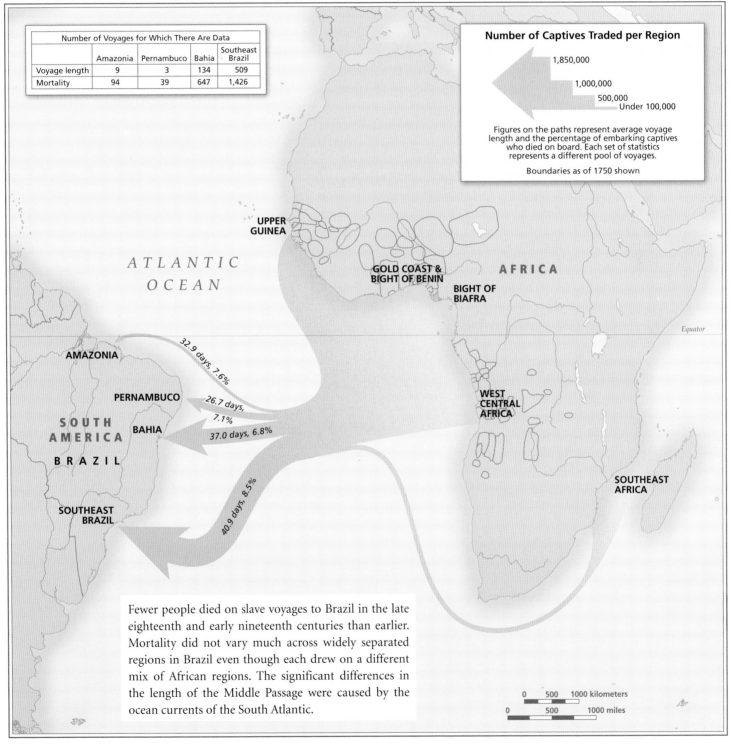

Number of Voyages for Which There Are Data				
	Amazonia	Pernambuco	Bahia	Southeast Brazil
Voyage length	9	3	134	509
Mortality	94	39	647	1,426

Number of Captives Traded per Region

1,850,000
1,000,000
500,000
Under 100,000

Figures on the paths represent average voyage length and the percentage of embarking captives who died on board. Each set of statistics represents a different pool of voyages.

Boundaries as of 1750 shown

ATLANTIC OCEAN

UPPER GUINEA

GOLD COAST & BIGHT OF BENIN

AFRICA

BIGHT OF BIAFRA

Equator

AMAZONIA

32.9 days, 7.6%

PERNAMBUCO

26.7 days, 7.1%

SOUTH AMERICA

BAHIA

37.0 days, 6.8%

WEST CENTRAL AFRICA

BRAZIL

40.9 days, 8.5%

SOUTHEAST AFRICA

SOUTHEAST BRAZIL

Fewer people died on slave voyages to Brazil in the late eighteenth and early nineteenth centuries than earlier. Mortality did not vary much across widely separated regions in Brazil even though each drew on a different mix of African regions. The significant differences in the length of the Middle Passage were caused by the ocean currents of the South Atlantic.

0   500   1000 kilometers
0   500   1000 miles

Map 129: Slave Mortality and Voyage Length for Slaves Leaving African Regions for Brazil, 1831–1851

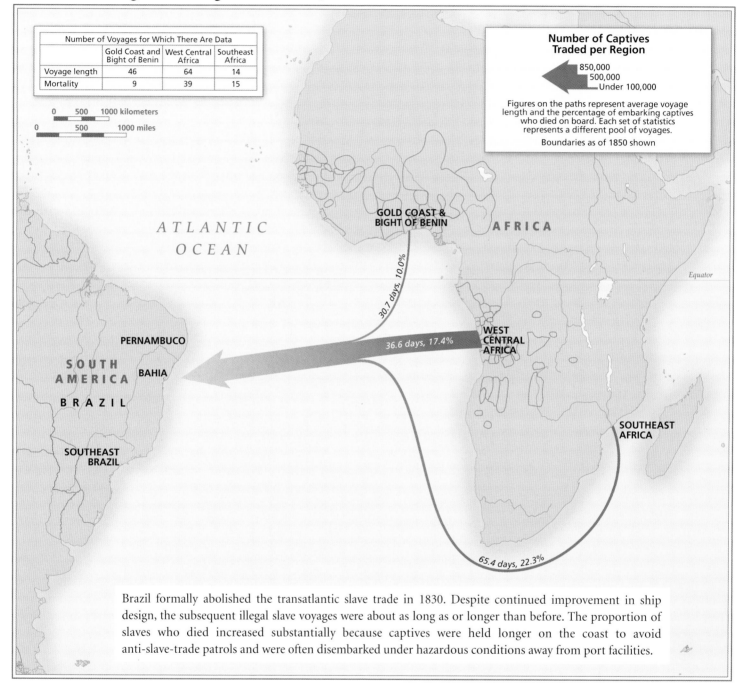

Number of Voyages for Which There Are Data			
	Gold Coast and Bight of Benin	West Central Africa	Southeast Africa
Voyage length	46	64	14
Mortality	9	39	15

0   500   1000 kilometers

0   500   1000 miles

Number of Captives Traded per Region

850,000
500,000
Under 100,000

Figures on the paths represent average voyage length and the percentage of embarking captives who died on board. Each set of statistics represents a different pool of voyages.

Boundaries as of 1850 shown

ATLANTIC OCEAN

AFRICA

Equator

GOLD COAST & BIGHT OF BENIN

30.7 days, 10.0%

WEST CENTRAL AFRICA

36.6 days, 17.4%

PERNAMBUCO

SOUTH AMERICA   BAHIA

BRAZIL

SOUTHEAST BRAZIL

SOUTHEAST AFRICA

65.4 days, 22.3%

Brazil formally abolished the transatlantic slave trade in 1830. Despite continued improvement in ship design, the subsequent illegal slave voyages were about as long as or longer than before. The proportion of slaves who died increased substantially because captives were held longer on the coast to avoid anti-slave-trade patrols and were often disembarked under hazardous conditions away from port facilities.

Map 130: Slave Mortality and Voyage Length for Slaves Arriving in Brazilian Regions from Africa, 1831–1851

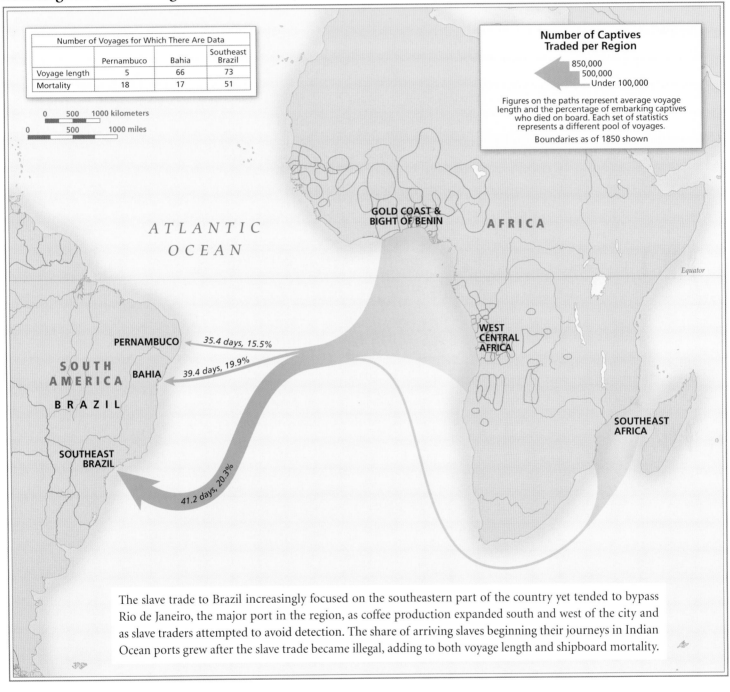

Number of Voyages for Which There Are Data			
	Pernambuco	Bahia	Southeast Brazil
Voyage length	5	66	73
Mortality	18	17	51

0 500 1000 kilometers

0 500 1000 miles

Number of Captives Traded per Region

850,000
500,000
Under 100,000

Figures on the paths represent average voyage length and the percentage of embarking captives who died on board. Each set of statistics represents a different pool of voyages.

Boundaries as of 1850 shown

ATLANTIC OCEAN

GOLD COAST & BIGHT OF BENIN

AFRICA

Equator

WEST CENTRAL AFRICA

SOUTHEAST AFRICA

PERNAMBUCO

35.4 days, 15.5%

SOUTH AMERICA

BAHIA

39.4 days, 19.9%

BRAZIL

SOUTHEAST BRAZIL

41.2 days, 20.3%

The slave trade to Brazil increasingly focused on the southeastern part of the country yet tended to bypass Rio de Janeiro, the major port in the region, as coffee production expanded south and west of the city and as slave traders attempted to avoid detection. The share of arriving slaves beginning their journeys in Indian Ocean ports grew after the slave trade became illegal, adding to both voyage length and shipboard mortality.

June 6th 1770   The Slaves made an Insurrection, wch. Was soon quelled, with ye [the] Loss of two Women

Saturday June 22nd 1770   the Slaves attempted an Insurrection, lost a man of Capt. Monypenny's Purchase No. 1 who jumped overboard & was drown'd[. We were] Employ'd securing ye. Men in Chains, and gave ye. women concerned 24 Lashes each

Tuesday 26 June.   The slaves this Day proposed making an Insurrection and a few of them got off their Handcuffs, but were detected in Time

Wednesday 27th June   the Slaves attempted to force up ye Gratings [from the hold] in ye Night, with a design to murder ye whites or drown themselves, but were prevented by ye watch in ye morning they confessed their Intention, and that ye women as well as the men were determin'd if dissapointed of cutting off ye whites, to jump overboard, but in Case of being prevented by their Irons were resolved as their last resource to burn the Ship. their Obstinacy put me under ye Necessity of shooting ye Ringleader.

Wednesday July 11th 1770   A Man no. 3 A Woman No. 4 of Capt Monypenny Purchase Died Mad. they had frequently attempted to drown themselves since their Views were dissapointed in ye Insurrection.

Excerpt from A Journall of a Voyage in the Ship Unity of Liverpool bound to Holland, Africa & Jamaica, kept by Robert Norris, master, commencing at Liverpool Sunday July 23rd 1769 & ending at Liverpool Tuesday May 21st 1771. Earle Family and Business Archive, National Maritime Museum on Merseyside, Liverpool. Published with permission of the National Maritime Museum on Merseyside.

Map 131: Slave-Ship Revolts and Percentage of Slaves Who Embarked, by African Region of Departure, 1566–1865

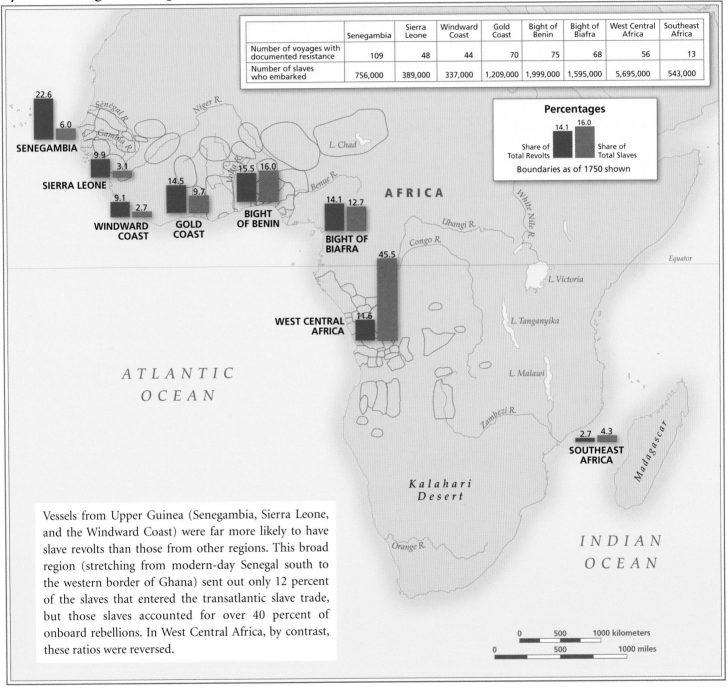

	Senegambia	Sierra Leone	Windward Coast	Gold Coast	Bight of Benin	Bight of Biafra	West Central Africa	Southeast Africa
Number of voyages with documented resistance	109	48	44	70	75	68	56	13
Number of slaves who embarked	756,000	389,000	337,000	1,209,000	1,999,000	1,595,000	5,695,000	543,000

Percentages

14.1 Share of Total Revolts 16.0 Share of Total Slaves

Boundaries as of 1750 shown

22.6 / 6.0 **SENEGAMBIA**

9.9 / 3.1 **SIERRA LEONE**

9.1 / 2.7 **WINDWARD COAST**

14.5 / 9.7 **GOLD COAST**

15.5 / 16.0 **BIGHT OF BENIN**

14.1 / 12.7 **BIGHT OF BIAFRA**

45.5 / 11.6 **WEST CENTRAL AFRICA**

2.7 / 4.3 **SOUTHEAST AFRICA**

AFRICA

Niger R. *Sénégal R.* *Gambia R.* *Benue R.* *L. Chad* *Ubangi R.* *Congo R.* *White Nile R.* *L. Victoria* *Equator* *L. Tanganyika* *L. Malawi* *Zambezi R.* *Madagascar*

ATLANTIC OCEAN

Kalahari Desert *Orange R.* *INDIAN OCEAN*

Vessels from Upper Guinea (Senegambia, Sierra Leone, and the Windward Coast) were far more likely to have slave revolts than those from other regions. This broad region (stretching from modern-day Senegal south to the western border of Ghana) sent out only 12 percent of the slaves that entered the transatlantic slave trade, but those slaves accounted for over 40 percent of onboard rebellions. In West Central Africa, by contrast, these ratios were reversed.

0   500   1000 kilometers
0   500   1000 miles

Map 132: Phases of Slave Voyages during Which Slaves Rebelled, 1566–1865

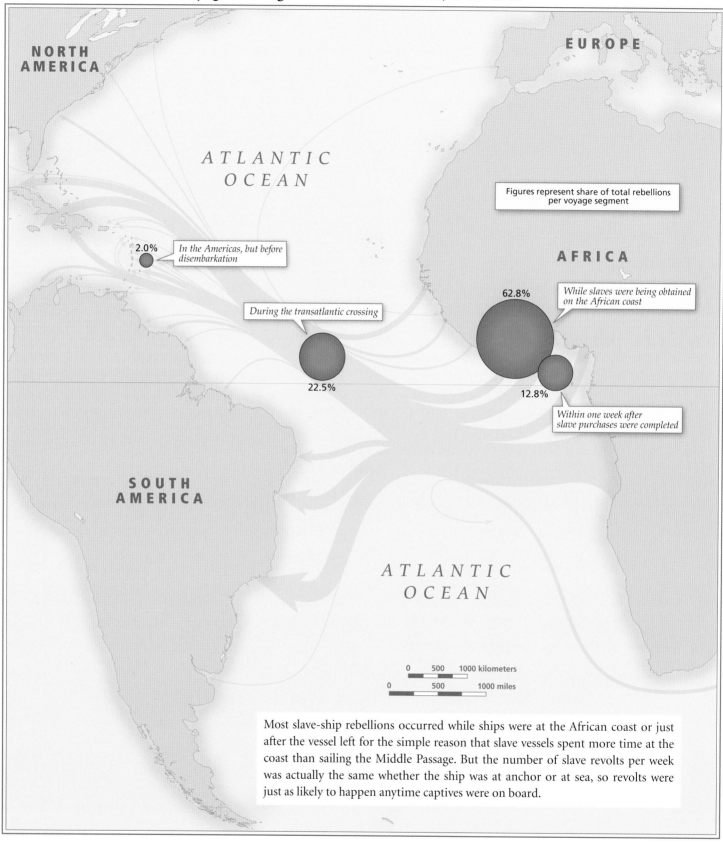

NORTH AMERICA

EUROPE

ATLANTIC OCEAN

Figures represent share of total rebellions per voyage segment

AFRICA

2.0% *In the Americas, but before disembarkation*

62.8% *While slaves were being obtained on the African coast*

During the transatlantic crossing

22.5%

12.8%

Within one week after slave purchases were completed

SOUTH AMERICA

ATLANTIC OCEAN

0   500   1000 kilometers
0   500   1000 miles

Most slave-ship rebellions occurred while ships were at the African coast or just after the vessel left for the simple reason that slave vessels spent more time at the coast than sailing the Middle Passage. But the number of slave revolts per week was actually the same whether the ship was at anchor or at sea, so revolts were just as likely to happen anytime captives were on board.

Insurrection on Board a Slave Ship, 1851

Aquatint by W. L. Walton, from William Fox, *A Brief History of the Wesleyan Missions on the Western Coast of Africa* (London: Aylott and Jones, 1851), p. 116. Image courtesy of the Division of Rare and Manuscript Collections, Cornell University Libraries.

Death of Capt. Ferrer, the Captain of the Amistad, July, 1839.

Don Jose Ruiz and Don Pedro Montez, of the Island of Cuba, having purchased fifty-three slaves at Havana, recently imported from Africa, put them on board the Amistad, Capt. Ferrer, in order to transport them to Principe, another port on the Island of Cuba. After being out from Havana about four days, the African captives on board, in order to obtain their freedom, and return to Africa, armed themselves with cane knives, and rose upon the Captain and crew of the vessel. Capt. Ferrer and the cook of the vessel were killed; two of the crew escaped; Ruiz and Montez were made prisoners.

Death of Capt. Ferrer, the Captain of the *Amistad,* July, 1839

Color lithograph from John Warner Barber, *A History of the Amistad Captives* (New Haven, Conn.: E. L. Barber and J. W. Barber, 1840), frontispiece. Manuscripts, Archives and Rare Books Division, Schomburg Center for Research in Black Culture, The New York Public Library, Astor, Lenox and Tilden Foundations.

Rebellions occurred whenever captives were on board ship. In the aquatint by W. L. Walton, the crew, sheltered behind a barricade that spans the deck, are firing down on rebellious Africans. Several Africans are shown diving overboard. Many others are hidden in clouds of gunsmoke. The image of the *Amistad* mutiny is a contemporary representation of the celebrated uprising. The *Amistad* was engaged in intra-American slave trafficking when the captives, led by Cinque, overpowered the crew, killed the captain, and seized control of the vessel. It eventually reached the United States, where, after a lengthy legal process, the captives were freed and returned to Africa.

Map 133: Linguistic Identifications of Liberated Africans Who Embarked in Cameroon, 1822–1837

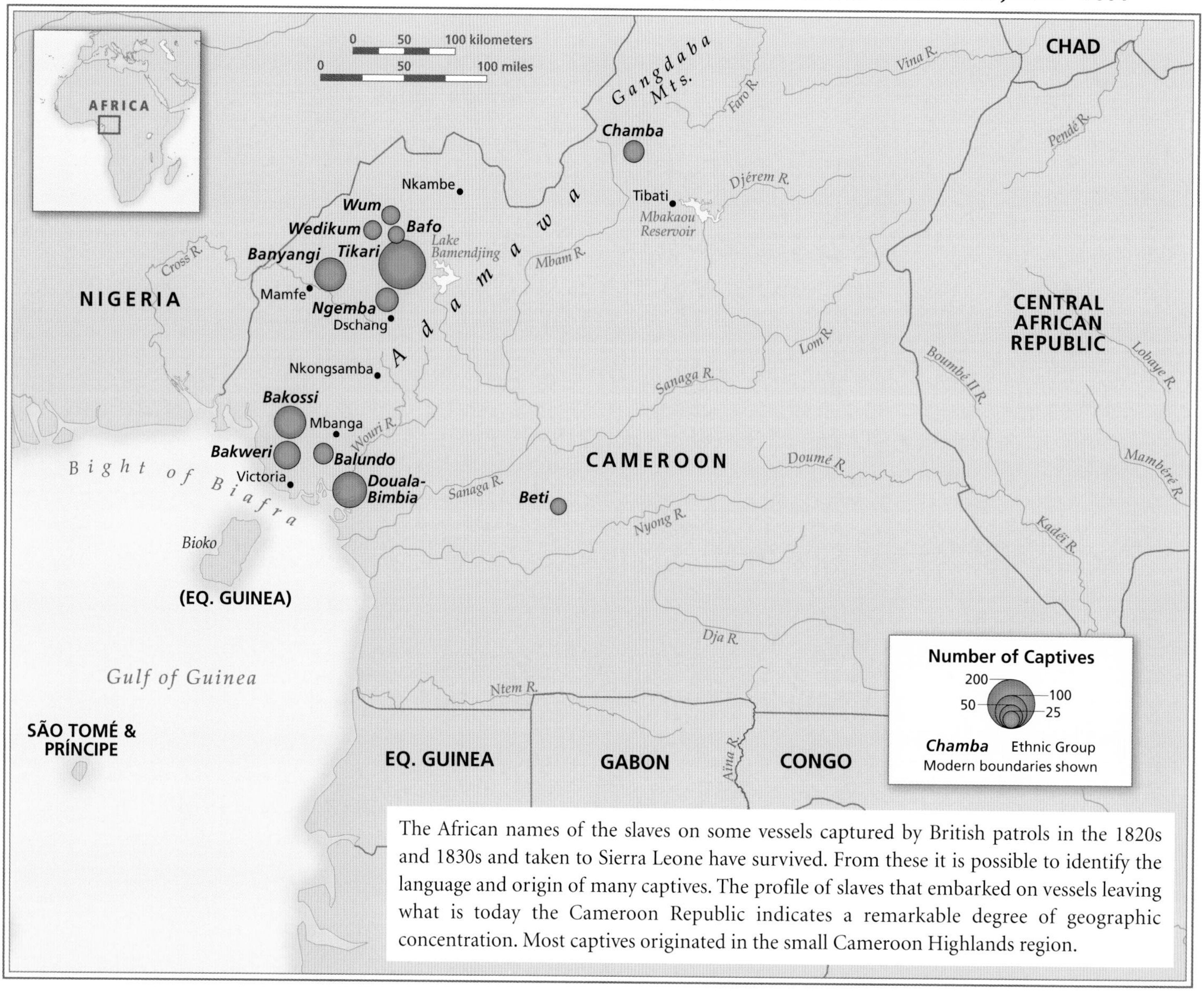

The African names of the slaves on some vessels captured by British patrols in the 1820s and 1830s and taken to Sierra Leone have survived. From these it is possible to identify the language and origin of many captives. The profile of slaves that embarked on vessels leaving what is today the Cameroon Republic indicates a remarkable degree of geographic concentration. Most captives originated in the small Cameroon Highlands region.

Nº	Name	Sex	Age	Stature (ft. in.)		Description
4385	Ahmirah	Man	22	5	10	Yellow complexion, cuts on he[...]
4386	Dahunny	„	25	5	3	do do do
4387	Iggie	„	22	5	5	Cuts on face and body
4388	Agelarbugee	„	19	5	0	No marks
4389	Oneirdie	„	24	5	5	Cuts on face, back and belly
4390	Janai	„	22	5	6	No marks
4391	Adoo	„	23	5	6	Tattooed on Arms & Back
4392	Chaibee	„	20	5	4	Cuts on face and belly
4393	Achelookoo	„	19	5	4	do do do
4394	Auchau	„	28	5	6	do do do
4395	Auchau	„	18	5	3	do do do
4396	Chokailoo	„	30	5	6	do do do
4397	Barbarogah	„	20	5	7	do do Breast
4398	Abbochah	„	22	5	8½	do do do b[...]
4399	Dukulm	„	28	5	8	do do do
4400	Tirarmor	„	19	5	4	No marks
4401	Bubikah	„	22	5	4	Cuts on body and Arms
4402	Koodibarkie	„	26	5	4	do do
4403	Monamarootoo	„	22	5	5	do all over body
4404	Kootie	„	20	5	5	Cuts on belly, back & Cheek[...]
4405	Auchau	„	21	5	3	do face
4406	Dussomor	„	26	5	5	do do back and che[...]
4407	Neorgum	„	19	5	7	do do do

Register of Liberated Africans, 1824

Extract from the Portuguese brig *Dois Amigos Brasileiros* register of slaves, 1824. Foreign Office, FO 84/3, p. 321, The National Archives of the UK. Published with permission of The National Archives of the UK.

Courts of Mixed Commission were created at several venues in the Atlantic basin after 1817 as part of the British-led effort to suppress international slave trading. The courts passed judgment on those suspected of illegal slaving activities, who were detained by naval vessels in international waters. Captives on board ships condemned for illegal trade were liberated, and registers with their name, age, height, and body marks, including scarifications, were kept in an effort to prevent their subsequent reenslavement. Among the earliest and most important of these courts was the one established at Freetown, Sierra Leone, the slave registers of which cover 1819 to 1845 and provide the largest source of data on identities of Africans forced into the Atlantic slave trade. Shown here is a page of the slave register arising from the seizure and condemnation of the brig *Dois Amigos Brasileiros* (voyage id 2945) at Freetown in 1824.

Map 134: Linguistic Identifications of Liberated Africans Who Embarked in the Sierra Leone Region, 1819–1844

Number of Captives

200 — 100
50 — 25

KAABU   Historical State
Mende   Ethnic Group
Galinhas●   Embarkation Point
Boundaries as of 1850 shown

Africans on board captured slave vessels who were taken to Sierra Leone and Havana supplied their names and places of origin. The 1,557 slaves from the Sierra Leone area represented all major language groups and came from all across the region. As in Cameroon, most captives came from within 150 miles of the coast. In West Central Africa other kinds of evidence suggest that slaves traveled much longer distances prior to embarkation. (See Philip Misevich, "The Origins of Slaves Leaving the Upper Guinea Coast in the Nineteenth Century," in David Eltis and David Richardson, eds., *Extending the Frontiers: Essays on the New Transatlantic Slave Trade Database* [New Haven: Yale University Press, 2008].)

To make mankind labour beyond their wants,
to make one part of a state work to maintain the
other gratuitously, could only be brought about
by slavery, and slavery was therefore introduced
universally. Slavery was then as necessary towards
multiplication, as it would now be destructive of
it. The reason is plain. If mankind be not forced
to labour, they will labour for themselves only;
and if they have few wants, there will be little
labour . . . . From these principles it appears,
that slavery in former times had the same effect
in peopling the world that trade and industry
have now. Men were then forced to labour because
they were slaves to others; men are now forced to
labour because they are slaves to their own wants.

Excerpt from Sir James Steuart, *An Inquiry into the
Principles of Political Economy* (London: A. Millar and T.
Cadell, 1767), book 1, chap. 7.

The experience of all ages and nations, I believe,
demonstrates that the work done by slaves,
though it appears to cost only their maintenance,
is in the end the dearest of any. A person who can
acquire no property can have no other interest
but to eat as much and to labour as little as
possible. Whatever work he does beyond what is
sufficient to purchase his own maintenance, can
be squeezed out of him by violence only, and not
by interest of his own.

Excerpt from Adam Smith, *An Inquiry into the Nature and
Causes of the Wealth of Nations,* new ed. (1776; London:
Routledge, 1900), p. 298.

Maps 135 and 136: Black Populations of the Caribbean and the North American Mainland in 1750 and 1830 with Prior Inflows of Slaves from Africa

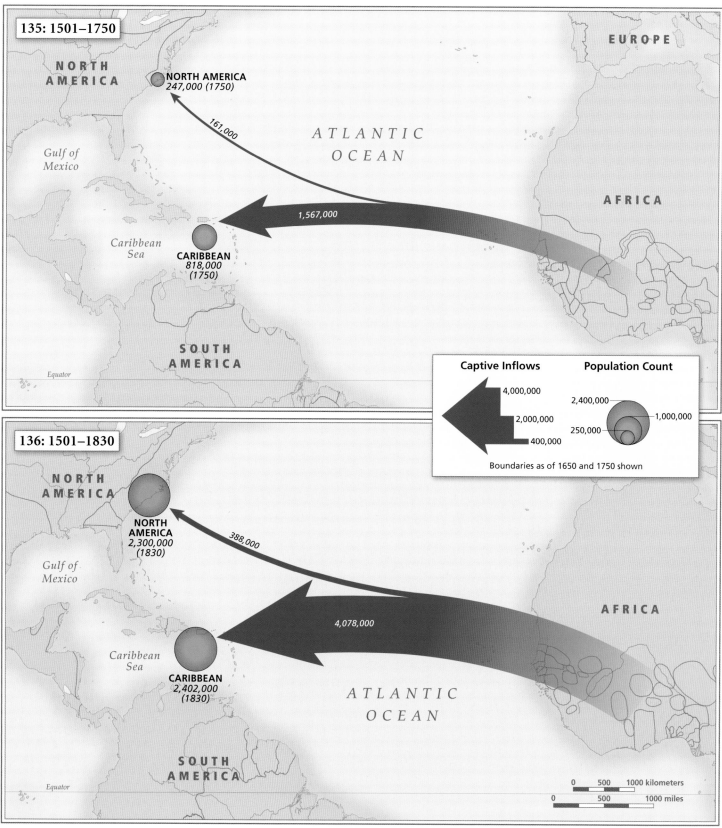

135: 1501–1750

EUROPE

NORTH AMERICA

NORTH AMERICA
247,000 (1750)

ATLANTIC OCEAN

Gulf of Mexico

161,000

AFRICA

1,567,000

Caribbean Sea

CARIBBEAN
818,000
(1750)

SOUTH AMERICA

Equator

Captive Inflows

4,000,000

2,000,000

400,000

Population Count

2,400,000

1,000,000

250,000

Boundaries as of 1650 and 1750 shown

136: 1501–1830

NORTH AMERICA

NORTH AMERICA
2,300,000
(1830)

Gulf of Mexico

388,000

AFRICA

4,078,000

Caribbean Sea

CARIBBEAN
2,402,000
(1830)

ATLANTIC OCEAN

SOUTH AMERICA

Equator

0 500 1000 kilometers
0 500 1000 miles

The slave trade to the Caribbean was much larger than the slave trade to the North American mainland. By 1750, the Caribbean had received nine times as many Africans, yet the mainland population of African origin was already almost a third the size of the black population in the Caribbean. By 1830, over ten times the number of captives had arrived in the Caribbean as in North America. Nevertheless, in that year the black populations in the two regions were just about equal. The Caribbean had a large black population because of huge inflows of slaves; the mainland, by contrast, had grown mostly because of a positive natural growth rate – a product of a healthier and more nutritionally secure environment.

Part V
The Destinations of Slaves in the Americas and Their Links with the Atlantic World

We use 1501 as the starting date of an uninterrupted slave trade, but African captives may have arrived in the Americas on Columbus's third voyage in 1498. The first transatlantic slaves came by way of Europe rather than directly from Africa until 1525. It is estimated that a total of 10.7 million captives arrived from Africa, or about 30,000 a year over three and a half centuries. (See the *Voyages* Web site for details.) Table 6 shows the distribution of these arrivals over regions of the Americas; an "Africa" category accounts for those whose transatlantic voyages were diverted as a result of a slave revolt or interception by a naval cruiser attempting to suppress the trade in the nineteenth century. Until 1830 and the beginning of mass migrations from Europe, between three and four Africans crossed the Atlantic for every European, making the Americas more a demographic extension of Africa than of Europe before the nineteenth century. The first Africans to arrive were probably personal servants, but with the discovery of gold in Hispaniola and the collapse of the Amerindian population in the West Indies, the Spanish soon began to bring in slave labor, primarily to generate commodity exports. For the first century of the transatlantic slave trade, the production of precious metals—first gold, then silver—dictated the involvement of the Western Hemisphere in the slave trade, even though the mining labor force mainly comprised American Indians. Until the 1590s and the full development of the silver mines in Potosi, Bolivia, the number of Africans brought in was modest—probably between 1,000 and 2,000 a year. Over the long run, the principal source of demand for captives was not precious metals but sugar. For the two centuries during which both the size and the range of the transatlantic slave traffic expanded dramatically, it was the plantations of the Americas, not the mines, that created the demand for labor. Within the plantation sector, it was sugar that pulled in 80 percent of the captives unloaded from the crowded slave ships. During the eighteenth century, Caribbean islands led the economic growth of the Americas, and captive African laborers made that possible.

The sugar plantation complex moved to the Americas via the Mediterranean, the Atlantic Mediterranean, and São Tomé in the Gulf of Guinea (see map 2). It was established first in northeastern Brazil (1560s) and then in the eastern Caribbean (1630s and 1640s); by the mid-1600s it had become apparent that the conditions under which sugar was grown meant that some form of coerced labor was essential if consumers were to get their preferred sweetener for prices they could afford. European laborers could choose not to work on sugar plantations, and the indigenous population had declined too much to be a feasible alternative source of labor. Slave arrivals from Africa expanded from 2,000 a year in the 1570s to 7,000 a year in the early 1600s to 18,000 annually by the time sugar was well established in the eastern Caribbean in the 1660s. The number tripled in size over the next seventy years as the sugar complex spread to the western Caribbean, then almost doubled again in the 1780s and 1790s, when the traffic reached its all-time peak of nearly 80,000 arrivals each year. The most important of the non-sugar commodities in this story of expansion was Brazilian gold, extracted after discoveries in Minas Gerais in the mid-1690s and in Goiás later. Coffee, whose production in the Americas began in the French Caribbean in the early eighteenth century, also grew in importance. After 1807, coffee cultivation in the states of Rio de Janeiro and São Paulo temporarily surpassed the sugar sectors of Brazil and the Caribbean as the main driver of demand for African labor in the Americas.

Most of the captives carried off from Africa ended up in the Caribbean and Brazil. The two temperate areas of the Americas that also required slave labor—north of the Florida border and south of Paranaguá, mainly in the Río de la Plata region—together absorbed only about 4 percent of the captives who arrived in the Americas. The rice, tobacco, beef jerky, and indigo produced in these regions were of small economic significance compared to sugar. The massive cotton crops of the southern United States in the nineteenth century were produced for the most part without labor purchased directly from Africa. Table 7 shows the relative distribution of arrivals by port (rather than by region, as in table 6). Slaves passed through a wider range of ports in the Americas than on the African coast, but the importance of Rio de Janeiro, Salvador da Bahia, Recife, Kingston (Jamaica), Bridgetown (Barbados), Havana, and Cap-Français (St.-Domingue, or Haiti) is immediately obvious. Six out of ten captives passed through these seven ports, and more than three-quarters passed through just twenty ports. None of the top seven ports and only one of the top twenty, Charleston, was located in what became the United States.

The port information points indirectly to a central feature of the slave trade that has yet to be fully documented: the intra-American slave trade—that is, the movement of captives after they arrived in the Americas. All of the top seven ports shown in table 7 were transit points for captives subsequently dispatched to other parts of the Americas. Most of this traffic occurred after the transatlantic slave trade ended—for example, from the Chesapeake and the Carolinas to New Orleans after 1807 in the United States, and from northeast to southeast Brazil after 1851. This intra-American trade was a result of the suppression of the transatlantic trade, and a substitute for it. But even when the transatlantic traffic was most active, there were always markets for slave labor that were too small or too remote for direct delivery from Africa, and some markets were not fully accessible for political reasons (for example, Spanish American protectionist policies before 1789). It seems likely that about one in four Africans who survived the Middle Passage had to endure a further journey, sometimes lasting as long as the Middle Passage itself, before they reached their final destination.

A steady stream of captives went from Brazilian ports to the Río de la Plata over the course of two centuries, and even then, most captives arriving in the Río de la Plata region faced a long journey overland (although a few went by sea around the southern tip of the continent) to what are now Bolivia, Peru, and even Chile. Within Brazil, the gold-producing areas of Minas Gerais and Goiás received captives overland from such major ports as Salvador da Bahia and Rio de Janeiro. For 150 years Peru and New Spain (the Spanish territory in the southwestern United States, Mexico, Central America, the West Indies, and the Philippines, combined) received African captives by way of an intra-Caribbean trade based in Jamaica, Barbados, and Curaçao. The North American mainland received probably 15 percent of its captives from ports in the Caribbean, especially the eastern Caribbean. Even within the Caribbean, such islands as Dominica, St. Vincent, St. Eustatius, and tiny St.-Barthélemy distributed captives recently arrived from Africa to other islands.

Table 6   Number of Slaves Estimated to Have Arrived at Major Regions in the Atlantic World, 1501–1867

	Europe	Mainland North America					Dutch Caribbean		Danish West Indies
		Northern United States	Chesapeake Bay	Carolinas / Georgia	Gulf Coast	Unspecified	Dutch West Indies	Dutch Guianas	
1501–1525	500	0	0	0	0	0	0	0	0
1526–1550	0	0	0	0	0	0	0	0	0
1551–1575	0	0	0	0	0	0	0	0	0
1576–1600	200	0	0	0	0	0	0	0	0
1601–1625	90	0	0	0	0	0	0	0	0
1626–1650	0	0	100	0	0	0	0	0	0
1651–1675	1,300	1,100	2,900	0	0	0	38,000	14,000	0
1676–1700	1,600	1,700	9,200	0	0	100	46,000	26,000	18,000
1701–1725	200	1,300	30,000	5,500	2,500	0	29,000	24,000	8,100
1726–1750	4,000	12,000	54,000	36,000	4,700	900	13,000	60,000	4,500
1751–1775	1,100	11,000	31,000	76,000	1,600	0	16,000	102,000	18,000
1776–1800	20	300	500	27,000	2,900	400	7,700	43,000	38,000
1801–1825	0	300	70	67,000	10,000	500	0	25,000	17,000
1826–1850	0	0	0	0	90	0	0	0	5,000
1851–1866	0	0	0	300	100	0	0	0	0
Total*	9,010	27,700	127,770	211,800	21,890	1,900	149,700	294,000	108,600

British Caribbean

	Jamaica	Barbados	Antigua	St. Kitts	Grenada	Dominica	British Guiana	St. Vincent	Montserrat / Nevis	Trinidad / Tobago	Other
1501–1525	0	0	0	0	0	0	0	0	0	0	0
1526–1550	0	0	0	0	0	0	0	0	0	0	0
1551–1575	0	0	0	0	0	0	0	0	0	0	0
1576–1600	0	0	0	0	0	0	0	0	0	0	0
1601–1625	100	0	0	0	0	0	0	0	0	500	0
1626–1650	0	26,000	0	800	0	0	0	0	0	0	0
1651–1675	18,000	63,000	0	1,000	200	0	0	0	2,300	1,500	1,300
1676–1700	73,000	93,000	6,000	1,700	0	0	0	0	20,000	0	2,900
1701–1725	135,000	96,000	25,000	7,100	500	0	0	0	13,000	0	4,600
1726–1750	188,000	74,000	38,000	48,000	500	0	0	0	7,000	0	1,600
1751–1775	232,000	107,000	53,000	60,000	50,000	42,000	0	14,000	4,400	1,900	16,000
1776–1800	300,000	28,000	12,000	13,000	71,000	60,000	31,000	36,000	200	19,000	23,000
1801–1825	69,000	6,800	4,800	2,700	4,600	8,600	42,000	8,400	500	20,000	17,000
1826–1850	2,400	400	0	0	1,100	0	300	0	0	1,300	5,200
1851–1866	0	0	0	0	0	0	0	0	0	0	0
Total*	1,017,500	494,200	138,800	134,300	127,900	110,600	73,300	58,400	47,400	44,200	71,600

Table 6 (continued)

	French Caribbean					Spanish America				
	St.-Domingue	Martinique	Guadeloupe	French Guiana	Unspecified	Cuba	Puerto Rico	Spanish Caribbean Mainland	Río de la Plata	Unspecified
1501–1525	0	0	0	0	0	0	0	0	0	8,900
1526–1550	0	0	0	0	0	0	0	1,900	0	34,000
1551–1575	0	0	0	0	0	0	0	3,600	0	37,000
1576–1600	0	0	0	0	0	0	0	45,000	0	40,000
1601–1625	0	0	0	0	0	0	0	106,000	0	12,000
1626–1650	0	500	0	0	0	0	0	53,000	700	8,000
1651–1675	0	7,700	3,100	1,100	4,900	300	300	19,000	5,500	6,700
1676–1700	4,900	10,000	300	1,400	4,500	0	0	14,000	100	0
1701–1725	43,000	33,000	1,200	1,300	3,600	2,400	0	19,000	17,000	200
1726–1750	141,000	68,000	900	2,600	800	1,000	400	3,700	11,000	1,200
1751–1775	244,000	30,000	29,000	3,500	3,300	8,400	9,800	800	900	1,200
1776–1800	340,000	30,000	13,000	6,300	1,900	56,000	500	1,900	6,700	3,900
1801–1825	800	24,000	22,000	10,000	6,100	229,000	3,700	600	22,000	400
1826–1850	0	14,000	3,500	4,400	1,300	318,000	12,000	0	3,800	0
1851–1866	0	0	0	0	0	164,000	0	0	0	0
Total*	773,700	217,200	73,000	30,600	26,400	779,100	26,700	268,500	67,700	153,500

	Brazil					Africa[†]	Total for All Regions by Quarter-Century*
	Amazonia	Bahia	Pernambuco	Southeast Brazil	Unspecified		
1501–1525	0	0	0	0	0	0	9,400
1526–1550	0	0	0	0	0	0	35,900
1551–1575	0	0	2,500	0	0	0	43,100
1576–1600	0	5,600	16,000	4,800	300	0	111,900
1601–1625	0	46,000	77,000	32,000	700	0	274,390
1626–1650	0	69,000	45,000	48,000	1,400	200	252,700
1651–1675	0	94,900	41,000	68,000	100	2,500	399,700
1676–1700	1,100	103,000	83,000	72,000	0	500	594,000
1701–1725	2,500	185,000	111,000	122,000	3,100	0	926,100
1726–1750	1,700	231,000	73,000	160,000	2,900	500	1,245,900
1751–1775	23,000	176,000	71,000	205,000	1,400	400	1,644,700
1776–1800	45,000	224,000	75,000	270,000	8,100	1,400	1,796,720
1801–1825	59,000	256,000	170,000	500,000	28,000	32,000	1,667,870
1826–1850	10,000	158,000	89,000	776,000	8,380	99,900	1,514,070
1851–1866	0	1,000	400	5,600	0	18,000	189,400
Total*	142,300	1,549,500	853,900	2,263,400	54,380	155,400	10,705,850

Source: Voyages Web site, http://www.slavevoyages.org/tast/assessment/estimates.faces?yearFrom=1501&yearTo=1866: set cells = "only slaves disembarked" and columns = "specific regions of disembarkation."

* The column and row totals in this table differ slightly from the data on the *Voyages* Web site because of the rounding rules used throughout this volume and explained in "About This Atlas."

† Refers to African captives liberated from slave ships en route to the Americas.

Table 7   Estimated Number of Slaves Carried on Vessels Arriving at the Largest Twenty Ports of Disembarkation in the Americas, 1501–1867

Port*	Number of Slaves
Rio de Janeiro	1,839,000
Salvador da Bahia	1,550,000
Kingston, Jamaica	886,000
Recife	854,000
Barbados (Bridgetown)	493,000
Havana	464,000
Cap-Français (now Cap-Haïtien)	406,000
Suriname (Paramaribo)	256,000
Martinique (St.-Pierre)	217,000
Charleston, South Carolina	186,000
Cartagena	150,000
Antigua (St. John's)	138,000
St. Kitts (Basseterre)	134,000
Port-au-Prince	130,000
Grenada (St. George's)	129,000
Curaçao (Willemstad)	122,000
Dominica (Roseau)	110,000
Maranhão	98,000
Léogane, St.-Domingue / Haiti	90,000
Guadeloupe (Basse-Terre)	73,000
Total	8,325,000
All 179 known slave-trade ports of disembarkation combined	10,706,000

Source: Voyages Web site, http://www.slavevoyages.org/tast/database/search.faces?yearFrom= 1514&yearTo=1866&mjslptimp=21302.31312.32110.32241.33400.33500.33800.34200.34400.35114 .35199.35304.36100.36200.36403.36404.36412.41207.50100.50200.50300.50422.50423: go to the tables tab and create table of "specific disembarkation regions" and "sum of disembarked slaves." The ratios derived from the numbers of disembarked slaves in each port are applied to the regional totals from http://www.slavevoyages.org/tast/assessment/estimates.faces to obtain estimates for the major ports.

Note: Table 6 derives from the Estimates interface on the *Voyages* Web site, whereas table 7 derives from actual voyage records available on the Search the Voyages Database interface; for details about the estimates see "About This Atlas" in this volume.

* Where data are for an island as a whole, the main port on the island is given in parentheses.

Map 137: Captive Flows between African and North American Mainland Regions, 1619–1860

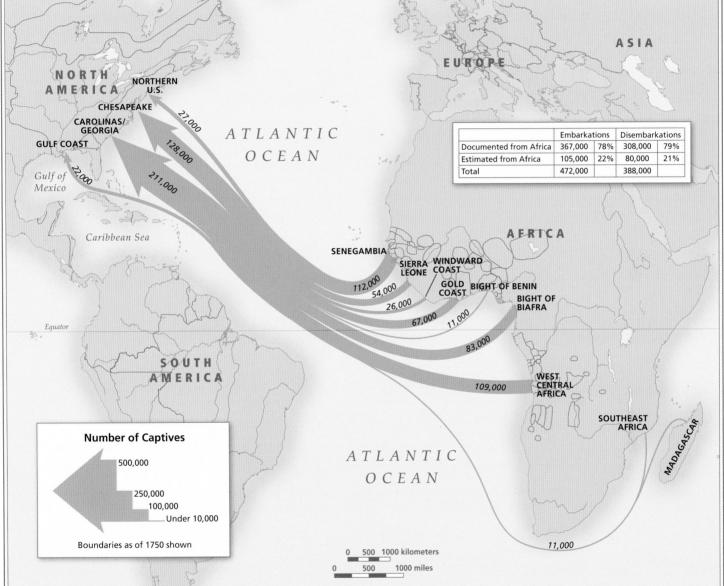

	Embarkations		Disembarkations	
Documented from Africa	367,000	78%	308,000	79%
Estimated from Africa	105,000	22%	80,000	21%
Total	472,000		388,000	

Number of Captives

500,000
250,000
100,000
Under 10,000

Boundaries as of 1750 shown

0   500   1000 kilometers
0   500   1000 miles

Fewer than one in thirty of all Africans forced into the Atlantic slave trade landed in mainland North America. Although enslaved Africans reached North America before 1620, a regular trade began only in the late seventeenth century and had largely ended in most of the colonies by the American Revolution. African captives arrived either indirectly via the Caribbean (especially before 1720) or, increasingly, directly from Africa (principally West Central Africa and Senegambia). Maryland and Virginia, both bordering the Chesapeake Bay, and South Carolina and Georgia received the most enslaved Africans. Most slaves arrived in British or British colonial (later U.S.) vessels, but those landing in the Gulf Coast region came mainly under the French flag.

Map 138: Slaves Arriving at North American Mainland Ports, 1619–1710

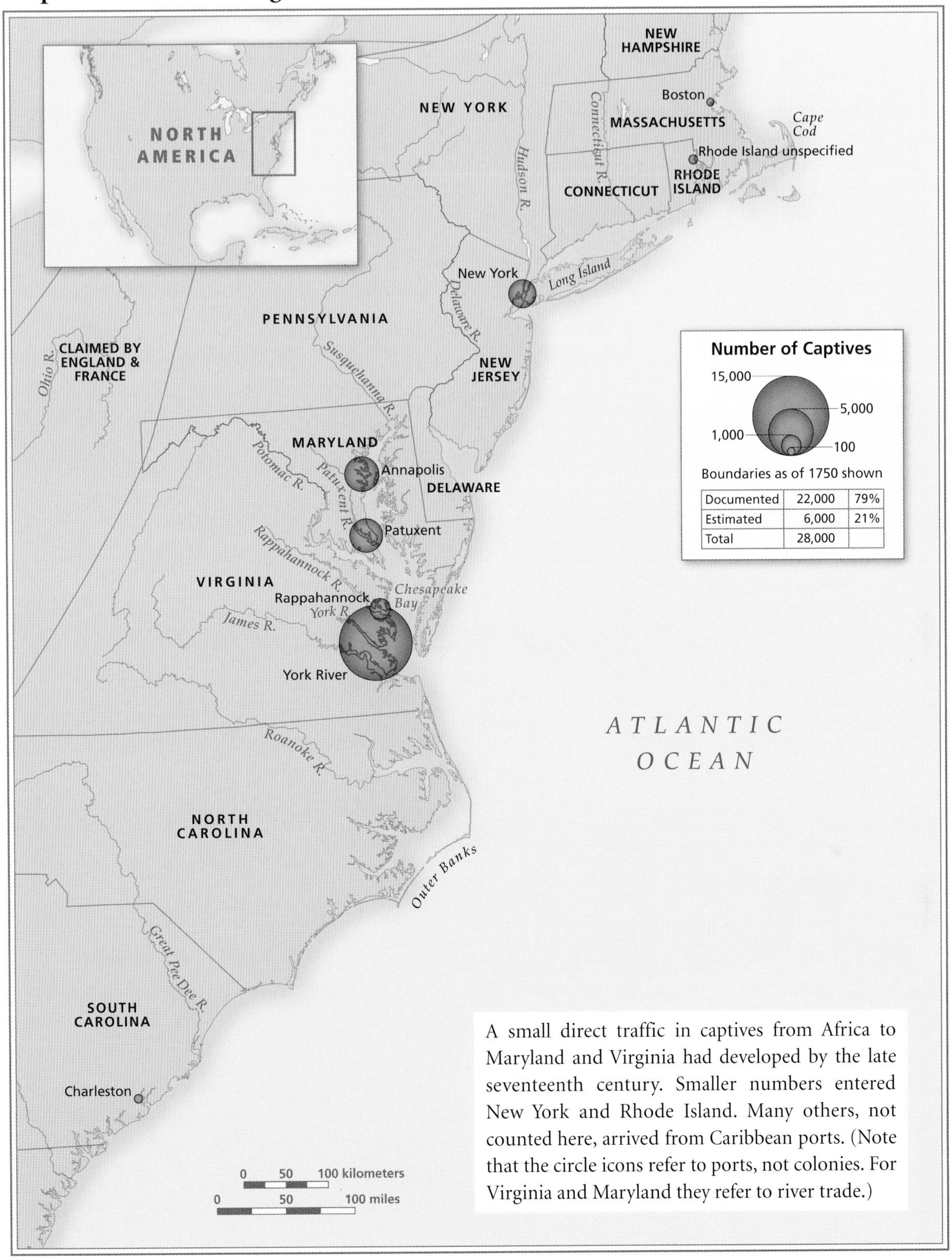

NEW HAMPSHIRE

NORTH AMERICA

NEW YORK

Boston
MASSACHUSETTS

Cape Cod

Rhode Island unspecified

Connecticut R.

Hudson R.

CONNECTICUT

RHODE ISLAND

New York

Long Island

PENNSYLVANIA

Delaware R.

Susquehanna R.

NEW JERSEY

CLAIMED BY ENGLAND & FRANCE

Ohio R.

MARYLAND

Annapolis

DELAWARE

Potomac R.

Patuxent R.

Patuxent

Rappahannock R.

VIRGINIA

Rappahannock

Chesapeake Bay

York R.

James R.

York River

Roanoke R.

ATLANTIC OCEAN

NORTH CAROLINA

Outer Banks

Great Pee Dee R.

SOUTH CAROLINA

Charleston

Number of Captives

15,000

5,000

1,000

100

Boundaries as of 1750 shown

Documented	22,000	79%
Estimated	6,000	21%
Total	28,000	

A small direct traffic in captives from Africa to Maryland and Virginia had developed by the late seventeenth century. Smaller numbers entered New York and Rhode Island. Many others, not counted here, arrived from Caribbean ports. (Note that the circle icons refer to ports, not colonies. For Virginia and Maryland they refer to river trade.)

0   50   100 kilometers

0   50   100 miles

Map 139: Slaves Arriving at North American Mainland Ports, 1711–1775

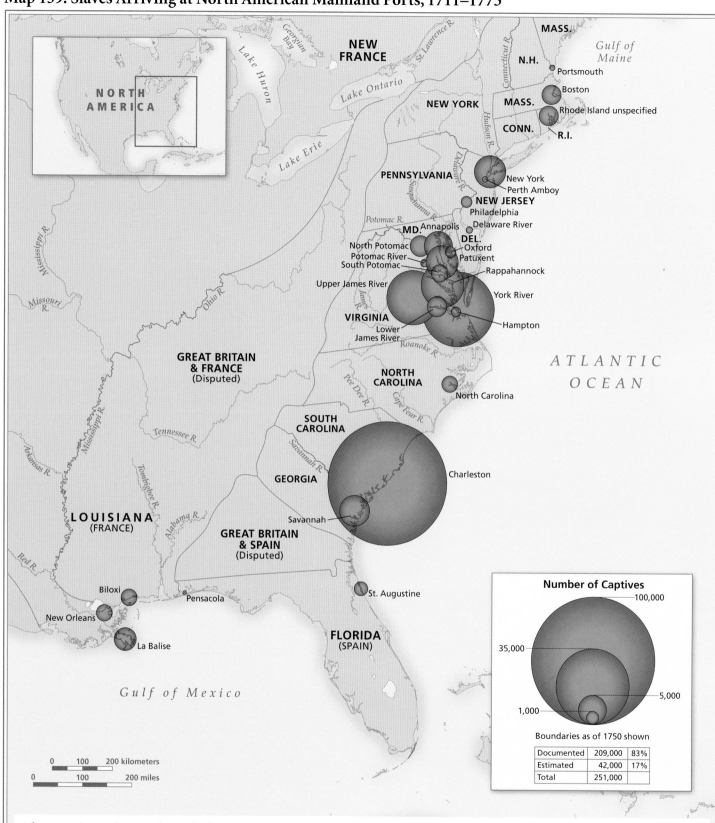

After 1710 increasing numbers of African slaves arrived in mainland North America through more entry points. The proportion of captives arriving directly from Africa, mostly in British and British colonial vessels, rose sharply. Through 1730 most slaves disembarked at points around the Chesapeake Bay as tobacco growing expanded. Arrivals in Virginia fell away before the American Revolution, partly because demand for enslaved labor in the Chesapeake region was met by natural reproduction and partly because there were competing demands for labor in South Carolina and Georgia for rice and indigo cultivation.

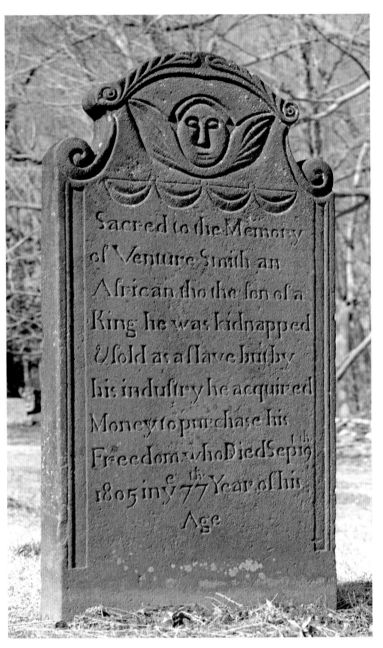

Tombstone of Venture Smith (d. 1805)

Courtesy of the Documenting Venture Smith Project.

The great majority of African captives lived and died in obscurity, but some, like Venture Smith, succeeded in creating an identity in the historical record. Born Broteer Furor in Africa, enslaved as a child, and taken from Anomabu on the Gold Coast in 1738 by the Rhode Island ship *Charming Susanna* to Newport, Rhode Island, Venture Smith became successively the property of three American masters, from the last of whom—Oliver Smith, whose surname he adopted—he bought his freedom in 1765. Through industry and skill, he became a landowner and trader in Connecticut, establishing a family dynasty that continues today. He recounted his life in Africa and his journey through slavery and freedom in a narrative published in 1798. When Venture Smith died in 1805, he was buried in East Haddam, Connecticut. His is one of the very few gravestones of an African-born slave to survive in the Americas.

Map 140: Slaves Arriving at North American Mainland Ports, 1776–1860

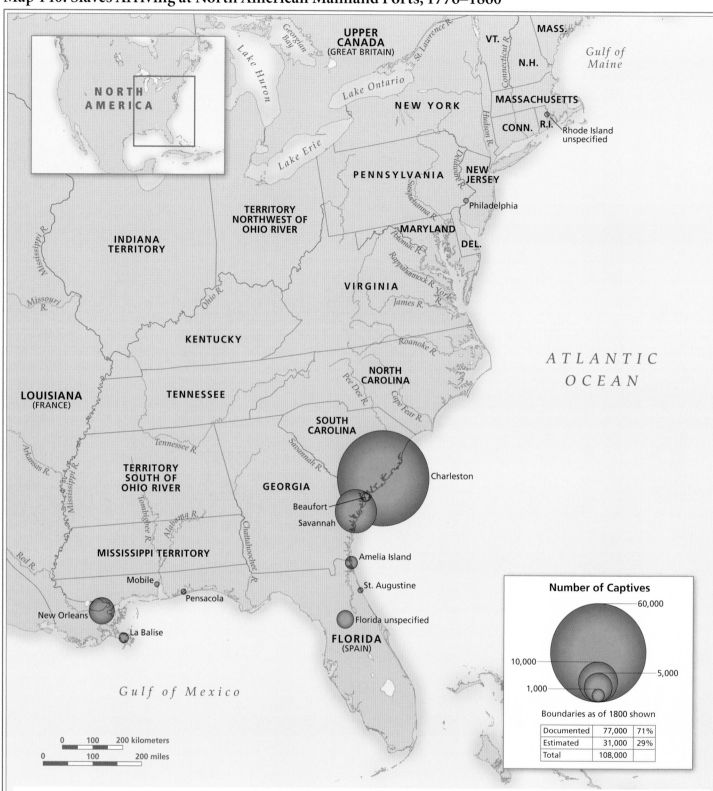

Number of Captives

60,000
10,000
5,000
1,000

Boundaries as of 1800 shown

Documented	77,000	71%
Estimated	31,000	29%
Total	108,000	

The American Revolution curtailed arrivals of enslaved Africans in mainland North America. Among the newly independent states, only Georgia for a brief period after 1783 and later South Carolina in 1804–1807, as cotton growing was becoming important, opened their borders to vessels bringing captives directly from Africa. The number of slaves coming to mainland North America through Florida (under Spanish control until 1818) and Louisiana (under French control until 1803) also shrank after 1775. A few vessels brought in captives to the United States directly from Africa until 1860 even though it was illegal to do so after 1808.

11 Mch 1718 [1719]	Woman, apoplexy
14 Mch	Boy, convulsions
21 Mch	man, mortification of the vicula [vincula? sing. vinculum: tendon of foot]
24 Mch	man, stubborn & w[oul]d not eat
5 Ap 1719	man, flux
	man, flux
8 Ap	man, of flux and astma [asthma], woman of consumption
9	negro man, flux
13	man, flux & malignant fever
28	boy, consumption & astma
14 May	man, malignant fever
17	boy, malignant fever
20	boy, flux
21	woman, lethargy
28	woman, malignant fever
30	woman, disentry [dysentery]
3 June	woman, apoplexy
4	man, consumption
13	woman, flux
15	boy, an anasarea [extreme edema]
19	man, fever
20	man, epilepsy
22	man, flux
27	2 negro women, one flux, one scurvy
29	negro woman, violent blow to head
7 July	negro woman, Diarea & falling down
9	boy, convulsions
13	woman, flux

Acct [by surgeon] of Slaves Died on Elizabeth, 1719, Humphry
Morice Papers, Bank of England Archives, London, M6/69.
Published with permission of the Bank of England.

Map 141: Chesapeake:
African Coastal Origins of Slaves and Home Ports of Vessels Carrying Them, 1619–1775

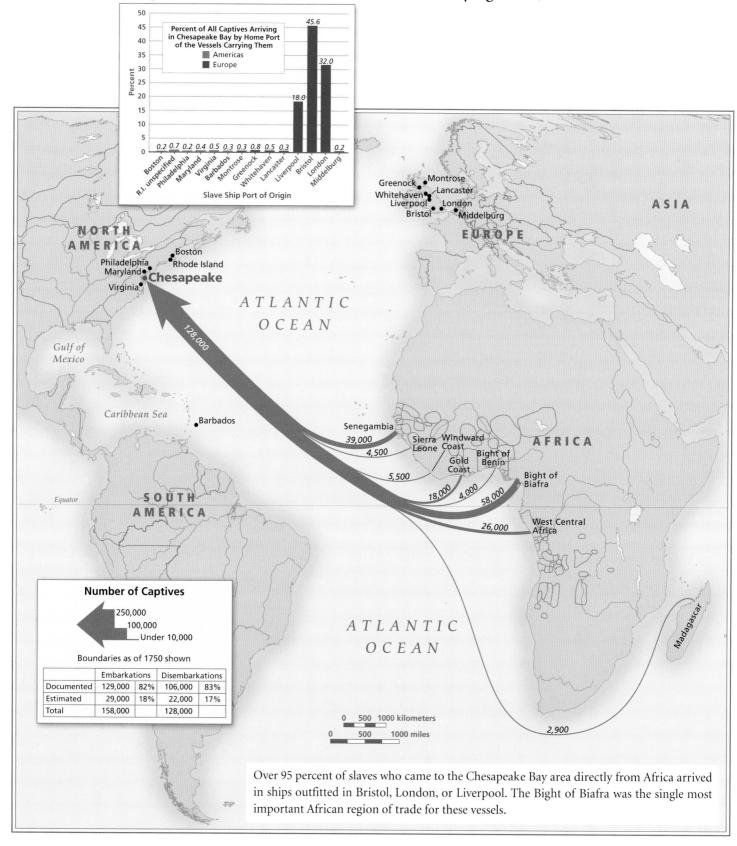

Percent of All Captives Arriving in Chesapeake Bay by Home Port of the Vessels Carrying Them

■ Americas
■ Europe

Slave Ship Port of Origin

Boston 0.2, R.I. unspecified 0.7, Philadelphia 0.2, Maryland 0.4, Virginia 0.5, Barbados 0.3, Montrose 0.3, Greenock 0.8, Whitehaven 0.5, Lancaster 0.3, Liverpool 18.0, Bristol 45.6, London 32.0, Middelburg 0.2

Number of Captives

250,000
100,000
Under 10,000

Boundaries as of 1750 shown

	Embarkations		Disembarkations	
Documented	129,000	82%	106,000	83%
Estimated	29,000	18%	22,000	17%
Total	158,000		128,000	

128,000

Senegambia 39,000
Sierra Leone 4,500
Gold Coast 5,500
Windward Coast 18,000
Bight of Benin 4,000
Bight of Biafra 58,000
West Central Africa 26,000
Madagascar 2,900

Over 95 percent of slaves who came to the Chesapeake Bay area directly from Africa arrived in ships outfitted in Bristol, London, or Liverpool. The Bight of Biafra was the single most important African region of trade for these vessels.

Map 142: Middle Colonies:
African Coastal Origins of Slaves and Home Ports of Vessels Carrying Them, 1655–1775

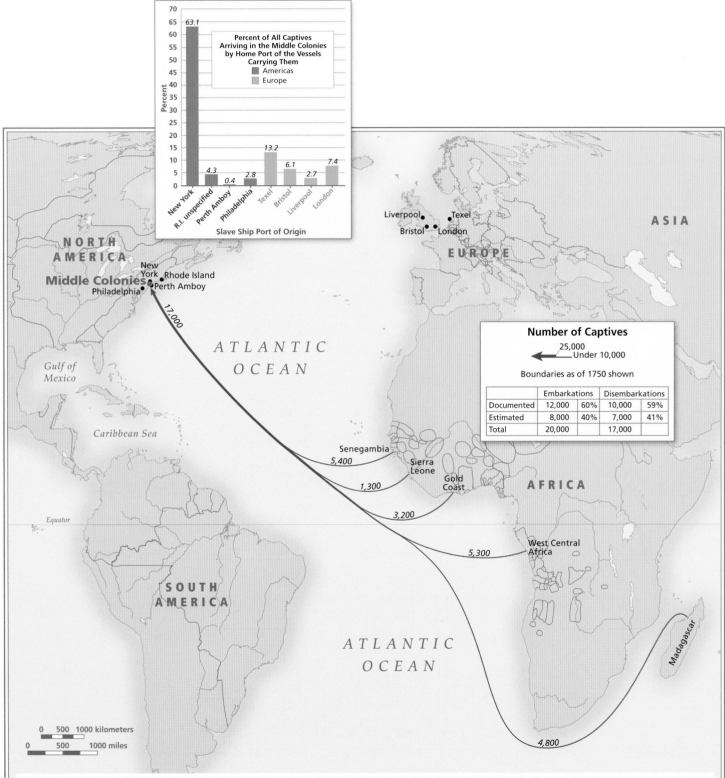

Percent of All Captives Arriving in the Middle Colonies by Home Port of the Vessels Carrying Them

- Americas
- Europe

Percent

Slave Ship Port of Origin

New York 63.1 / R.I. unspecified 4.3 / Perth Amboy 0.4 / Philadelphia 2.8 / Texel 13.2 / Bristol 6.1 / Liverpool 2.7 / London 7.4

Number of Captives

25,000
Under 10,000

Boundaries as of 1750 shown

	Embarkations		Disembarkations	
Documented	12,000	60%	10,000	59%
Estimated	8,000	40%	7,000	41%
Total	20,000		17,000	

Slaves from Africa first arrived in what became New York before 1667, during the Dutch period of control. Ninety percent of those brought into the Middle Colonies – which became New York, Pennsylvania, New Jersey, and Delaware – arrived in New York City and Perth Amboy (New Jersey), with the remainder going to Philadelphia. The number of captives rarely exceeded 500 a year overall, although there was a modest concentration between 1750 and 1775. Sixty percent of the slaves were landed by vessels owned by New Yorkers, not by the British merchants who supplied most of the coerced labor to mainland North America. To avoid higher customs dues, many captives destined for New York markets were landed in Perth Amboy.

Phillis Wheatley, Negro Servant to Mr. John Wheatley of Boston, 1773

Copperplate engraving by Scipio Moorhead, 1773, from Phillis Wheatley, *Poems on Various Subjects, Religious and Moral* (London: Printed for A. Bell, bookseller, Aldgate, 1773), frontispiece. Courtesy of the Library of Congress, Rare Book and Special Collections Division, Washington, D.C.

Phillis Wheatley (1753–1784) took her name from the slave ship *Phillis,* which made four voyages to Africa, on the second of which (voyage id 25481) she was forcibly taken as a child from Gambia to Boston. In Boston she became servant to John Wheatley. Literary success allowed her to gain her freedom before the American Revolution. The first documented African American poet, Wheatley, who styled herself "Afric's muse," published her first book in London after being denied the opportunity to do so in Boston. To mark the event, she commissioned the African American artist Scipio Moorhead to produce her portrait. She died in New England in 1784, aged around thirty.

Map 143: New England:
African Coastal Origins of Slaves and Home Ports of Vessels Carrying Them, 1676–1802

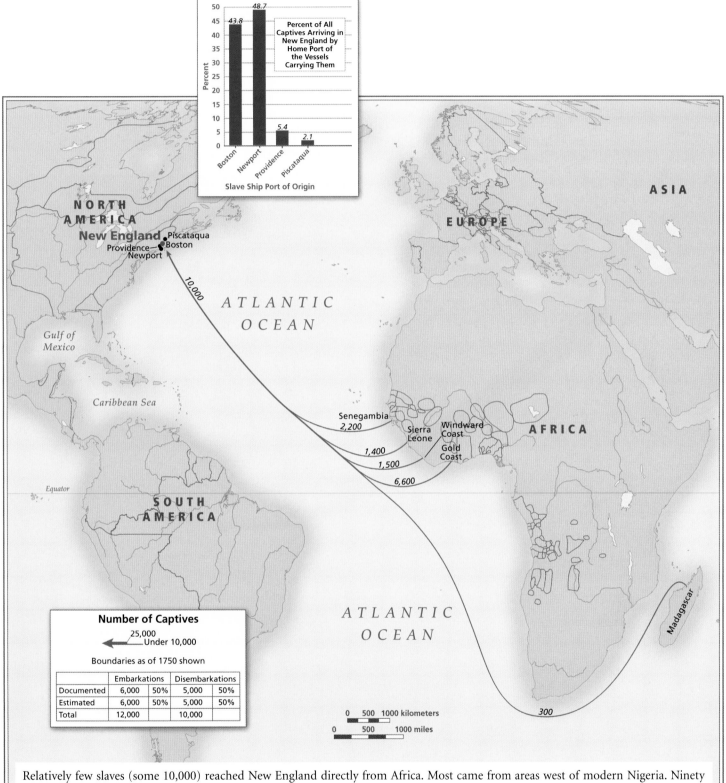

Percent of All Captives Arriving in New England by Home Port of the Vessels Carrying Them

Slave Ship Port of Origin	Percent
Boston	43.8
Newport	48.7
Providence	5.4
Piscataqua	2.1

Number of Captives

25,000
Under 10,000

Boundaries as of 1750 shown

	Embarkations		Disembarkations	
Documented	6,000	50%	5,000	50%
Estimated	6,000	50%	5,000	50%
Total	12,000		10,000	

Senegambia 2,200
1,400
1,500
6,600
300
10,000

0 500 1000 kilometers
0 500 1000 miles

Relatively few slaves (some 10,000) reached New England directly from Africa. Most came from areas west of modern Nigeria. Ninety percent arrived in Boston- and Newport-owned vessels. More African captives reached New England through intercolonial trafficking or as the residual of a larger group of slaves sold from New England transatlantic vessels in the West Indies.

Map 144: South Carolina:
African Coastal Origins of Slaves and Home Ports of Vessels Carrying Them, 1701–1808

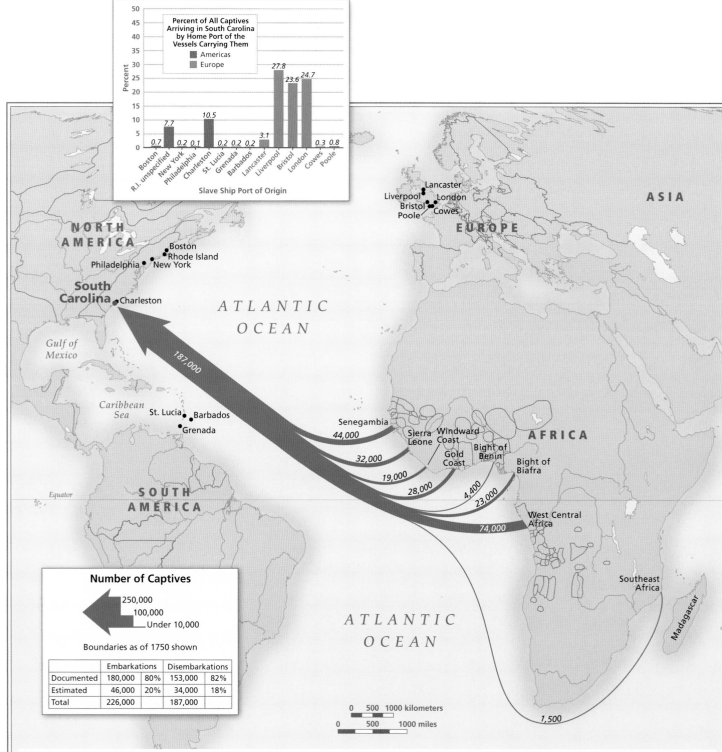

Percent of All Captives Arriving in South Carolina by Home Port of the Vessels Carrying Them
- Americas
- Europe

(Bar chart values: Boston 0.7, R.I. unspecified 7.7, New York 0.2, Philadelphia 0.1, Charleston 10.5, St. Lucia 0.2, Grenada 0.2, Barbados 0.2, Lancaster 3.1, Liverpool 27.8, Bristol 23.6, London 24.7, Cowes 0.3, Poole 0.8)

Slave Ship Port of Origin

Number of Captives
- 250,000
- 100,000
- Under 10,000

Boundaries as of 1750 shown

	Embarkations		Disembarkations	
Documented	180,000	80%	153,000	82%
Estimated	46,000	20%	34,000	18%
Total	226,000		187,000	

(Map flow values: 187,000; Senegambia 44,000; 32,000; 19,000; 28,000; 4,400; 23,000; West Central Africa 74,000; Southeast Africa 1,500)

Charleston, South Carolina, became the main entry point for African captives coming to mainland North America from the 1730s through 1808. Although many slaves came to South Carolina via the West Indies before 1720, after 1720 the vast majority came directly from Africa, most in the four decades before the American Revolution and again in 1804–1807, when South Carolina permitted resumption of the transatlantic slave trade. West Central Africa was the largest single regional supplier, notably before 1740 and again in 1804–1807, with Senegambia, Sierra Leone, and the Gold Coast supplying most of the rest, mainly between 1750 and 1775.

TO BE SOLD on board the Ship *Bance-Yland*, on tuefday the 6th of *May* next, at *Afhley-Ferry*; a choice cargo of about 250 fine healthy

NEGROES,

juft arrived from the Windward & Rice Coaft. —The utmoft care has already been taken, and fhall be continued, to keep them free from the leaft danger of being infected with the SMALL-POX, no boat having been on board, and all other communication with people from *Charles-Town* prevented.

Auftin, Laurens, & Appleby.

N. B. Full one Half of the above Negroes have had the SMALL-POX in their own Country.

Advertisement for a Slave Sale, Charles-Town, South Carolina, 1760

Sale of Africans from the Windward & Rice Coast.
Photographs and Prints Division, Schomburg Center for Research in Black Culture, The New York Public Library, Astor, Lenox and Tilden Foundations.

By the eighteenth century, slave traders typically relied on specialist "slave factors" in American ports to sell African captives and to recover and pay the proceeds of the sales. Slave factors were paid a commission for their services. In the advertisement here, the slave factors Austin, Laurens & Appleby of Charleston, South Carolina, are giving potential buyers notice of the time and place of the impending sale of a "choice cargo" of Africans recently arrived on a ship from the "Windward & Rice Coast" (voyage id 77723). Because Charleston was currently undergoing a smallpox epidemic, the slave factors sought to reassure buyers that the captives were neither infected nor likely to catch the disease.

Map 145: Georgia:
African Coastal Origins of Slaves and Home Ports of Vessels Carrying Them, 1766–1858

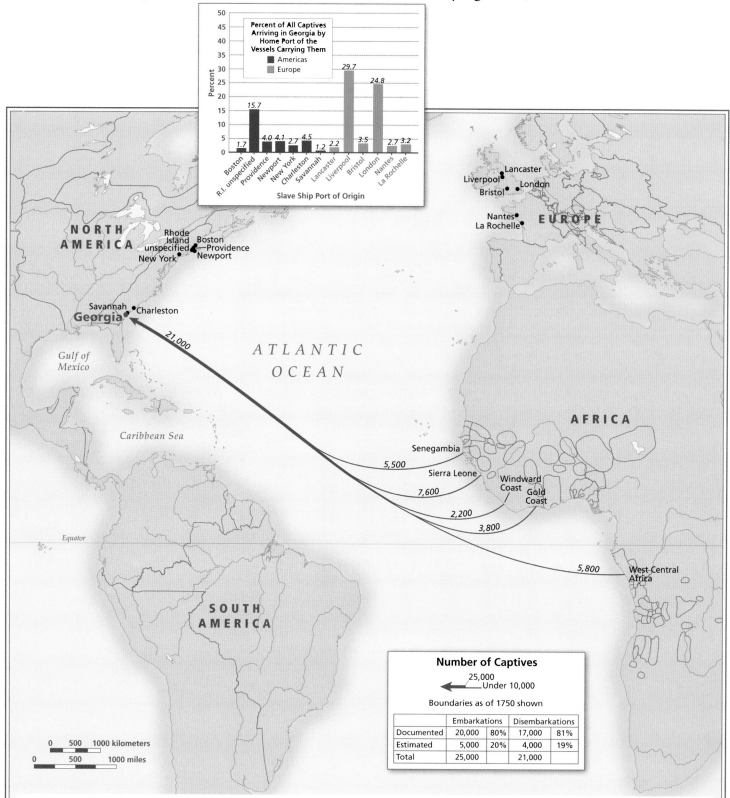

Percent of All Captives Arriving in Georgia by Home Port of the Vessels Carrying Them
- Americas
- Europe

Boston 1.7 · R.I. unspecified 15.7 · Providence 4.0 · Newport 4.1 · New York 2.7 · Charleston 4.5 · Savannah 1.2 · Lancaster 2.2 · Liverpool 29.7 · Bristol 3.5 · London 24.8 · Nantes 2.7 · La Rochelle 3.2

Slave Ship Port of Origin

Number of Captives

25,000 / Under 10,000

Boundaries as of 1750 shown

	Embarkations		Disembarkations	
Documented	20,000	80%	17,000	81%
Estimated	5,000	20%	4,000	19%
Total	25,000		21,000	

Although Georgia repealed its original prohibition on importing and using slaves in 1749, the colony received slaves directly from Africa only in the mid–1760s; it had previously relied on slaves from the West Indies and South Carolina for labor for its growing rice economy. A mix of British, British colonial, and, from 1783, U.S. vessels accounted for arrivals of captives in Savannah, the principal point of entry. Almost all came from either West Central Africa or regions west of the Gold Coast. Liverpool and London merchants accounted for well over half of the trade, particularly since they probably also owned the privateers that captured the Nantes and La Rochelle slave vessels shown in the bar graph.

Goray Le mardy 27 Juillet 1723
Embarqué nos Noirs 60 malles Tant grand naigre que Naigrillons
40 Naigraisse avec 4: ou 5 petite Enfans a la Mamelle

Gorée, Tuesday 27 July 1723
Embarked our Blacks 60 males as many large men as children
40 women with 4 or 5 small infants at the breast.

Le vouiage de france au Senegalle pour Y prandres des Noirs Et les Porter au Micicipy Dans le Vaisseau Le Courier de Bourbon de la Roialle Compagnie commandé par Monsieur de La Lande Boulon Menard [1723] [The voyage from France to Senegal to take in Blacks and Carry them to Mississippi in the Vessel *Le Courier de Bourbon* of the Royal Company commanded by Monsieur La Lande Boulon Menard, 1723], 4 JJ 15, 21 bis. National Archives, Paris. Translated by David Richardson.

Map 146: Gulf Coast:
African Coastal Origins of Slaves and Home Ports of Vessels Carrying Them, 1719–1860

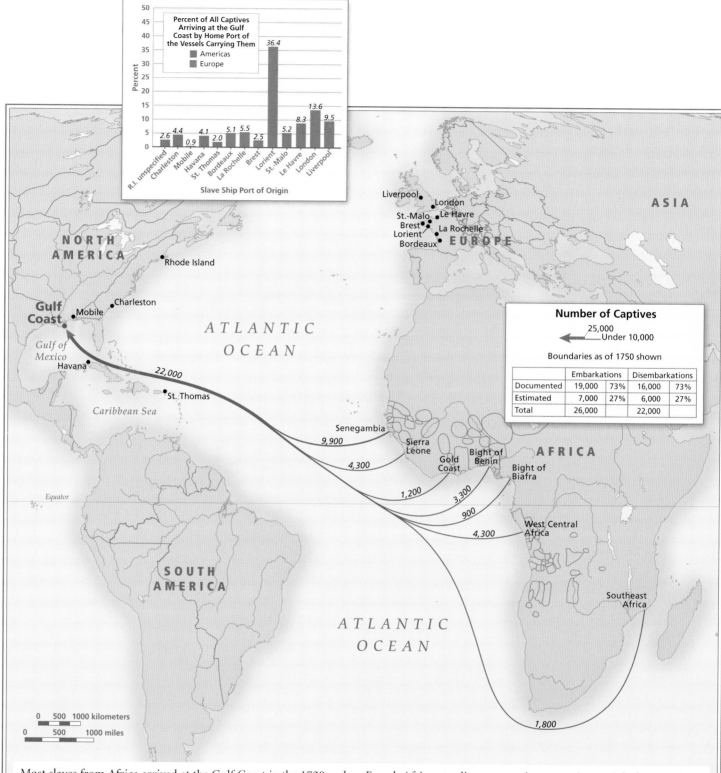

Most slaves from Africa arrived at the Gulf Coast in the 1720s, when French African trading companies, operating mainly from Lorient, on France's west coast, dominated the region's slave trade. An irregular traffic in captives continued thereafter by vessels from other ports, supplemented by arrivals through intercolonial trafficking, notably after 1791. Nearly three-quarters of the first generation of slaves (arriving before 1740) came from what is now Senegal, and most of the remainder came from the Bight of Benin.

Abaché [Clara Turner] and Cudjoe Kazoola Lewis, 1914

Photograph from Emma Langdon Roche, *Historic Sketches of the South,* 1914. General Research and Reference Division, Schomburg Center for Research in Black Culture, The New York Public Library, Astor, Lenox and Tilden Foundations.

The last known U.S. slave ship to bring Africans as slaves across the Atlantic was the *Clotilde* (voyage id 36990). It landed in Mobile, Alabama, in 1860 with 110 Africans on board. They had been taken from Ouidah, on the Bight of Benin. Among them were Cudjoe and Abaché, otherwise known as Cudjoe Kazoola Lewis and Clara Turner, respectively, who, after being liberated in 1865, joined other *Clotilde* survivors to establish Africatown at Plateau, Alabama. There they sought to rebuild the culture of their homeland. A bust of Cudjoe still sits in front of the Union Missionary Baptist Church in Africatown.

Map 147: Captive Flows between African Regions and Caribbean Regions, 1501–1867

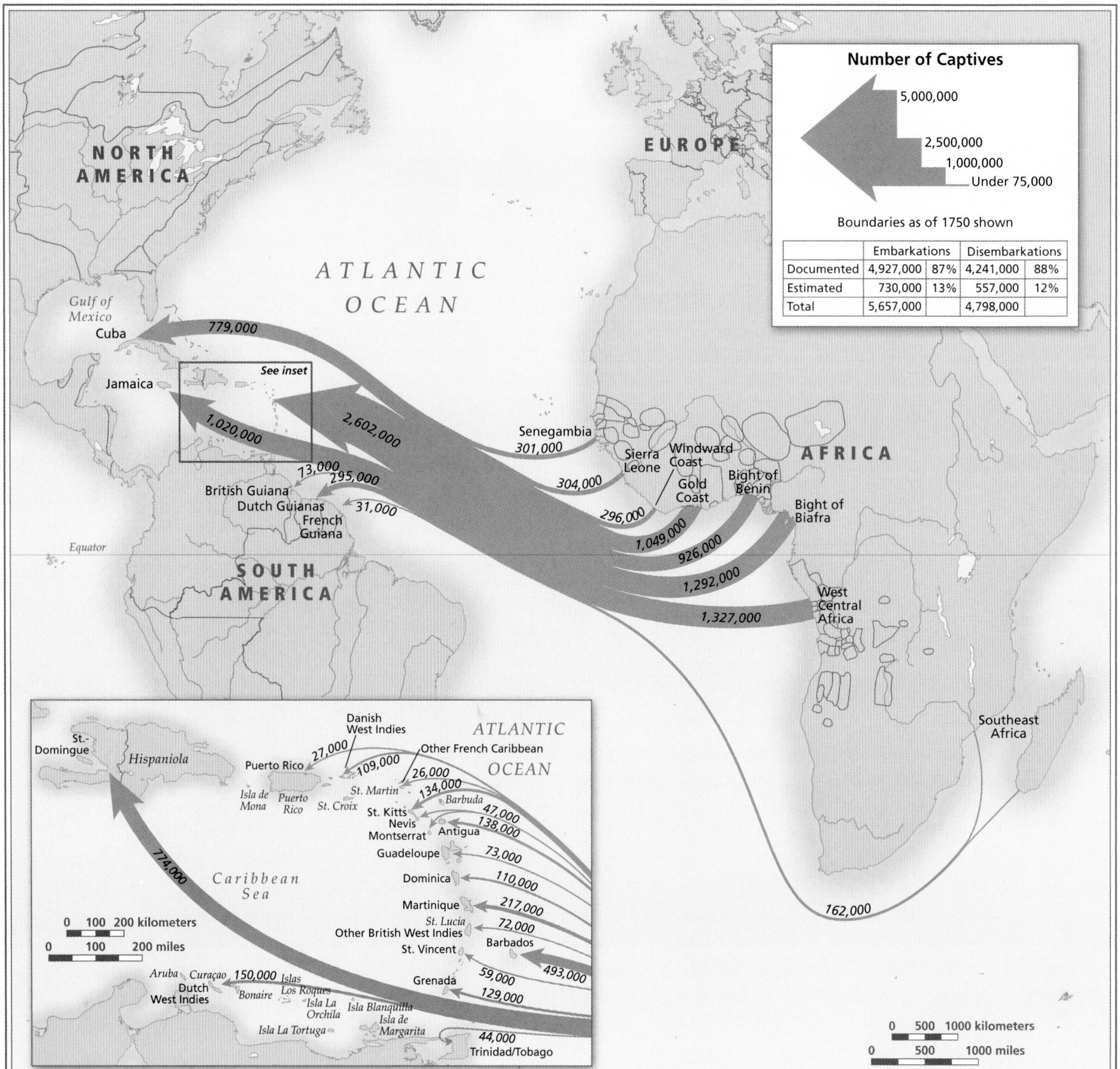

Number of Captives

5,000,000
2,500,000
1,000,000
Under 75,000

Boundaries as of 1750 shown

	Embarkations		Disembarkations	
Documented	4,927,000	87%	4,241,000	88%
Estimated	730,000	13%	557,000	12%
Total	5,657,000		4,798,000	

The West Indies islands and the adjacent areas of South America received almost as many slaves directly from Africa as did Brazil. Arrivals rose substantially from the sixteenth century to the 1790s and generally shifted west to Jamaica, St.-Domingue, and Cuba, where just over half of all enslaved Africans coming to the region landed. West Africa was the major source for Caribbean markets.

How the Negro Slaves Work and Look for Gold in the Mines of the Region Called Varaguas [Veraguas in modern-day Panama], late 16th century

Watercolor by an unknown artist, from *Histoire naturelle des Indes* (Natural History of the Indies), the "Drake Manuscript," late 16th century, folio 100. The Pierport Morgan Library / Art Resource, NY.

Large numbers of African captives in Spanish America worked in gold and silver mines in the sixteenth century and later. Many entered the Spanish colonies through Central America, where some were sold locally. Others were taken south as far as modern-day Bolivia. This early drawing of slaves looking for gold in Panama shows four Africans working under the supervision of an overseer, who receives and weighs gold delivered by one of them. An accompanying description says, "The Spaniards buy a great number of Negroes from Africa to serve them as slaves and when the Negroes have finished a day's work in a group of eight or ten, there is at the exit of these mines half a barrel filled with water in which they wash the gold."

Map 148: Slaves Arriving in the Caribbean, 1501–1641

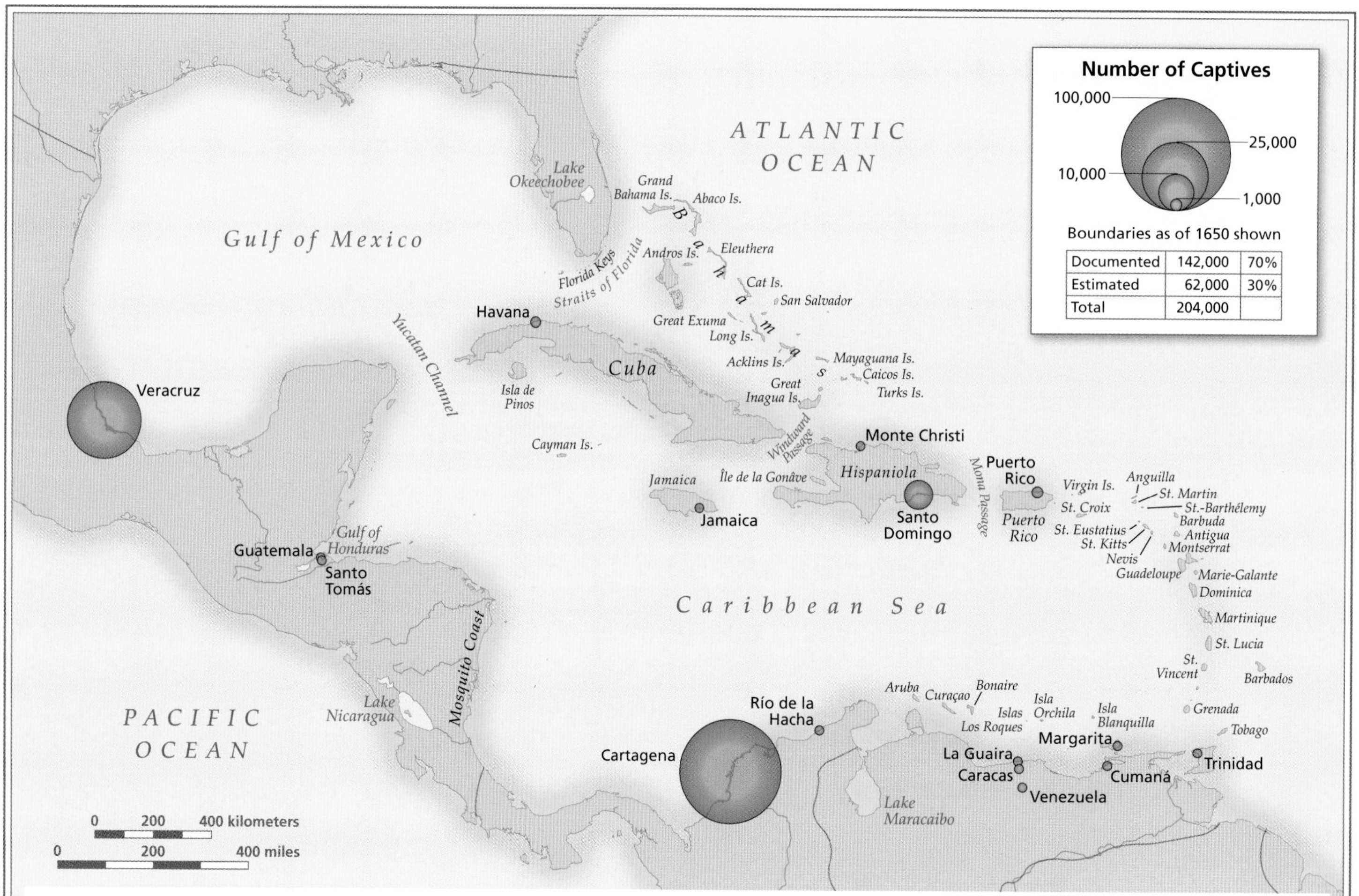

Spain dominated the colonization of the Caribbean region until 1641. Slaves arriving in Spanish America before the 1520s were Africans who had previously been taken to Spain, but after that time the Spanish authorities issued contracts (*asientos*) to traders to carry slaves directly to Spanish American markets. Although some captives disembarked in the Spanish-controlled islands, including Jamaica (which was Spanish through 1655), most landed at Veracruz and Cartagena on the Spanish colonial mainland, with many traveling on to Peru and places south.

LIVERPOOL, May 31 [1765]

ARRIVALS. The Sam, Captain Powell, with 250 slaves, and the Hannah, Capt. Prescott, with 297, both from Angola at Barbadoes.—The Industry, Capt. Erskine, with 173, from Africa at Jamaica; she purchased 186 slaves and buried 13.—The Plumper, Capt. Edward Brown, arrived at St. Kitts, March 19, with 296 slaves and would sail for Jamaica that evening; she left the Coast Feb. 8, with 304 Slaves.—Capt. Dobb, in the Captain, sailed from the Coast Feb. 6, with 290 Slaves; they left at Bassa the Essex, Capt. Seaman, with 168 Slaves; the Anton, Capt. Brettargh, with 40 Slaves; the Swallow, Capt. Ewings, with 150 Slaves; a Vessel from Whitehaven with 60; and a number of other Vessels, both to Windward and Leeward.—Slaves were at a great Price on the Coast, and many Ships would fall short of their Cargoes proposed.—Capt. Brown has buried his second Mate, Boatswain, Carpenter, Carpenter's Mate, and Eight Seamen.

Williamson's Liverpool Advertiser and Mercantile Chronicle, issue 471, 31 May 1765.

Map 149: Slaves Arriving in the Caribbean, 1642–1807

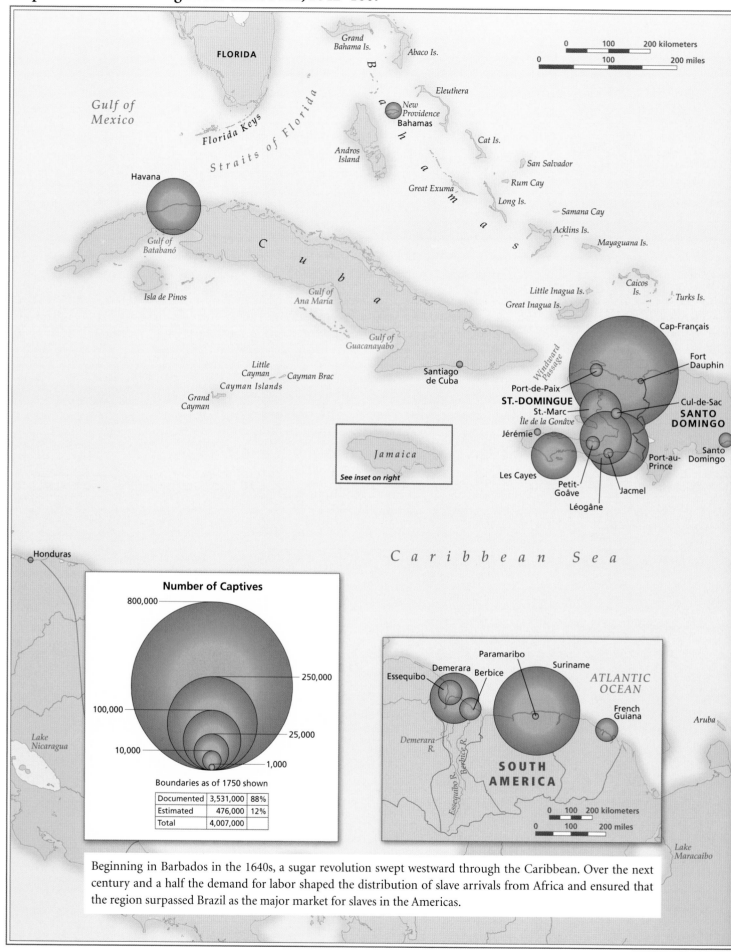

Number of Captives

800,000
250,000
100,000
25,000
10,000
1,000

Boundaries as of 1750 shown

Documented	3,531,000	88%
Estimated	476,000	12%
Total	4,007,000	

Beginning in Barbados in the 1640s, a sugar revolution swept westward through the Caribbean. Over the next century and a half the demand for labor shaped the distribution of slave arrivals from Africa and ensured that the region surpassed Brazil as the major market for slaves in the Americas.

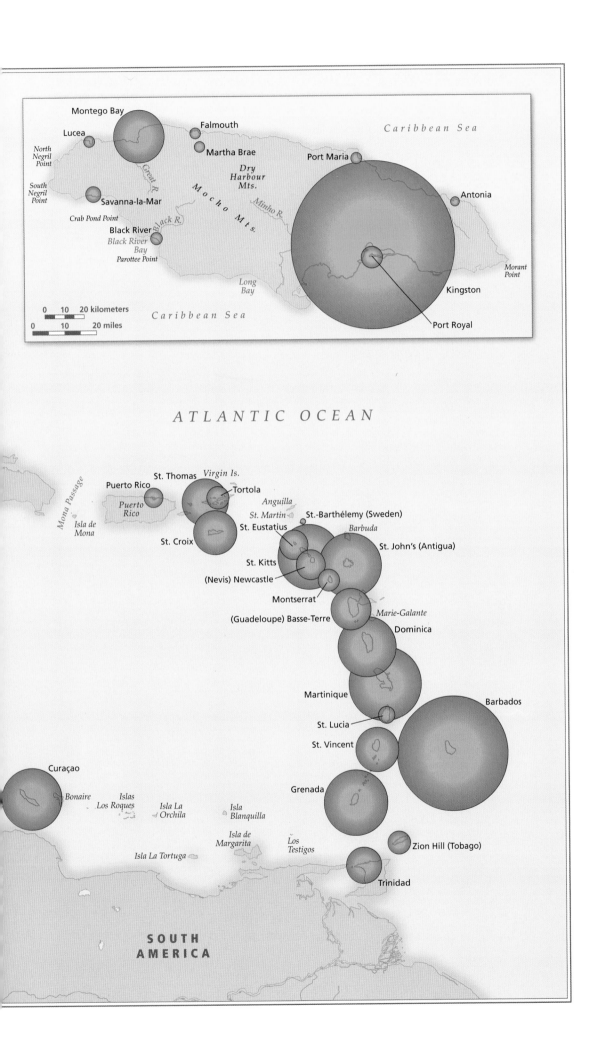

Montego Bay
Falmouth
Lucea
Martha Brae
North Negril Point
Dry Harbour Mts.
Port Maria
Caribbean Sea
Antonia
Great R.
Mocho Mts.
Minho R.
South Negril Point
Savanna-la-Mar
Crab Pond Point
Black River
Black R.
Black River Bay
Parottee Point
Kingston
Port Royal
Long Bay
Morant Point

0   10   20 kilometers
0   10   20 miles

Caribbean Sea

ATLANTIC OCEAN

St. Thomas
Virgin Is.
Puerto Rico
Tortola
Mona Passage
Anguilla
Puerto Rico
St. Martin
St.-Barthélemy (Sweden)
St. Eustatius
Barbuda
Isla de Mona
St. Croix
St. John's (Antigua)
St. Kitts
(Nevis) Newcastle
Montserrat
(Guadeloupe) Basse-Terre
Marie-Galante
Dominica
Martinique
Barbados
St. Lucia
Curaçao
St. Vincent
Bonaire
Islas Los Roques
Isla La Orchila
Isla Blanquilla
Grenada
Isla de Margarita
Los Testigos
Zion Hill (Tobago)
Isla La Tortuga
Trinidad

SOUTH AMERICA

Map 150: Slaves Arriving in the Caribbean, 1808–1867

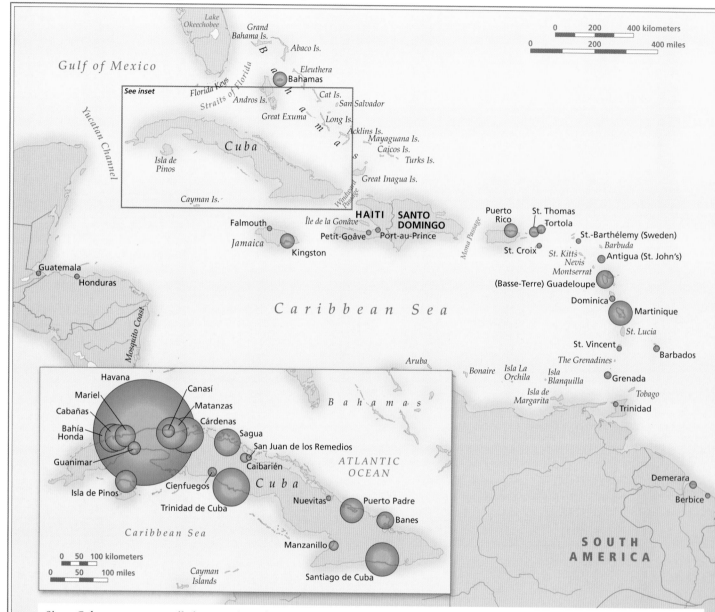

Since Cuba was open to all slave carriers after 1788, most African slaves who came to the Greater Caribbean after 1808 landed there. The market for slaves in St.-Domingue had collapsed after the slave uprising in 1791 and the subsequent independence of Haiti in 1804, and two leading importing nations, Britain and the United States, had outlawed slave trading under their flags in 1807. The French islands, which had received almost no slaves since 1793 owing to the long war with Britain, began again to participate in the traffic in 1814. The slave trade there ended in 1831.

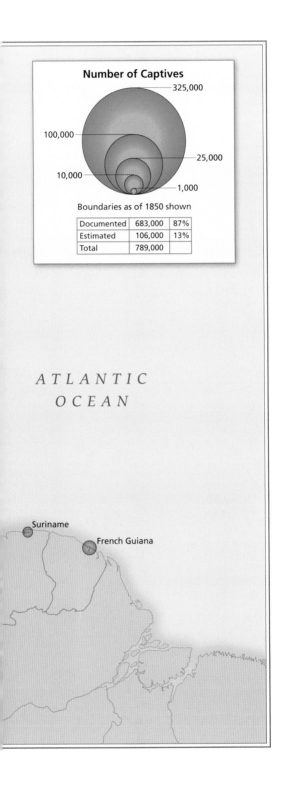

Number of Captives

325,000

100,000

25,000

10,000

1,000

Boundaries as of 1850 shown

Documented	683,000	87%
Estimated	106,000	13%
Total	789,000	

ATLANTIC
OCEAN

Suriname

French Guiana

Map 151: Cuba: African Coastal Origins of Slaves and Home Ports of Vessels Carrying Them, 1526–1867

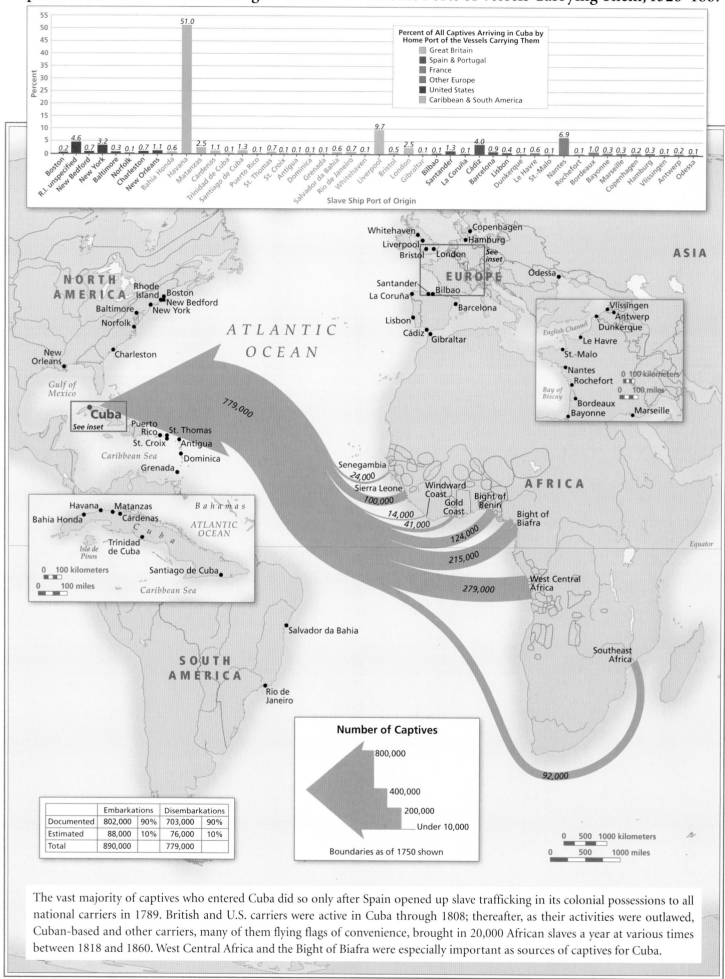

The vast majority of captives who entered Cuba did so only after Spain opened up slave trafficking in its colonial possessions to all national carriers in 1789. British and U.S. carriers were active in Cuba through 1808; thereafter, as their activities were outlawed, Cuban-based and other carriers, many of them flying flags of convenience, brought in 20,000 African slaves a year at various times between 1818 and 1860. West Central Africa and the Bight of Biafra were especially important as sources of captives for Cuba.

Map 152: Puerto Rico:
African Coastal Origins of Slaves and Home Ports of Vessels Carrying Them, 1527–1842

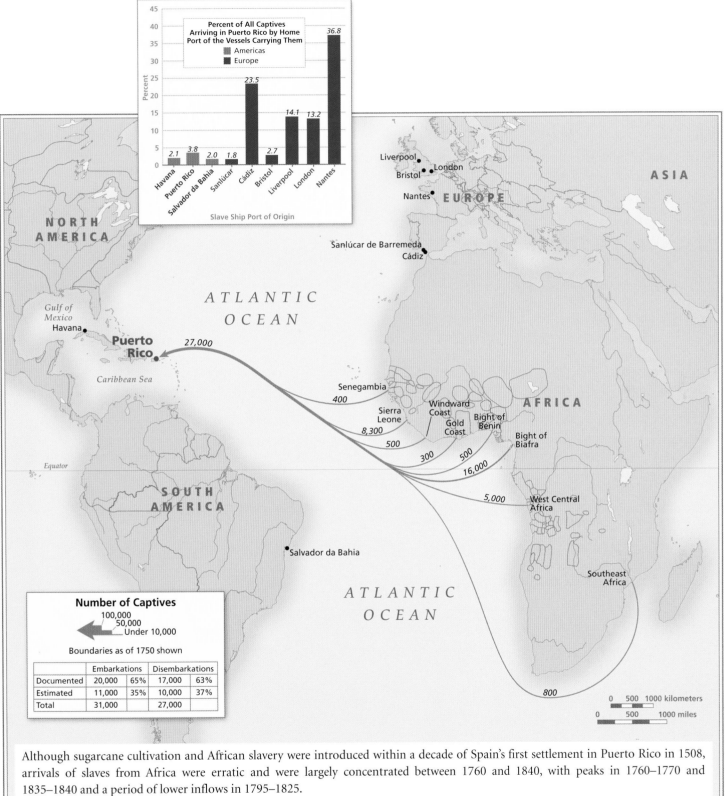

Percent of All Captives Arriving in Puerto Rico by Home Port of the Vessels Carrying Them

- Americas
- Europe

	Havana	Puerto Rico	Salvador da Bahia	Sanlúcar	Cádiz	Bristol	Liverpool	London	Nantes
Percent	2.1	3.8	2.0	1.8	23.5	2.7	14.1	13.2	36.8

Slave Ship Port of Origin

Number of Captives

100,000
50,000
Under 10,000

Boundaries as of 1750 shown

	Embarkations		Disembarkations	
Documented	20,000	65%	17,000	63%
Estimated	11,000	35%	10,000	37%
Total	31,000		27,000	

Senegambia 400
Sierra Leone 8,300
Windward Coast 500
Gold Coast 300
Bight of Benin 500
Bight of Biafra 16,000
West Central Africa 5,000
Southeast Africa 800

Puerto Rico 27,000

Although sugarcane cultivation and African slavery were introduced within a decade of Spain's first settlement in Puerto Rico in 1508, arrivals of slaves from Africa were erratic and were largely concentrated between 1760 and 1840, with peaks in 1760–1770 and 1835–1840 and a period of lower inflows in 1795–1825.

Map 153: Trinidad and Tobago:
African Coastal Origins of Slaves and Home Ports of Vessels Carrying Them, 1606–1833

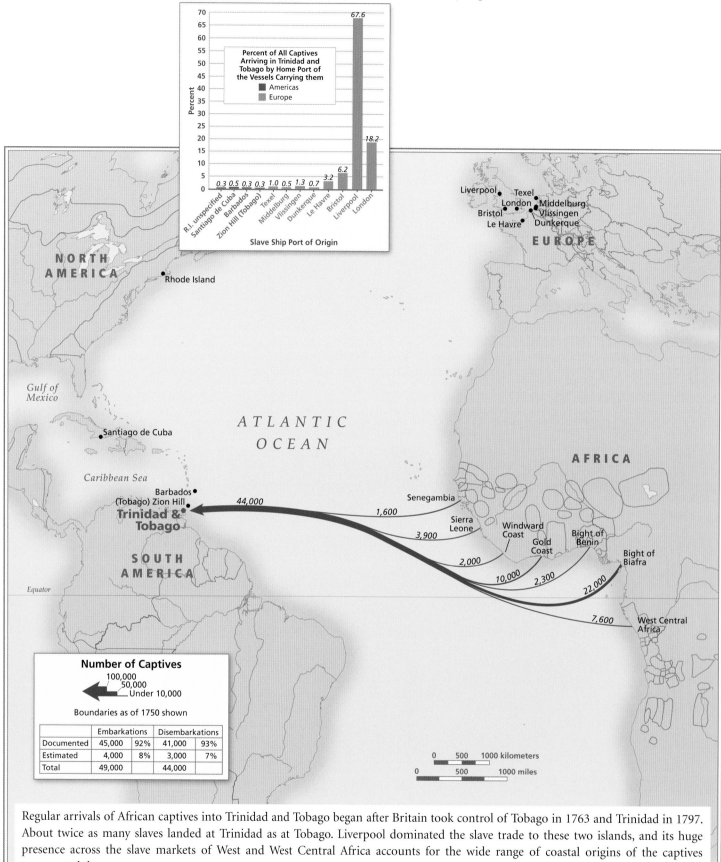

Regular arrivals of African captives into Trinidad and Tobago began after Britain took control of Tobago in 1763 and Trinidad in 1797. About twice as many slaves landed at Trinidad as at Tobago. Liverpool dominated the slave trade to these two islands, and its huge presence across the slave markets of West and West Central Africa accounts for the wide range of coastal origins of the captives transported there.

Monday 13 Decr. [1773, Kingston, Jamaica]

       Monday & Tuesday mere Store days, having now 3 Ships, viz: the Robert, the M[arquis]. of Rockingham & the Jenny. Some of the Captains generally dine with us. On Wednesday we agree Sale of the Jenny and sell only four Negroes; much mortified by it. On Thursday my Brother goes to Spa[nish]. Town, and we sell 40 out of the Jenny to Lewis Vassall, and eight to Doctor Simpson. Vassall dines with us. Spaniards make another proposal which is accepted. On Friday young Barral very sick. Old Barral, the Spaniards and myself are most of the day on board the two Guinea vessels; they choose out of both 164. On Saturday the three Captains dine with us and my Bro. returns from Spanish Town. On Sunday J. Kenyon & I go over to the Pallisades with Hughes, Dennison, etc. to fish the Robert being then heaving down. H. Cunniffe, Rob Jackson, Nixon, Walter, etc. dine with us. R. Jackson stays supper.

Excerpt from Robert Hibbert Diaries, 1771–1778, private collection. Published with the permission of Nick Hibbert Steele and Ken Cozens.

Map 154: Jamaica: African Coastal Origins of Slaves and Home Ports of Vessels Carrying Them, 1607–1857

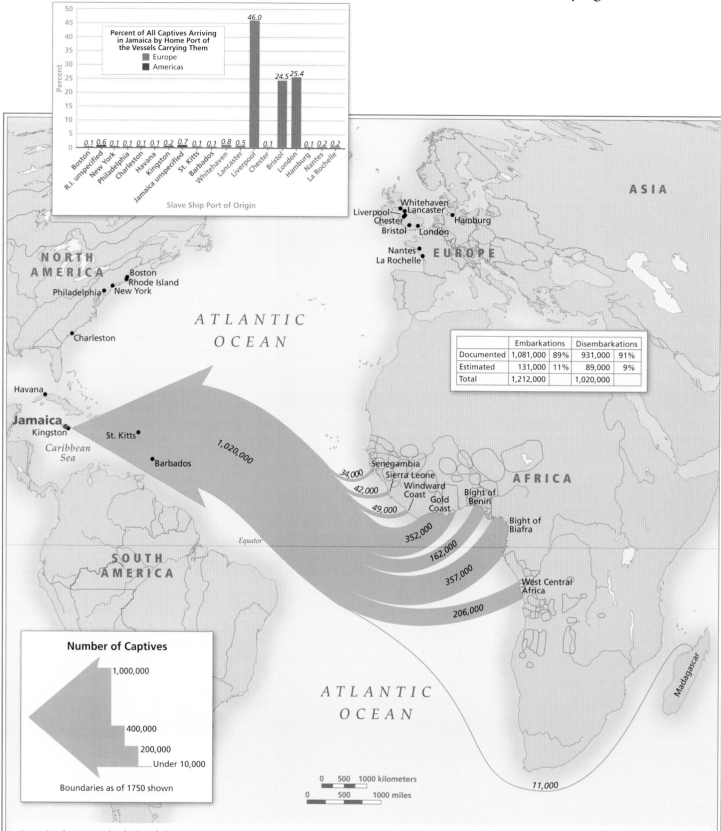

Percent of All Captives Arriving in Jamaica by Home Port of the Vessels Carrying Them

Europe
Americas

Slave Ship Port of Origin

Boston 0.1, R.I. unspecified 0.6, New York 0.1, Philadelphia 0.1, Charleston 0.1, Havana 0.1, Kingston 0.2, Jamaica unspecified 0.7, St. Kitts 0.1, Barbados 0.1, Whitehaven 0.8, Lancaster 0.5, Liverpool 46.0, Chester 0.1, Bristol 24.5, London 25.4, Hamburg 0.1, Nantes 0.2, La Rochelle 0.2

	Embarkations		Disembarkations	
Documented	1,081,000	89%	931,000	91%
Estimated	131,000	11%	89,000	9%
Total	1,212,000		1,020,000	

ASIA

Whitehaven
Liverpool · Lancaster
Chester · · Hamburg
Bristol · London
EUROPE
Nantes ·
La Rochelle

NORTH
AMERICA
Boston
Rhode Island
Philadelphia · New York
Charleston

ATLANTIC
OCEAN

Havana

Jamaica
Kingston
Caribbean
Sea
St. Kitts
Barbados

1,020,000

34,000
42,000
49,000

Senegambia
Sierra Leone
Windward
Coast
Gold
Coast
Bight of
Benin

AFRICA

Bight of
Biafra

352,000
162,000
357,000

West Central
Africa

206,000

Equator

SOUTH
AMERICA

ATLANTIC
OCEAN

Madagascar

Number of Captives

1,000,000

400,000

200,000

Under 10,000

Boundaries as of 1750 shown

11,000

0   500   1000 kilometers
0   500   1000 miles

Jamaica became the hub of the British West Indian slave economy, and a base for British slave trafficking with Spanish America. From the 1720s Jamaica provided the largest single market for African captives in British America, with arrivals peaking at 16,000 a year in the 1790s; reexport of slaves to Spanish America was important at times, notably in 1713–1739. British ships carried most arriving slaves, with leadership passing from London by 1720 to Bristol in the following three decades and to Liverpool from 1750 to 1807. Two out of three captives entering the island before 1720 came from the Bight of Benin and the Gold Coast; from 1720 to 1807 the Bight of Biafra contributed up to 40 percent of arrivals.

Map 155: Barbados:
African Coastal Origins of Slaves and Home Ports of Vessels Carrying Them, 1641–1837

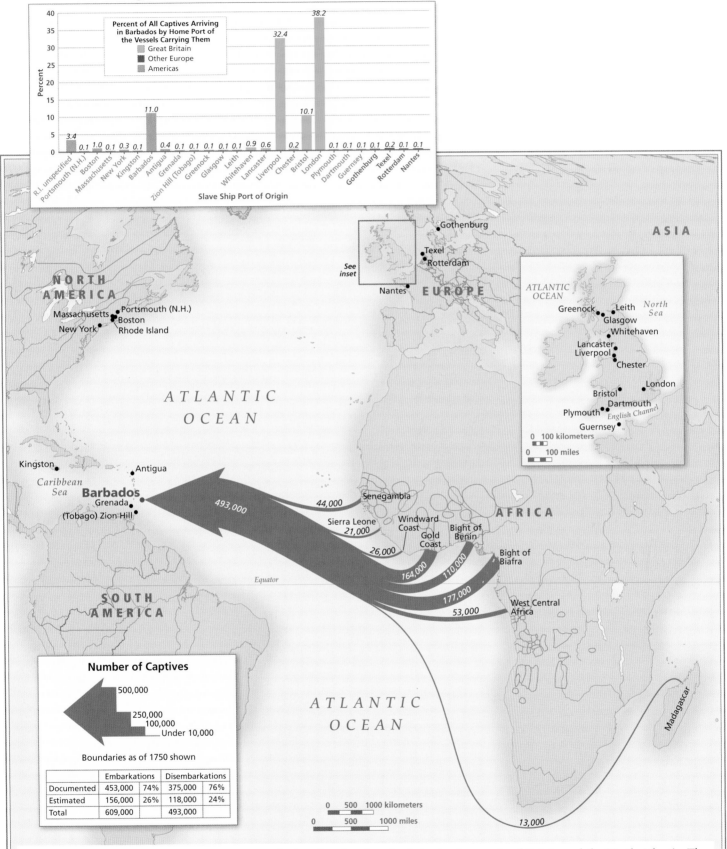

Percent of All Captives Arriving in Barbados by Home Port of the Vessels Carrying Them
- Great Britain
- Other Europe
- Americas

Chart values (Slave Ship Port of Origin):
R.I. unspecified 3.4; Portsmouth (N.H.) 0.1; Boston 1.0; Massachusetts 0.1; New York 0.3; Kingston 0.1; Barbados 11.0; Antigua 0.4; Grenada 0.1; Zion Hill (Tobago) 0.1; Greenock 0.1; Glasgow 0.1; Leith 0.1; Whitehaven 0.9; Lancaster 0.6; Liverpool 32.4; Chester 0.2; Bristol 10.1; London 38.2; Plymouth 0.1; Dartmouth 0.1; Guernsey 0.1; Gothenburg 0.1; Texel 0.2; Rotterdam 0.1; Nantes 0.1

Number of Captives

500,000
250,000
100,000
Under 10,000

Boundaries as of 1750 shown

	Embarkations		Disembarkations	
Documented	453,000	74%	375,000	76%
Estimated	156,000	26%	118,000	24%
Total	609,000		493,000	

Flow values: 493,000; 44,000; 21,000; 26,000; 164,000; 110,000; 177,000; 53,000; 13,000

Under continuous British rule from 1625 on, Barbados played a pivotal role in the slave trade of Britain and the North Atlantic. The Caribbean sugar revolution of the 1640s made Barbados the center of the first prolonged traffic in African captives coming into the region. London vessels carried most arrivals through the 1720s, and Liverpool ships carried most of them later in the eighteenth century. Barbados itself became a center for outfitting slave ships, notably before 1720. This small island sent out more slave vessels to Africa in this period than were dispatched from any other port in North America. A large proportion of slaves came from the Gold Coast and the Bight of Biafra.

Map of Barbados, 1673

A Topographicall Description and Admeasurement of the Yland of Barbados in the West Indyaes with the M[an]ys Names of the Severall plantacons, from Richard Ligon, *A True and Exact History of the Island of Barbadoes* (London: Peter Parker and Thomas Guy, 1657; 2nd ed., 1673), frontispiece. Beinecke Rare Book and Manuscript Library, Yale University.

As the first island in the West Indies to undergo the sugar revolution, Barbados provided a model of plantation development that was copied in the rest of the region over the following two centuries and that, with the spread of sugarcane cultivation in Brazil, created the major single source of demand for enslaved African labor in the Americas. This map, published in the 1673 edition of Richard Ligon's history of Barbados, shows the extent to which sugar planting, and the slaves who cultivated and processed it, had come to dominate life on the island since the crop was introduced in the 1640s. According to Ligon, Africans were "more than double the numbers of Christians that are there." Buyers chose African workers, he reported, "as they do Horses in a Market; the strongest, youthfullest, and most beautiful, yield the greatest prices. Thirty pounds sterling is a price for the best man *Negroe;* and twenty five, twenty six or twenty seven pounds for a Woman; the Children are at easier rates."

Map 156: St. Kitts: African Coastal Origins of Slaves and Home Ports of Vessels Carrying Them, 1644–1807

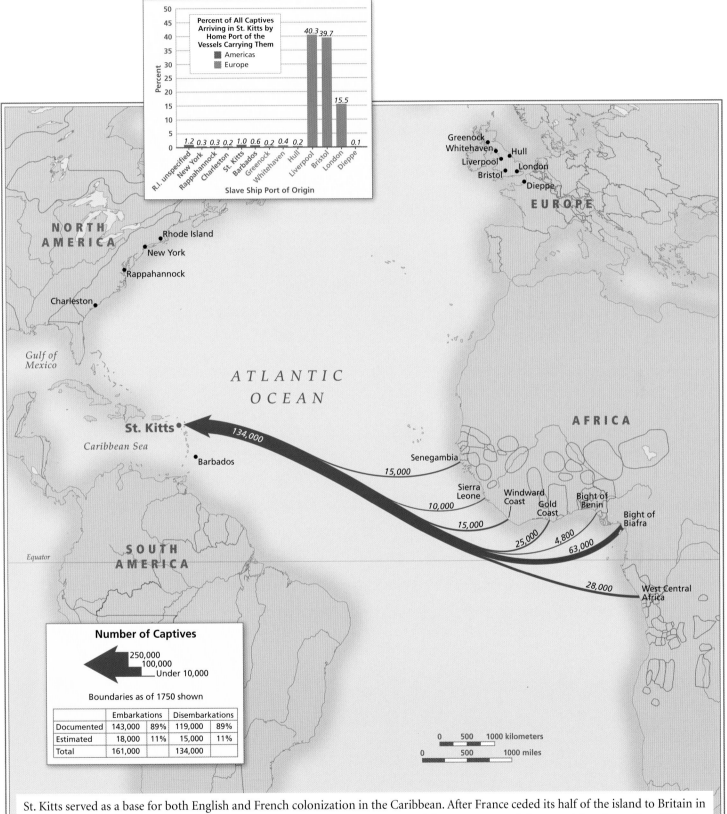

St. Kitts served as a base for both English and French colonization in the Caribbean. After France ceded its half of the island to Britain in 1713, sugar output grew rapidly, and Bristol and Liverpool vessels accounted for 80 percent of slaves arriving there. Two-fifths the embarkations for St. Kitts were at ports in the Bight of Biafra.

Map 157: French Eastern Caribbean Islands:
African Coastal Origins of Slaves and Home Ports of Vessels Carrying Them, 1653–1831

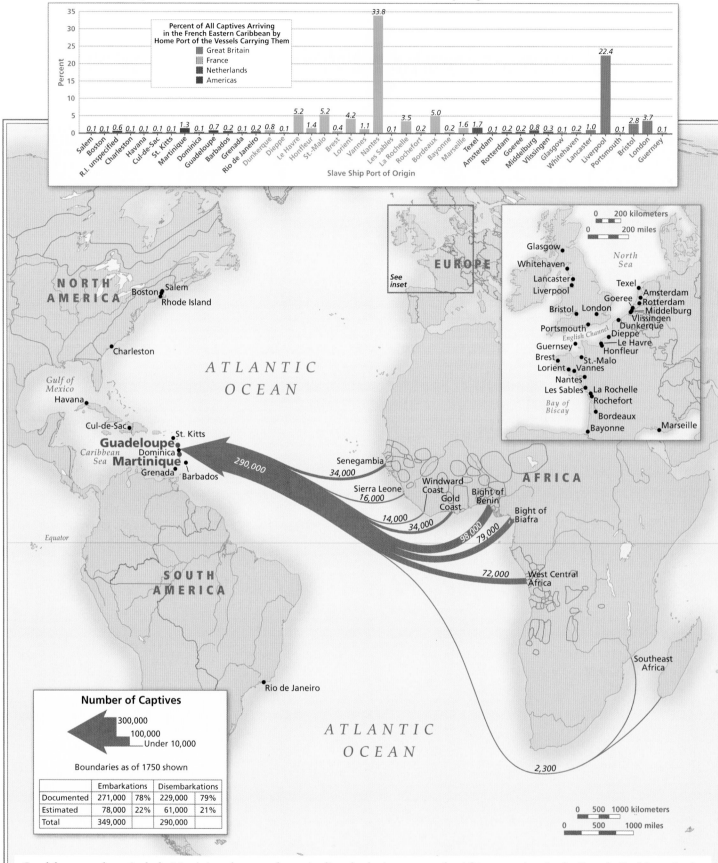

Guadeloupe and particularly Martinique became the main disembarkation centers for African captives in the French Caribbean in the late seventeenth century. Thereafter, Guadeloupe declined as a slave market and imported most of its slaves by way of Martinique. This pattern was reversed only in 1759–1763 when Guadeloupe was under British control. Martinique became an important venue for French traders during the illegal period of French slaving, 1814–1831. French dominance in the Bight of Benin and West Central Africa ensured that these regions accounted for over half of the slaves arriving in these French islands.

Map 158: Dutch West Indies:
African Coastal Origins of Slaves and Home Ports of Vessels Carrying Them, 1657–1794

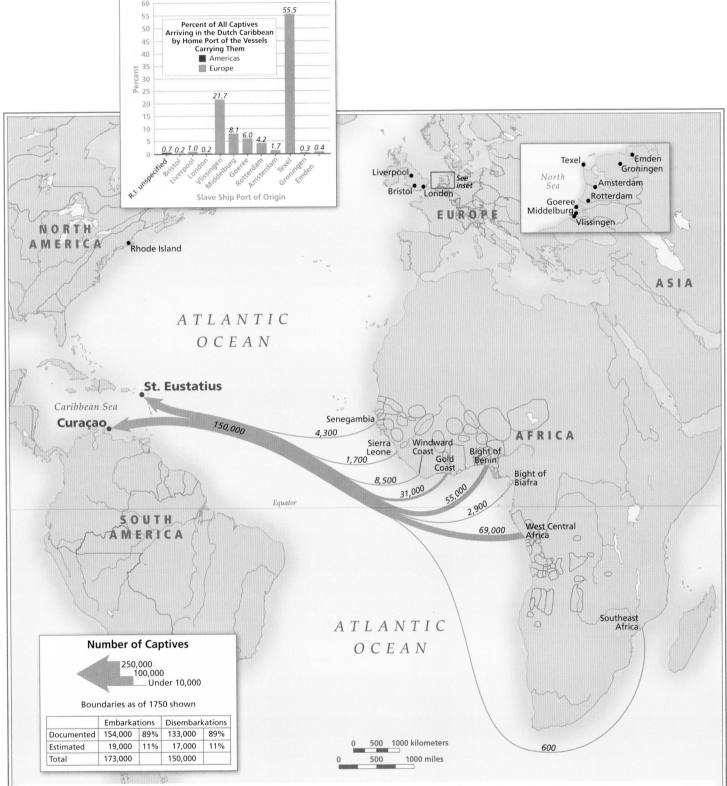

Percent of All Captives Arriving in the Dutch Caribbean by Home Port of the Vessels Carrying Them

- Americas
- Europe

Slave Ship Port of Origin

R.I. unspecified 0.7 Bristol 0.2 Liverpool 1.0 London 0.2 Vlissingen 21.7 Middelburg 8.1 Goeree 6.0 Rotterdam 4.2 Amsterdam 1.7 Texel 55.5 Groningen 0.3 Emden 0.4

Number of Captives

- 250,000
- 100,000
- Under 10,000

Boundaries as of 1750 shown

	Embarkations		Disembarkations	
Documented	154,000	89%	133,000	89%
Estimated	19,000	11%	17,000	11%
Total	173,000		150,000	

Senegambia 4,300
Sierra Leone 1,700
Windward Coast / Gold Coast 8,500
31,000
Bight of Benin 55,000
Bight of Biafra 2,900
West Central Africa 69,000
Southeast Africa 600

150,000

0 500 1000 kilometers
0 500 1000 miles

Curaçao and St. Eustatius became significant venues for reshipment of recent arrivals from Africa to Spanish America and the rest of the Caribbean, Spanish or not, notably between 1670 and 1730 and again from the late 1750s to the mid-1780s. The coastal origins of the slaves disembarking at Curaçao and St. Eustatius reflected the concentration of Dutch traders in West Central Africa and on the Bight of Benin before 1730.

List
Slaves purchased by trade
and sold in Suriname
Year 1758

Running Total	Number per Purchase	Slave	Suriname Purchaser	Guilders
2	2	Boys	Steeven Boon	220
8	6	Women	Barlon	1840
13	5	Men	Polak	1000
16	3	Boys	Klienhans	300
20	4	Women		
24	4	Men	Krans	2900
26	2	Boys		
27	1	Boy	Wife [widow?] of Lemmers	100
30	3	Girls	Benelle	300
34	4	Boys	Kirker	700
35	1	Boy	Schellinger	100
45	10	Men		
47	2	Girls	Cellier	3400
49	2	Boys		
53	4	Boys	Folljer	700
54	1	Boy	Van Vark	180
60	6	Boys	Kemmers	1000
61	1	Woman	Wager Heijm	130
63	2	Women	Du Plaifer	500
65	2	Boys	Bogel	250
75	10	Men	Van Son	2500
76	1	Boy	Nap	100
77	1	Boy	Van Velfen	100
78	1	Woman	Kruijs	150
79	1	Boy	Guttelman	130
91	12	Mixed Group	Knuffel	2000
93	2	Sick Boys	Teckenaar	119, 10

Total 93   **Total Cost 18719, 10**

Excerpt from Journal of Daily Trade Negotiations recorded by Captain Adriaan Jacobze, on behalf of Ship Prins Willem V, 1758, Middelburgshe Commercie Compagnie, item 985, Middelburg Archives, The Netherlands. In the last column, prices are given in guilders and stuivers. Twenty stuivers equals one guilder. We are grateful to Stacey Sommerdyk for help in translating this document.

Map 159: Dutch Guianas:
African Coastal Origins of Slaves and Home Ports of Vessels Carrying Them, 1658–1825

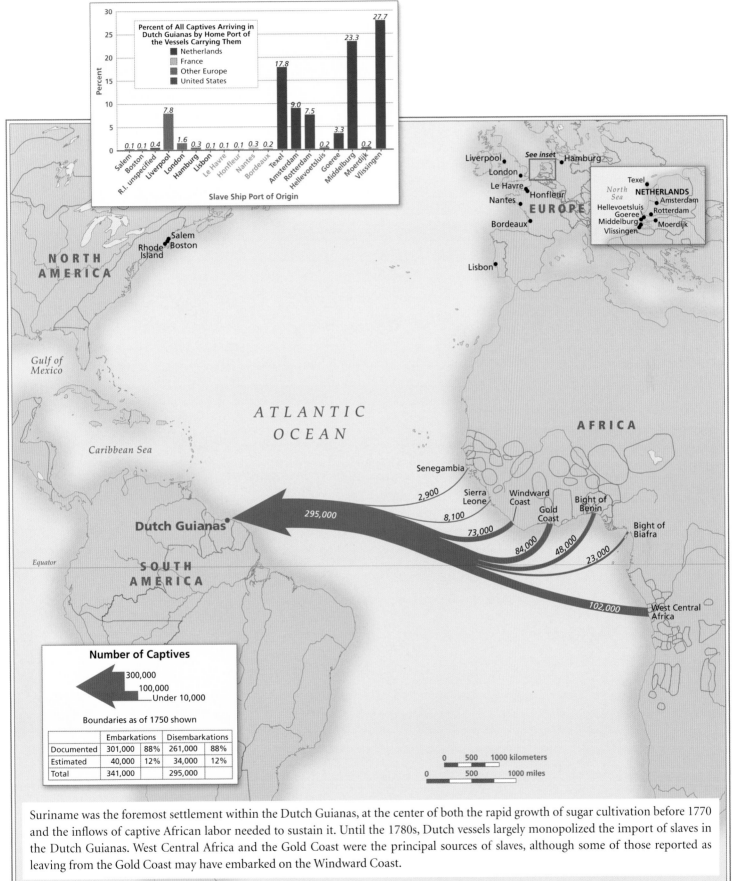

Percent of All Captives Arriving in Dutch Guianas by Home Port of the Vessels Carrying Them

- ■ Netherlands
- ▨ France
- ▨ Other Europe
- ■ United States

Slave Ship Port of Origin

Salem 0.1, Boston 0.1, R.I. unspecified 0.4, Liverpool 7.8, London 1.6, Hamburg 0.3, Lisbon 0.1, Le Havre 0.1, Honfleur 0.1, Nantes 0.3, Bordeaux 0.2, Texel 17.8, Amsterdam 9.0, Rotterdam 7.5, Hellevoetsluis 0.2, Goeree 3.3, Middelburg 23.3, Moerdijk 0.2, Vlissingen 27.7

Number of Captives

300,000
100,000
Under 10,000

Boundaries as of 1750 shown

	Embarkations		Disembarkations	
Documented	301,000	88%	261,000	88%
Estimated	40,000	12%	34,000	12%
Total	341,000		295,000	

Senegambia 2,900
Sierra Leone 8,100
Windward Coast 73,000
Gold Coast 84,000
Bight of Benin 48,000
Bight of Biafra 23,000
West Central Africa 102,000
295,000

Suriname was the foremost settlement within the Dutch Guianas, at the center of both the rapid growth of sugar cultivation before 1770 and the inflows of captive African labor needed to sustain it. Until the 1780s, Dutch vessels largely monopolized the import of slaves in the Dutch Guianas. West Central Africa and the Gold Coast were the principal sources of slaves, although some of those reported as leaving from the Gold Coast may have embarked on the Windward Coast.

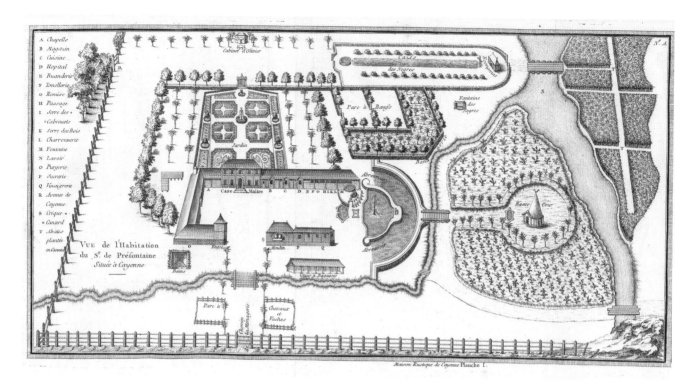

Plan of a Large Plantation, Cayenne (French Guiana), 1763

Vue de l'Habitation du Sr. de Préfontaine, from Chevalier de Préfontaine, *Maison rustique, à l'usage des habitans de la partie de la France équinoxiale, connu sous le nom de Cayenne* (Paris: J. B. Bauche, 1763), plate 1. Courtesy of the John Carter Brown Library at Brown University.

Sugar plantations spread widely in the three centuries after they were established in Brazil in the sixteenth century. Many plans of sugar plantations have survived. The plantation depicted here was in Cayenne, an outpost of French sugarcane cultivation on mainland South America in the later eighteenth century. As the plan shows, sugar plantations required major investments in buildings and equipment as well as African slave labor. The slaves, who typically numbered 100–200 or more, lived in rows of huts. The work exacted a heavy toll; plantation owners commonly had to buy new recruits from Africa to sustain their labor force instead of relying on natural reproduction.

Map 160: French Guiana:
African Coastal Origins of Slaves and Home Ports of Vessels Carrying Them, 1664–1829

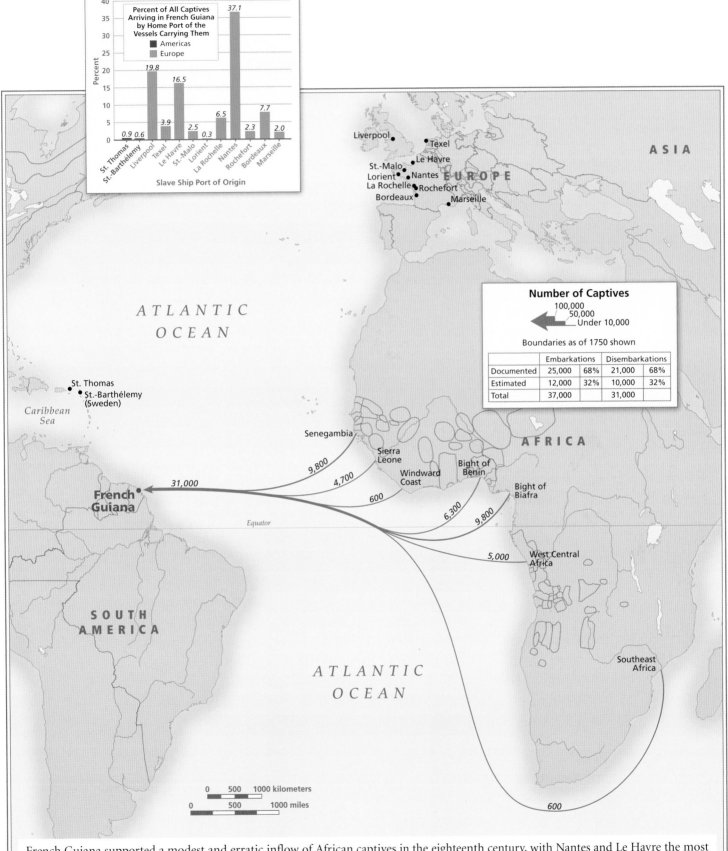

Percent of All Captives Arriving in French Guiana by Home Port of the Vessels Carrying Them

- ■ Americas
- ■ Europe

St. Thomas 0.9
St.-Barthélemy 0.6
Liverpool 19.8
Texel 3.9
Le Havre 16.5
St.-Malo 2.5
Lorient 0.3
La Rochelle 6.5
Nantes 37.1
Rochefort 2.3
Bordeaux 7.7
Marseille 2.0

Slave Ship Port of Origin

Number of Captives

100,000
50,000
Under 10,000

Boundaries as of 1750 shown

	Embarkations		Disembarkations	
Documented	25,000	68%	21,000	68%
Estimated	12,000	32%	10,000	32%
Total	37,000		31,000	

French Guiana supported a modest and erratic inflow of African captives in the eighteenth century, with Nantes and Le Havre the most prominent outfitting ports. Liverpool traders briefly became suppliers of slaves to Cayenne, the former island and now capital city, in 1796–1807, when the colony fell under British control. French rule was restored in 1814, and a final brief inflow of captives occurred in the 1820s. Slaves arriving in Cayenne came from most African coastal regions, probably because almost every slave vessel heading to the large Caribbean market from Africa passed by French Guiana, and many sold a few slaves there.

This Lord of Hosts, in his great providence, and in great mercy to me, made a way for my deliverance from Grenada. Being in this dreadful captivity and horrible slavery, without any hope of deliverance, for about eight or nine months, beholding the most dreadful scenes of misery and cruelty, and seeing my miserable companions often cruelly lashed, and, as it were, cut to pieces, for the most trifling faults; this made me often tremble and weep, but I escaped better than many of them. . . . Thus seeing my miserable companions and countrymen in this pitiful, distressed, and horrible situation, with all the brutish baseness and barbarity attending it, could not but fill my little mind with horror and indignation. But I must own, to the shame of my own countrymen, that I was first kidnapped and betrayed by some of my own complexion, who were the first cause of my exile, and slavery; but if there were no buyers there would be no sellers. So far as I can remember, some of the Africans in my country keep slaves, which they take in war, or for debt; but those which they keep are well fed, and good care taken of them, and treated well; and as to their clothing, they differ according to the custom of the country. But I may safely say, that all the poverty and misery that any of the inhabitants of Africa meet with among themselves, is far inferior to those inhospitable regions of misery which they meet with in the West-Indies, where their hard-hearted overseers have neither Regard to the laws of God, nor the life of their fellow-men.

Thanks be to God, I was delivered from Grenada, and that horrid brutal slavery. A gentleman coming to England took me for his servant, and brought me away, where I soon found my situation become more agreeable. After coming to England, and seeing others write and read, I had a strong desire to learn, and getting what assistance I could, I applied myself to learn reading and writing, which soon became my recreation, pleasure, and delight; and when my master perceived that I could write some, he sent me to a proper school for that purpose to learn. Since, I have endeavoured to improve my mind in reading, and have sought to get all the intelligence I could, in my situation of life, towards the state of my brethren and countrymen in complexion, and of the miserable situation of those who are barbarously sold into captivity, and unlawfully held in slavery

Excerpt from *Narrative of the Enslavement of Ottobah Cugoano, a Native of Africa, Published by Himself in the Year 1787* (1787; London: Printed for the author and sold by Hatchard and Co., 1825).

Map 161: Grenada: African Coastal Origins of Slaves and Home Ports of Vessels Carrying Them, 1669–1808

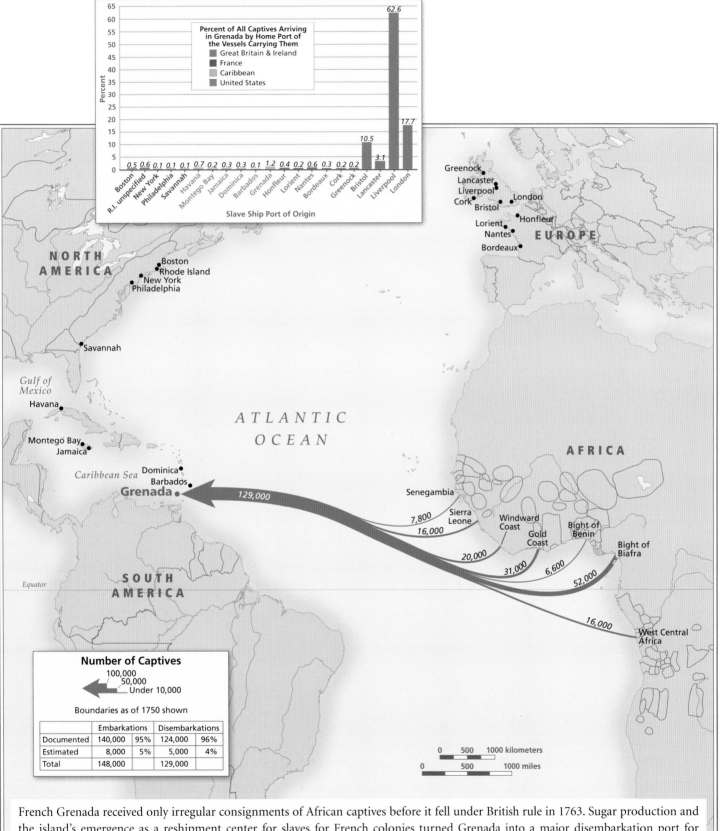

French Grenada received only irregular consignments of African captives before it fell under British rule in 1763. Sugar production and the island's emergence as a reshipment center for slaves for French colonies turned Grenada into a major disembarkation port for African captives in British ships. Liverpool ships accounted for more than 60 percent of arrivals. Over a third of the slaves transported to Grenada came from ports on the Bight of Biafra.

Map 162: Nevis: African Coastal Origins of Slaves and Home Ports of Vessels Carrying Them, 1674–1806

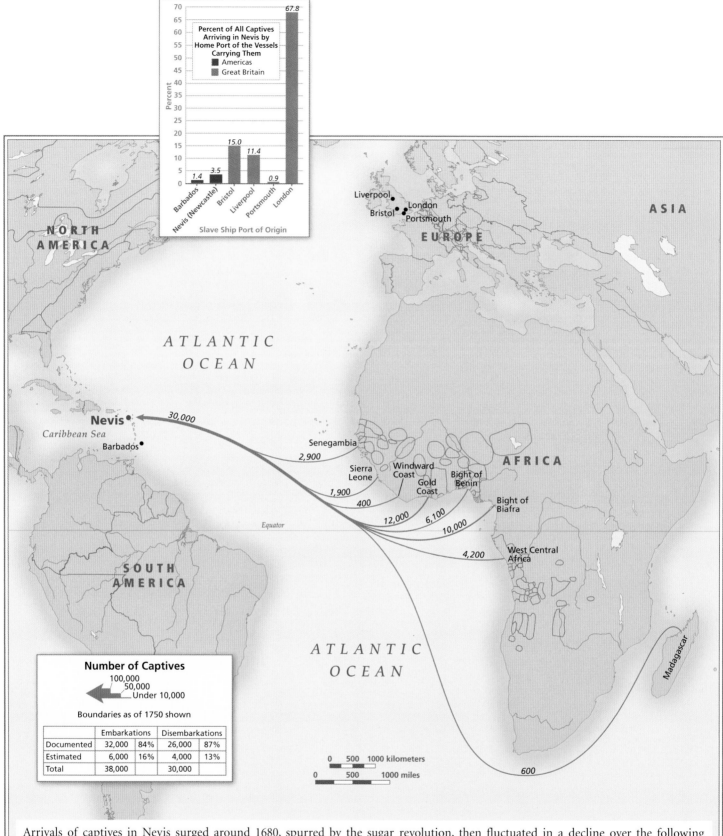

Percent of All Captives Arriving in Nevis by Home Port of the Vessels Carrying Them
- Americas
- Great Britain

	Barbados	Nevis (Newcastle)	Bristol	Liverpool	Portsmouth	London
Percent	1.4	3.5	15.0	11.4	0.9	67.8

Slave Ship Port of Origin

Number of Captives

100,000
50,000
Under 10,000

Boundaries as of 1750 shown

	Embarkations		Disembarkations	
Documented	32,000	84%	26,000	87%
Estimated	6,000	16%	4,000	13%
Total	38,000		30,000	

Arrivals of captives in Nevis surged around 1680, spurred by the sugar revolution, then fluctuated in a decline over the following century. London vessels brought most of the slaves until 1730, carrying them mainly from ports on the Gold Coast, the Bight of Benin, and the Bight of Biafra.

Map 163: Antigua: African Coastal Origins of Slaves and Home Ports of Vessels Carrying Them, 1677–1820

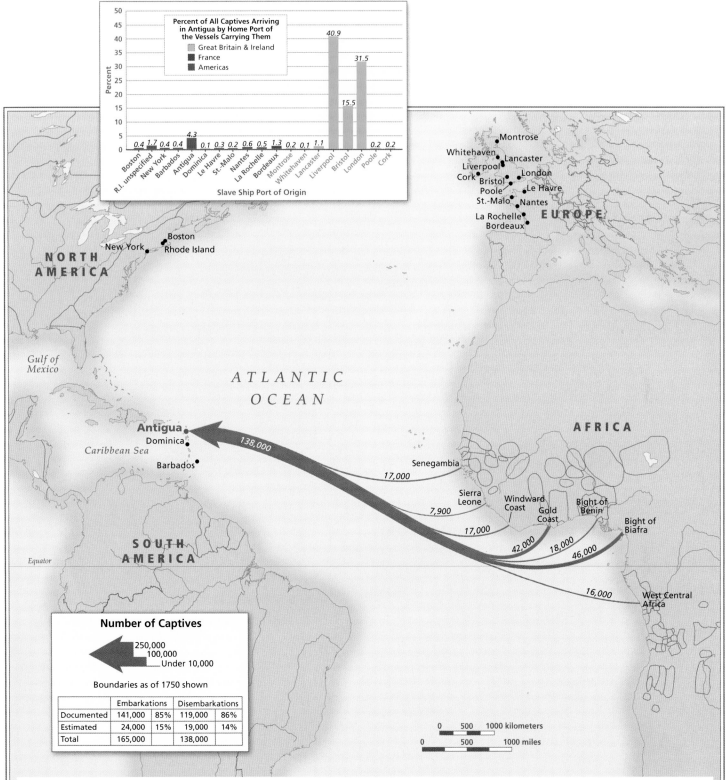

Settled by the English in 1632, Antigua supported a traffic in captives from Africa that peaked at over 5,000 slaves a year in the mid-1750s and late 1760s and persisted, at a lower level, through 1808. London ships dominated the traffic to the island before 1730, and Liverpool ships did later in the eighteenth century, but the island fitted out a significant number of ships itself and attracted vessels fitted out at many ports. Slaves arriving after 1808 did so because their vessels had been shipwrecked or captured while en route to Spanish-owned Caribbean islands. The Gold Coast was a major source of captives through 1720, giving way to the Bight of Biafra and the Windward Coast in later years.

Map 164: St.-Domingue/Haiti:
African Coastal Origins of Slaves and Home Ports of Vessels Carrying Them, 1679–1819

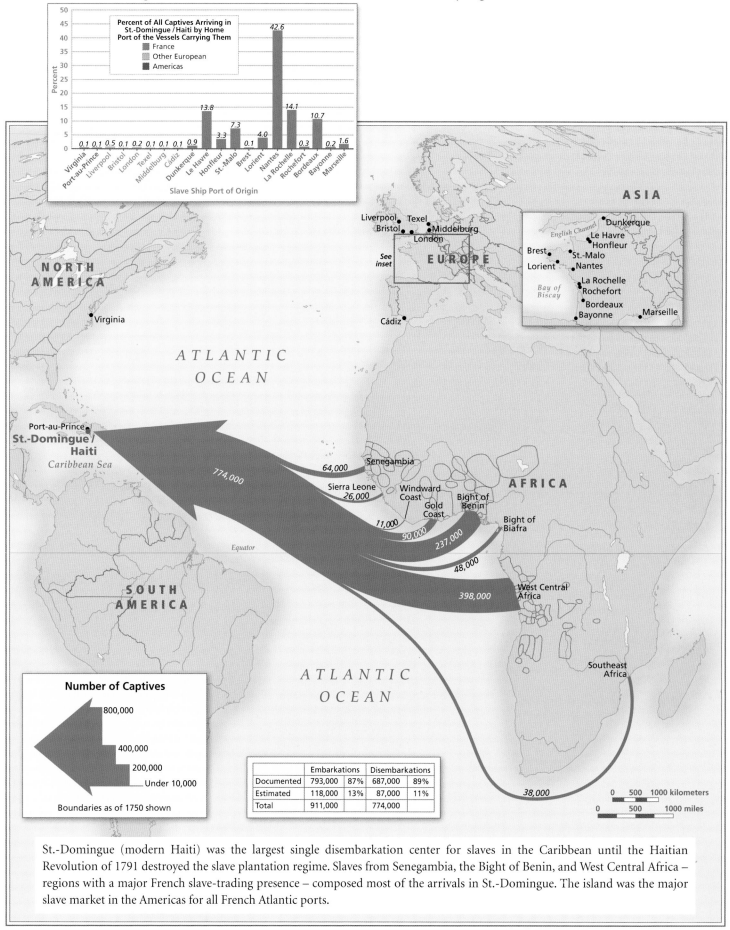

Percent of All Captives Arriving in St.-Domingue/Haiti by Home Port of the Vessels Carrying Them

- France
- Other European
- Americas

Virginia 0.1, Port-au-Prince 0.1, Liverpool 0.5, Bristol 0.1, London 0.2, Texel 0.1, Middelburg 0.1, Cádiz 0.1, Dunkerque 0.9, Le Havre 13.8, Honfleur 3.3, St.-Malo 7.3, Brest 0.1, Lorient 4.0, Nantes 42.6, La Rochelle 14.1, Rochefort 0.3, Bordeaux 10.7, Bayonne 0.2, Marseille 1.6

Slave Ship Port of Origin

Number of Captives

- 800,000
- 400,000
- 200,000
- Under 10,000

Boundaries as of 1750 shown

	Embarkations		Disembarkations	
Documented	793,000	87%	687,000	89%
Estimated	118,000	13%	87,000	11%
Total	911,000		774,000	

St.-Domingue (modern Haiti) was the largest single disembarkation center for slaves in the Caribbean until the Haitian Revolution of 1791 destroyed the slave plantation regime. Slaves from Senegambia, the Bight of Benin, and West Central Africa – regions with a major French slave-trading presence – composed most of the arrivals in St.-Domingue. The island was the major slave market in the Americas for all French Atlantic ports.

Map 165: Tortola, Montserrat, St. Lucia, and the Bahamas: African Coastal Origins of Slaves and Home Ports of Vessels Carrying Them, 1679–1860

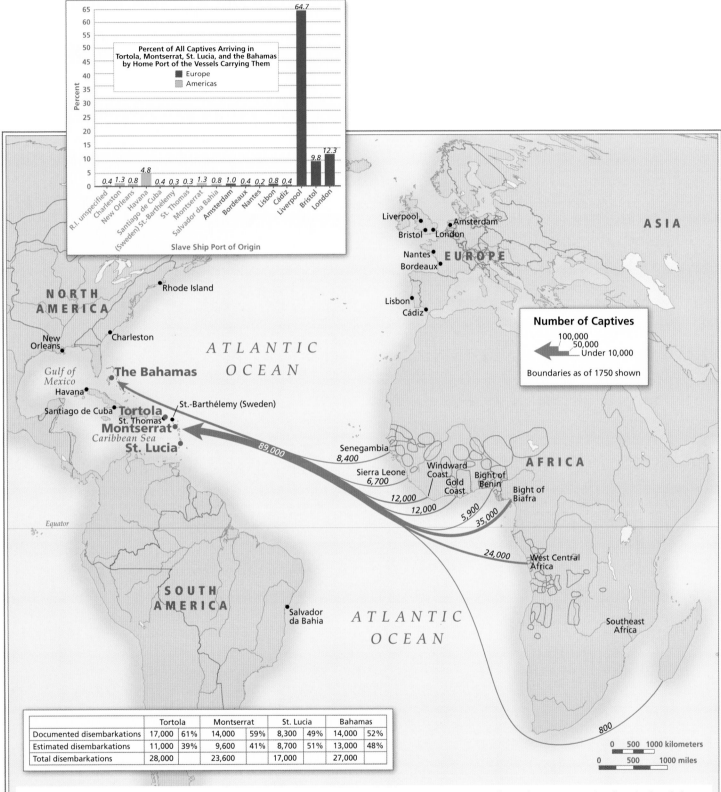

	Tortola		Montserrat		St. Lucia		Bahamas	
Documented disembarkations	17,000	61%	14,000	59%	8,300	49%	14,000	52%
Estimated disembarkations	11,000	39%	9,600	41%	8,700	51%	13,000	48%
Total disembarkations	28,000		23,600		17,000		27,000	

Montserrat, in the British Leeward Islands, developed a significant sugar-producing sector dependent on sustained arrivals of slaves between 1689 and 1730, during which time first London and then Bristol accounted for most arrivals. The chief slaveholders by 1730 were descendants of Irish indentured servants brought to the island in the seventeenth century. A less systematic pattern of slave arrivals, with some concentration in wartime, developed for St. Lucia, Tortola, and the Bahamas. These islands relied mostly on Liverpool ships to bring new captives before 1807, a high proportion of whom came from the Bight of Biafra in St. Lucia's case and from West Central Africa in the case of the Bahamas.

Map 166: Danish West Indies:
African Coastal Origins of Slaves and Home Ports of Vessels Carrying Them, 1680–1807

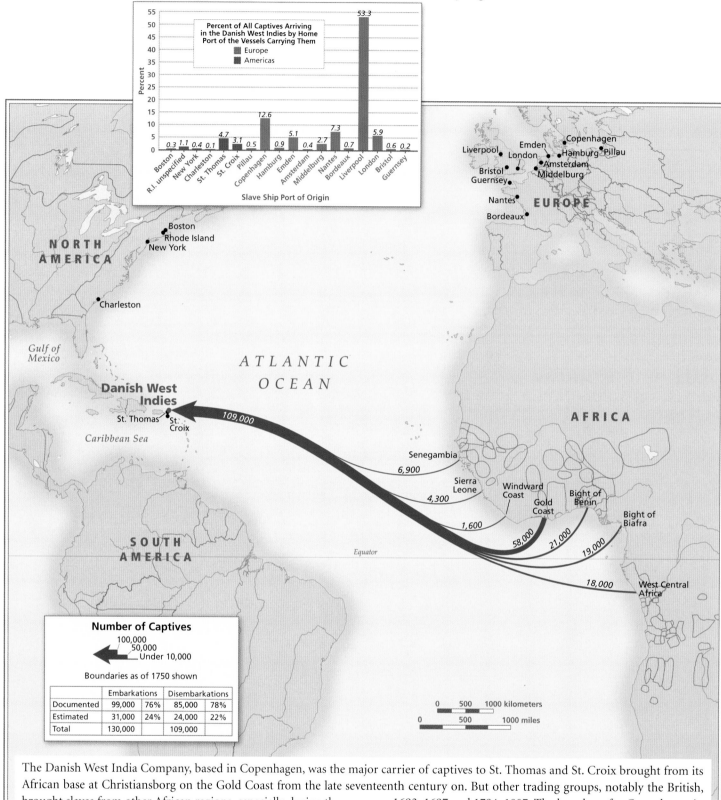

The Danish West India Company, based in Copenhagen, was the major carrier of captives to St. Thomas and St. Croix brought from its African base at Christiansborg on the Gold Coast from the late seventeenth century on. But other trading groups, notably the British, brought slaves from other African regions, especially during the war years 1693–1697 and 1794–1807. The low share for Copenhagen in the bar graph reflects very poor departure port information, especially for the early years of the trade.

Grenada 24 May 1784, Campbell Baillie & Co to Messrs. Will[iam]. Davenport & Co.

Your favour of the 1st Febry came to our hands at St Vincent the 17th Ulto. And we left a letter there for Capt. Potter of your ship Essex, giving him no great encouragement to proceed to this Island, in case he should [missing: meet?] any demand on tolerable good terms for his slaves at St Vincent—in consequence whereof our mutual friends Messrs Baillie & Hamilton advise us of his arrival there, and that they had undertaken to sell the Cargo on the 28th inst. they do not say on what terms—we enclose you their advertisement, with a sincere wish they may sell to your Content—good Windward or Gold coast slaves may yet average £35 @ [to] £40 here, provided the buyers can have credit to include the whole of next years Crop, for this Crop is already so fully engaged, that tho the Estates want Negroes much the best of them cannot even commence their payments till the next Crop is shipped—and to Remit from such payments, a Guarantee House here cannot with safety & Credit draw at less than 15 @ [to] 24 Months.

St Vincent 26th May 1784 Baillie & Hamilton to Messrs. William Davenport & Co.

We wrote you the 16th Instant advising you of the arrival of your Ship Essex Capt. Potter with 291 Slaves, at which time we did not expect he would stop here, but finding that his Slaves were to small for the Carolina Market he accepted of our offer to put his Cargo into our hands to dispose of to the best advantage in our power, giving Bills at 12, 15 & 18 Months for the Nt [net] Proceeds, we have fixed upon Fraiday the 28th Instant for the Sale, and have every prospect of turning them out to a good account, but we cannot flatter you with the hopes of a high average, as about half of the Cargo consist of Old, Thin & a large proportion of small slaves under size, we expect Capt Potter will get nearly loaded for your port, there is a ship to sail from here the 30th by which we shall write you.

St Vincent June 12th 1784 Baillie & Hamilton to Messrs. William Davenport & Co.

Since we wrote you the 29th Ultimo, we have disposed of the remainder of the Essex's Cargo of Slaves, Inclosed you have a copy of the Sales, by which you will see that the average is reduced to £34–1/ St[erlin]g which we hope you will be satisfyed with, we have done the utmost in our power for your Interest, & had it not been for the number of refuse & small Slaves under size, the average woud have been very high, Captain Potter has no doubt informed you that he has lost Eleven since his Arrival. We expect he will be ready to leave this about the 5th July with a full Load, he writes you by this conveyance to which beg leave to refer, there will be a demand for Slaves in this Island during the Months of September, October November and December, and should any Vessels arrive here about that time from the Windward Coast, gold Coast or Bonny they cannot fail of coming to a good Market.

Correspondence from Slave Factors to William Davenport & Co of Liverpool regarding the disposal of captives from ship Essex at St Vincent, 1784, William Davenport Archives, National Maritime Museum on Merseyside, Liverpool. Published with permission of the National Maritime Museum on Merseyside.

Map 167: St. Vincent:
African Coastal Origins of Slaves and Home Ports of Vessels Carrying Them, 1764–1808

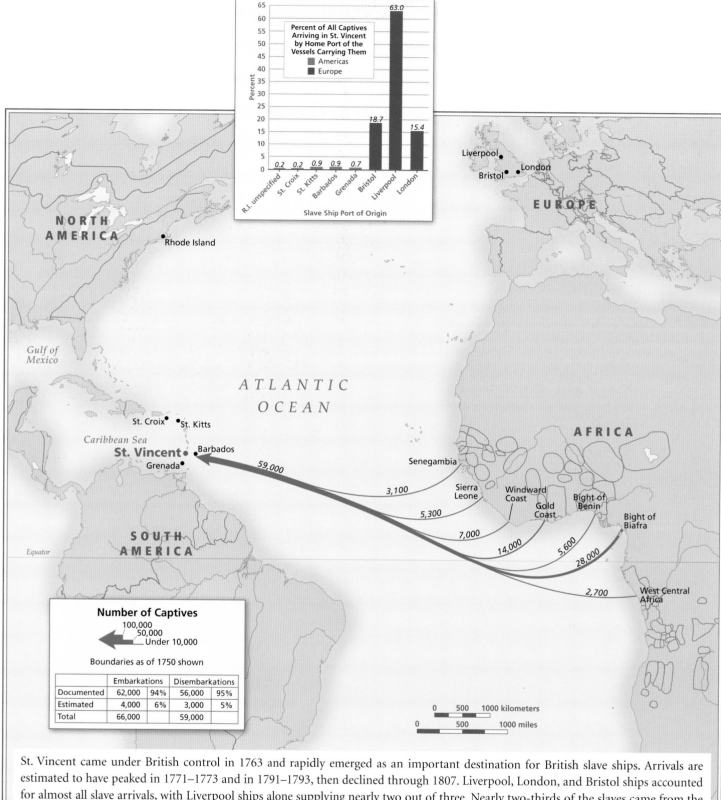

St. Vincent came under British control in 1763 and rapidly emerged as an important destination for British slave ships. Arrivals are estimated to have peaked in 1771–1773 and in 1791–1793, then declined through 1807. Liverpool, London, and Bristol ships accounted for almost all slave arrivals, with Liverpool ships alone supplying nearly two out of three. Nearly two-thirds of the slaves came from the Gold Coast and the Bight of Biafra.

Map 168: Dominica:
African Coastal Origins of Slaves and Home Ports of Vessels Carrying Them, 1764–1837

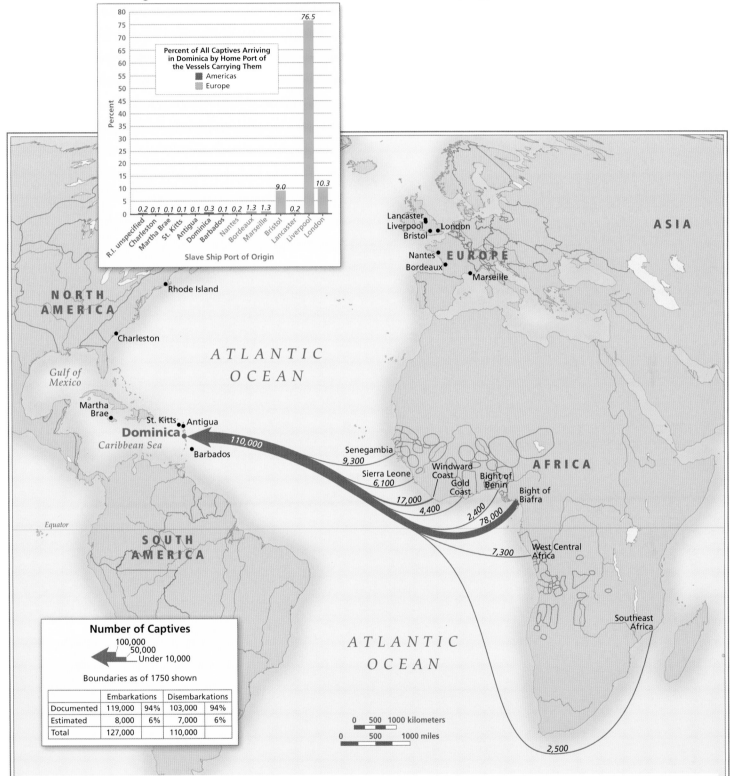

Percent of All Captives Arriving in Dominica by Home Port of the Vessels Carrying Them

- Americas
- Europe

Slave Ship Port of Origin

R.I. unspecified	Charleston	Martha Brae	St. Kitts	Antigua	Dominica	Barbados	Nantes	Bordeaux	Marseille	Bristol	Lancaster	Liverpool	London
0.2	0.1	0.1	0.1	0.1	0.3	0.1	0.2	1.3	1.3	9.0	0.2	76.5	10.3

Number of Captives

- 100,000
- 50,000
- Under 10,000

Boundaries as of 1750 shown

	Embarkations		Disembarkations	
Documented	119,000	94%	103,000	94%
Estimated	8,000	6%	7,000	6%
Total	127,000		110,000	

Senegambia 9,300
Sierra Leone 6,100
Windward Coast 4,400
Gold Coast 17,000
Bight of Benin 2,400
Bight of Biafra 78,000
West Central Africa 7,300
Southeast Africa 2,500

110,000

After the British conquered Dominica in 1761, the island quickly became a major center of British slaving activity, with peaks of arrivals from Africa in 1771 and 1785. Liverpool ships accounted for three in four of the captives who disembarked; three in five of all those taken on board in Africa came from ports in the Bight of Biafra. In addition to providing local employment for slaves, Dominica became a major reexport center for slaves, supplying many other colonies with forced labor.

Map 169: British Guiana:
African Coastal Origins of Slaves and Home Ports of Vessels Carrying Them, 1796–1842

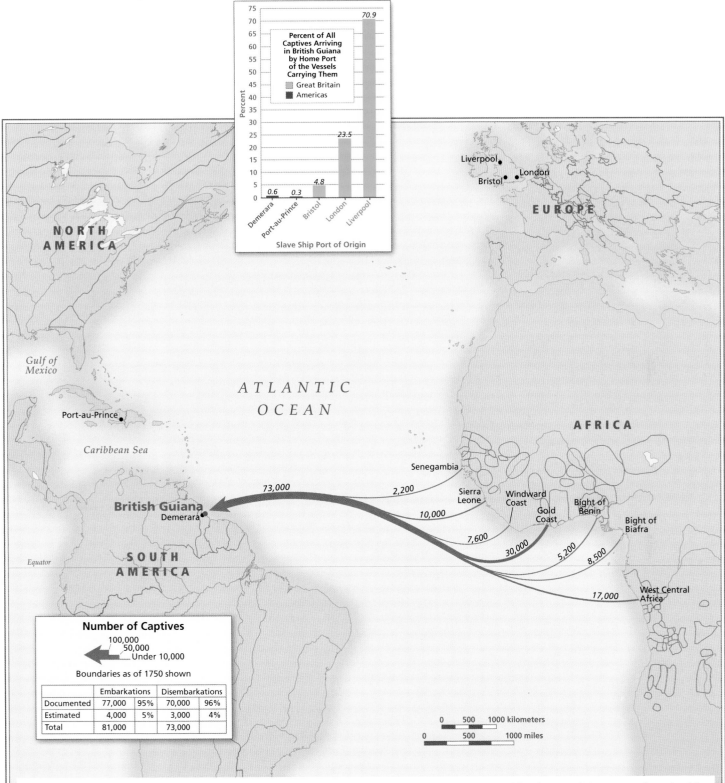

Percent of All Captives Arriving in British Guiana by Home Port of the Vessels Carrying Them

- Great Britain
- Americas

Slave Ship Port of Origin	Percent
Demerara	0.6
Port-au-Prince	0.3
Bristol	4.8
London	23.5
Liverpool	70.9

Number of Captives

100,000
50,000
Under 10,000

Boundaries as of 1750 shown

	Embarkations		Disembarkations	
Documented	77,000	95%	70,000	96%
Estimated	4,000	5%	3,000	4%
Total	81,000		73,000	

British Guiana comprised the former Dutch colonies of Demerara, Essequibo, and Berbice, seized by the British in 1796 and retained by them after the 1815 peace treaty that ended the Napoleonic wars. The British seizure triggered a large influx of African captives for plantation work, over 70 percent of whom arrived in Liverpool vessels. The slaves came from all regions of Atlantic Africa, reflecting Liverpool's dominance of the European-based slave trade from 1797 to 1807.

CANAV·POVR·PECHER·LES·PERLES

Canoe for Pearl-Fishing, Margarita Island, Venezuela, late 16th century

Watercolor by an unknown artist, from *Histoire naturelle des Indes* (Natural History of the Indies), the "Drake Manuscript," late 16th century, folio 57. The Pierpont Morgan Library / Art Resource, NY.

Slaves dived for pearls in the waters off Venezuela. Together with precious metals, pearls were among the exports from Spanish America to Europe that paid for imports of Africans. A description accompanying this ink drawing describes how pearls were gathered: "in three or four fathoms of water . . . the negroes . . . dive into the sea, holding a hoop-net to descend to the bottom where they scrape the soil where oysters are, in order to find the pearls. And the deeper they descend in the water, the larger are the pearls they find. Not being able to hold their breath longer than a quarter of an hour, they come up again and pull their hoop-net. The fishing from morning to evening being completed, they return to . . . where they live." Pearl fishing in this way was hazardous and cost lives.

Map 170: Captive Flows between African and South American Regions, 1561–1856

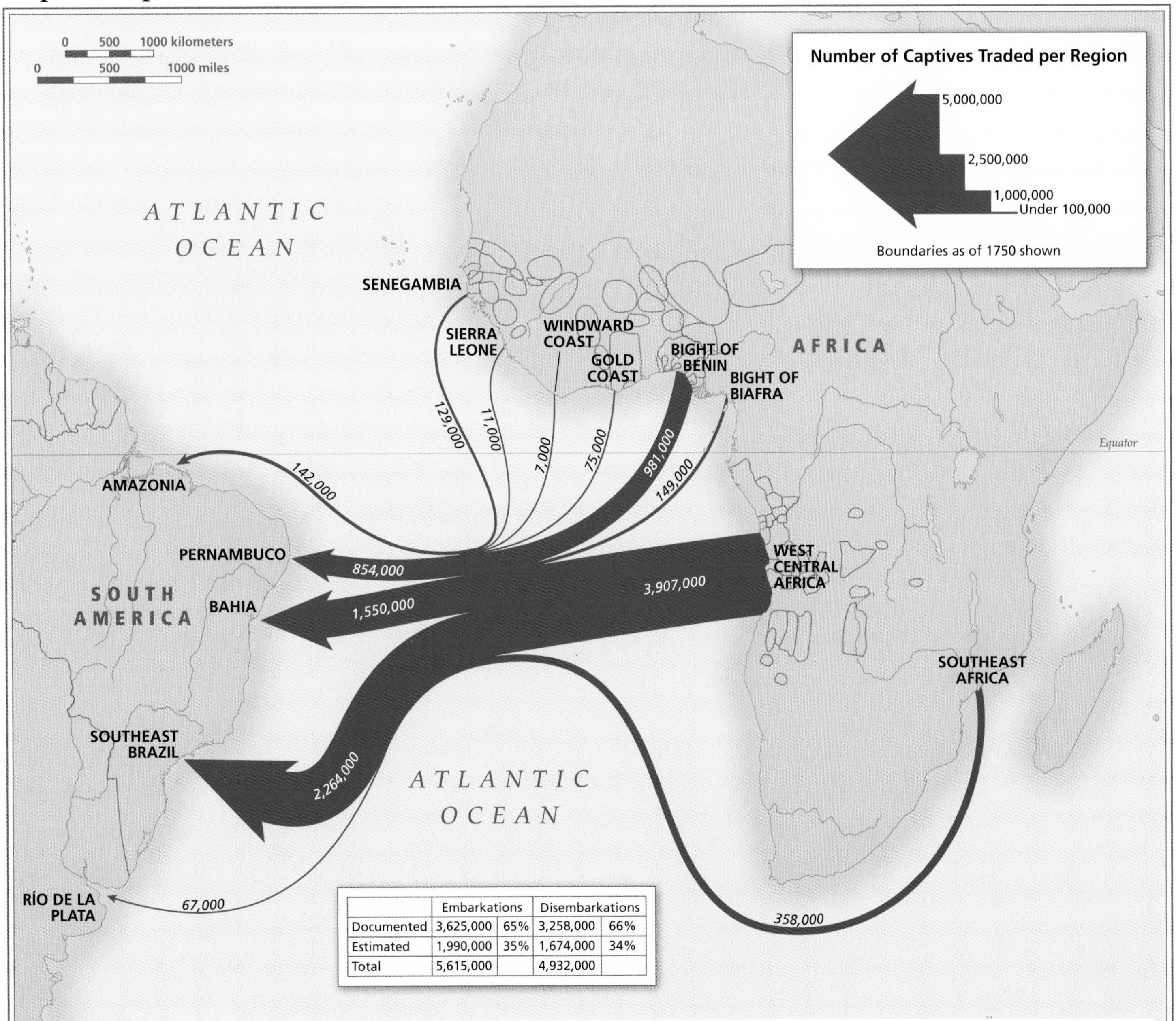
0 500 1000 kilometers
0 500 1000 miles
Number of Captives Traded per Region
5,000,000
2,500,000
1,000,000
Under 100,000
Boundaries as of 1750 shown
ATLANTIC OCEAN
SENEGAMBIA
SIERRA LEONE
WINDWARD COAST
GOLD COAST
BIGHT OF BENIN
BIGHT OF BIAFRA
AFRICA
Equator
AMAZONIA
142,000
129,000
11,000
7,000
75,000
981,000
149,000
PERNAMBUCO
854,000
WEST CENTRAL AFRICA
3,907,000
SOUTH AMERICA
BAHIA
1,550,000
SOUTHEAST AFRICA
SOUTHEAST BRAZIL
2,264,000
ATLANTIC OCEAN
RÍO DE LA PLATA
67,000
358,000

	Embarkations		Disembarkations	
Documented	3,625,000	65%	3,258,000	66%
Estimated	1,990,000	35%	1,674,000	34%
Total	5,615,000		4,932,000	

West Central Africa was the major source of slaves for all the Americas, but in South America it was particularly dominant, especially in Rio de Janeiro and Río de la Plata. Winds and ocean currents allowed slave ships sailing to Rio de Janeiro to sell some of their captives in Pernambuco or Bahia and facilitated an important intra-American traffic between Brazilian ports and Río de la Plata. Note that the paths do not represent the 55,000 slaves who arrived in Brazil at unspecified places.

Slave sales Brazil 1640
1640-12-31

List of slaves from Guinea, Ardra and Calabar, transported on the ship Wapen van Delf, and sold publicly (with names of buyers)

No. of Slaves	Price per slave (Patacas)	Total Guilders	Buyers	Extra
10	161	3864	Reynier Menssen et Compe.	Bought
10	172	4128	Francisco Farinha	Bought
10	174	4156	Abraham Quereido	Bought
10	162	3888	Joseph de Solis	Bought
10	175	4200	Jacob Secuto	Bought
10	162	3888	Gaspar Dias Ferreira	Bought
10	179	4296	Gaspar Dias Ferreira	Bought
10	167	4008	Gaspar Dias Ferreira	Bought
10	205	4920	Gaspar Dias Ferreira	Bought
10	177	4248	Gaspar Dias Ferreira	Bought
10	213	5112	Moses Netto	Bought
10	187	4488	Simon van der Neese	Bought
10	188	4512	Simon van der Neese	Bought
10	190	4560	Pr. Marissinqs [?]	Bought
10	199	4776	Jacob Aboaff	Bought
10	236	5664	Diogo Carvalho et Compe.	Bought
10	200	4800	Godefrey van Wessem	Bought
10	180	4320	Vicento Rodrigues	Bought
10	177	4248	Aaram Tovar	Bought
10	168	4032	Jean d'Aragon	Bought
10	190	4560	Tjercq. Tode	Bought
9	210	4536	Cosmo de Torres et Compe.	Bought
2	—	900	Frederiq Janssen	Bought
221				

Oude Westindische Compagnie [Old West India Company], *Overgekomen brieven en papieren van Brazilie*, no. 56, microfilm 7, National Archief, The Hague, The Netherlands. We are grateful to Filipa da Silva Ribeiro for help in translating this document.

Maps 171 and 172: Slaves Arriving in Brazil, 1561–1790

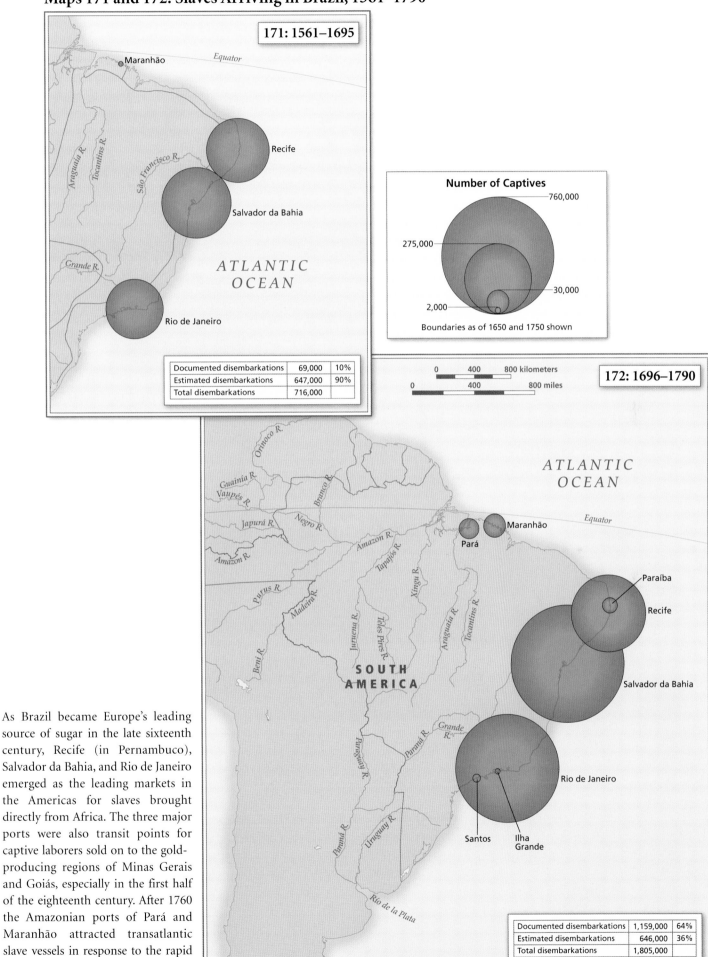

171: 1561–1695

Maranhão

Equator

Araguaia R.

Tocantins R.

São Francisco R.

Recife

Salvador da Bahia

Grande R.

ATLANTIC OCEAN

Rio de Janeiro

Number of Captives

760,000

275,000

30,000

2,000

Boundaries as of 1650 and 1750 shown

Documented disembarkations	69,000	10%
Estimated disembarkations	647,000	90%
Total disembarkations	716,000	

0   400   800 kilometers
0   400   800 miles

172: 1696–1790

Orinoco R.

Guainia R.

Vaupés R.

Japurá R.

Negro R.

Branco R.

ATLANTIC OCEAN

Amazon R.

Tapajós R.

Equator

Maranhão

Pará

Amazon R.

Purus R.

Madeira R.

Juruena R.

Teles Pires R.

Xingu R.

Araguaia R.

Tocantins R.

Paraíba

Recife

Beni R.

SOUTH AMERICA

Salvador da Bahia

Paraguay R.

Grande R.

Paraná R.

Rio de Janeiro

Paraná R.

Uruguay R.

Santos

Ilha Grande

Rio de la Plata

As Brazil became Europe's leading source of sugar in the late sixteenth century, Recife (in Pernambuco), Salvador da Bahia, and Rio de Janeiro emerged as the leading markets in the Americas for slaves brought directly from Africa. The three major ports were also transit points for captive laborers sold on to the gold-producing regions of Minas Gerais and Goiás, especially in the first half of the eighteenth century. After 1760 the Amazonian ports of Pará and Maranhão attracted transatlantic slave vessels in response to the rapid growth of demand for cotton.

Documented disembarkations	1,159,000	64%
Estimated disembarkations	646,000	36%
Total disembarkations	1,805,000	

Slaves Carrying a Covered Hammock in Brazil, 1630s

Watercolor from Cristina Ferrão and José Paolo Monteiro Soares, eds., *Dutch Brazil,* 3 vols. (Rio de Janeiro: Editoria Index, 1997), vol. 2, *The Thierbuch and Autobiography of Zacharias Wagener,* plate 104. Courtesy of the Yale University Library.

A Planter and His Wife on a Journey, 1816

Etching and aquatint by Henry Koster, from Koster, *Travels in Brazil* (London: Longman, Hurst, Rees & Brown, 1816), frontispiece. Courtesy of the John Carter Brown Library at Brown University.

Throughout the Americas, enslaved Africans were used not only to produce coffee, gold, sugar, tobacco, cotton, and other goods for market but also to work as servants and to display their owners' status—that is, they were both producers and symbols of their owners' wealth. Zacharias Wagener, a German mercenary who lived in Brazil in 1634–1641 during the Dutch West India Company's occupancy of Recife, reported that, as in the watercolor here, "the wives and children of notable and wealthy Portuguese are transported . . . by two strong slaves, to the houses of their friends or to the church; they hang the beautiful cloths of velvet or damask over the poles so that the sun does not burn them strongly." Two hundred years later, slaves were still carrying wealthy owners. Here, a Brazilian planter riding a horse is accompanied by his wife carried in a type of sedan chair held by two enslaved African men. An African woman is in attendance.

Map 173: Slaves Arriving in Brazil, 1791–1856

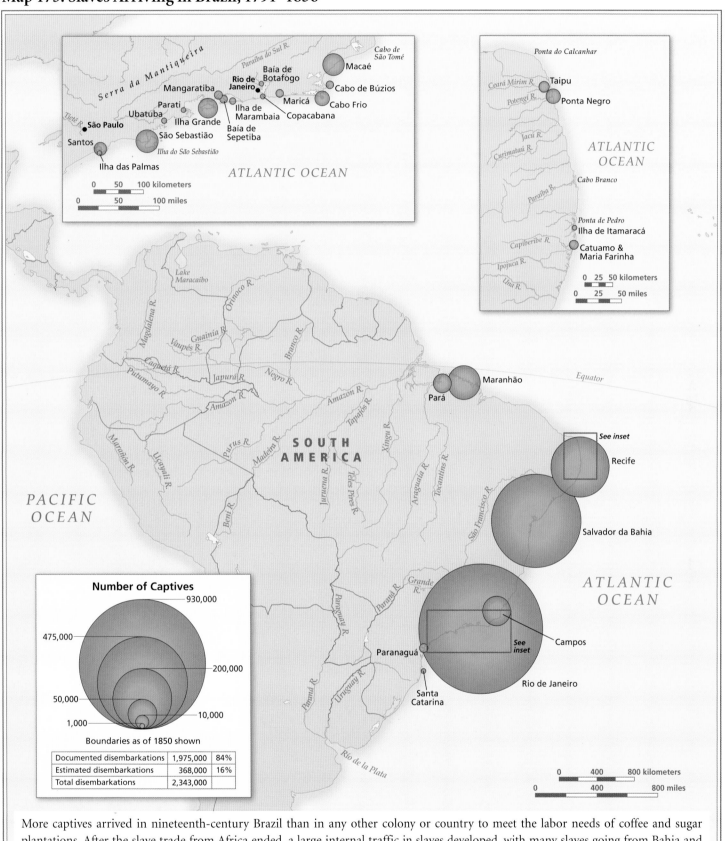

Number of Captives

930,000
475,000
200,000
50,000
10,000
1,000

Boundaries as of 1850 shown

Documented disembarkations	1,975,000	84%
Estimated disembarkations	368,000	16%
Total disembarkations	2,343,000	

More captives arrived in nineteenth-century Brazil than in any other colony or country to meet the labor needs of coffee and sugar plantations. After the slave trade from Africa ended, a large internal traffic in slaves developed, with many slaves going from Bahia and Pernambuco and Amazonia in the north to the southeastern coffee regions. Rio de Janeiro continued to be a center of the slave trade, but after 1838, with the slave trade illegal in Brazil, slave vessels disembarked their captives surreptitiously outside the port and, increasingly, closer to the new coffee frontier to the southeast.

Map 174: Slaves Arriving in the Río de la Plata, 1620–1835

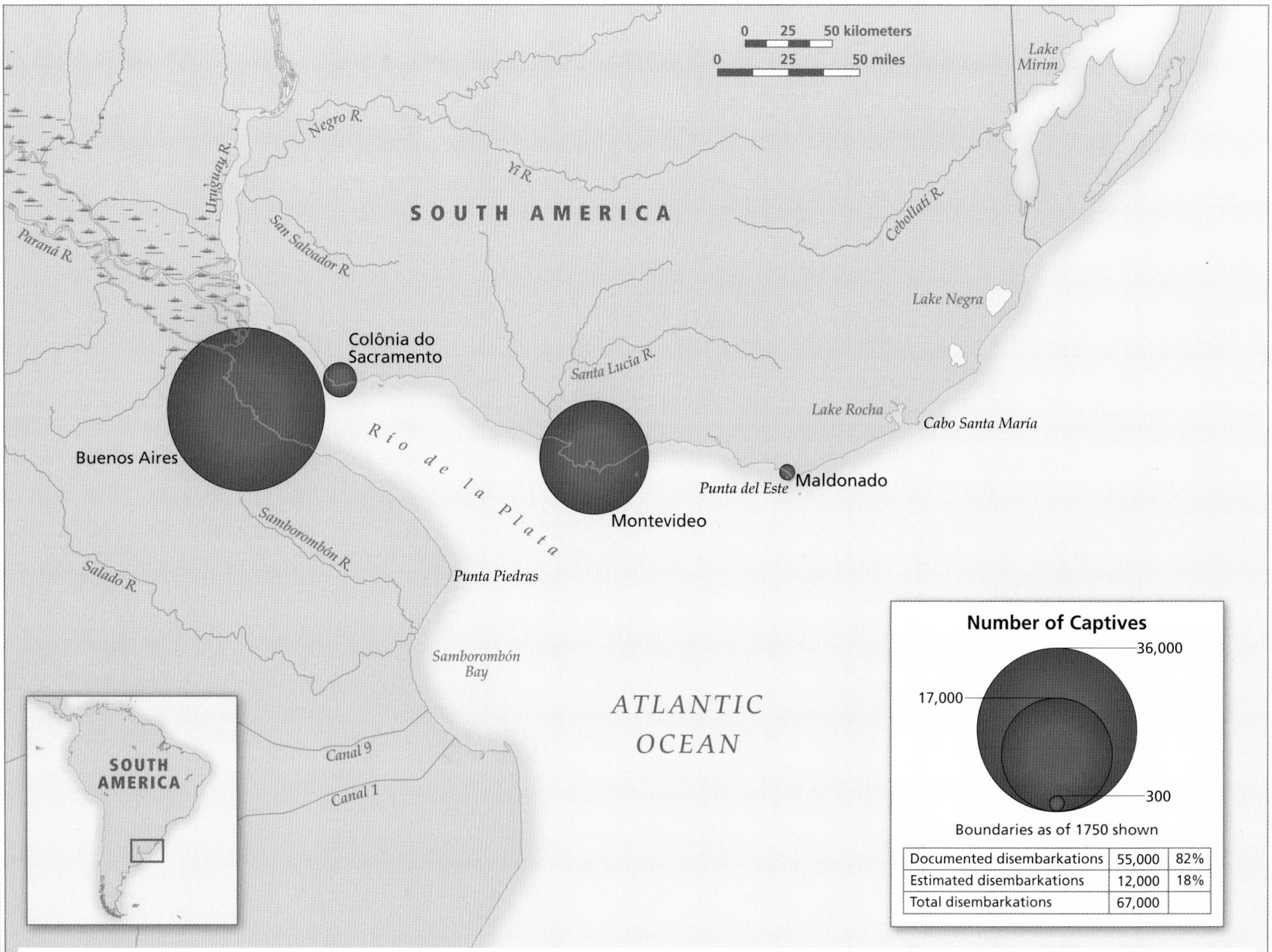

| | 0 | 25 | 50 kilometers |
| | 0 | 25 | 50 miles |

SOUTH AMERICA

Negro R.

Uruguay R.

Yí R.

Cebollatí R.

Lake Mirim

Paraná R.

San Salvador R.

Lake Negra

Colônia do Sacramento

Santa Lucía R.

Lake Rocha

Cabo Santa María

Buenos Aires

Río de la Plata

Punta del Este   Maldonado

Montevideo

Samborombón R.

Salado R.

Punta Piedras

SOUTH AMERICA

Samborombón Bay

ATLANTIC OCEAN

Canal 9

Canal 1

Number of Captives

36,000

17,000

300

Boundaries as of 1750 shown

Documented disembarkations	55,000	82%
Estimated disembarkations	12,000	18%
Total disembarkations	67,000	

The Río de la Plata was an early destination in the slave trade. Buenos Aires merchants sought slaves from Angola in 1585, within five years of the founding of the port. African slaves continued to arrive into the mid-1830s in what was by then Uruguay. Most of the captives faced a long journey overland to silver mines in what are today Bolivia and Peru. In the eighteenth century the Portuguese presence at Colônia do Sacramento facilitated an intra-American slave traffic with Brazil (not included in the estimates here).

Mahommah G. Baquaqua, 1854

Engraved portrait on the cover of Mahommah G. Baquaqua and Samuel Moore,
Biography of Mahommah G. Baquaqua, a Native of Zoogoo, in the Interior of Africa
(Detroit: Geo. E. Pomeroy & Co., 1854). Manuscripts, Archives and Rare Books Division,
Schomburg Center for Research in Black Culture, The New York Public Library, Astor,
Lenox and Tilden Foundations.

Enslaved in the interior of the Bight of Benin region in 1845 at the age of about twenty,
Mahommah Gardo Baquaqua was deported to Pernambuco, where he was sold to a baker,
and then he was resold in Rio de Janeiro, where a ship's captain bought him. He escaped
the latter's employ in New York City in 1847 and fled to Haiti before returning to New York
to study. By 1854 he had moved to Chatham, Canada, where he finished his autobiography.
His irrepressible search for freedom and his capacity to adapt culturally are evident in
the story of his life. Following the publication of the autobiography, Baquaqua moved to
Britain, where he lived until at least 1857. What happened thereafter remains a mystery. In
his autobiography we read of his desire, as a convert to Christianity, to return to Africa as a
missionary.

Map 175: Pernambuco:
African Coastal Origins of Slaves and Home Ports of Vessels Carrying Them, 1561–1851

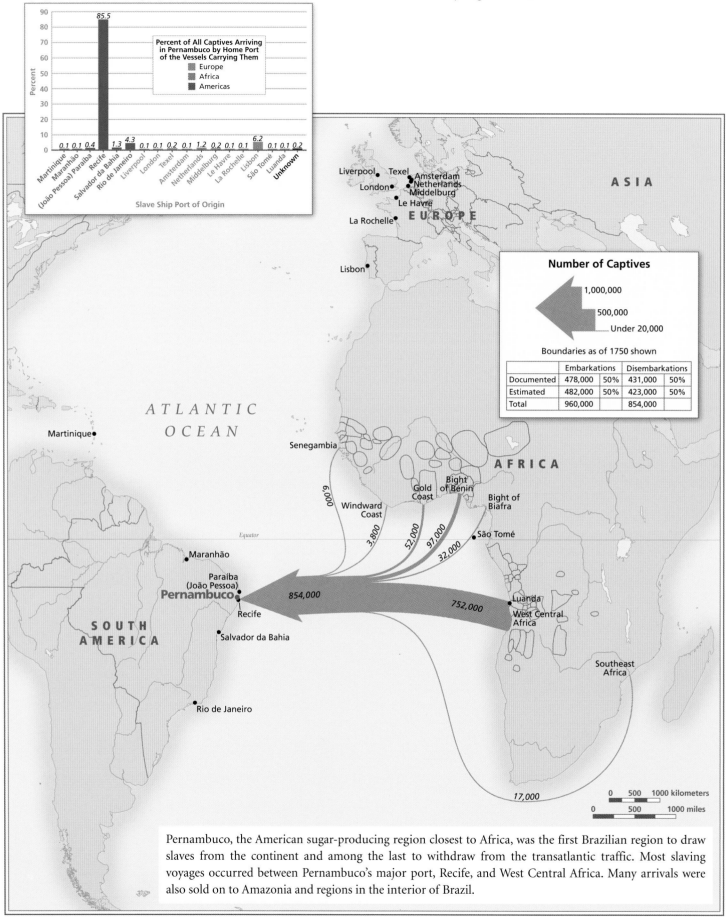

Percent of All Captives Arriving in Pernambuco by Home Port of the Vessels Carrying Them

- Europe
- Africa
- Americas

Slave Ship Port of Origin

Martinique 0.1 | Maranhão 0.1 | Paraíba (João Pessoa) 0.4 | Recife 85.5 | Salvador da Bahia 1.3 | Rio de Janeiro 4.3 | Liverpool 0.1 | London 0.1 | Texel 0.2 | Amsterdam 0.1 | Netherlands 1.2 | Middelburg 0.2 | Le Havre 0.1 | La Rochelle 0.1 | Lisbon 6.2 | São Tomé 0.1 | Luanda 0.1 | Unknown 0.2

Number of Captives

1,000,000
500,000
Under 20,000

Boundaries as of 1750 shown

	Embarkations		Disembarkations	
Documented	478,000	50%	431,000	50%
Estimated	482,000	50%	423,000	50%
Total	960,000		854,000	

ASIA

EUROPE

Liverpool · Texel · Amsterdam
London · Netherlands
Middelburg
Le Havre

La Rochelle

Lisbon

AFRICA

ATLANTIC
OCEAN

Martinique

Senegambia

Windward Coast

Gold Coast

Bight of Benin

Bight of Biafra

São Tomé

6,000
3,800
52,000
97,000
32,000

Equator

Maranhão

Paraíba (João Pessoa)

Pernambuco

Recife

854,000

752,000

Luanda
West Central Africa

SOUTH AMERICA

Salvador da Bahia

Southeast Africa

Rio de Janeiro

17,000

0 500 1000 kilometers
0 500 1000 miles

Pernambuco, the American sugar-producing region closest to Africa, was the first Brazilian region to draw slaves from the continent and among the last to withdraw from the transatlantic traffic. Most slaving voyages occurred between Pernambuco's major port, Recife, and West Central Africa. Many arrivals were also sold on to Amazonia and regions in the interior of Brazil.

Map 176: Southeast Brazil:
African Coastal Origins of Slaves and Home Ports of Vessels Carrying Them, 1581–1856

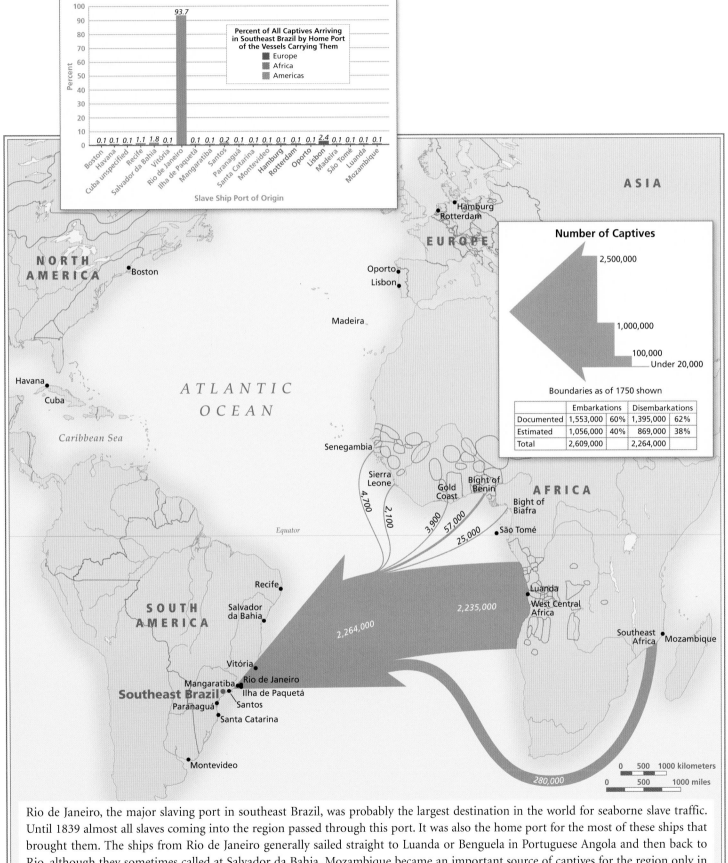

Rio de Janeiro, the major slaving port in southeast Brazil, was probably the largest destination in the world for seaborne slave traffic. Until 1839 almost all slaves coming into the region passed through this port. It was also the home port for the most of these ships that brought them. The ships from Rio de Janeiro generally sailed straight to Luanda or Benguela in Portuguese Angola and then back to Rio, although they sometimes called at Salvador da Bahia. Mozambique became an important source of captives for the region only in the nineteenth century.

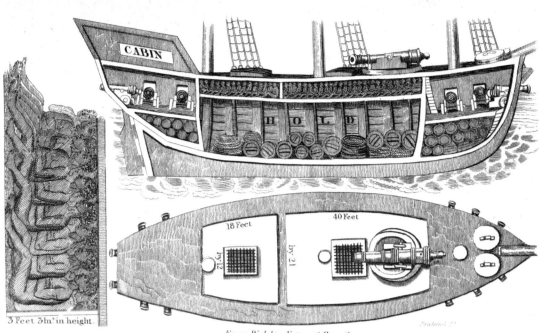

From Walsh's Notes of Brazil.

Sections of a Slave Ship, 1829

Engraving by Mathew Carey, from the Reverend R[obert] Walsh, *Notices of Brazil in 1828 and 1829,* 2 vols. (London: Frederick Westley and A. H. Davies, 1830; Boston: Boston Press, 1831), opposite the title page. Manuscripts, Archives and Rare Books Division, Schomburg Center for Research in Black Culture, The New York Public Library, Astor, Lenox and Tilden Foundations.

This Brazilian slaver—possibly the *Feloz* (or *Veloz,* voyage id 895), with José Barbosa as captain—accommodated seated rather than just prone slaves. Robert Walsh, chaplain to the British Embassy in Rio de Janeiro, boarded the ship in 1829 and supplied this image in his book on Brazil, published in 1830–1831. The ship completed its voyage, and the surviving slaves were sold at Bahia.

The first object that struck us, was an enormous gun, turning on a swivel, on deck, the constant appendage of a pirate; and the next, were large kettles for cooking, on the bows, the usual apparatus of a slaver. Our boat was now hoisted out, and I went on board with the officers. When we mounted her decks, we found her full of slaves. She was called the Veloz [Feloz], commanded by Captain José Barbosa, bound to Bahia. She was a very broad-decked ship, with a mainmast, schooner rigged, and behind her foremast was that large formidable gun, which turned on a broad circle of iron, on deck, and which enabled her to act as a pirate, if her slaving speculation failed. She had taken in, on the coast of Africa, 336 males, and 226 females, making in all 562, and had been out seventeen days, during which she had thrown overboard fiftyfive. The slaves were all enclosed under grated hatchways, between decks. The space was so low, that they sat between each other's legs, and stowed so close together, that there was no possibility of their lying down, or at all changing their position, by night or day. As they belonged to, and were shipped on account of different individuals, they were all branded, like sheep, with the owners' marks of different forms, ⟨mark⟩, or ⟨mark⟩, or ⟨mark⟩. These were impressed under their breasts, or on their arms, and, as the mate informed me with perfect indifference, "queimados pelo ferro quento—burnt with the red-hot iron." Over the hatchway stood a ferocious-looking fellow, with a scourge of many twisted thongs in his hand, who was the slave driver of the ship, and whenever he heard the slightest noise below, he shook it over them, and seemed eager to exercise it. I was quite pleased to take this hateful badge out of his hand, and I have kept it ever since, as a horrid memorial of reality, should I ever be disposed to forget the scene I witnessed.

Excerpt from Robert Walsh, "On boarding a slave ship, 1829," in the Reverend R[obert] Walsh, *Notices of Brazil in 1828 and 1829,* 2 vols. (London: Frederick Westley and A. H. Davies, 1830; Boston: Boston Press, 1831), vol. 2, p. 262.

Map 177: Bahia:
African Coastal Origins of Slaves and Home Ports of Vessels Carrying Them, 1581–1851

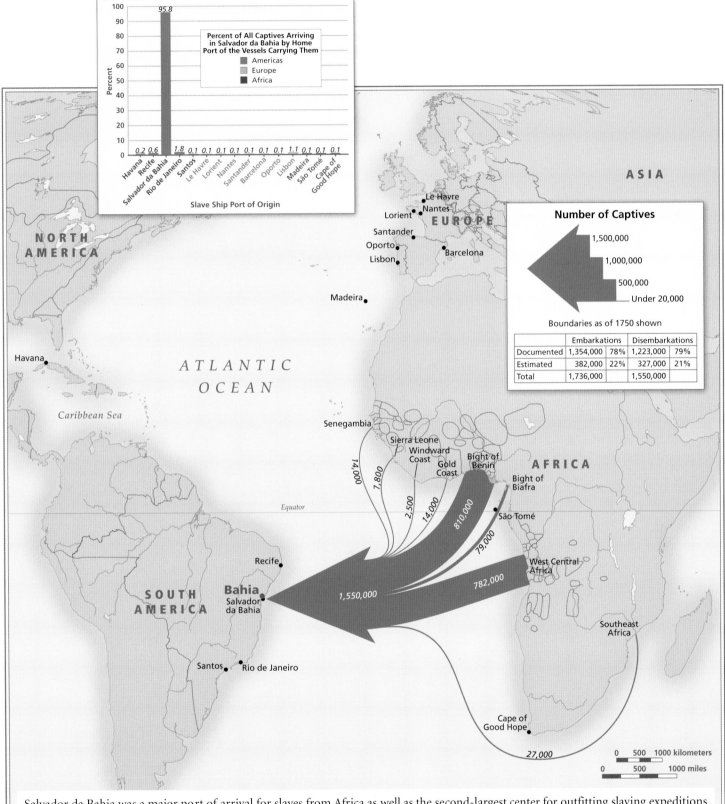

Percent of All Captives Arriving in Salvador da Bahia by Home Port of the Vessels Carrying Them

- Americas
- Europe
- Africa

Slave Ship Port of Origin

	Embarkations		Disembarkations	
Documented	1,354,000	78%	1,223,000	79%
Estimated	382,000	22%	327,000	21%
Total	1,736,000		1,550,000	

Number of Captives

1,500,000
1,000,000
500,000
Under 20,000

Boundaries as of 1750 shown

Salvador da Bahia was a major port of arrival for slaves from Africa as well as the second-largest center for outfitting slaving expeditions to Africa. The region of Bahia was a major producer of sugar and tobacco, but slaves were also sold on to the inland gold-producing regions of Brazil. Unlike other Brazilian regions, Bahia drew most of its captives from embarkation points on the Bight of Benin, although West Central Africa was also an important source of slaves.

Map 178: Amazonia:
African Coastal Origins of Slaves and Home Ports of Vessels Carrying Them, 1693–1846

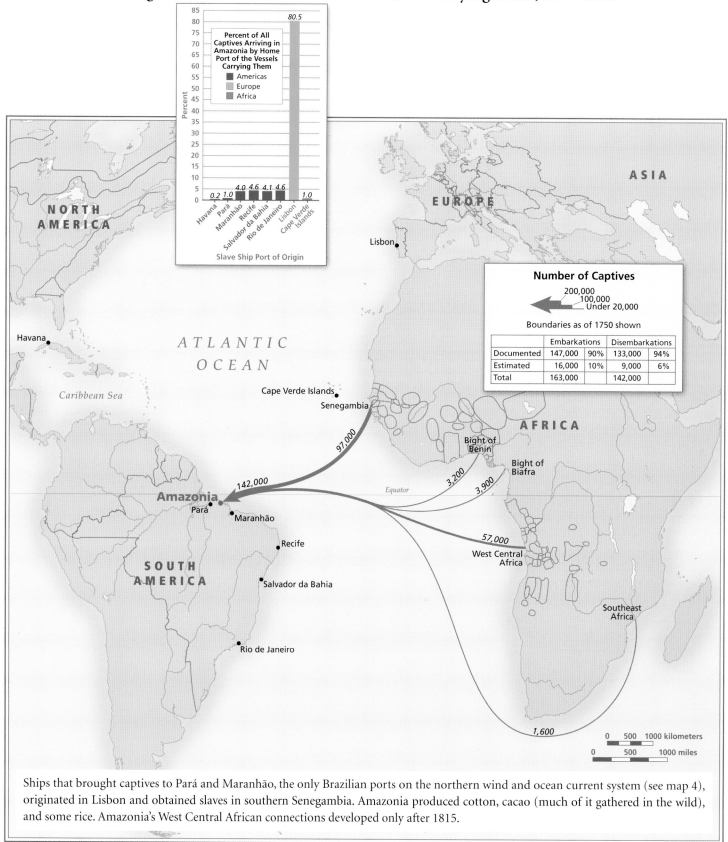

Ships that brought captives to Pará and Maranhão, the only Brazilian ports on the northern wind and ocean current system (see map 4), originated in Lisbon and obtained slaves in southern Senegambia. Amazonia produced cotton, cacao (much of it gathered in the wild), and some rice. Amazonia's West Central African connections developed only after 1815.

Map 179: Río de la Plata:
African Coastal Origins of Slaves and Home Ports of Vessels Carrying Them, 1620–1835

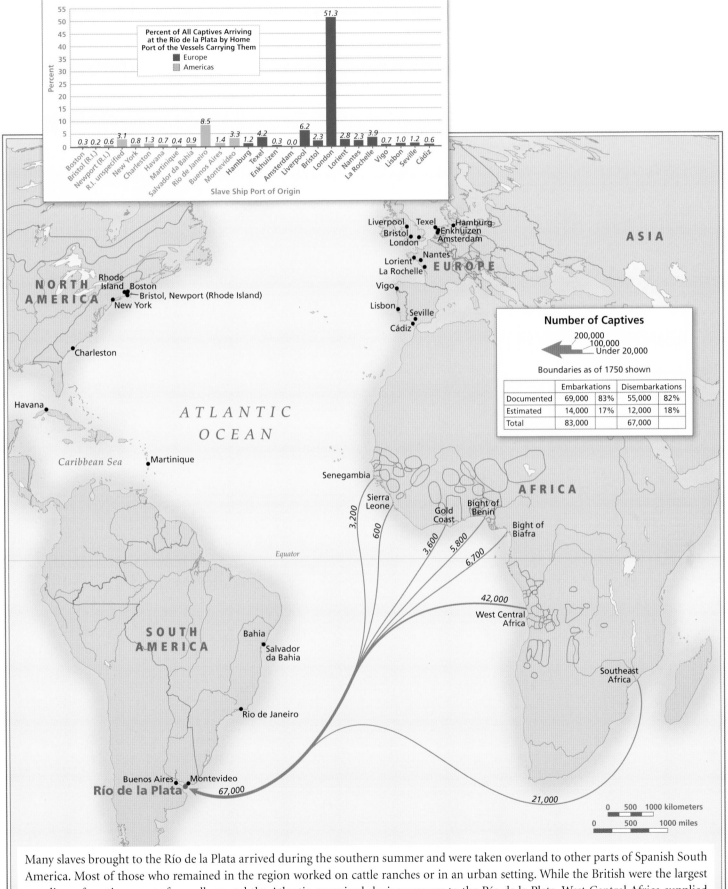

Percent of All Captives Arriving at the Río de la Plata by Home Port of the Vessels Carrying Them
- Europe
- Americas

Slave Ship Port of Origin

Number of Captives				
	Embarkations		Disembarkations	
Documented	69,000	83%	55,000	82%
Estimated	14,000	17%	12,000	18%
Total	83,000		67,000	

200,000
100,000
Under 20,000

Boundaries as of 1750 shown

Many slaves brought to the Río de la Plata arrived during the southern summer and were taken overland to other parts of Spanish South America. Most of those who remained in the region worked on cattle ranches or in an urban setting. While the British were the largest suppliers of captives, ports from all around the Atlantic organized slaving voyages to the Río de la Plata. West Central Africa supplied most of these slaves, but captives from Southeast Africa were more important here than anywhere else in the Americas. The intra-American trade in slaves from Brazil (not shown here) was also an important source of slaves, however.

Part VI
Abolition and Suppression of the Transatlantic Slave Trade

In a very real sense, captives on board slave vessels attempted to suppress the slave trade by attempting to capture the vessels taking them away from Africa. European nations took action against the slave trade from 1792, when Denmark outlawed its slave trade, a ban effective in 1803. Both Britain and the United States outlawed theirs in 1807, with their bans effective the next year, but in most countries abolition came about in two stages. The first was the struggle to pass formal laws against transatlantic slave trading, and the second was the fight to make the laws effective. Unlike the fight against slavery itself, which took place largely within the confines of the state, the campaign against the slave trade always had a strong international dimension. Many nations took action against the slave trade only after signing treaties agreeing to do so. The issue became inextricably intertwined with the emergence of international law, the definition of piracy, and the thorny question of intervention by one sovereign state in the affairs of another in the face of what today would be called human rights abuses.

The narrative of the formal abolition of the transatlantic slave trade is straightforward. Portugal was the last nation in the Atlantic world to abolish the slave trade—in 1836. But once all nations had agreed that it should end, it did, in just over three decades—even though long-distance slave trading had probably been acceptable since before the first written records were kept. Individual states in the United States prohibited the slave trade before the 1807 federal act. Those actions aside, we can say it took thirty-three years for all Atlantic nations to move to stop the traffic (from Denmark's implementation in 1803 to Portugal's ban in 1836). Except with the British and Dutch abolitions in 1807 and 1814, respectively, however, there was a gap, measured in decades, between the bans themselves and their effective enforcement. Since the last transatlantic slave vessel probably landed slaves in Cuba in 1867, we can also say that it took a further three decades after 1836 to suppress the traffic. As a result, at least a million slaves arrived in the Americas in violation of the various laws against the slave trade. Table 8 shows the post-1836 pattern of arrivals.

The slave trade from Africa was by definition an international activity, and laws governing international activity were still very much evolving in the early nineteenth century. Several nations declared slave trading to be piracy, an offense in international waters that in theory any nation could suppress. But to this day the international community has never succeeded in making slave trading piracy. As an alternative, Britain, the Netherlands, Spain, Portugal, and several minor maritime powers eventually set up joint courts to adjudicate instances of suspected slave-trading. These were called Courts of Mixed Commission because the courts included a mix of representatives from different states; they were located at various times in Freetown (Sierra Leone), Havana (Cuba), Luanda (Angola), Cape Town (South Africa), Rio de Janeiro (Brazil), Paramaribo (Suriname), Kingston (Jamaica), and New York. The courts could confiscate vessels, equipment, and merchandise, as well as release slaves, but could exact no penalties against crews or owners. France, Sardinia, and, until 1862, the United States would not go even this far. Like other nations, they were prepared to arrest and try their own nationals, but they allowed foreign powers (usually, in practice, Britain) only to hand over any suspects for adjudication in their own domestic courts.

The British played a large role in suppression. By the mid-1840s more than sixty British, French, American, and Portuguese warships were patrolling the African coast. No anti-slave-trade treaty was signed in the nineteenth century that did not have Britain as one of the signatories. Further, nearly 90 percent of all captured slave vessels fell into the hands of the British. Nearly 200,000 slaves were liberated from the holds of those captured ships. Many of the so-called recaptives did not live to experience their new freed status, however. Those who did survive were often moved again after adjudication and generally lived out their lives in British territory either as peasants in villages in Sierra Leone, the Bahamas, and Trinidad or as indentured servants in the British Caribbean after slavery was abolished there in 1833. Another group became unpaid municipal workers in Brazilian cities. The least fortunate were spirited away to Cuban sugar plantations, where they effectively remained slaves, or, worse, were kidnapped from the Sierra Leone villages where they had been resettled, and sold a second time into the slave trade.

The British actions of suppression were legally ambivalent. Indeed, some actions were clearly against international law as it was then understood. The British attempted to negotiate, first, a right of search and, second, an anti-slave-trade treaty with every other maritime nation. When the Brazilian and the Portuguese governments refused to comply or, in one case, to extend a treaty already agreed upon, the British Parliament passed legislation allowing the British navy to take foreign slave vessels into English courts anyway, an unprecedented extension of British law to foreign nationals. A British foreign secretary, Lord Palmerston, used secret-service funds to bribe Brazilian politicians, paid surreptitious subsidies to Brazilian newspapers, and hired a vast network of spies around the Atlantic world. In 1850 he authorized the navy to invade Brazilian waters and destroy the property of slave traders—an action that was clearly grounds for war.

The British also aggressively pursued treaties with African powers, beginning on the east coast with the sultan of Zanzibar in 1838. The treaty provisions included not only the ending of the slave trade but also most-favored-nation status for Britain with regard to commerce, freedom for British merchants to trade with any individual or group on African territory, and freedom of religion. The early treaties were signed under the guns of a British fleet, and in one instance, refusal to sign led to the occupation of Lagos and the foundation (ultimately) of Nigeria, Britain's largest African colony.

British diplomatic and naval measures, except in part the assault on Brazil in 1850, usually were not successful, even though 10 percent of the British navy was deployed against the slave trade by the mid-1840s. As the data in table 9 suggest, the number of captives released from slave vessels was always a small share of the total transatlantic traffic. Naval officers might detain vessels, but unless the crew of the slave vessel were of the same nationality as those carrying out the detention, those who captured the slave vessel could exact no penalties except confiscation of the ship and its contents. Like slave revolts, naval actions raised the cost of doing business and therefore the prices of slaves in the Americas, which reduced the number of slaves purchased and carried across the Atlantic. But naval actions could not in themselves halt the slave trade. So unsuccessful was the navy that in the late 1840s a parliamentary campaign to withdraw British cruisers from anti-slave-trade duties came very close to success.

The key initiatives that ended the transatlantic slave trade came from shifts in public opinion in one country after another, which resulted in support for attempts to enforce the laws against national slave trading. Although the Brazilian government had agreed in 1826 to ban the trade starting in 1830, abolition was not proclaimed as law until 1831, and the government did not begin to take serious action against slave merchants until 1850; its efforts culminated in the expulsion of Portuguese citizens involved in the business. In Cuba, the other major market for African slaves in the mid-nineteenth century, a repressive regime meant that public opinion had much less opportunity to make an impact; but in 1862 the new captain-general of the island began to expel slave traders and dismiss officials who had been bribed to permit the arrival of slave ships.

The transatlantic slave trade began five centuries ago, and through much of the early modern era people accepted slavery and the slave trade as legitimate and moral. By the early nineteenth century, values had shifted, and it became clear that for the international community neither full chattel slavery nor a trade in human beings could ever again be given legal sanction.

Table 8 Number of Slaves Who Embarked Illegally, 1837–1867, by Region of Arrival in the Americas

	1837–1846	1847–1856	1857–1867	Total[†]
Carolinas / Georgia	0	0	400	400
Gulf Coast	0	0	100	100
Jamaica	2,600	0	0	2,600
Barbados	400	0	0	400
Grenada	300	0	0	300
British Guiana	400	0	0	400
Bahamas	3,300	0	0	3,300
Danish West Indies	300	0	0	300
Cuba	138,000	82,000	131,000	351,000
Puerto Rico	5,700	0	0	5,700
Amazonia	4,200	0	0	4,200
Bahia	47,000	43,000	0	90,000
Pernambuco	46,000	8,500	0	54,500
Southeast Brazil	373,000	216,000	0	589,000
Brazil unspecified	4,400	1,600	0	6,000
Africa*	36,000	25,000	20,000	81,000
Total[†]	661,600	376,400	152,000	1,189,500

Source: Calculated from the *Voyages* Web site, http://www.slavevoyages.org/tast/assessment/estimates
.faces?yearFrom=1837&yearTo=1866.

* Refers to African captives liberated from slave ships en route to the Americas.

[†] The column and row totals in this table differ slightly from the data on the *Voyages* Web site because of the rounding rules used throughout this volume and explained in "About This Atlas."

Table 9 Recaptives (Africans Liberated from Slave Vessels) Who Embarked from Africa, 1808–1863, by Decade

	Number of Recaptives	Recaptives in Decade as Percent of Total Number of Recaptives	Number of Captives Who Embarked from Africa	Recaptives as Percent of Total Number of Captives Who Embarked
1808–1817	23,239	11.7	603,000	3.9
1818–1827	20,969	10.6	795,000	2.6
1828–1837	62,109	31.3	721,000	8.6
1838–1847	47,044	23.7	643,000	7.3
1848–1857	28,296	14.2	308,000	9.2
1858–1863	17,053	8.6	135,000	12.6
Total	198,710	100	3,205,000	6.2

Source: Data derived from tastdb-exp-2009.sav at the *Voyages* Web site, http://www.slavevoyages.org/
tast/database/download.faces. For an immediate approximation of column 1, readers can paste in
http://www.slavevoyages.org/tast/database/search.faces?yearFrom=1808&yearTo=1866&fate=56.102
.103.104.106.108.110.112.118.120.121.122.124.126.128.130.132.134.138.142.144.148.161.201, and go to the tables
tab to generate departures of slaves from Africa who were subsequently liberated from slave ships.
This generates 205,000 departures—slightly more than is shown in column 1. Making decisions about
who was liberated and who was not, especially for cases involving non-British vessels, requires more
sophisticated programming than the *Voyages* search interface allows. For the exact figures readers will
have to use the downloadable SPSS version of the data.

Map 180: Transatlantic Routes of Slaves, 1786–1790, Prior to the Abolitionist Era

	Embarkations		Disembarkations	
Documented	442,000	88%	383,000	87%
Estimated	63,000	12%	59,000	13%
Total	505,000		442,000	

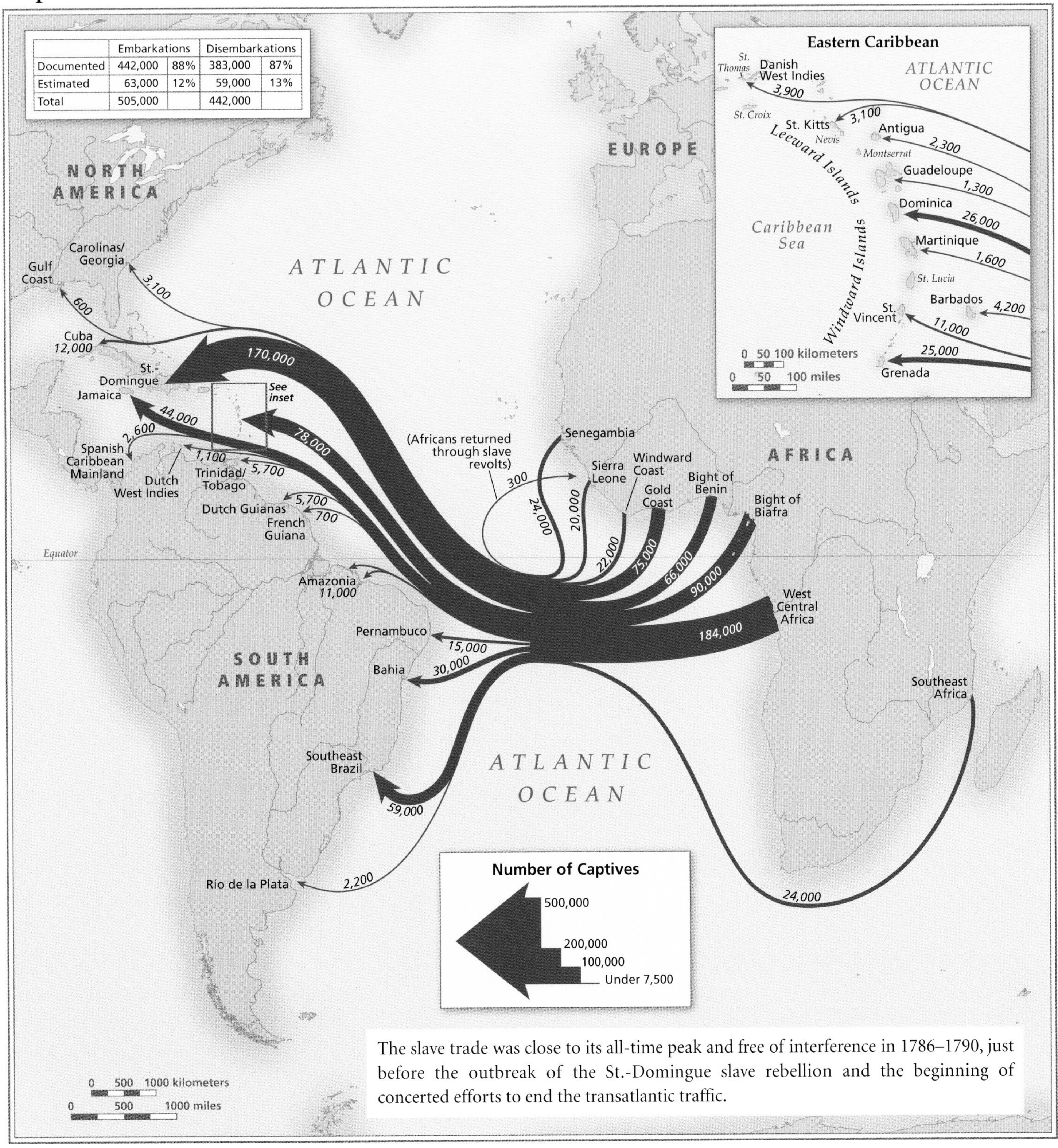

Eastern Caribbean

St. Thomas
Danish West Indies
3,900
St. Croix
St. Kitts
3,100
Nevis
Antigua
2,300
Montserrat
Guadeloupe
1,300
Dominica
26,000
Martinique
1,600
St. Lucia
Barbados
4,200
St. Vincent
11,000
25,000
Grenada

Leeward Islands
Windward Islands
Caribbean Sea
ATLANTIC OCEAN

0 50 100 kilometers
0 50 100 miles

NORTH AMERICA
ATLANTIC OCEAN
EUROPE
AFRICA

Gulf Coast
600
Carolinas/Georgia
3,100
Cuba 12,000
St. Domingue
Jamaica
44,000
2,600
Spanish Caribbean Mainland
1,100
Dutch West Indies
Trinidad/Tobago
5,700
Dutch Guianas
French Guiana
5,700
700
170,000
See inset
78,000

(Africans returned through slave revolts)
300
Senegambia
24,000
Sierra Leone
20,000
Windward Coast
Gold Coast
22,000
75,000
Bight of Benin
66,000
90,000
Bight of Biafra
West Central Africa
184,000

Equator

Amazonia 11,000
SOUTH AMERICA
Pernambuco
15,000
Bahia
30,000

Southeast Africa

Southeast Brazil
59,000
ATLANTIC OCEAN

Río de la Plata
2,200
24,000

Number of Captives

500,000
200,000
100,000
Under 7,500

0 500 1000 kilometers
0 500 1000 miles

The slave trade was close to its all-time peak and free of interference in 1786–1790, just before the outbreak of the St.-Domingue slave rebellion and the beginning of concerted efforts to end the transatlantic traffic.

I presume the popular clamour [in Britain] respecting the Trade to Africa has ere this subsided and that we may expect supplies as usual. It is lucky that the Rumour of this intended Novelty [i.e., abolition of the slave trade] which spread like Wild Fire amongst our own Negroes, and to which great additions were made, no less than that there was to be an Abolition of Slavery altogether, has had hitherto no very fatal effects, but our Alarms are not yet over, and whether the Idea was originally dictated by Malignity or Enthusiasm, certain it is that Nothing was ever more calculated to raise Commotions amongst a Set of People naturally peaceable and harmless, but who, if they knew their Power have our Lives and property entirely at their Mercy.

Hibbert, Robert, to James Brydges, 3rd Duke of Chandos, 1788, May 20, STB Box 26(29), The Huntington Library, San Marino, California. This item is reproduced by permission of the Huntington Library, San Marino, California.

To Preserve Their Freedom, 1937–1938

By Jacob Lawrence. Silk screen print, 1988. Toussaint L'Ouverture Series, Aaron Douglas Collection, Amistad Research Center at Tulane University.

The uprising by enslaved Africans under the leadership of Toussaint L'Ouverture in St.-Domingue in 1791 was the most successful slave revolt in history. It destroyed the thriving French colony's plantation regime and, despite military intervention from Europe, resulted in the creation of an independent Haiti in 1804. In 1937–1938 the African American painter Jacob Lawrence (1917–2002) depicted the events in a series of forty-one paintings. The one shown here shows the defeat of Napoleon's efforts to restore slavery by force in St.-Domingue in 1802–1803. The revolt succeeded because ordinary men, women, and children of African descent took up arms "to preserve their freedom."

Map 181: Transatlantic Routes of Slaves, 1796–1800, after the St.-Domingue Revolution Began

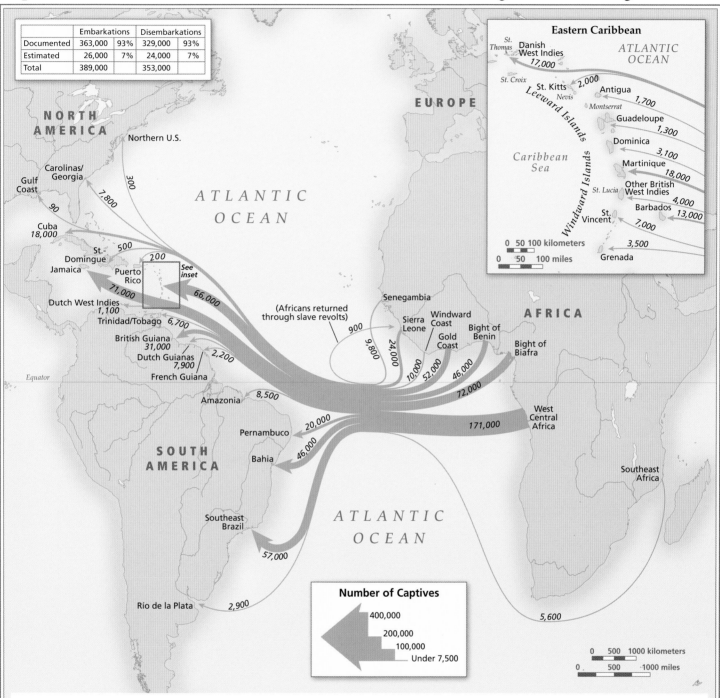

	Embarkations		Disembarkations	
Documented	363,000	93%	329,000	93%
Estimated	26,000	7%	24,000	7%
Total	389,000		353,000	

Eastern Caribbean

St. Thomas · Danish West Indies 17,000
St. Croix
Leeward Islands
St. Kitts 2,000
Nevis
Antigua 1,700
Montserrat
Guadeloupe 1,300
Dominica 3,100
Martinique 18,000
Other British West Indies 4,000
St. Lucia
Barbados 13,000
St. Vincent 7,000
Grenada 3,500
Caribbean Sea
Windward Islands
ATLANTIC OCEAN
0 50 100 kilometers
0 50 100 miles

NORTH AMERICA
Northern U.S.
Carolinas/Georgia 7,800
Gulf Coast 90
300
Cuba 18,000
St.-Domingue 500
Jamaica 71,000
Puerto Rico 200
See inset
Dutch West Indies 1,100
Trinidad/Tobago 6,700
British Guiana 31,000
Dutch Guianas 7,900
French Guiana 2,200
Amazonia 8,500
Pernambuco 20,000
Bahia 46,000
Southeast Brazil 57,000
Río de la Plata 2,900

ATLANTIC OCEAN

Equator

SOUTH AMERICA

ATLANTIC OCEAN

EUROPE

AFRICA
Senegambia
(Africans returned through slave revolts) 900
Sierra Leone 24,000
Windward Coast
Gold Coast 52,000
Bight of Benin 46,000
Bight of Biafra 72,000
9,800
10,000
West Central Africa 171,000
Southeast Africa 5,600
66,000

Number of Captives
400,000
200,000
100,000
Under 7,500

0 500 1000 kilometers
0 500 1000 miles

After the St.-Domingue Revolution (1791–1804), the number of slaves arriving in St.-Domingue (now Haiti) dropped dramatically (see map 180). Those who did arrive were on slave ships captured by the Haitian navy. The revolution was not primarily aimed at suppressing the slave trade, although it closed down the biggest slave market in the Caribbean. Increasing numbers of slaves arrived in other parts of the Americas as a consequence. The net effect was to begin a shift in the center of gravity of the traffic southward, away from the Caribbean and West Africa and toward Brazil and West Central Africa.

Map 182: Transatlantic Routes of Slaves, 1816–1820, after Danish, U.S., and British Abolition Laws

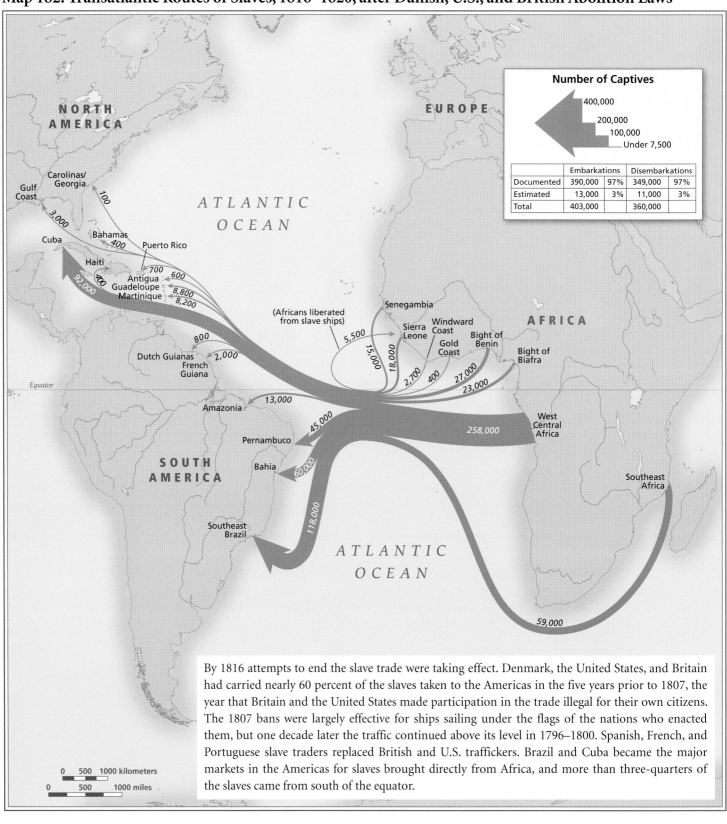

	Embarkations		Disembarkations	
Documented	390,000	97%	349,000	97%
Estimated	13,000	3%	11,000	3%
Total	403,000		360,000	

Number of Captives

400,000
200,000
100,000
Under 7,500

By 1816 attempts to end the slave trade were taking effect. Denmark, the United States, and Britain had carried nearly 60 percent of the slaves taken to the Americas in the five years prior to 1807, the year that Britain and the United States made participation in the trade illegal for their own citizens. The 1807 bans were largely effective for ships sailing under the flags of the nations who enacted them, but one decade later the traffic continued above its level in 1796–1800. Spanish, French, and Portuguese slave traders replaced British and U.S. traffickers. Brazil and Cuba became the major markets in the Americas for slaves brought directly from Africa, and more than three-quarters of the slaves came from south of the equator.

Slave Ship, 1840

By Joseph Mallord William Turner, English (1775–1851), *Slave Ship (Slavers Throwing Overboard the Dead and Dying, Typhoon Coming On)*, 1840; oil on canvas, 90.8 × 122.6 cm (35 3/4 × 48 1/4 in.). Museum of Fine Arts, Boston, Henry Lillie Pierce Fund, 99.22. Photograph © 2010 Museum of Fine Arts, Boston.

J. M. W. Turner's painting of a slave ship jettisoning its dead and dying human cargo as a typhoon approaches is thought to be based on the notorious voyage of the British slave ship *Zong* in 1781–1782 (voyage id 84106), when, concerned over levels of provisions during the Atlantic crossing, the ship's officers threw overboard 132 living Africans, assuming that their loss would be recoverable through insurance. Claims for compensation were subsequently rejected, largely on legal technicalities, but the judge's insistence in *Gilbert vs. Gregson* (1785) that in maritime law "the case of the slaves was as if horses had been thrown overboard" outraged many and helped ignite British abolitionism. Half a century later, memories of the *Zong* became, through Turner's *Slave Ship,* a means to promote abolition more generally.

Map 183: Transatlantic Routes of Slaves, 1836–1840, after French, Brazilian, and Spanish Abolition Measures

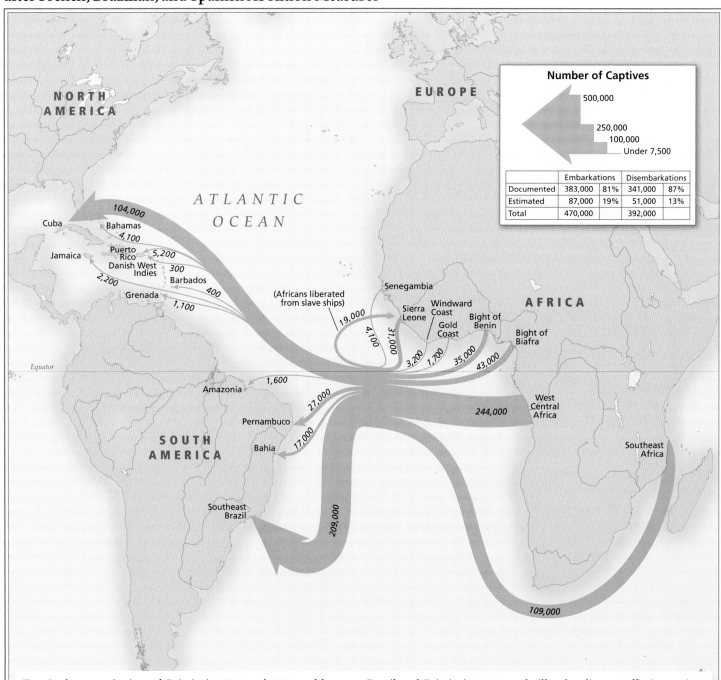

	Embarkations		Disembarkations	
Documented	383,000	81%	341,000	87%
Estimated	87,000	19%	51,000	13%
Total	470,000		392,000	

Treaties between Spain and Britain in 1817 and 1835 and between Brazil and Britain in 1826 made illegal a direct traffic in captives between Africa and Cuba, and Africa and Brazil, in 1820 and 1830, respectively. In addition, France began to enforce suppression in its remaining colonies after its 1830 revolution. The British captured slave vessels sailing to Cuba and Brazil, and the now recaptive Africans on board were mostly taken to Sierra Leone.

Map 184: The Transatlantic Slave Trade, 1861–1865, after Brazilian Suppression

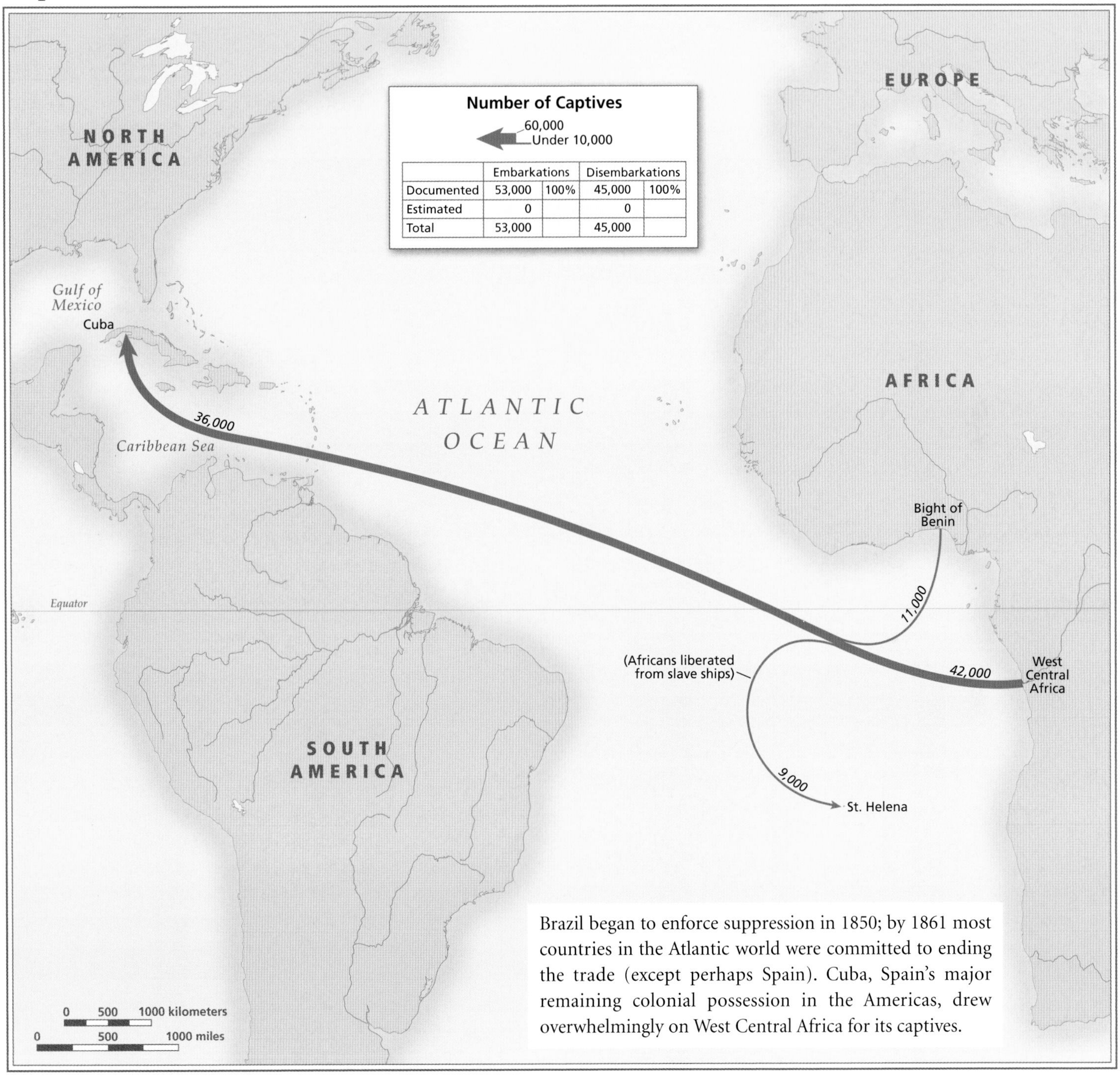

NORTH AMERICA

EUROPE

Number of Captives

60,000
Under 10,000

	Embarkations		Disembarkations	
Documented	53,000	100%	45,000	100%
Estimated	0		0	
Total	53,000		45,000	

Gulf of Mexico

Cuba

AFRICA

36,000

Caribbean Sea

ATLANTIC OCEAN

Bight of Benin

Equator

11,000

(Africans liberated from slave ships)

West Central Africa

42,000

SOUTH AMERICA

9,000

St. Helena

Brazil began to enforce suppression in 1850; by 1861 most countries in the Atlantic world were committed to ending the trade (except perhaps Spain). Cuba, Spain's major remaining colonial possession in the Americas, drew overwhelmingly on West Central Africa for its captives.

0   500   1000 kilometers
0   500   1000 miles

Map 185: Vessels Captured and Africans Liberated by Naval Vessels of Nations Attempting to Suppress the Slave Trade, 1808–1867

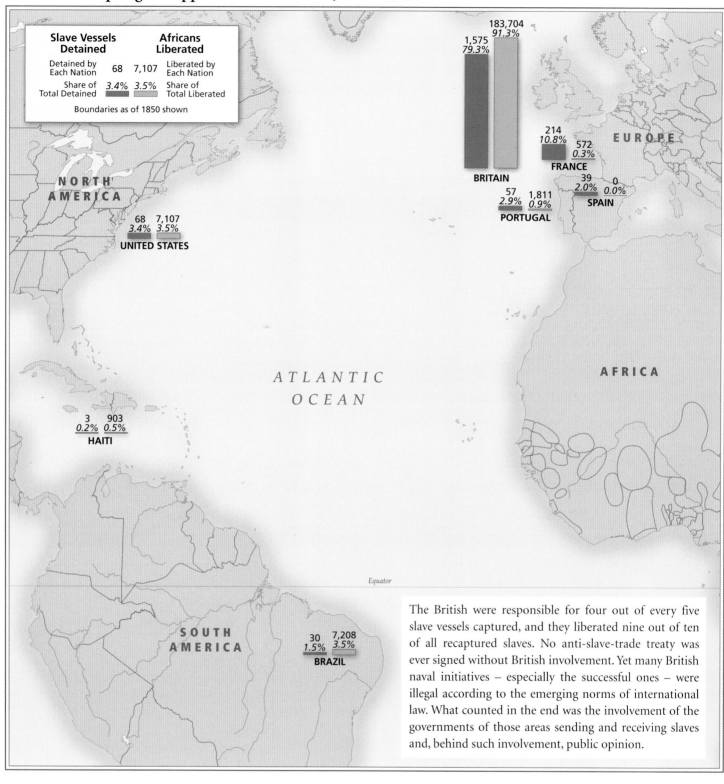

Slave Vessels Detained | **Africans Liberated**

Detained by Each Nation 68 | 7,107 Liberated by Each Nation

Share of Total Detained 3.4% | 3.5% Share of Total Liberated

Boundaries as of 1850 shown

183,704
91.3%

1,575
79.3%

BRITAIN

214
10.8%
FRANCE

572
0.3%

EUROPE

39
2.0%
SPAIN

0
0.0%

57
2.9%

1,811
0.9%
PORTUGAL

NORTH AMERICA

68   7,107
3.4%   3.5%
UNITED STATES

ATLANTIC OCEAN

AFRICA

3   903
0.2%   0.5%
HAITI

Equator

SOUTH AMERICA

30   7,208
1.5%   3.5%
BRAZIL

The British were responsible for four out of every five slave vessels captured, and they liberated nine out of ten of all recaptured slaves. No anti-slave-trade treaty was ever signed without British involvement. Yet many British naval initiatives – especially the successful ones – were illegal according to the emerging norms of international law. What counted in the end was the involvement of the governments of those areas sending and receiving slaves and, behind such involvement, public opinion.

Slaves Below Deck on Board the Captured Spanish Ship *Albaroz* [*Albañez*], 1845

Watercolor by Lieutenant Francis Meynell. © National Maritime Museum, Greenwich, London.

Francis Meynell, a British naval officer serving in West Africa, painted an album of watercolors reflecting his experience on slave-trade-suppression patrol in 1845. When he painted Africans belowdecks on the captured Spanish slaver *Albanez* (voyage id 3483), the captives were evidently under naval protection and free of shackles, but Meynell could not disguise their youthful yet emaciated and despondent state.

Map 186: Slave-Ship Captures by the British African Squadron, 1847–1848

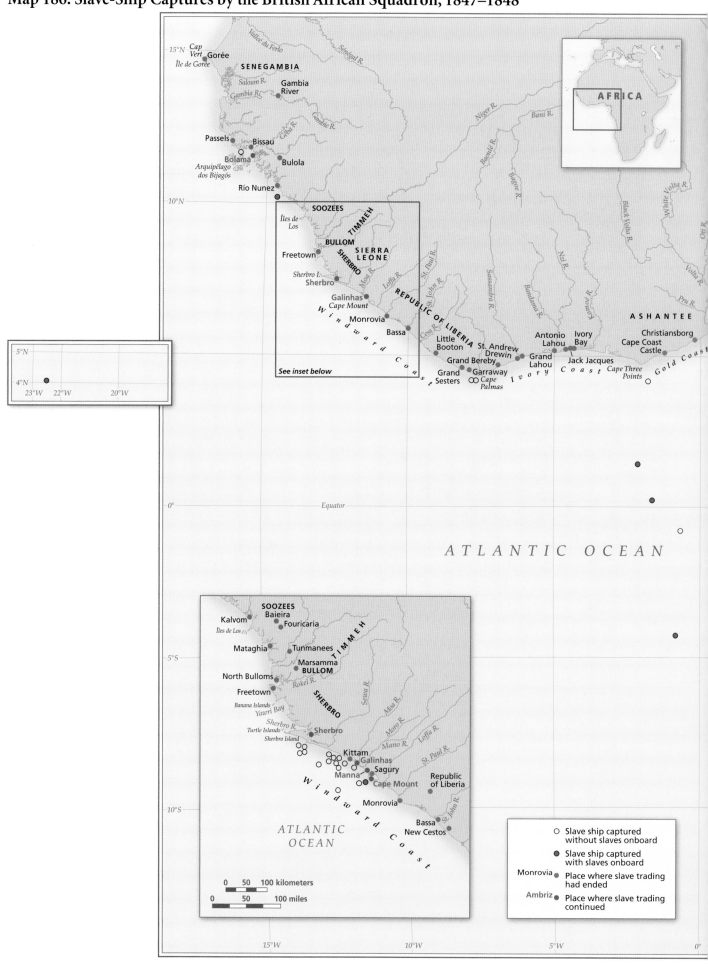

Legend:

○ Slave ship captured without slaves onboard

● Slave ship captured with slaves onboard

Monrovia ● Place where slave trading had ended

Ambriz ● Place where slave trading continued

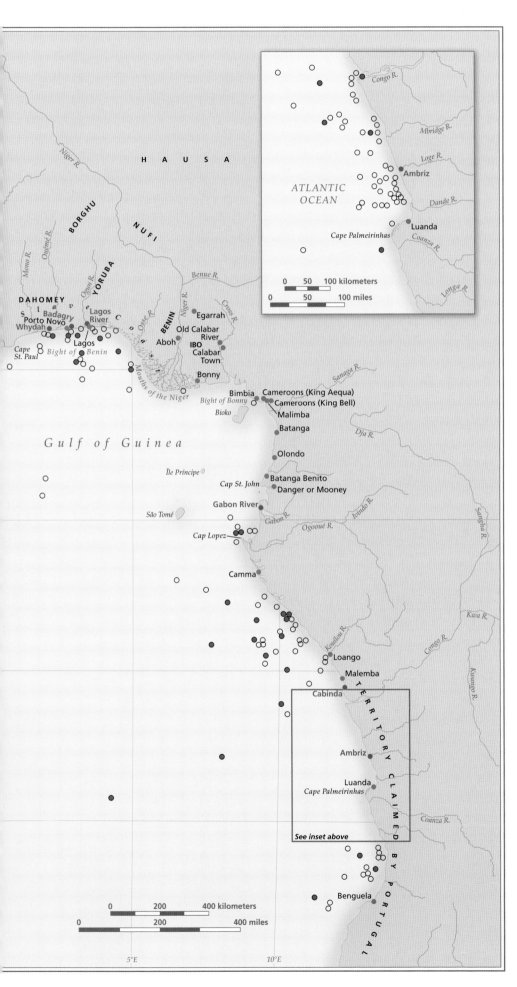

HAUSA

ATLANTIC
OCEAN

Congo R.

Mbridge R.

Loge R.

Ambriz

Dande R.

Luanda

Cape Palmeirinhas

Coanza R.

Longa R.

| 0 | 50 | 100 kilometers |
| 0 | 50 | 100 miles |

Niger R.

BORGHU

NUFI

Oueme R.

Mono R.

Ogun R.

YORUBA

Benue R.

DAHOMEY
I
a   v
S   e   Lagos
Badagry   River
Porto Novo
Whydah   BENIN   Egarrah
Cape   Lagos   C   Old Calabar
St. Paul   *Bight of Benin*   Aboh   River
IBO   Calabar
Town
Bonny

Mouths of the Niger

Gulf of Guinea

Ile Príncipe

São Tomé

Bimbia   Cameroons (King Aequa)
Bight of Bonny   Cameroons (King Bell)
Bioko   Malimba
Batanga

Olondo

Batanga Benito
Cap St. John   Danger or Mooney
Gabon River
Gabon R.   *Sanaga R.*

Dja R.

Ogooué R.   *Ivindo R.*

Sangha R.

Cap Lopez

Camma

Koulou R.

Congo R.

Kwa R.

Loango
Malemba

Cabinda

T E R R I T O R Y   C L A I M E D   B Y   P O R T U G A L

Ambriz

Luanda
Cape Palmeirinhas

Coanza R.

Kwango R.

See inset above

Benguela

| 0 | 200 | 400 kilometers |
| 0 | 200 | 400 miles |

5°E   10°E

Of the 1,575 transatlantic slave vessels captured by the British navy after 1807, no fewer than one in nine were seized in 1847 and 1848. The naval campaign against the slave trade (mainly the blockading of major ports of embarkation) was at its peak in these years, with close to 10 percent of the total strength of the Royal Navy stationed off Africa. About 90 percent of all captures took place off Africa. Captures were for the most part near major ports of embarkation. It is clear that the naval strategy was to establish a blockade wherever possible, rather than patrol well offshore. The place-names here are not always consistent with those shown on other maps in this atlas.

THE AFRICAN STATION.—The following is an extract from a letter written by an Officer on board the Squadron on the west coast of Africa:—"Her Majesty's Ship ———, West Coast, Africa, July 26, 1845. Here we are, on the most miserable station in the wide world—nigger hunting—attempting an impossibility—the suppression of the slave trade. We look upon the affair as complete humbug. You may make treaties in London, and send the whole combined Squadrons of England and France to this coast, and then you will have gained your object. So long as a slave, worth only a few dollars here, fetches 8ol. or 1ool. in America, men and means will be found to evade the strictest blockade. The French ships trouble themselves so little about the affair, that they have never yet been known to take a prize. The absurdity of blockading a coast 2,000 miles in extent must be obvious to the meanest capacity. Even if successful, you must be prepared to continue the force for ever and a day, or your labor is lost; for the moment the ships are removed, the business recommences. The market is the true centre to aim at; put an end to that, and the supplies will not be required. The loss of life and demoralizing effect to our Service are very great, the climate and service being of that nature to prevent the proper exercise of discipline, and ships are anything but men of war; and many Officers acquire habits neither beneficial to themselves nor ornamental to the Navy. The best method of suppressing the trade we may leave to speculative theorists; but the naked fact of our exertions in favor of the African slave having increased his miseries to an awful extent, with an immense sacrifice of life, is uncontradicted by the best-informed advocates of slave measures—I mean men of practical information employed on the coast."

Press cutting of 16 January 1846 from an unidentified newspaper found in the letters and cuttings of Lieutenant Francis Meynell sent to his father, MEY/5, National Maritime Museum, Greenwich, London. Published with permission of the National Maritime Museum, Greenwich, London. We are grateful to Mary Wills for drawing this source to our attention.

Maps 187 and 188: African Regional Origins of Slaves Liberated from Slave Ships, 1808–1867

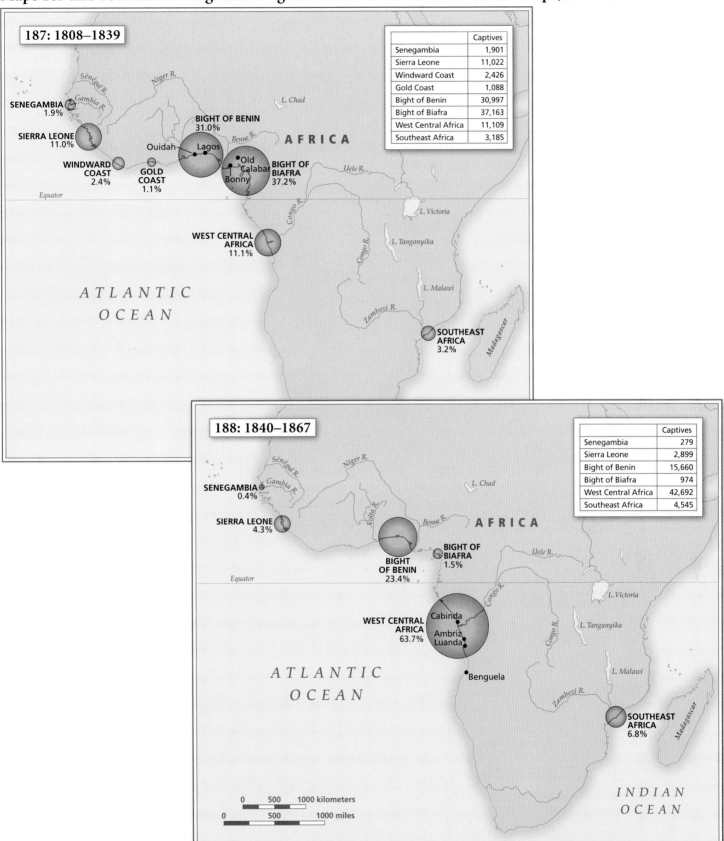

187: 1808–1839	Captives
Senegambia	1,901
Sierra Leone	11,022
Windward Coast	2,426
Gold Coast	1,088
Bight of Benin	30,997
Bight of Biafra	37,163
West Central Africa	11,109
Southeast Africa	3,185

188: 1840–1867	Captives
Senegambia	279
Sierra Leone	2,899
Bight of Benin	15,660
Bight of Biafra	974
West Central Africa	42,692
Southeast Africa	4,545

The formal restrictions on the trade were first passed and enforced north of the equator; an overwhelming proportion of vessels were captured coming from West Africa. Sierra Leone and the Bights of Benin and Biafra provided the departure points for over four out of every five captives who, for the most part, managed to avoid plantation chattel slavery in the Americas in the first three decades after British and U.S. abolition of the slave trade. Most passed through Ouidah, Lagos, Bonny, and Old Calabar, all located in modern-day Benin and Nigeria. After 1839 the sanctions against the traffic were applied throughout the South Atlantic as well as the North Atlantic, making liberated Africans much more representative of the mix of people who were pulled into the slave trade. They exited Africa mainly through Ambriz, Luanda, and Cabinda, in the Congo River area, and through Benguela.

Samuel Adjai Crowther
Bishop, Niger Territory
Oct. 19 1888

Samuel Adjai Crowther, Bishop, Niger Territory, Oct. 19, 1888

Engraving from Jesse Page, *Samuel Crowther: The Slave Boy Who Became Bishop of the Niger,* 3rd ed. (New York: F. H. Revell, [1890?]), frontispiece. Courtesy of the Yale Divinity School Library.

Born in Yorubaland (which is now part of Benin, Nigeria, and Togo), Samuel Adjai Crowther was forced into the Atlantic slave trade as a young man but was rescued by the British navy and freed by the Court of Mixed Commission at Freetown, Sierra Leone, in 1821. There he converted to Christianity. After training in London and Fourah Bay (Sierra Leone), he was ordained in London in 1841. In 1864 he was appointed the first African Anglican bishop. To this remarkable achievement Crowther coupled extraordinary educational and linguistic accomplishments. He produced primers in Igbo and Nupe, a Yoruba dictionary, and Yoruba translations of the Anglican Book of Common Prayer and the Bible. He married Asano, another convert to Christianity, whom he met on the slave ship from which they were rescued. He died in 1891.

Map 189: First Places of Disembarkation for Slaves Liberated from Slave Ships, 1808–1867

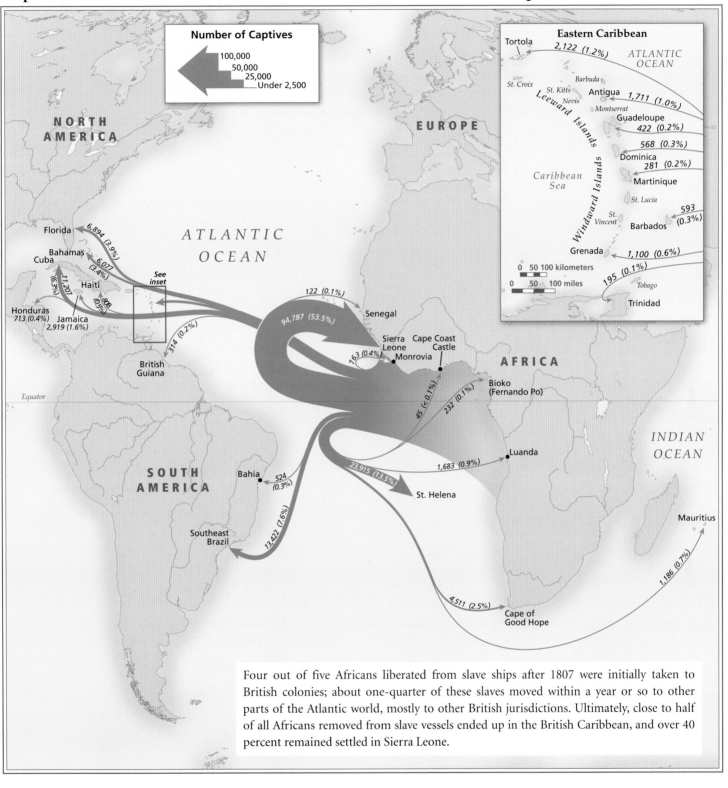

Number of Captives

100,000
50,000
25,000
Under 2,500

NORTH AMERICA

EUROPE

ATLANTIC OCEAN

Eastern Caribbean

Tortola

ATLANTIC OCEAN

2,122 (1.2%)

St. Croix

Barbuda

St. Kitts
Nevis

Antigua 1,711 (1.0%)

Montserrat

Guadeloupe 422 (0.2%)

568 (0.3%)

Dominica 281 (0.2%)

Caribbean Sea

Martinique

St. Lucia

Leeward Islands

Windward Islands

St. Vincent

593 (0.3%)

Barbados

Grenada 1,100 (0.6%)

0   50 100 kilometers

0   50 100 miles

195 (0.1%)

Tobago

Trinidad

Florida 6,894 (3.9%)

Bahamas 6,077 (3.4%)

Cuba 11,207 (6.3%)

Haiti 838 (0.5%)

Honduras 713 (0.4%)

Jamaica 2,919 (1.6%)

British Guiana 314 (0.2%)

Equator

ATLANTIC OCEAN

122 (0.1%)

Senegal

94,787 (53.5%)

163 (0.4%)

Sierra Leone
Monrovia

Cape Coast Castle

AFRICA

45 (<0.1%)

232 (0.1%)

Bioko (Fernando Po)

INDIAN OCEAN

SOUTH AMERICA

Bahia 524 (0.3%)

23,915 (13.5%)

1,683 (0.9%)

Luanda

13,422 (7.6%)

St. Helena

Southeast Brazil

Mauritius

4,511 (2.5%)

1,186 (0.7%)

Cape of Good Hope

Four out of five Africans liberated from slave ships after 1807 were initially taken to British colonies; about one-quarter of these slaves moved within a year or so to other parts of the Atlantic world, mostly to other British jurisdictions. Ultimately, close to half of all Africans removed from slave vessels ended up in the British Caribbean, and over 40 percent remained settled in Sierra Leone.

Afterword

DAVID W. BLIGHT

Its high walls of dark brown stone still stand guard after five centuries, looking toward the Atlantic Ocean on one side and looking inland on the other, toward vast river systems, rain forests, and some of the most important trade routes in West Africa. Built by the Portuguese in 1482–1483, Elmina Castle (São Jorge da Mina, or St. George of the Mine) is an imposing square structure with steep stone stairways, forbidding dungeons, a large interior courtyard, and the ever-present sound of waves. In the fifteenth century it declared by its presence that Europeans had come to the coast of Africa to do business and stay. Elmina, wrote one ship captain early in its history, was "justly famous for its beauty and strength, having no equal in all the coasts of Guinea." Beneath Elmina's base a large cistern supplied water to slave ships for more than three centuries. And from its waiting rooms and out its back door (referred to now as the door of no return), thousands of Africans were herded into vessels bound for the Americas as well as other ports in Africa. Elmina was a crossroads of commerce, culture, and human bondage. It is still a crossroads of history and memory.

Elmina is in modern Ghana, west of the capital, only a morning's drive down the coastline, in the region the Europeans came to know as the Gold Coast. Today it sits on its promontory, a major tourist attraction, with a busy fishing and market town behind it. In early evening or early morning, from the height of Elmina Castle, visitors have a stunning view of fishing boats swarming in and out of the small harbor. When I visited Elmina in 2007 for a major international conference commemorating the 200th anniversary of the end of the slave trade in the British Empire, I finished my tour, like most others, by ducking and stepping through the door of no return.

The door opens onto a small beach. Here boats waited to take captive Africans out to anchored slave ships. On my afternoon I emerged to see several fishermen lounging on their tied-up boats. In the eyes of those tired, bored fishermen I saw a certain knowing, practiced contempt. "What is it you want to see here?" they seemed to be asking. "What is it you hope to feel here?" That I was a historian, that I might make some special claim to be there to enhance my teaching or writing, made not a whit of difference. But some kind of exchange took place. In the fishermen's eyes, and in my discomfort that my fellow tourists and I had invaded their workspace, that we were indulging a wish to meditate on our world-historical notions of the slave trade, present met past, and I could, for a moment, see, smell, breathe, feel, and hear the past imposing itself on the present. Deep in my bones I felt a trembling sense of what a legacy actually is. Nothing further happened. I walked around the small beach for a few minutes, nodded and waved to a few of the indifferent fishermen, and went back through the door. I felt then, and still do, that although I could have reached out and shaken the hands of the fishermen, the distance between us that day was too great—greater than the distance of the centuries during which Elmina Castle had stood.

In 1996, Orlando Bagwell, the executive producer of *Africans in America,* a PBS documentary on slavery, arrived with his crew to film at Elmina. In his journal he wrote of his feelings as an African American. "Today at Elmina Castle I saw other people from other countries walk through the dungeons but none responded like those from my country. Master and slave, enslaved and enslaver, we have all been changed and molded by this shared past." Bagwell clearly felt the same visceral collision of past and present that I later did. As he encountered slave-trade tourists, Bagwell observed special reactions among Americans. Every visitor seemed to experience anguish inside Elmina's walls. "But for those of us from the Americas, white and black," he wrote, "there were even more questions that this place conjured up. Maybe we or our ancestors came from the same town or country? Maybe we even shared family, possibly even blood? Our story of slavery is so complicated and complex. . . . In the dungeons of Elmina we all cried."

Many Americans to go to Africa in search of roots, in search of understanding, in search of the character and meaning of the slave trade. But how this vast trade in human beings was even possible—that remains elusive. Americans often do not understand the nature of fifteenth- to eighteenth-century West Africa, where African societies themselves were deeply involved in the exchange between economies rich in technology and desperate for labor (Europe) and economies rich in the raw material of people and desperate for technology (Africa). Because Americans and other westerners tend to measure history by a moral yardstick, the slave trade can seem inscrutable in its terror and inhumanity. The place to start to understand this epic history is with its physical, political, and moral geography.

Bagwell was well informed. But he declared himself "unsure" just how to face this past, even as one responsible for re-creating it on film. He admitted to feelings of anger, guilt, fear, and shame in seeing the physical remains of the slave trade in which his own ancestors participated on both sides of the ledger. Elmina and other slave-trade fortresses can haunt those who visit them. And they should. "All I knew," wrote Bagwell, "was that I wanted to find within me a way toward understanding, toward closure, a way toward the future." Whether history can really provide us with closure is an open question. Whatever the answer, understanding the past is our only secure way to build a future.

The Portuguese established a trading base near the gold mines of the interior. As the centuries passed and the slave trade boomed in so many regions and ports, Elmina came under the control of the Dutch and then the British. Gold supplies waned, and slave trading thrived in the seventeenth century. By the

Elmina Castle, 2005

Photographs © Cheryl Finley. Reproduced by permission.

The former slave-trading post is now a historic site and tourist destination in Ghana. Clockwise from top, the photographs show the castle viewed from the coastal road, the Portuguese church in the castle courtyard, fishing boats outside the castle, and tour guide Ato Eshun showing the "door of no return."

eighteenth century, when the British dominated the Atlantic slave trade, Europeans had built nearly fifty slaving forts of varying sizes (some much larger than Elmina) along the long coast of Africa, from the Senegambia basin on the tip of West Africa to Angola in the south, a shoreline distance of 3,400 miles. By 1710, from Elmina alone, about 1,350 slaves per year crossed the Atlantic for the Americas, and as the magnificent maps in this volume illustrate in rich detail, Elmina was only one small site of embarkation in the slave trade. When captives from the interior entered Elmina across a drawbridge over a moat, they were gathered in the open courtyard and inspected, forced to exercise, and often branded. They frequently had to wait for weeks to be traded to one of the ships waiting to fill its hold in the harbor. They were black pilgrims, racked with fear, suffering from dislocation, and awaiting, in agony, an unknown fate. When they saw a ship on the immediate water's horizon, they were about to enter a hell in motion, a savage commerce in flesh, disease, and valuable labor. There, in what one historian, Vincent Harding, has called one of "the cramped and fetid waiting rooms of history," they could hardly know that they were part of the largest forced oceanic migration of people in history.

When Europeans arrived on the west coast of Africa in the fifteenth century, they were unprepared for the diversity of the people and the vastness of the land. The same might be said of the Europeans and their African captives as they colonized, settled, and exploited the Americas over the next centuries. If the West African slaving coastline was longer than the United States is wide, the distance from Río de la Plata in South America to New England in North America was much longer still. As this book demonstrates in stunning detail, the ports of embarkation and disembarkation numbered in the hundreds. In an important sense, the history and significance of the Atlantic slave trade is tied to geography, then, to the mingling and collision of peoples, cultures, and economic imperatives, encounters impelled by greed, empire, ocean currents, and the desire to convert the bodies of human beings into cash crops. The power, even the beauty, of the maps in this book mask the horror of the trade even as they elucidate its sources, its destinations, its scope: the ruthless and amazing conquest of time and space on water and land.

In the slave trade a thousand African places became forever linked to a thousand American places. And it was the slave ships, making nearly 35,000 now-documented voyages, that connected this far-flung system. Slave ships were creations of capitalist calculations, the white-sailed messengers of European ambitions and African fates. They were like guided missiles launched into the space of the sea, designed to bring back the lucre of the Indies and of the Brazilian sugar plantations. But they were also prisons bobbing on the water, chambers of human suffering with the power to destroy or corrupt everyone they touched.

The Middle Passage gained its name from being the second leg—the most dangerous leg—of the infamous triangular trade: a ship went from Europe to Africa with goods to sell for slaves; from Africa to the Americas with slaves; and from the Americas back to the European port of origin with goods and money. The slaves' survival of the Middle Passage depended on the journey's success, as did the profits of investors. Slave-ship companies were state-sponsored enterprises as well as private businesses, and in their operation over so long a time we can see some of the roots of modern capitalism. By the eighteenth century all major European countries were involved in slaving. Crown-sanctioned monopolies were granted to certain companies, and great houses and fortunes were built in the major port cities of London, Bristol, and Liverpool in England, Nantes in France, Lisbon in Portugal, Seville in Spain, Middelburg in Holland, and Charleston and Providence in North America, among others. The typical trader was involved in all kinds of commerce besides slaves—whaling, banking, the China trade (tea, opium)—and sometimes owned plantations in the West Indies. Often slave ships were financed by partnerships of venture capitalists, and many owner-merchants started as slave-ship captains. All European religions were involved in this human commerce, and many slave traders and financiers were members of the British Parliament, the U.S. Congress, or, after 1789, the French National Assembly.

When the trade regularized and increased its share of Atlantic commerce, slave ships were especially designed to carry larger cargoes of captives, as shown in maps and statistics in this book. A French critic of the slave trade, Abbé Raynal, wrote satirically in 1782 about the builders of the ships. "Look at that shipbuilder who, bent over his desk, determines, his pen in hand, how many crimes he can make occur on the coast of Guinea; who examines at leisure the number of guns he will have need of to obtain a black, how many chains he will need to have him garroted on his ship, how many strokes of the whip to make him work." Countless African rulers supplying slaves for the trade upon which they became ever more dependent engaged likewise in cost-benefit analyses as they acquired captives by intrigue, normal trade, and, especially, raiding and warfare.

Words and imagination are sometimes all we have to enter the transatlantic slave-trading world. An English passenger on a Portuguese ship carrying 562 slaves to Brazil in the early eighteenth century described the Africans' place of confinement as "so low that they sat between each other's legs," and they were "stowed so close together that there was no possibility of their lying down . . . by night or day." When the slaves came out on deck, they were "fellow creatures of all ages and sexes, some children, some adults, some old men and women, all in a state of total nudity, scrambling out together to taste the luxury of a little fresh air and water. They came swarming up like bees from an aperture of a hive." The former slaving captain and future composer, after repentance, of the famous hymn "Amazing Grace," the Reverend John Newton, left this description of the holds of slave ships:

> The cargo of a vessel of a hundred tons or a little more is calculated to purchase from 220 to 250 slaves. Their lodging rooms below deck are sometimes more than five feet high and sometimes less. . . . The slaves lie in two rows, one above the other, on each side of the ship, close to each other like books upon a shelf. I have known them so close the shelf would not contain one more. The poor creatures, thus cramped, are likewise in irons for the most part which makes it difficult for them to turn or move or attempt to rise or to lie down without hurting themselves or each other. Every morning, perhaps, more instances than one are found of the living and the dead fastened together.

Sometimes only through art can we gain access to the full agony of this story. Nearly 200 years later, the American poet Robert Hayden captured the meaning and the horror of the slave ships in a poem entitled "Middle Passage":

Shuttles in the rocking loom of history,
the dark ships move, the dark ships move,
their bright ironical names
like jests of kindness on a murderer's mouth;
plough through thrashing glister toward
fata morgana's lucent melting shore,
weave toward New World littorals that are
mirage and myth and actual shore.

Voyage through death,
                    voyage whose chartings are unlove.

A charnel stench, effluvium of living death
spreads outward from the hold,
where the living and the dead, the horribly dying,
lie interlocked, lie foul with blood and excrement.

Deep in the festering hold thy father lies,
the corpse of mercy rots with him,
rats eat love's rotten gelid eyes.

But, oh, the living look at you
with human eyes whose suffering accuses you,
whose hatred reaches through the swill of dark
to strike you like a leper's claw.

You cannot stare that hatred down
or chain the fear that stalks the watches
and breathes on you its fetid scorching breath;
cannot kill the deep immortal human wish,
the timeless will.

Modern moral outrage, clinical statistics, a tragic sensibility, racism and antiracism, the story of human commerce, survival, and transcendence—all have been evoked in calculations of the human suffering and loss represented by the slave trade. Many weights have teetered uneasily in the scales of historical justice. Today, as individuals and as nations, we still struggle to "repair" this past.

The slave trade has to be assessed for what it was: a massive economic enterprise that helped build the colonial Atlantic world, a story of the enormous human cruelty and exploitation that helped forge modern capitalism, a tale of migration and cultural transplantation that brought African peoples and folkways to all New World societies. Hayden offers a simple and timeless definition of the slave trade: a "voyage through death to life upon these shores."

Sometimes history "accuses" us, and we cannot "stare . . . down" our moral responsibilities. But history also forces us to interpret, explain, describe, and imagine ourselves into the events of the past. Africans transported to the Americas—to Brazilian and Caribbean ports and to Charleston, South Carolina—experienced a physical, psychological, and cultural "rupture" from their known universe, to use the historian Nathan Huggins's words. And lest we forget, the slave trade was about *people* who were ripped out of the "social tissue" that gave meaning to their lives, and converted into "marketable objects." We must imagine them lost, writes Huggins, lost "in a process, the end of which was impossible to see from its onset," its "precise beginnings lost forever to recall." So at the most fundamental level, this book offers a way to see a withering story of loss.

But more than 10.7 million people survived the cruel "filter" of forced migration; they adjusted, coped, and labored to make meaning of their fate and to make new homes. The Middle Passage was dehumanizing, but many transplanted Africans were not dehumanized. Into Kingston, Trinidad, Havana, Bahia, Baltimore, and Boston they carried their memories and languages, their drums and musical styles and instruments, their habits and cuisine, their gods, their immune systems, and their DNA. They carried culture and creativity, their potential for heroism and roguery, their loves and hatreds—and their desire to be recognized, not rendered nameless and self-less. They carried skills and knowledge to help cultivate New World soils and crops. They were colonists too, however reluctant— essential contributors to the burgeoning colonial economies. They helped found and change American republics, including the one that became the United States. Immigrants, changing as they survived, they made the landscapes in the Americas their own. The world they had known had been profoundly unmade through their suffering. In the New World they remade themselves.

Timeline

1501–1641

1501	The transatlantic slave trade from Europe to the Americas begins.
1525	The first slave ship sails directly from Africa to the Americas.
1560	Steady slave trading from Africa to Brazil begins.
1630	The Dutch occupy Pernambuco (Brazil) and begin slave trading from Africa.
1640	The Iberian Union (Spain and Portugal ruled by a single monarch) comes to an end after sixty years. Portuguese ships can no longer legally deliver slaves to Spanish territories.
1641	Sugar exports from the eastern Caribbean become significant.

1642–1807

1672	The English Royal African Company, the largest single slave-trading business, is founded.
1674	The Dutch West Indies Company is reorganized and becomes a major slave-trading business.
1695	Gold is discovered in Minas Gerais (Brazil).
1697	The French obtain St.-Domingue (now Haiti) in the Treaty of Ryswick, which ended the Nine Years' War in Europe.
1756	The Seven Years' War begins.
1775	The American Revolutionary War begins. The end of the war, in 1783, brings a resurgence in the slave trade.
1780s	The movement to abolish the slave trade begins.
1789	The Spanish monarchy allows free entry of foreign ships to Spanish colonial ports, making unlicensed arrivals of slaves into Spanish America legal.
1791	The St.-Domingue Revolution begins. The colony declares its independence as Haiti in 1804.
1792	Denmark abolishes its slave trade. The ban takes effect in 1803.
1793	The French Revolutionary wars close down the French slave trade.
1794	France abolishes slavery only to reinstitute it in 1802.
1804–1807	South Carolina permits resumption of the slave trade after banning it in 1802.

1807–1808 British and U.S. laws abolish slave trading by their nationals, effective in 1808.

1810 An Anglo-Portuguese treaty with an anti-slave-trade clause is the first of many international treaties to proscribe the slave trade.

1814 The Dutch abolish the slave trade.

1817 An Anglo-Spanish anti-slave-trade treaty is signed in which Spain undertakes to halt its slave trade in 1820. Both Portugal and Spain join with Britain to establish Courts of Mixed Commission to adjudicate the cases of captured slave ships.

1826 The first Anglo-Brazilian treaty is signed. It contains an undertaking by the newly independent nation of Brazil to abolish the slave trade.

1830 The 1826 Anglo-Brazilian treaty takes effect.

1831 Brazil formally abolishes the slave trade. The new French monarchy suppresses the remnants of the French slave trade.

1835 An Anglo-Spanish treaty allows naval cruisers to detain slave ships with slave-trading equipment on board, which allows ships with no slaves on board to be condemned as slavers.

1836 Portugal abolishes the slave trade, the last European nation to do so.

1839 Britain authorizes its navy and its domestic Vice Admiralty Courts to detain and condemn suspected Portuguese slave ships.

1850 Brazil suppresses its slave trade.

1860 The *Clotilde,* the last known slave ship to introduce slaves into the United States from Africa, arrives in Mobile, Alabama.

1867 The slave trade to Cuba ends in response to Spanish, British, and U.S. pressure.

Glossary

Abolition of the slave trade   Initiatives to end the legal trade in enslaved people. This is not to be confused with the abolition of slavery itself. France abolished its slave trade in 1794 but reinstituted it legally in 1802, almost coincidentally with Denmark's effective abolition of its slave trade permanently. Britain spearheaded an international abolition movement, which culminated in the termination of the British slave trade in 1807, but the slave trade of other countries continued legally thereafter. The Spanish government ended the legal slave trade to Cuba in 1820. Brazil took similar action for its own traffic in 1831, although an illegal trade continued for several decades thereafter.

Adults   In the slave trade, African men and women were generally defined as older than thirteen or fourteen years of age or taller than four feet four inches (132 centimeters). Over the 366-year history of the transatlantic slave trade, captains purchased more adults than children for transport. Specific age ratios differed by time and place.

Adult-to-child ratio   The proportion of children to adult Africans shipped in the transatlantic slave trade. Approximately 26 percent of all slaves carried to the Americas were classified as children, a ratio unmatched in any pre-twentieth-century migration.

Africa   The continent that was the source of 12.5 million captives carried off to the Americas after the Spanish and the Portuguese opened the Americas to European trade and colonization circa 1500. Most enslaved Africans embarked from what are today Nigeria, Congo, Zaire, and Angola. Europeans purchased enslaved Africans mostly along the Atlantic coastline of Africa from the Sénégal River to Benguela (Angola), that is, in West and West Central Africa, but also in Madagascar and Mozambique, in Southeast Africa.

Africans   People born or living in Africa. Europeans believed Africans to be ideal slaves because of their supposed docility, ability to work in tropical climates, and the biblical "curse of Ham." Europeans also believed that enslaving Africans was legitimate because the institution of slavery existed in Africa. Ideas of European racial superiority increased through the era of the slave trade.

American Indian, Amerindian   The pre-Columbian indigenous inhabitants of the Americas. The Spanish and the Portuguese destroyed many of the native societies; entire regions, such as the Bahamas, were depopulated within a generation. Between 1492 and 1550 the Amerindian population of the West Indies was reduced by 90 percent owing to massacres, the importation of Old World diseases, such as smallpox and measles, and the destruction of local agriculture.

Within a decade of Columbian contact, colonists in need of labor demanded that the Spanish Crown authorize shipments of enslaved Africans to work on the plantations and in the mines of the New World.

American Revolutionary War (1775–1783)   The transatlantic slave trade declined steeply during the war, leaving only the traffic to Brazil unaffected. Naval squadrons and privateers raided shipping, destroyed African trading posts, and captured Caribbean ports. Between 1777 and 1782 the Dutch, American, and French commerce in slaves virtually ended.

Americas   The landmasses and islands of North America, Central America, and South America: the New World. The Americas were the destination for the vast majority of captive Africans transported overseas, and most were put to work in the plantations and mines of the European colonies.

Anglo-Portuguese Treaty of 1810   The first of several hundred treaties between the British and a wide range of other polities in Europe, Africa, and the Americas intended to end the slave trade. The 1810 treaty contained a clause in which the Portuguese gave up the slave trade north of the equator except between their African possessions. The British wrongly interpreted this as allowing them to detain Portuguese slave ships north of the equator.

Angola   *See* West Central Africa.

Arrivals   The number of slaves arriving at the first port of sale. The number of arrivals was typically lower than the number of departures because of mortality during the voyage.

Asiento   A contract between the Spanish Crown and an individual or company granting a license to introduce slaves into Spanish America. The *asiento* system continued until a policy of free trade was instituted in the Spanish colonial world, effective from 1789.

Atlantic islands   Here, islands off Africa, in the eastern Atlantic Ocean, principally the Azores, the Madeira Islands, the Canaries, the Cape Verde Islands, São Tomé, Príncipe, and Bioko. Some of these islands also served as prototypes of plantation economies. When the Caribbean islands became one of the primary destinations for enslaved Africans, the Canaries were an important provisioning stop.

Baltic States   Countries bordering the Baltic Sea, mainly Denmark and the other Scandinavian countries but also sometimes including parts of northern Germany, cities of the Hanseatic League (or Hanse), and other geographical units.

Bight of Benin   A bay of the Atlantic Ocean, part of the Gulf of Guinea, on the coast of western Africa, which gave its name to a slaving region. The Bight of Benin slaving region stretched about 400 miles along the coast, from Cape St. Paul east to the Nun River (an extension of the Niger). Today the coastline is part of eastern Ghana, Togo, Benin, and western Nigeria. Europeans also referred to the region as the Slave Coast.

Bight of Biafra   A bay of the Atlantic Ocean, part of the Gulf of Guinea, on the coast of western Africa, which gave its name to a slaving region. The Bight of Biafra slaving region stretched about 370 miles, from the Nun River (an extension of the Niger) to Cap Lopez (at the southern end of the Gulf of Guinea). Today the coastline belongs to eastern Nigeria, Cameroon, Equatorial Guinea, and northern Gabon. The region includes Bimbia Island (Cameroon) and the Gulf of Guinea islands Príncipe, São Tomé, and Bioko.

Boys   Immature male slaves. Generally, slave traders classified male slaves as boys if they were younger than thirteen or fourteen or shorter than four feet four inches.

Brazil   The center of the transatlantic slave trade for most of the years between 1570 and 1850, whether under the Portuguese flag or, after independence in 1822, under the Brazilian flag. More slaving voyages were outfitted in Rio de Janeiro and Salvador da Bahia than in any other ports. About 44 percent of all Africans forced into the slave trade ended their lives in Brazil. In the late 1820s more enslaved Africans were imported into Rio de Janeiro than into any other port in the history of the trade.

Captain   The commander of a slaving vessel and the legal authority on board. Slaving captains had a broad range of responsibilities, including navigating the ship; trading with African merchants for slaves, provisions, and produce; and selling slaves in the Americas. Merchants paid captains commissions and bonuses and gave them "privilege slaves" and other emoluments.

Captive   A person who is forcibly confined, restrained, or subjugated as a prisoner. Most enslaved Africans were taken captive by other Africans. As this implies, an African identity did not exist in the era of the slave trade.

Captor   A person who takes or keeps another person as a captive. Raiders acted as captors when taking slaves; traders acted as captors when purchasing slaves.

Capture of a slave ship   The taking of a slave ship by a naval vessel, by privateers or pirates, by Africans (free or enslaved), or by crewmen (in a mutiny). The transatlantic slave trade declined during wartime because of the heightened risk of capture.

Caribbean   Islands of the Caribbean basin and the adjacent territories of what are now Guyana, Suriname, and French Guiana.

Castle (or fort)   Fortified structure on the African coast—for example, Elmina Castle in what is now Ghana.

Children   Slaves younger than thirteen or fourteen or shorter than four feet four inches were defined as children. Over the whole era of the transatlantic slave trade captains purchased more adults than children. Specific age ratios differed by time and place.

Condemnation of a slave ship   A decision by a state official or, where none was available, a committee of captains that a slaving vessel was no longer seaworthy or that it had been detained according to law. Most condemnations occurred in the Americas.

Court of Mixed Commission   Commission formed to hear cases concerning captured slave ships, created in 1817 by British-sponsored international treaties. The court included officials from a mix of countries to ensure impartiality. The first court sat in Freetown (Sierra Leone) in 1819. The courts failed to suppress the slave trade and adjudicated no cases after 1845.

Crew   Personnel manning a slave ship. The need to guard, feed, and clean African captives, coupled with the high mortality suffered by Europeans on a slaving voyage, meant that slaving vessels typically carried more crew than did similarly sized vessels in other trades. Slave-ship crew suffered high death rates from tropical diseases.

Departures   Departures from ports where voyages were organized or from ports where vessels obtained slaves. By 1820 almost all slaving voyages were organized in the Americas.

Disembarkation of slaves   The removal of slaves from a vessel. Slaves could be disembarked at any of several ports in the Americas, given that slave-ship captains often searched for the best price for their captives prior to their sale to plantation or mine owners.

Embarkation of slaves   The loading of African captives into a slave ship. In West Africa, where slaving vessels had to anchor offshore because of a lack of natural harbors, slaves were taken to the slave ship by canoe and often remained belowdecks for weeks after embarkation.

Factory   A trading base, usually incorporating storehouses and pens for slaves.

Flag of a ship   National registration papers carried aboard a ship. After 1810, as one nation after another banned the traffic, a slave ship often sailed under a flag different from that of its actual country of ownership.

Geophysical map   A map that displays topographical features, such as rivers and mountains, or oceanographic features, such as winds and currents. The clockwise North Atlantic and counterclockwise South Atlantic wind and current systems helped to order the routes and timing of the voyages in the transatlantic slave trade.

Girls   Immature female slaves. Generally, slave traders classified female slaves as girls when they were younger than thirteen or fourteen or shorter than four feet four inches (132 centimeters). Captains confined "girls" to specific below-deck compartments toward the stern.

Gold Coast   Slaving region of West Africa that stretched along the coast from east of Axim to the Volta River. Most of the region today is in Ghana. Europeans built most of their trading forts along this 400-mile coastline, several of which, including Elmina Castle, remain important historic sites.

Gyre   A major circular, rotating ocean current created by the movement of the earth.

Haitian Revolution   *See* St.-Domingue or Haitian Revolution.

Iberian Peninsula   The peninsula of southwestern Europe comprising Spain and Portugal. The Iberian countries dominated the slave trade in Africa and the Americas during its infancy (1450–1650).

Indentured servants   Europeans, mostly males between the ages of eighteen and twenty-five, who contracted themselves to employers in the Americas for three to seven years, after which time they were free to work for themselves. The small number of servants relative to the demand for workers in the Americas was one of the key factors behind the importation of enslaved Africans.

Ivory Coast   The easternmost section of the Windward Coast, broadly equivalent to the modern Côte d'Ivoire.

Liberated slaves / liberated Africans   Captives freed from slave ships. Following anti-slave-trade treaties, the first in 1810, the British Royal Navy policed the African Atlantic coast to search for ships undertaking illegal slaving voyages. Navy ships escorted captured slaves to Sierra Leone, St. Helena, or the Cape of Good Hope and there liberated the Africans. The navies of other countries disembarked any slaves they captured in Havana, Rio de Janeiro, or Luanda. The *Voyages* Web site contains several pictures of liberated slaves in the Images section, in addition to pictures of Royal Navy ships approaching or capturing slaving vessels. *See also* Court of Mixed Commission.

Logbook   A book in which a ship captain kept the daily navigational log and details of some occurrences on board, including crew deaths and acts of resistance by slaves. Captains noted wind direction, hull speed, latitude, and longitude as they plotted their course.

Male-to-female ratio   The number of male slaves relative to the number of female slaves.

Men   Adult male Africans sold into the transatlantic slave trade. On most slaving vessels captains confined and chained men to specific below-deck compartments toward the center and the bow of the vessel.

Middle Passage   The transatlantic voyage between Africa and the Americas. The Middle Passage, notorious because of the cramped, unhygienic conditions suffered by the slaves belowdecks, became a key reference point for the anti-slave-trade movement.

Minas Gerais   In the 1690s, gold and some diamonds were discovered in Brazil. Minas Gerais—in Portuguese, "general mines"—and Goiás formed one of the largest riverine goldfields ever exploited; it required thousands of workers to extract its riches. After exploiting Amerindian labor in the mines, the Portuguese turned to enslaved Africans, purchased mostly from West Central Africa and the Bight of Benin. Minas Gerais remained an important mining region through the mid-eighteenth century.

Mortality   *See* Shipboard mortality.

National carrier   *See* Flag of a ship.

Old World   Here, Africa and Europe. Between 1445 and 1756, an Old World slave trade organized by Europeans, mainly Portuguese, shipped enslaved Africans between African coastal locations, between the African coast and such eastern Atlantic islands as Madeira, and between the African coast and Europe.

Plantation   A large estate or farm on which cash crops are grown, usually by slave workers. Plantations were the destination of the majority of Africans brought to the Americas. Plantation workers faced long hours of planting, cultivating, and harvesting crops like sugarcane, tobacco, and rice. The poor conditions on plantations, especially in the Caribbean, typically resulted in high mortality rates.

Pound sterling   The currency of the United Kingdom of Great Britain and Ireland. Colonial currencies, such as Jamaican pounds, were valued at 40 percent below the value of the British pound sterling.

Price / standardized price   The price of a slave at a port of sale in the Americas, standardized in pounds sterling. Such a price was normally the present value of a slave's lifetime output. Just before British and U.S. abolition, a newly arrived adult male slave might fetch up to £100 sterling in the Caribbean. In today's terms such a price would be equal to several hundred thousand dollars.

Privateer   A ship privately owned and operated but authorized by a government during wartime to attack and capture enemy vessels. Armed slaving vessels often purchased letters of marque during wartime so they could, with government sanction, capture enemy shipping on their own account.

Recaptive   African captive aboard a slave ship off Africa or en route to the Americas who was liberated from slavery, usually when a British navy vessel captured the slave ship.

Resistance   Actions by slaves or crewmen to gain freedom or improve shipboard conditions. Most Africans resisted their slave status and shipboard confinement. Many crewmen were impressed into service, and some sailors resisted tyrannical and cruel officers.

Río de la Plata   The "Plate" or "Silver" River, which flows through Argentina and Uruguay. Its estuary was the southernmost disembarkation point for enslaved Africans in the Americas. Enslaved Africans sent to the Río de la Plata were often transported overland to the Andean colonies of Bolivia and Peru, where they worked in silver mines.

Royal African Company   A London-based publicly traded chartered company with a (British) monopoly on African trade. It began operations in 1672 and was the last and largest of several such British African companies, but it eventually came to be subsidized by taxpayers. The termination of the company's monopoly privileges in 1698 and 1712 accelerated its decline; it was dissolved in 1752.

Senegambia   Slaving region on the West African coast, including offshore islands—a region comprising Guinea-Bissau, Gambia, and Senegal.

Seven Years' War (1756–1763)   A war fought between all the major powers of Europe that transformed the colonial New World. The main victor, Britain, gained a large part of France's possessions in both North America and the Caribbean.

Shipboard mortality   The number of Africans and crewmen who died on board a ship while it was anchored off the coast of Africa, traversing the Middle Passage, or lying in American harbors. Crew mortality was highest along the African coast. Slaves died at greater rates than crewmen did, and mortality rose during long voyages because of water shortages, starvation, and diet-related diseases. The mortality statistics in the maps take into account the deaths of Africans, not crew.

Sierra Leone (region)   Slaving region on the African coast, including offshore islands. Stretching south from Guinea-Bissau to just west of Cape Mount (Liberia), the region today is in Guinea-Bissau, Sierra Leone, and western Liberia. Europeans often included this stretch of coastline when they spoke of the Windward Coast.

Slave ship / slaver   A sailing ship refitted for the slave trade, known also as a Guineaman after Guinea, a major source of slaves. Most slave ships were secondhand vessels that were also used in other trades. Owners sought to purchase fast-sailing vessels or ones that could be retooled below the main deck to maximize the number of Africans who could be imprisoned.

Southeast Africa   Slaving region along the African coast east of the Cape of Good Hope (South Africa) and including the islands of Madagascar and Zanzibar. The center of the slave trade in Southeast Africa was Mozambique. Some maps refer simply to Madagascar when it was the only recorded embarkation center in the region.

Spanish Caribbean mainland   The Spanish-ruled mainland territories bordering the Caribbean that today make up Mexico, other parts of Central America, Colombia, and Venezuela. After the conquest of the Aztec and Inca Empires in the sixteenth century, the Spanish consolidated an empire that comprised most of the Americas. Slaves entered this empire mainly through Veracruz (Mexico), Cartegena (Colombia), and Buenos Aires, the first two being by far the most important. Many of the slaves were destined for the silver mines of central Mexico and the region around Potosi, "the Silver Mountain," located in modern-day Bolivia.

St.-Domingue or Haitian Revolution (1791–1804)   In 1697, Spain ceded the western half of the island of Hispaniola to France in the Treaty of Ryswick. By the mid-1700s the French colony there, St.-Domingue, had become the leading sugar, coffee, and indigo producer in the Caribbean owing to the efforts of the colony's enslaved African workforce. The slave rebellion that broke out in August 1791 soon turned into a revolution, leading to the freedom of 500,000 enslaved Africans and to the creation of the Republic of Haiti (1804).

Sugar   The principal cash crop grown on plantations in the Americas during the era of the transatlantic slave trade. Sugar-production techniques were transferred from the Mediterranean to the Atlantic world—specifically, in the mid-sixteenth century, from the Portuguese island-colony São Tomé to Portuguese Brazil. Four in five Africans shipped to the Americas between the 1620s and the 1860s entered sugar-growing areas.

Transatlantic slave trade   The coerced migration of 12.5 million enslaved Africans to the Americas between between 1501 and 1867. They were captured in Africa and transported across the Atlantic to ports in the Americas where they were sold.

Triangular trade   Slave trade that followed the northern gyre of the Atlantic Ocean. It was conducted by a slave ship whose voyage had three legs. The ship traveling to Africa from a European or North American port carried goods to sell or trade for African captives. Then it carried the captives to a port in the Americas (the Middle Passage) and, after selling them, returned to its home region, often carrying plantation produce.

Upper Guinea   The combined slaving regions of Senegambia, Sierra Leone, and the Windward Coast.

Voyage   Voyage by a slave-trading vessel, generally here the transatlantic voyage with African captives aboard: the Middle Passage. The voyage needed to be organized and financed. The vessel was fitted out with goods in demand in regional African markets to exchange for slaves. The ship owners and captain hired crewmen to work as sailors, craftsmen, and guards. Outfitting took time and money, as did the voyages themselves, because of the distances traveled and the time spent waiting for goods and slaves in European, African, and American ports. Voyages often took a year or more to complete on the North Atlantic circuit. Return voyages from Brazil to Africa took less than a year. On average, slave vessels had 350 captives on board when leaving Africa. *See also* Triangular trade.

War   Period of conflict often marked by a drop in slave voyages, as in 1688–1697 (Nine Years' War, or War of the League of Augsburg; in America, King William's War), 1740–1748 (War of Austrian Succession, or King George's War), and 1793–1794 (the beginning of the French Revolution). *See also* American Revolutionary War; Seven Years' War.

West Africa   Slaving region that comprised all of the slaving regions of Atlantic Africa down to Cap Lopez (Gabon): Upper Guinea (Senegambia, Sierra Leone, and the Windward Coast), the Gold Coast, and the Bights of Benin and Biafra. That is, it included sub-Saharan Africa north of West Central Africa.

West Central Africa   Slaving region along the western African coast from Cap Lopez (Gabon), at the southern end of the Gulf of Guinea, to the southern tip of Africa. The southernmost slaving port in Atlantic Africa was approximately midway, at Benguela (Angola), and Europeans often called the whole region Angola. This region today includes Gabon, the Republic of Congo, the Democratic Republic of Congo, and Angola.

West Indies   Islands of the Caribbean basin, including the Bahamas and the Greater and Lesser Antilles.

Windward Coast   European name for a slaving region west of the Gold Coast. It stretched along the African coast from Cape Mount east to Cap Lahou. The region today is in Liberia and Côte d'Ivoire.

Women   Adult female Africans sold into the transatlantic slave trade. On most slaving vessels captains confined women to below-deck compartments toward the stern of the ship. Female slaves were kept separate from the male slaves on board, and because they were usually not shackled, they occasionally broke into chests of arms, located in or near captains' cabins, also near the stern, and helped instigate insurrections. Crewmen occasionally raped female slaves.